The Triangle Fire, the
Protocols of Peace, and
Industrial Democracy
in Progressive Era New York

In the series
Labor in Crisis,
edited by Stanley Aronowitz

The Triangle Fire, the Protocols of Peace, and Industrial Democracy

in Progressive Era New York

RICHARD A. GREENWALD

TEMPLE UNIVERSITY PRESS
Philadelphia

Richard A. Greenwald is the Director of the Business, Society, and Culture Program and Associate Professor of History at Drew University, Madison, NJ. He is co-editor of *Sweatshop USA: The American Sweatshop in Historical and Global Perspective* and serves on the editorial board of the journal *Working USA*.

Temple University Press
1601 North Broad Street
Philadelphia PA 19122
www.temple.edu/tempress

⊗ The paper used in this publication meets the requirements of the American National Standard for Information Sciences—Permanence of Paper for Printed Library Materials, ANSI Z39.48-1992

The author expresses appreciation to the University Seminars at Columbia University for their help in publication. Material in this work was presented to the University Seminar on Globalization, Labor, and Popular Struggles.

Illustrations (pp. 1, 21, 126) are from UNITE Archives, courtesy of the Kheel Center, Cornell University.

Library of Congress Cataloging-in-Publication Data

Greenwald, Richard A.
   The Triangle fire, the protocols of peace, and industrial democracy in progressive era New York / Richard A. Greenwald.
       p. cm. — (Labor in crisis)
   Includes bibliographical references and index.
   ISBN 1-59213-174-3 (cloth : alk. paper) — ISBN 1-59213-175-1 (pbk. : alk. paper)
   1. Clothing trade—New York (State)—New York—History—20th century.
2. Management—Employee participation—New York (State)—New York—
History—20th century.   3. Industrial relations—New York (State)—New York—
History—20th century.   4. Triangle Shirtwaist Company—Fire, 1911.   I. Title.
II. Series.

HD6976.C62U64   2005
331.88'09747'109041—dc22

2004062010

2 4 6 8 9 7 5 3 1

For Danny and Debbie

Contents

Acknowledgments

In the course of writing this book, I have accumulated many debts, both large and small. And while I can never adequately repay them, I can acknowledge the kindnesses shown to me. This book started at New York University as a dissertation. My dissertation committee—Danny Walkowitz, Liz Cohen, Dave Reimers, Paul Mattingly and Edward Johanningsmeier—deserves special thanks for reading a very early and rough draft of this project. Both Danny Walkowitz and Dave Reimers read multiple drafts. Dave sent me detailed comments and made several important suggestions for how to turn the dissertation into a book. My fellow graduate students, Janet Green, Adina Back, Dan Bender, David Quigley and the late Greg Raynor kept my spirits high and my mind fueled. I owe a special thanks to Liz Cohen, who stayed with me even after she left NYU. I entered NYU with one thought in mind, to study labor history with Danny Walkowitz. This proved a great decision. In so many ways, Danny is a great teacher, an ideal advisor, and a wonderful mentor. He created an intellectual community at NYU that made it exciting to study history. More importantly, I am so glad that he has become a true friend.

Thanks must go to the History Department, Graduate School of Arts and Science, and the Metropolitan Studies Department at NYU for financial support. Additional financial support came from Morrisville State College, SUNY, the United States Merchant Marine Academy, the Franklin Delano Roosevelt Institute's Lubin Fellowship in Labor Relations, the Styskal Fellowship in Labor-Management Policy Studies at CUNY, and the Seminars at Columbia University.

I must thank the great folks at the Kheel Center at the New York State School of Industrial Labor Relations at Cornell University. They provided an ideal research center for labor scholars. The greatest thanks need to go to the staff at the Wagner Labor Archives at the Tamiment Library, NYU. I always felt at home there. Much of the spirit and energy of Wagner emanated from Debra Bernhardt. Her death was a great blow to all labor historians and she will be forever missed. Additionally, I am grateful to Marc Fasanella, who allowed me the wonderful honor to use his father's image as the cover of this book.

Since 1995, I have had the great fortune of being an employed academic. No small feat in this job market. In four years of teaching at Morrisville State College, SUNY, I learned the value of good teaching. I also made great friends, who helped keep me sane amidst all the snow of upstate New York and pushed me to finish my dissertation while teaching full time. Thanks to Allen Levinsohn, Elizabeth Grant, Louisa Richards, Roxanna Pisiak, Paul Griffin, Ray and Betsy Lasch-Quinn, and Maurice Isserman. Their support and encouragement are appreciated.

This work has been presented over the years at several conferences. I want to thank those who listened and commented on my work at the Organization of American Historians, the American Historical Association, Policy History Conference, Social Science History Association, the North American Labor History Conference, the Business History Conference, the Columbia University Seminar on Labor, Globalization, and Popular Struggles, and the New York State History Association. Part of Chapter 4 originally appeared in the Winter 2002 issue of *New York History* and I thank Daniel Goodwin for permission to use it here. I was also fortunate to present the key ideas of this project at a critical moment in the writing to the Pittsburgh Working Class History Seminar. Special thanks are owed to Marcus Rediker, Maurine Greenwald, and Dick Oestreicher for clarifying my thinking and reading through a large draft of the manuscript.

Dan Bender, Liz Faue, Roseanne Currarino, Eileen Boris, Ruth Percy, Mel Dubofsky, Colin Gordon, Julie Greene, Shel Stromquist, David Offenhall, Joe McCartin, Andy Wax, and Jim Barrett not only strengthened my thinking by commenting on parts of the manuscript, but challenged me to clarify in my mind the meaning of industrial democracy. Labor lawyers Ken Kimerling and Jim Reif found a way to use my historical work on sweatshops in today's antisweatshop fight, giving me a way to connect the past with the present and helping make history relevant. I would also like to thank Mike Wallace, Josh Freeman, Suzanne Wasserman, and Marci Reaven for widening my intellectual circles once I moved back to New York City and for forcing me to think big about Gotham.

My students and colleagues at the U.S. Merchant Marine Academy deserve special thanks. It is an honor to teach these midshipmen; they challenge my thinking on labor and always keep me on my toes. My chair, Jane Brickman, my dean, Warren Mazek, and the Academy's Superintendent, Vice Admiral Joseph Stewart, have been supportive of my scholarship. Thanks to my colleagues Jeff Taffet, Josh Smith, Laury Magnus, Roseanne Wassermann, Art Donovan, Melanie Ross, Georgia Durrant, Dianne Taha, Charles Schultheiss, Howard Weiner, George Billy, Elliot Lumbard, and Bob Gardella for making the Academy a true intellectual home. I would be remiss if I did not thank the interlibrary loan staff at the U.S. Merchant Marine Academy. I have had the pleasure of working with one of the best librarians, Donald Gill, who went out of his way to ensure that I got the materials I needed to finish this book.

I have some old debts to repay as well. I was privileged to attend Queens College, CUNY, as an undergraduate. There, I had great teachers who encouraged me to see scholarship as an engaged public practice. Mike Wreszin and Frank Warren—first-rate historians —by their example taught me how to be a historian. That I now can count them as friends is an honor. Before NYU, I briefly attended CUNY's Graduate Center. There I met Alan Brinkley and David Rosner, two of the most gifted and generous people one can encounter. It was in their seminars that the idea for this project was born. While at CUNY, I will forever be grateful to have worked with labor leader Victor Gotbaum. Vic had just retired from leading District Council 37, AFSME and created the Center for Labor-Management Policy Studies, CUNY–a rolling think tank of sorts. As a young grad student, Vic pushed me to see connections between scholarship and unions. He fostered in me an interest in labor relations that I hope is evident in this book. While a Fellow at the Center, I meet Richard Styskal, a gifted political scientist. Dick introduced me to the serious study of political economy and forced a historian to read across the disciplines. He created an intellectual community at the Center that I have not since encountered but am still longing for. He died tragically and I miss our wide-ranging 7:30 breakfast seminars and him.

I need to thank Stanley Aronowitz. Anyone who studies modern American labor needs to grabble with Stanley's ideas and his many works. He has been a warm and generous supporter of my work and a terrific series editor—taking time to discuss this book with me while running for governor of New York State. I owe a very special thanks to Micah Kleit, my editor at Temple University Press. He believed in this project and helped push me to complete it. Melissa Messina did a superb job copyediting the manuscript and saved me from some embarrassment. Any errors in style or substance that remain are of course mine alone.

My parents, Richard and Rosalie Greenwald, taught me that unions are important and that politics is what you discuss at dinner. They made me proud to be from a union home. They along with my grandparents gave me my love of New York and they encouraged me in every way. The greatest thanks are to my wife Debbie, who has been a co-conspirator on life's journey. She has lived with this project as long as she has lived with me and has been a source of constant support. She has put up with my endless discussions of sweatshops, industrial democracy, and academic politics with good spirits. She has been the perfect partner in all ways. While revising this book, our son Daniel was born. He is too small to realize how much he is loved. His existence gives me hope. As I write this, it is my wish that he grows up in a world where social justice is not just something he reads in history books, but is his lived reality.

The Triangle Shirtwaist Factory, at the corner of Greene Street and Washington Place, was the epicenter of the struggle for industrial democracy in Progressive Era New York. It was at the center of the "Uprising of Twenty Thousand" in 1909 and in March of 1911, the factory became the sight of one of the largest factory fires in New York. While some saw the fire as a "natural disaster," workers saw these two events as linked to their struggles for industrial democracy.

Introduction
Laboring Democracy

THE LABOR QUESTION

This book is about an important but woefully neglected historical subject, namely industrial democracy. Industrial democracy, at its core, was an effort to square free market capitalism with democracy to provide a fair and just workplace. While important, industrial democracy has been largely missing from debates about Progressive Era democracy. What has been missing specifically is a concrete understanding of political economy. We need to understand economic justice as the cornerstone of political democracy; to see it as part of the struggle to develop, implement, and refine a just political economy in the United States. This study sheds light on the interconnected struggles for political and economic justice. Nowhere was the connection between economic and political reform more clear than in Progressive Era New York. Gotham witnessed a series of important yet historically neglected experiments in industrial democracy. New York witnessed the creation of a unique and important industry-wide trade agreement in the ladies' garment industry that had a lasting impact in industrial relations for years to come: the Protocol of Peace. In addition, in 1911, New York was the site of the terrible Triangle Factory Fire, which killed 146 garment workers. The fire sparked a second experiment: the Factory Investigating Commission (FIC). These two interrelated experiments, the subject of this book, illustrate the ambiguities and limits, as well as the successes of industrial democracy as a vehicle to square free market capitalism with ideas of democracy. Through a study of the process of industrial relations (IR), we glimpse the intersection of labor, the state, and industry in important ways. In addition, we develop a more complicated understanding of not just the three, but also the increasing interdependency among them.

Writing a book today on industrial democracy might seem to some an exercise in futility. Labor union strength is at an all-time low. In countless

3

ways, this is a cynical and tough time for labor. History, however, can offer us a lesson for in 1900, labor was also weak. Careful study of work reveals important assumptions about how a society values it workers. One hundred years ago, the labor question seemed to have a special urgency as the nation witnessed waves of large and often violent strikes. Many worried that increased industrial violence would tear America apart. Others worried that the increasingly unequal distribution of wealth and power, coupled with a vast army of poor immigrant workers, had created social inequities that desperately needed readdressing. The position of labor in Progressive Era America hid within larger, ongoing discussions about democracy and social justice. This was hardly the abstract democracy of philosophers. Progressive Era debates about democracy were concrete and revolved around a new understanding of economic justice that was, for participants, equally as important as political participation. This economic focus seems not to have survived the Progressive Era. Can democracy have real meaning if it is stripped of economic justice? Can politics alone solve labor's problems? Progressive Era reformers and trade unionists debated these points and we can learn much from their struggles.[1]

Where one stood on the labor issue was central to the identity, scope, and meaning of the Progressive Era. In the days before World War I, no less an authority than Louis D. Brandeis, future Supreme Court Justice and leading Progressive Era industrial reformer, said labor "is and for a longtime must be the paramount economic question in this country." To reformers such as Brandeis, economic justice was a central pillar of democracy. From the vantage point of 2005, it is difficult to imagine a world such as the Progressive Era, where the cause of labor and economic and social justice were serious matters deserving focused and sustained attention from political and social leaders. Progressives possessed a powerful faith and optimism in America's ability to correct all its ills. The notion that labor was a problem that could and should be solved helped define the age. This struggle to square labor-management conflict in a democratic manner was a defining effort for the era.[2]

Labor historians have taught us a great deal about workers' lives and their shop-floor struggles. However, what we know all too little about are workers' equally important struggles revolving around IR. Clearly, any understanding of the labor question must deal with IR. Yet, the literatures on IR and labor history are like two ships that pass unnoticed in the night. Their concerns, however, are not unconnected. We need to follow the recent dictum of IR scholar and labor economist Bruce Kaufman, who claimed that "industrial relations should be defined broadly and inclusively."[3] I argue that not only do we need to more broadly define IR, but we need to ground the study of IR in labor and working-class history and in the lives and struggles of ordinary American workers. We need to cross-pollinate the fields of labor history and IR to not only deepen our understanding of both fields but to see the intersections that have been missed. This study seeks to broadly define IR during the Progressive Era as a struggle over industry democracy. The struggle over democracy in industry in New York City provides both a model for an inclusive IR history and a case study of one of the most significant sites of such struggles.

Labor historians, who have been interested in reclaiming the social history of ordinary Americans, have marginalized IR. This was not always the case, as modern labor history was born out of a rejection of the work of Progressive Era labor economist John R. Commons and his students. This "Wisconsin School" of labor history saw history as a tool for shaping labor policy. While much of the Wisconsin approach has been criticized for its overly narrow focus on institutions and political economy, as well as for ignoring the vast majority of unorganized American workers, labor historians have essentially thrown the baby out with the bathwater.[4]

Workers all too readily know that their experiences on the job are greatly shaped by whether they have a union and by how strong that union is in protecting their interests at the bargaining table. Therefore, the ability of unions to function within and shape IR is central to the lives of American workers. Yet, you would not know this by reading most labor histories. Until very recently, labor historians all but abandoned the study of unions and institutions.[5] The avoidance of institutional studies by labor historians has left far too many important unions unstudied. The ILGWU (International Ladies' Garment Workers Union), for instance, does not have a modern history, for which we remain all the poorer. This study is an institutional history of a new system of IR, based on a concept of industrial democracy that involved workers, managers/owners, and the state/public in New York during the Progressive Era. The world made by this IR system had profound importance for each group. That there were three sides to this debate gave it a democratic form. How each group struggled to define its role and defend its interests is one of this book's primary focuses. How and why one vision of IR and industrial democracy won out over other competing visions will be the lesson learned. This history of IR and industrial democracy, however, is more than a case study. The story of this struggle for industrial democracy is in some ways the story of labor in the Progressive Era. Before we turn to a more formal discussion of industrial democracy, therefore, we need to explore why industrial democracy became so important to America by 1900.

SETTING THE STAGE FOR INDUSTRIAL DEMOCRACY

Rapid industrialization transformed the United States from a land of rural hamlets and small towns—what historian Robert Wiebe has called "island communities"—into an industrial giant in a few short decades.[6] In the process, the way Americans thought about themselves, their lives, their nation, and most importantly, their relationship to work forever changed. Gone were the (dream of) independent yeoman-farmers and artisans, owners of land and tools, men (rarely women) in control of their own destiny. "That [new] productive system," according to historians Nelson Lichtenstein and Howell Harris, "depended [instead] upon a vast blue-collar working class, a social group mid-century [20th] contemporaries often referred to as the 'armies of industry,'"—an army composed mainly of immigrant and unskilled workers living increasingly in American cities.[7]

Beginning in the Gilded Age, millions of immigrants poured into American cities. These "new" immigrants entered American industry predominately at the lowest rungs of the economy, as unskilled machine operators and manual laborers. Their dependence on wages and their poor working and living conditions marked them as different, even inferior, when compared with native-born, American workers.[8] Rather than meeting the boss as equals or in fraternity, as an older generation of republican workers had, these new workers engaged in a constant struggle for what historian David Montgomery has called "control" over the production process.[9] Their weapons were collective rather than individual: strikes, boycotts, and cooperatives.[10] These clashes were often bitter, violent, and usually hard fought. This battle for the hearts and minds of industrial America (the future of America) frightened so many

because it threatened the very fabric of American identity: democracy.
Simply told, this lack of harmony foretold terrible events to come.[11] "Labor conflict attended by significant violence," writes historian Shelton
Stromquist, "seemed to spread unchecked from one mass production
center to another, taking root especially among new immigrant unskilled
workers."[12] Violence was becoming so endemic that clearly, something
had to be done.

Work was not the only thing that changed during this period. America
transformed from a series of albeit loosely connected local economies
and states into a single national economy with a federal, centralizing state. America, throughout the nineteenth century, was a "well-
regulated society," according to historian William Novak. But, it was
at its core a localized society. Local self-government and a weak federalism predominated. Political scientist Stephen Skowronek has called
our national government in the nineteenth century a government of
"courts and [political] parties." This had huge implications for the ways
in which the economy was viewed and the position of workers within
this society.[13]

American labor history has told the story of the terrible violence that
accompanied workers' quests for higher wages, better working conditions, and simple justice. American history is littered with the names
Ludlow, Pullman, Haymarket, and countless other so-called industrial
disasters or conflicts.[14] Management's ability to rely on courts, and when
that failed, guns, to break strikes placed workers at a decidedly weak
position at the bargaining table. This legal system, according to a generation of labor law scholars, deeply affected the way unions developed.
The federated nature of unions and the reliance on legally enforceable
contracts signaled a recognition of the power of the courts in America.[15]

The public nature of IR in the Gilded Age and Progressive Era focused attention on the plight of workers. Reformers and religious and
civic leaders, as well as middle-class political activists were drawn to
labor's cause for a myriad of complex reasons. Some sought to help ameliorate the miserable conditions millions toiled under out a sense of noblesse oblige and humanitarianism. Others were afraid that capitalism
left to its own unguarded devises would push workers recklessly toward
radicalism and revolution. These reformers, whom Gabriel Kolko and
others have called "corporate liberals," sought to tame capitalism and
bring labor to the table as a palative measure.[16] A third group sought

to "fit" workers into a new system of production, one that would be more efficient, profitable, and hence modern; in the process they agreed to share some of the newfound profits with a more responsible labor movement.[17] And still others worried about the rise of monopoly capitalism for an American democracy based on small property holders, small businessmen, family farmers, and small manufacturers.[18] For a myriad of reasons then, labor became an important political issue that received national attention.

Progressives were armed with a new tool to solve the labor problem: social science. This tool suggested new ways to understand both social and economic relationships, offering objectivity by making reform rational, and thereby seeming to take away the moral and emotional aspects that guided previous generations of reformers. Historians of social science have reminded us how much social scientists contributed to this burgeoning reform movement. Old ways of looking at the world, such as laissez-faire economic theory, as historian Dorothy Ross so astutely states, "collapsed as a credible basis for policy" in the late nineteenth century.[19] These "professionals" applied their knowledge to shape society. The Panic of 1893 proved a turning point in economic thought as much as in social reform, because it was national in scope, rather than regional, and completely overwhelmed the limited voluntary social safety net, as charities were incapable of dealing with the volume of problems.[20] The collapse of the economy brought with it a renewal of working-class self-activity (both workplace centered and through political organization of working-class communities). The strikes and radical politics that accompanied the late nineteenth century were staging grounds for what historian Lawrence Goodwyn has called "democratic moments," moments of true democratic possibilities.[21] The Panic and accompanying worker self-activity had simply shifted the ground of public discourse and opened room in the debate for discussions about labor.[22]

At the core of these efforts to redemocratize America were a series of experiments in IR and a new ideology: industrial democracy.[23] Historian Steve Fraser has called industrial democracy "the Marxism of the professional Middle Class, [because it was] wise to the class antinomies of industrial society but sanguine enough to believe in their pacific supersession by science and abundance."[24] It was central for at least one segment of Progressive Era reform, the professional middle class, who though not Marxist in the traditional sense, nevertheless had class on the brain. Class for these professionals and their allies—whom I collectively refer to as industrial democrats—was a problem science could solve. Professionals relying on science joined by interested parties thought they could bring industrial peace, restore social harmony, and raise productivity through increased efficiency, thus improving not only American life for all, but also revitalizing American democracy in the process.

Labor historians, but for a relative few, have largely ignored the study of the "labor problem," leaving it instead to historians of social policy and intellectual history and scholars of industrial relations. Labor historians have therefore missed an important opportunity to deal with a significant historical phenomenon. After all, the way the labor problem was dealt with affected the lives of American workers in important and fundamental ways. Surprisingly, the few accounts of the "labor question" that do exist focus solely on the role of experts and elites.[25] Forgotten from this history is the role workers played (or did not play) in the discussions about labor and democracy. Workers, however, were active participants in this process; they had agency. As historian Herbert Gutman long ago reminded us, the central question for good social history is to determine not "what 'one' has done to man, but what man does with what 'one' has done to him."[26] This book seeks to correct that historical silence through an exploration of the ideology of industrial democracy as it developed in two important experiments in New York State during the Progressive Era. By perceiving workers as actors in the drama of labor relations policy formation, we learn that workers placed limits on what elites could and could not do. In addition, we see how workers were ultimately constrained by the system they themselves helped to create.

Labor historians, especially those writing about garment workers, have taught us much about workers' social and cultural worlds. However, we still have an incomplete understanding of their work lives because we know next to nothing about the system of labor they toiled under and helped shape. This book, accordingly, seeks to address this silence. Therefore, it will not deal with the world of the workers outside of work, but not because this is unimportant. I ignore this area, to my own peril perhaps, because I privilege labor relations to offer a new avenue to understand this lost world of work and industry.[27]

INDUSTRIAL DEMOCRACY

Industrial democracy provides an important lens through which to view IR during the Progressive Era. Industrial democracy was one of a handful of ideas that defined Progressive Era reformers. It signaled a new scientific approach to labor in America as well as a fundamental recommitment to democratic principles.[28] Historian Howard Dickman has argued that the term was so pervasive that by 1914, "there was hardly anyone who didn't have a good word for it."[29] For many, it was nothing less than an effort to revitalize American democracy. "Political freedom," wrote Basil Manly in 1916 for the U.S. Commission on Industrial Relations, "can only exist where there is industrial freedom; political democracy only where there is industrial democracy."[30]

Yet, for all its touting, it was such an amorphous term that its meaning was constantly in flux and therefore always contested. It meant different things to different people at different times.[31] "It referred to a variety of schemes," according to historians Lichtenstein and Harris, "involving the spread of producers' cooperatives and workers' control, or public ownership and the gradual socialization of the economy, or trade union recognition and collective bargaining, or simply the improvement of workers' participation in, and acceptance of, the organizational purposes of the firms where they worked."[32] How did industrial democracy come to be central to American efforts to reform IR? To understand this we must first understand industrial democracy.

Many American progressives were keenly aware of European experiences with labor problems. They studied Europe for guidance or a model.[33] Industrial democracy, one such import, is most often associated with Sidney and Beatrice Webb and their circle of British Fabian socialists. The Webbs, in their seminal 1897 book *Industrial Democracy*, called for a reinvigorated democracy, one where unions played a central role. For the Webbs, modern capitalist industry had put an undue strain on democratic society. Unions could bring democracy to industry because they were (or at least could be) representational bodies for workers. As democratic institutions themselves, they offered the best hope of bringing democracy to industry by providing a countermeasure to unchecked industry. In the process, they could bring democracy to society.[34] Historian David Montgomery suggests that the Webbs hoped that collective bargaining would become the linchpin of democratic reform in industry and thereby the basis for a revitalized political economy. Montgomery's reading of the Webbs correctly places collective bargaining at the center of industrial democracy. Collectively bargained trade agreements would replace what they called "primitive democracies," which included workers' reliance on work rules and communal and ethnic ties.[35] Collective bargaining, a term and idea the Webbs pioneered, was therefore central to industrial democracy. These trade agreements would, in the best of all possible worlds, have the status of law because they would have government sanction as legally enforceable contracts. Ultimately, the Webbs believed that unions would bargain directly with the state in industry-wide agreements, thereby ensuring the betterment of society as a whole. "But at its best," writes the Webbs' biographer Royden Harrison, "democracy [in industry of otherwise] meant a form of government in which assent and efficiency were mutually reinforcing." While collective bargaining is normally thought of as private, the Webbs saw it as semipublic. After all, the community had a stake in the outcome. Therefore, both public opinion and the powers of the state could and should be marshaled to influence the arbitration of labor disputes in the best interest of the community as a whole.[36] Who, however, would look out for the interests of the community? For the Webbs and their American counterparts, Harrison states, it was "the professional expert, whether civil servant or representative, [who] was of decisive importance" in bringing about industrial democracy.[37] Americans quickly noticed the idea, as it appealed to their newly found sense of rational or objective science as a means to solve social and economic problems.[38] American adherents to industrial democracy, including future Supreme Court Justice Louis Brandeis, saw in it a vehicle to rationalize American industry within a democratic framework.

Economist Selig Perlman, writing critically of the Webbs in 1928, smartly called these industrial democrats "social efficiency" intellectuals. "Instead of stressing the injustice of the existing order of things," writes Perlman, "he [the typical Fabian Socialist] condemns it on the grounds of its inefficiency, its general irrationality, and its waste of human energy and of material resources." In a sense, Perlman was right. What attracted many to the ideology was its promise of rationality and efficiency.[39] Many had a blind faith in the scientific progress precisely because it seemed to depoliticize the process. They believed that workplaces needed reform and that workers could pay for the higher costs associated with better wages and conditions through increased rationality and efficiency. Industrial democracy therefore provided a more democratic and progressive twist to Taylorite notions of efficiency and industry. Democracy in industry would essentially pay for itself, making it all the more attractive. In the process, they hoped, it would also revitalize American democracy.

Perlman argued there were two types of "efficiency socialists," or what I would call industrial democrats. The first, "generally have no connection with the labor movement, except for the few who 'arbitrate' disputes in the clothing industry, sponsor 'union-management co-operative plans', [sic] or advise labor unions on their economic policies." The second type, according to Perlman is "the political type," whose "program always leans heavily to governmentalism and political action—to state-guaranteed 'minima', [sic] and eventually to an organization of industry by the political community instead of by the private profit sector." Perlman could have, and most likely was, speaking directly about those involved in industrial democracy experiments in Progressive Era New York City.[40]

The Webbs also called for a new unionism to accompany industrial democracy. These unions were new in that they would uphold high wage rates and rational production, yet at the same time let go of union control of work rules, which interfered with efficient production. This new "Common Rule" system, as the Webbs called it, would drive inefficient producers out of business, as inefficient produces could only stay in business by sweating labor. This became a critical aspect in selling the idea of industrial democracy to large garment manufacturers who were then at war with small producers. According to this notion, unions should organize entire industries and the state should outlaw "sweatshops," thus making industry and the nation efficient.[41] Economist Bruce Kaufman has argued that the Webbs' Common Rule was designed to get rid of the "downward pressure on wages and labor standards . . . and place a floor under labor standards below which no employer could go." The Webbs believed this could be done through one of two methods: "the method of collective bargaining" or "the method of legal enactment (protective labor legislation)." These were at the center of the Webbs' philosophy of industrial democracy, and in turn became the basic underlying assumptions behind the New York City experiments.[42]

Central to industrial democracy, as legal scholar Christopher Tomlins argues, was the need "to obtain the consent of employees to their continued participation in the further development of the capitalist mode."[43] With this, industrial peace and acceptance brought stability, which allowed for increased productivity, and above all increased profits. To get there one had to deal constructively with labor. Therefore, some saw unions for the first time as constructive institutions rather than economic obstacles.

The unions of the Progressive Era, however, were a mixed lot.[44] There was the radical Industrial Workers of the World (IWW) with its direct-action methods, the conservative and highly skilled American Federation of Labor (AFL), and a handful of "new unions" (the Amalgamated Clothing Workers Union [ACWU], the United Mine Workers Union [UMW], and the International Ladies' Garment Workers Union [ILGWU]).[45] It was these so-called new unions that industrial democrats looked to for partners in their experiments. New unions were institutions that went beyond the narrow issues of wages—so-called bread-and-butter issues. "What was new about it," writes historian Steve Fraser, "was precisely . . . [a] sense of . . . [themselves] as an institution responsible not only for the material well-being of its members, but for the efficient and equitable functioning of the industrial order as a whole." New unions played a large role in shaping their industries and setting a new political agenda for their members. In short, they shaped political economy.[46] Some new unions, such as the UMW and ACWU, as well as their leaders John L. Lewis and Sidney Hillman, have received a great deal of attention. The experiments in IR that these unions engaged in were indeed important and had far-reaching consequences.[47] Far less attention, oddly enough, has been paid to the ILGWU as both an institution and a leader in IR experimentation. After all, it was the ILG who arguably had one of the most significant roles in shaping modern political economy in the Progressive Era. This might be more because the ILGWU lacked a charismatic leader than because of its historical importance.

We know a great deal about the rich lives of Jewish and Italian garment workers, but surprisingly little about the workings of their union and next to nothing about their experiences with industrial democracy.[48] Of all the major unions of the twentieth century, the ILGWU still lacks a historian. Its history is crucial, because the effort of the ILG to try to forge democracy in Progressive Era New York offers us a window into the workings of a new IR paradigm. New York City was in fact a laboratory for industrial democracy during the Progressive Era. It was not just the center of progressive reform, it was also the media and financial capital of the nation.[49]

Louis Brandeis, the embodiment of Perlman's "efficiency" industrial democrat, fused industrial democracy and Taylorism into a powerful new American ideology. Speaking in 1915 before the Taylor Society, he said, "In a democratic community men who are affected by a proposed change of conditions should be consulted and the innovators must carry the burden of convincing others at each stage on the process of change that what is being done is right."[50] "Scientific management," declared industrial efficiency expert Fredrick W. Taylor, "democratizes industry."[51] What the Taylorites did, according to historian Howell Harris, was to create a "redefinition of 'democracy' to allow for the inequalities of knowledge and expertise and to permit [a] technocratic elite to play an undisputed leading role." All that was needed, Harris says of the Taylorites "to fit trade unions into this blueprint was a confidence that ... they could be employed as scientific managers' chosen instruments for rationalization through representation."[52] In short, Brandeis and company saw unions as the most effective means available to rationalize industry.[53]

In New York City's garment industry, reformers found what was arguably the nation's most primitive industry. Cutthroat competition, layers of subcontracting, and a poorly paid mass of immigrant workers, among other things, locked garment manufacturing in a nineteenth-century production model. It therefore offered a perfect laboratory for people such as Louis Brandeis. The ladies' garment industry had an established, but weak, new union. It had a core of willing industrial democrats within the industry led by Julius Henry Cohen, a noted corporate lawyer. The result, Brandeis's creation, the Protocol of Peace, was one of the most significant labor-management cooperation schemes of the Pre–New Deal Era. So impressive was the Protocol that when the Wilson Administration created the U.S. Commission on Industrial Relations in 1913, Brandeis was the president's first choice to chair it.[54] New York also was the site of the terrible Triangle Factory Fire of March 25, 1911, when 146 mainly young, immigrant women garment workers died. The fire sparked a reform effort that in four years remade New York into the model of a progressive state.[55]

The Protocol and the Triangle Fire have for too long been seen as two unrelated and unconnected events.[56] In reality, however, they were two sides of the same coin. As the Webbs noted, industrial democracy involved two interrelated activities: collective bargaining coupled with active state involvement in IR. The Protocols provided the first, while the New York State Factory Investigating Commission (FIC), formed after the fire, performed the second. Therefore, to understand the new labor relations, one has to have a deep comprehension of these two interrelated events. New York, quite simply, offers us a remarkable opportunity for a case study.

Two factors connected these events. The first was the developing and shifting philosophy of industrial democracy. The second was a new political elite (reformers, trade unionists, and progressive politicians) who acted as a bridge connecting these two events. The ideology, together with the elites and workers, are narratives woven into one story: that of the making of modern IR and in the process shaping a new liberalism. The tool these elites used was the new administrative state, one that would play a major role in bringing industrial democracy to America.

Recent studies of the U.S. Commission on Industrial Relations, the work of John R. Commons and his students, and Joseph McCartin's remarkable study of World War I show that indeed New Deal labor policy had many antecedents. Commons and his "idea" involved professional expert panels "advising" state legislatures. The U.S. Commission on Industrial Relations, however, for all its importance, did not see any of its advice enacted by the federal government. Moreover, the experiences of World War I were as influenced by events in New York City as by other experiments. Therefore, it is important to understand New York City's experiences with industrial democracy as the premier Pre–New Deal labor-reform experiment.[57]

The Progressive Era witnessed a radical departure from the Gilded Age notion of laissez-faire economics. Traditionally, liberalism and economic thought cast labor relations as a purely private matter between two equal parties: employers and workers. The notion that the public had a stake in labor relations took hold during the Progressive Era. Not all manufacturers, of course, accepted this new idea, as the closed-shop movement and industrial violence demonstrate. Yet, from at least 1900 until 1919, enough reformers, politicians, trade unionists, and corporate-liberal businessmen did accept this model and fought for its implementation. It is within this larger framework that the events that unfolded in Progressive Era New York City revealed both the promise and limits of industrial democracy. In many ways, New York was a progressive laboratory for modern IR and what we now think of as modern liberalism.

Protocolism as Industrial Democracy

The father of the Protocol, Louis Brandeis, came to the labor question in 1892. It was then that the young MIT law professor, fresh from Harvard Law School, was transformed by the violence of the Homestead Strike at the Carnegie Steelworks in Pennsylvania.[58] "It was the affair at Homestead," Brandeis later recalled, "which first set me to thinking seriously about the labor problem .... It took the shock of battle ... to turn my mind definitely toward a searching study of the relations of labor to industry."[59] That event brought Brandeis to the attention of reformers working on the labor question, eventually bringing him to New York City and the ladies' garment industry.

In 1910, while New York was in the heat of the second in a series of general strikes in the garment industry, Brandeis came to the city to bring labor and management together in a novel agreement that became known as the Protocol of Peace. He heralded this agreement as ushering in a new day for labor relations. It was, he believed, the revolutionary embodiment of the Fabian ideal of industrial democracy connected to a Taylorite vision of efficiency. This book seeks to trace the meaning and significance of Protocolism and reclaim its historical importance.

Before Protocolism, American industrial relations was a violent, often bloody affair. The violence associated with the 1892 Homestead strike—the crushing defeat of the steelworkers' union at the hands of one the most powerful companies in the nation—while best known, was by no means unique. Workers faced difficult conditions, dangerous workplaces, company towns, hostile management, private armies, courts and police, and the militia. For most of the history of the republic, unions had been outlawed as conspiracies against the freedom of commerce of business owners. Just after the turn of the nineteenth century, workers began asserting themselves, demanding their citizenship rights. This culminated in the massive railroad strike of 1877, put down ultimately by the U.S. Army. Unions, after their defeat in 1877, struggled to hold on throughout the Gilded Age. Homestead was important precisely because it made all the more visible the socioeconomic inequalities of modern capitalism. It was a turning point because it forced many, including Brandeis, to deal with the contradictions of what it meant to be a democracy in an industrial world.[60]

Occurring in the largest city and the center of national media, the 1909 New York City garment strike was assured ample news coverage; occurring at the height of the Progressive reform movement, it was assured the interest of many middle-class reformers such as Brandeis.[61] The Uprising of 1909 was one of the first large-scale strikes that involved "outsiders" in its settlement. The involvement of middle-class reformers changed the relationship between employees and employers in important ways. It was not simply an attempt to level the playing field; it sought to tilt it in favor of labor. If the Uprising was the dress rehearsal for the reform of labor relations, then the Great Revolt of 1910 was the first act in a long performance. The Protocol of Peace, fashioned by Brandeis to settle the second strike, was a unique and revolutionary institution. It gave workers collective bargaining and brought about improved conditions, better wages and hours, safer and cleaner workplaces, and a host of other important reforms. It also brought labor into the political economy as a partner by giving it a voice in industry, ushering in a tripartite system of labor relations that would find its crowning fulfillment in the National Labor Relations Act of 1936 (Wagner Act). Brandeis and other reformers argued that the lessons of Homestead necessitated that the public take an active role in industrial relations.

The slow-moving bureaucracy that the Protocol set up, rising expectations, its inability to solve all the problems workers faced, its limited application to only one industry, and the Triangle Fire all provoked a rethinking of Protocolism shortly after it began. Its weakness was twofold. To succeed, it needed to include the entire industry, which it never could. In addition, as a purely voluntary code it lacked powerful enforcement mechanisms. In the aftermath of the Triangle Fire, reformers, politicians, and workers demanded that something be done to prevent other disasters. Reformers surrounding the Protocol—whom I call interchangeably Protocolists and industrial democrats—seized the moment. Through the state legislative body charged with investigating industry after the fire, the FIC, reformers grafted the idea of Protocolism to the state. If they charged the state with enforcement, and if reformers had access to the state, Protocolism would not only survive, it would thrive.

Part I of this book traces the origins of the Protocol and the new style of labor relations in the garment industry by looking at the two strikes of 1909 and 1910. The unique feature of the Protocol was that it required the organization of both labor and industry into strong, centralized institutions. Chapter 1 traces the rebirth of the ILGWU and the alliance of immigrant workers and middle-class reformers. The settlement of the 1909 strike was a success in that the union reached settlement with most shops. However, the very nature of the settlement—hundreds of individual shop contracts—proved problematic, as contracts varied widely. Chapter 1 also looks at the development of the industry and workers into powerful organizations, because of the 1910 strike. Workers and managers alike learned the importance of organization. Often seen as separate, unconnected events, I argue that the two strikes were part of a larger movement in industrial rationalization and that only through comparison can we see larger developments. Both workers and managers saw the strikes as an opportunity to rationalize this chaotic industry through an industry-wide agreement. This movement for an industry-wide agreement attracted the attention of reformers such as Brandeis who were already searching for solutions to industrial unrest. Thus, the Great Revolt became the test case for the ideas that Brandeis had been writing about for some time. Chapter 2 looks at the system of industrial democracy as it was embodied within the Protocol. By looking at the evolution and development of the Protocol, we can see how one set of meanings is privileged over others. Chapter 3 traces the contested terrain of the Protocol and looks specifically at the issue of representation and the changing relationship between workers and their union. Chapter 3 also explores the problems the Protocol encountered. The most pressing of these problems was the contradiction between the promise of industrial democracy inherent in the Protocol and the bureaucracy that the Protocol created. This contradiction was expressed most explicitly in the debates over who spoke for the rank-and-file workers covered by the Protocol: their local unions or the leaders of the International union. And lastly, Chapter 3 traces these debates through to the eventual collapse of the garment Protocol as an effective tool of labor relations.

Part II discusses the incorporation of Protocolism into the state. Chapter 4 looks at the Triangle Fire through the lens of industrial democracy and examines the formation of the Factory Investigating Commission in 1911 and the political atmosphere that engendered its creation. The FIC provided the larger political context that is often missing in studies of labor relations policy formation. Chapter 5 places the FIC within the political landscape of New York during the Progressive Era. It demonstrates that the FIC was not only shaped by the politics of the era, but most importantly, that it helped shape those politics. Chapter 6 looks at the early successes of the FIC in regulating industry, in sanitation, safety, the dangerous trades, and health. Finally, Chapter 7 traces the effort by the Protocolists to move beyond sanitation and health to larger issues of welfare: hours, wages, and protection. This book argues that the incorporation of the ideas of the Protocol into a legislative body, the FIC, transformed both the state and the working class in the process. It also brought into the state a group of reformers such as Frances Perkins and politicians like Robert Wagner who would continue to further parts of the Protocolist agenda during the New Deal.

The form of industrial democracy that emerged in Progressive Era New York, Protocolism, set the agenda for years to come and therefore is significant in and of itself. However, it would be wrong to see the Progressive Era, as some have, as a mere prelude or "dress rehearsal" for the New Deal. Protocolism captured the optimism of the time and merged various reform impulses into a more unified force. The shapers of Protocolism did not fully loose this optimism, as it would be reborn in the 1930s. While the events of Progressive Era New York clearly informed the New Deal, they are more correctly viewed as separate overlapping episodes. The experiences in New York set the stage for much that would follow, but also closed certain paths in the American political economy. What followed would be more limited, less shop-floor democratic, and more state sanctioned than the original promise of Protocolism. In this regard, Protocolism clearly influenced the New Deal by shaping the debate, but it would be wrong to see it as the New Deal's opening act. One can argue that Protocolism showed more democratic promise precisely because the range of possibilities had yet to be defined. The New Deal, however, because it built on previous reform efforts had more limited promise because the possibilities had already been narrowed.

The struggle for industrial democracy in New York is important for a number of reasons. One, it reveals the limits of a participatory industrial democracy that never really was. Second, it demonstrates the process through which form beat out function—structure trumped process.

Third, it illustrates the development of state systems of IR by looking at IR from the bottom up. Lastly, it speaks to the importance of economic justice for an understanding of industrial democracy. Protocolism illustrates the important connections between economic and political rights often missing from historical discussions of democracy.

What was gained by these struggles? Historian Steve Fraser has written eloquently on this new emerging IR paradigm. What Fraser says was clear by the 1930s can be correctly pushed back into the 1910s:

> The industrial relations compact worked out by the industrial union leadership and the scientific managerial-Keynesian milieu provided for job security, formal democratic grievance and representation procedures, and high wages and benefits, all in return for shop-floor stability self-consciously achieved at the expense of the less formal practices of shop-floor democracy.[62]

American workers, and garment workers in particular, were better off because of the Protocols and the FIC. Looking at these events as act one of the New Deal denies these struggles their rightful place in history. The Progressive Era witnessed an important development for industrial democracy and IR. Only by studying it for its own sake can we truly understand its meaning and how future generations were informed and shaped by it.

"March to City Hall." Workers marching to City Hall to make visible their demands for a fair contract, safe and sanitary working conditions, a living wage, and reasonable hours.

1 PRIVATE PROTOCOLISM: INDUSTRIAL DEMOCRACY IN NEW YORK'S LADIES' GARMENT INDUSTRY

INDUSTRIAL DEMOCRACY was a term that before 1909 had significant relevance only for reformers and intellectuals. Events in Progressive Era New York grounded this abstract theory into the streets of the Lower East Side. The conflicts in the ladies' garment industry provided a ready-made laboratory. The Protocols of Peace, a radical trade agreement in New York City's ladies' garment industry, ushered in a new experiment with industrial democracy. Strikes of 1909 and 1910 organized more than the workers, they organized the industry as well. The unity of the labor force, public support for workers, and pressure from industrial democrats brought management to the bargaining table. In many ways, the Protocol was a traditional trade agreement—addressing wages, hours, and conditions. What made it unique was that it created a complete system of labor relations, whose intent was to transform the industry. The Protocol was an industrial regime, something much larger than a mere trade agreement.

The spark for this new industrial relations system came from the workers themselves. The strikes in the industry set the stage and organized both workers and owners into powerful groups necessary for an industry-wide agreement. Industrial democrats used this canvas provided by workers to paint a new picture. Men and women such as Louis Brandeis, Robert Wagner, Frances Perkins, George Price, Henry Julius Cohen, Belle Moskowitz, John Dyche, and others marshaled the power of social science and used their influence to broker deals to gain a seat at the industrial relations table.

Over time, these industrial democrats exerted more and more control over the system of labor relations. In the process, they transformed the meaning of industrial democracy. What started as a grass-roots effort for more democracy on the shop floor quickly transformed into both a viable ideology and system that allowed industrial democrats to control labor relations. Over time, reformers became more important as workers were moved to the sidelines. Under the new regime, unions found a powerful new role as broker and controller of working-class interests, becoming more structured, more bureaucratic, and less democratic. Yet, the compromise that was offered provided for better wages, hours, and conditions. Workers proved to be marginally supportive of the new system as long as they benefited. The Triangle Fire, the subject of Part 2 of this book, demonstrates the inherent weakness in this system. In addition, it shows that the protocol system was only, at best, half the story. Chapter 1 traces the importance of the 1909 and 1910 strikes as critical to the formation of a new labor regime. Chapter 2 focuses on the creation of the Protocols of Peace, the radical new labor agreement. And Chapter 3 looks at the conflicts with the Protocol over the contested meaning of industrial democracy. In particular, it traces the debates about representation and the proper role of the union within the agreement.

1   Workers Organizing Industry
The New York City Garment Strikes
of 1909 and 1910

THE FIRST steps toward industrial democracy came from below, from the workers themselves. New York City's ladies garment workers in 1909, and again in 1910, forced labor into the public's consciousness, providing the spark reformers and industry activists needed to envision an alternative to the current industrial order. This chapter traces rank-and-file workers' efforts to improve their lot. In the process, workers created an important and effective vehicle to channel their demands: a mature, stable trade union, the International Ladies' Garment Workers Union (ILGWU or ILG). The ILG would become a major force in shaping the direction of industrial democracy within New York City. This chapter traces the development of the ILGWU from 1909 to 1910. It looks at the interaction between workers and industrial democrats that developed and how this complicated relationship served both. Through that relationship, workers received the public support, expert advice, and financial assistance that enabled them to make significant improvements in working and sanitary conditions, wages, hours, and other important areas of concern. Industrial democrats gained as well, finding an arena for experimentation in industrial relations (IR). The chaotic nature of the New York ladies' garment industry made it a natural laboratory for industrial reform. If experts could reform this industry in this city, they could reform any industry. In the end, this symbiotic relationship between workers and reformers, while mutually beneficial, transformed the industry.

Massive strikes in 1909 and 1910 provided the impetus for changes in the IR system/regime that have missed the radar of labor historians. In 1909, women workers had no access, real or imaginary, to a public forum that could allow them to combat employers. Middle-class women reformers, principally the Women's Trade Union League (WTUL), bridged that gap for them. Out of a sense of maternalism, the WTUL moved from doing public relations for the "girl" strikers to active leadership by 1910. By the time of the 1910 cloakmakers' "Great Revolt," male workers, who could by virtue of their gender already occupy public space, were never permitted that role by middle-class allies and union leaders.[1]

The great strike of mostly women shirtwaist makers in 1909, known as the Uprising of Twenty Thousand, together with the Great Revolt of mostly male tailors in 1910, redefined IR, proving the crucible in which modern twentieth-century industrial policy was forged. This new IR, what I call Protocolism, transformed the conditions of labor and the relationship between labor and the public, and empowered a new professional elite at the expense of rank-and-file democracy. The predominance of women in the 1909 strike has made it a landmark in both women's history and labor history. The focus of this vast scholarship has been on the cross-class alliances of middle-class women reformers with their trade union sisters.[2] By failing to follow up on the second garment strike, women's historians have missed an important opportunity to study the role of gender on the newly forming labor policies in the ladies' garment industry. These efforts by middle-class reformers to redefine IR, starting on the picket lines in 1909, were refined during the 1910 strike and would resonate for the next fifty years.[3] These two events have too often been studied in isolation from one another. In the process, an important scholarly opportunity has been lost. By reconnecting these two events and studying them as a whole, one can trace the development of an emerging IR system. Middle-class reformers, mainly reform-minded social-worker types, played an active role in the 1909 strike. However, it was a secondary, supporting role. By the 1910 strike, reformers were leading participants. How this happened is the story of this chapter.[4]

THE UPRISING

Garment workers in 1909 and 1910 complained about the petty abuses and systematic terrors such as espionage, tyrannical supervisors, rudeness, poor pay, and favoritism they suffered daily. These abuses were the norm, not the exception. In addition, workers had the added indignity of paying for needles, thread, and electricity. At the heart of these complaints, therefore, were issues that went beyond bread-and-butter concerns to matters of humane treatment, citizenship rights, and industrial democracy, best summed up in the Yiddish phrase *menghlekhe bahandlung* (humane treatment), which was a common rallying cry for the mainly Jewish garment workers.[5] Bertha Elkins, a striker and Russian immigrant, put it this way: "I want something more than work and more than money. I want *freedom* [italics mine]." Workers, in 1909 and again in 1910, were striking for nothing short of democracy in industry.[6] They demanded to be treated and recognized as people, and the strike was their vehicle for democracy.

Daily, workers faced an undemocratic system of arbitrary work rules, petty abuses, and poor pay, and miserable working conditions.[7] Most manufacturers instituted a system of fines for their workers. Workers were also charged for "damaged" goods or products deemed of poor quality. Most simply felt that these were ploys to pay them less.[8] Another clear abuse was the "ticket system." Working on a piece-rate system, after each finished piece, workers received small tickets to be exchanged for their pay. Workers had no place to collect their tickets; they simply piled them up on their benches before them. Many workers regularly lost or misplaced tickets because they had no place to keep them. Workers alleged that the tickets were intentionally small and that they were not permitted anything to collect them in so that they would lose them and therefore be cheated out of wages. When workers complained or challenged management, they could be fired, labeled as troublemakers, and blacklisted in the industry.[9] The system disempowered them, taking their dignity as well as their agency.

Clara Lemlich, a veteran worker and strike leader, recalled how badly workers were treated when they tried to stand up for themselves:

> The bosses in the shops are hardly what you would call educated men. They yell at the girls and they "call them down" even worse than I would imagine slaves were in the South. They don't use very nice language. They swear at us and sometimes they do worse.[10]

The analogy with slavery is a fairly common one for garment workers. Clearly, garment workers were not "enslaved," as African slaves had been in America. Garment workers used the term as a powerful metaphor to drive home both their powerlessness and their struggles for (industrial) freedom. Lemlich knew in her heart that, like slaves, garment workers too would have their emancipation proclamation someday. She hoped, as others did, that they could free themselves.

Against such treatment, women demanded respect as both work-ers and as women. Historian Annelise Orleck and others refer to these women as "industrial feminists," women such as Lemlich who came to a feminist consciousness through a worker consciousness. By 1909, a con-currence of oppressive conditions had created a combustible situation and raised workers' consciousness about their own situation.[11]

The spark that set off the Uprising occurred late in July 1909 at the Rosen Brothers shop, a large factory producing women's shirtwaists or blouses. Rosen Brothers operated its factory under the "inside contract-ing system." Inside contracting developed in large shops as a means to compete with small shops. Smaller shops constantly had a labor cost advantage over large shops through their sweating of labor. "Sweating labor" refers to the continual downward pressures on labor costs, that is, wages and conditions, that lead to sweatshops.[12] Through the use of cheap labor, small shops could undercut, and thereby undersell, the larger shops. In response, larger shops, in essence, brought the small shop inside through the inside contracting system.

Large factories such as Rosen Brothers designed clothing, hired skilled cutters to make patterns, and sold finished goods to retailers. They did not make clothes. Rather, they hired skilled workers under contract to make the garments, settling on a price per finished garment, or the piece-rate. These inside contractors, in turn, hired teams of their own workers who actually made the garments. The inside contractor contracted with these workers and negotiated their own piece-rate. All work, however, was done within the factory, under the supervision of the firm. The chief benefits of this system were that it allowed manage-ment to sweat labor, provided flexibility, and gave management insula-tion from labor conflict. Inside contracting allowed Rosen Brothers to ex-pand and contract production as needed, without worrying about hiring and firing workers. And, lastly but most importantly, inside contracting allowed firms to take advantage of sweated labor by continuously low-ering labor costs and wage rates. Rosen, and other shops, continually adjusted (or lowered) piece-rates in an attempt to remain competitive with the small sweatshops in the industry. In short, sweatshops were driving industry standards.[13]

The massive strike in 1909 started when Rosen Brothers refused to pay the negotiated price, or piece-rate, that was agreed upon with its inside or subcontractors. Instead, the firm sought to renegotiate the rate. The inside contractors at Rosen, however, convinced their 200 workers to walk out with them to demand a just price. Arguing that if the price they were paid was lowered, the wages they could pay the workers also would be lowered. The workers turned to Local 25, the shirtwaist-makers' local of the ILGWU and the United Hebrew Trades (UHT) for assistance. The five-week strike was typical of garment strikes in many ways. First, thugs hired by the firms assaulted strikers on the picket lines. Second, strikers were subjected to police brutality. Third, strikers relied on the support of other unionists. And finally, local leadership never fully gave up control to the national union—even if the ILGWU received most of the press coverage and appeared to the public to be in charge. Yet, in the face of insurmountable odds, and after a five-week struggle, Rosen Brothers settled with the union. The workers gained union recognition, a 20 percent piece-rate hike, and, more importantly, a shop-floor committee to give workers a democratic voice. The first significant victory for Local 25 was achieved, and with it, workers streamed into the union and strike talk spread.[14]

The ILG had seen all this before. But, in the past, workers had left the union as quickly as they joined. Garment workers, according to one industry historian, were "emotional strikers but disinterested unionists."[15] One ILGWU organizer put it this way: "[The] greatest stumbling block is the indifference of their own [union] members."[16] Abraham Cahan, editor of the *Jewish Daily Forward*, the socialist community paper of the Lower East Side and quasi-official organ of the ILGWU, recalled the cycle of boom and bust that the ILGWU experienced in these years: "When our movement gave birth to a child, somehow or other, the child did not live. No sooner was it born then it died and then a new child would have to be born and the same thing would occur."[17] Thus, during the Rosen Brothers' strike, the ILGWU, the American Federation of Labor (AFL), and Local 25 tried to impress upon workers to stay with the union for the long haul. Frank Morrison, AFL secretary, told the strikers in August 1909,

> You waistmakers are generally successful in all strikes, but as soon as a strike is over you drop from the union. Do not keep away from the union. Attend all meetings and help those in the union to carry out their plans for betterment of your condition.[18]

As the Rosen Brothers strike was being settled, strike fever spread to other shops throughout the city. These strikes were unorganized and spontaneous in that workers went out first, then, like the Rosen strike, contacted and joined the union. Two of these strikes, at the Leiserson and Triangle shops, became the focus in the industry. Leiserson and Triangle were the two biggest shops. If the union could crack them, it could crack the entire industry. The owners of Leiserson and Triangle knew this, and the battle lines were firmly drawn.[19] One hundred and fifty workers walked out of Leiserson's shop protesting starvation wages and, more importantly, the brutal tyranny of one Italian foreman. But it was the Triangle shop strike that soon became the union's focus.[20]

In an effort to circumvent the union, Triangle had created a company union in 1908 and stepped up its activities in the summer of 1909. By mid-September, the "Triangle Employés [sic] Benevolent Association" had itself become the source of employee grievances. Workers began to demand that the association distribute a ten-dollar "Passover Allowance" to every member, not just a select few who were loyal to management. Triangle management saw this as a maneuver to disrupt the association by liquidating its funds. Management stepped in and refused to let the association give out these allowances, demonstrating to the workers the true nature of the association. Instead, it permitted the association to only lend ten dollars to needy, "worthy" families.[21]

Some of the workers, about 100, became so aggravated by the company's actions that they began to discuss unionization seriously for the first time. A special meeting of Local 25, the UHT, and Triangle workers took place behind locked doors and drawn shades at the union's headquarters at 96 Clinton Street. Soon after, Triangle's spies singled out these workers and the firm laid them off, claiming a slack time in production. Espionage was nothing new for the garment industry. At the same time, the union learned that Triangle had placed ads in many of the city's papers calling for replacement workers. The union, recognizing this as a lockout, declared a strike against Triangle on September 27.[22]

By mid-October, it appeared to union leaders that unless something drastic was done the strikes at Leiserson and Triangle would be lost. Both firms hired thugs to disrupt pickets and kept their factories open with scab labor. Under these circumstances, Local 25 and the UHT began to contemplate a general strike. However, it was a risk. Local 25 had approximately 500 members and only $4 in its treasury. Still, the workers were driven by a hyperpassion for unionism that just might sustain a call for a general strike. Local 25's fifteen-member Executive

Board (including four women, one of whom was Clara Lemlich) met to discuss the idea of a general strike. At a general meeting of the local on October 21, the union voted for a general strike and appointed a Committee of Five (three men and two women) to put it into effect. As talk of a general strike spread from shop to shop, picket-line violence, police brutality, and use of thugs hired by shop owners increased. The union was in a precarious position.[23]

Early on in the strike, middle-class reform women became increasingly visible. Many, seeing these mainly young immigrant women strikers as "sisters" in the larger women's rights struggle, ran to the picket lines as a show of feminist solidarity. Others operated under an older sense of noblesse oblige, an effort to protect these fragile girl strikers. Middle-class female reformers, whatever their motivation, stepped up their activity as the strike wore on. The focus of these reformers' activities was the New York WTUL. The national WTUL was founded at the American Federation of Labor's Boston Convention in 1903 by the noted socialist William English Walling, labor organizer Mary Kenny, and Hull House's Jane Addams, along with others. The WTUL saw itself as filling a necessary void. The leaders believed in labor unions as a democratic necessity. But unions had ignored women workers. The WTUL's goal was to aid local and national unions in organizing women. It quickly established branches in Boston, Chicago, and New York. The NYWTUL therefore saw the 1909 strike as its opportunity.[24]

On November 15, the union's Committee of Five realized that shop-by-shop organizing would not work; only a general strike would offer a solution in an industry as fragmented as shirtwaists.[25] It called for a general meeting to be held at Cooper Union later that week. On the night of November 22, an overflow crowd had to be directed to other halls throughout the city, Beethoven Hall and the Manhattan Lyceum among them. "For two hours," the *New York World* reported, "attentive audiences were cautioned to use deliberation, to be sober in their decision, but to be loyal to each other, and when they did decide to strike to stand by their union until all demands were granted."[26]

The speakers that night also used the occasion to address the manufacturers. Samuel Gompers, president of the AFL, told the strikers, "If you cannot get the manufacturers to give you what you want then strike, and when you strike, let the manufacturers know that you are on strike." Gompers told workers to concentrate on three key demands: a

10 percent wage increase, union recognition, and an end to police brutality and thug violence. "Strike and let them know it," Gompers implored the workers, "use it as an opportunity to strengthen the union."[27]

After listening for two hours, Clara Lemlich rose to speak. While many of the reporters did not recognize her, the garment workers surely did. She was a member of Local 25's Executive Board, a leader of the Leiserson strike, and an equally fiery socialist. Rising and taking the floor, she said:

> I am a working girl, one of those who are on strike against intolerable conditions. I am tired of listening to speakers who talk in general terms. What we are here for is to decide whether we shall or shall not strike. I offer a resolution that a general strike be declared—now.

What Lemlich wanted was action, not words. With that, "the big gathering was on its feet," according to the *New York World*:

> [E]veryone shouting an emphatic affirmative, waving hats, canes, handkerchiefs, anything that came handy. For five minutes, perhaps, the tumult continued; then the chairperson, B. Feigenbaum [of the *Jewish Daily Forward*], made himself heard and asked for a seconder of the resolution. Again the big audience leaped to its feet, everyone seconding.[28]

Feigenbaum asked the audience to take the Jewish oath. "Do you mean faith?" he screamed. "Will you take the old Jewish oath?" The crowd rose and repeated the pledge: "If I forget thee oh Jerusalem, may my right hand wither, may my tongue forget speech." The Jerusalem Feigenbaum referenced was not merely a religious symbol, but a signifier for the union movement. It demonstrates the extent to which radical Jews replaced theology with the new ideology of unionism.[29]

The next day, 15,000 shirtwaist makers walked out. The first few days were simply chaotic, as thousands of workers tried to crowd into Clinton Hall, Local 25's headquarters, to join the union. Clinton Hall had the atmosphere of a religious revival meeting. In one corner, workers were dancing, in another, signing union cards, and in yet another, talking strategy.[30] It took days for Clinton Hall to gain some semblance of organization, thanks in part to the help of the WTUL, who sent in dozens of members to handle the flow of people.[31] Once things calmed down, Local 25 sent strike committees from location to location trying to settle all the strikes shop by shop. By November 26, 2,000 workers had settled and returned to work, but another 1,200 had walked out on strike.[32]

While the call for the strike might not have surprised many workers, the means by which it took place certainly confused many; it also demonstrated the level of solidarity between the workers. One worker recalled how her shop decided to go out:

> I did not know how many workers in my shop had taken the oath at that meeting. I could not tell how many would go on strike in our factory the next day. When we came back the next morning to the factory, though, no one went to the dressing-room. We all sat at the machines with our hats and coats beside us, ready to leave .... And there was whispering and talking softly all around the room among the machines: "shall we wait like this?" "There is a general strike." "Who will get up first?" Well, so we stayed whispering and no one knowing what the other would do, not making up our minds for two hours. Then I started to get up. And at just the same minute all—we all got up together, in a second. No one after the other, no one before. And when I saw it—that time—oh, it excites me so yet I can hardly talk about it.[33]

Many of the small and medium-sized shops settled with the union on all of the wage and hour demands. The strike occurred just at the tail end of the busy fall season. Therefore, many smaller shops with orders to fill and a hand-to-mouth existence sought a quick settlement. While these settlements differed from shop to shop, they had several main features: union recognition; shop-committee arbitration for piece-rates; a union shop, or at least union preferences when hiring; and an end to charges for thread, needles, and electricity. The agreements also instituted a system of fines against management for breaking agreements. While these fines were small, the highest being $300, the profit margins were so close at many shops that even the smallest fine could close down a shop.[34]

The seventy large manufacturers that dominated the trade, led by Triangle and Leiserson, however, stayed firm. Rather than go it alone or attempt to negotiate with the union, the owners of Triangle, Max Blanck and Isaac Harris, circulated a letter in early November to all shirtwaist manufacturers suggesting the formation of an Employers Mutual Protective Association " in order to prevent this irresponsible union in gain[ing] the upper hand . . . [and] dictating to us the manner of conducting our business."[35] According to most newspaper accounts, by the evening of November 24, two days after the call for a general strike, more than 20,000 workers remained on strike.[36]

Following Triangle's call, the new Association of Waist and Dress Manufacturers (the association) met on November 25 and 26 at the Broadway Central Hotel. It elected I. B. Hyman as chair and Charles Weinblatt as secretary and legal counsel.[37] Declaring open war on the union, Samuel Floersheimer, speaking for the association, stated that any contract signed with the ILGWU or Local 25 was not "worth the paper it was written upon . . . [for] the men connected with the union are a lot of irresponsible black guards."[38] The organization further called for all manufacturers who had already signed contracts to openly break them and lock out their workers. Firms, then, who joined the association, according to Floersheimer, would be striking a blow for "liberty." Yet, few small shops took this advice. During this brief chaotic period, these settled firms were doing a brisk business picking up the orders left unfilled by the larger shops, and they were not going to jeopardize it for the larger shops or for any matter of principle.[39]

Larger shops, such as Triangle, were able to fight the union effectively for several reasons. First, they never shut down production. Second, they were able to shift production to factories outside of New York. Triangle, for instance, had operations in Yonkers and Philadelphia. Third, these shops subcontracted with those smaller shops that had already settled to fill fall orders. Fourth, as the strike moved into the winter, entering the slack season, larger firms had the resources to simply wait out the strikers.[40]

In late November, members of Local 25 recognized that some of the larger manufacturers had shifted production to Philadelphia. It appeared as if the New York strike would be lost because of these "runaway shops." In an effort to shore up its flanks, Local 25 began to open discussions with the Philadelphia Shirtwaist Union. By mid-December, with the aid and prompting of Local 25, the Philadelphia waistmakers called their own general strike. In establishing working-class solidarity across geographic boundaries, the Philadelphia strike was an important turning point for the union. That the shirtwaist workers of Philadelphia would also walk out reaffirmed the New York strikers' faith in the union and signaled a new coordinated militancy to management. Finally, the industrial workforce was functioning as a *unified* workforce, setting the first stage for industrial democracy.[41]

Violence, Brutality, the WTUL, and the "Employer's Law"

Compounding the union's uneven success in combating ethnic divisiveness and other internal problems were external forces such as the law and middle-class attitudes. Strikers, for instance, were beaten and terrorized by toughs and prostitutes hired by management. They were regularly jailed for contempt of court. Moreover, many newspapers suggested that the strikers deserved this treatment. As one picketer recalled, "There was the law to protect the employer, but only the workers to protect the workers."[42]

Yet, it was this very violence that proved a turning point for the strike. As most of the strikers (80 percent) were young women, the violence aroused the maternalistic instincts among the middle-class reform women. These reformers entered the strike to protect their sisters from abuse and in the process played an unintentional role in transforming IR.[43]

Large manufacturers hired private security agents, mainly to keep their factories open with mostly nonunion Italian labor. In their circular letters, these agencies included the names of known gangsters, thugs, and toughs.[44] These services performed two main functions: to disrupt picketing and break the morale of the strikers, and to allow the use of scabs to keep their production going. On August 12, before the general strike, Rosen Brothers hired detectives to protect the "Italian girls" who remained inside the shop. During an altercation in front of the shop, several picketers were badly beaten. *The Jewish Daily Forward* published photos of the girls and the names of the toughs. These "detectives" all had lengthy criminal records.[45]

To many of the strikers and their allies, the courts seemed to be merely an extension of management. For example, after Clara Lemlich was beaten so badly that she was hospitalized for several days, the five men who beat her were acquitted by Magistrate Robert C. Cornell. At the hearing, the superintendent of the Rosen factory, a Mr. Ross, informed the judge that these men were hired simply to protect the "Italian girls" who remained at work.[46] At the arraignment on September 15, the men who beat Lemlich were arraigned together with a large group of strikers. The thugs—a prizefighter and several ex-convicts—were let go, even as Lemlich remained in the hospital. Six days earlier, the police had arrested four strikers for "assaulting" scabs. This was after the armed band of toughs had terrorized and beaten the four young workers. Again, they were let go while the girls were fined ten dollars apiece for disorderly conduct.[47]

Increased violence against young and teenaged women, coupled with the injustice of the court system, finally worked to the strikers' advantage, as it gained the waistmakers public support among the middle class. By the end of October, the police had arrested 77 strikers; by January 1, the number had reached 707.[48] For many affluent supporters of the strikers, the legal status of women was a straightforward issue demanding paternal intervention. To the elite, paternalism functioned through a complex lens of class and gender ideologies. These strikers needed protection not just because they were women, but also because they were poor and young. This paternalistic ideology saw the strikers as children needing help and support. However, for many strikers, the inequality of the legal system was explained solely as a class issue. As Theresa Malkiel's Mary, the young striker who narrates her fictionalized *Diary of a Shirtwaist Striker*, stated:

> [T]hey [middle-class women] try to tell us that it ain't lady-like to go out on strike. Why don't they say that it ain't lady-like to go out into the factories and work from morn until night and the same thing over again the next day til we get to see nothing but work and the machine before us.[49]

Still, the strikers, to hold the support of the middle class whom they desperately needed, never argued the point too loudly, lest they lose valuable allies.

The judges and magistrates, in front of whom came strikers and thugs alike, were almost of one mind on the strike. Typical were the words of Magistrate W. H. Olmstead. Addressing a fifteen- or sixteen-year-old striker in Children's Court, he declared: "You are on strike against God and nature." So, although peaceful picketing was legal in New York in 1909, municipal judges thought otherwise. They convicted scores of girls on vagrancy, solicitation, disorderly conduct, and assault charges. They fined hundreds and sentenced dozens more to the workhouse. It seems only one judge, Paul Krotel, dismissed some charges and made an attempt to remain neutral, while Magistrates Joseph E. Corrigan, Robert C. Cornell, Peter T. Barlow, and W. H. Olmstead did not.[50]

One magistrate announced that he would convict strikers just for using the word *scab*: "If these girls continue to rush around and cry 'scab' I shall convict them of disorderly conduct. There is no word in the English language as irritating as the word 'scab.'"[51] Magistrate Frederick B. House went so far as to oppose the Superior Court of New York's support for the right to picket:

> There has never been a strike in this city in which pickets have been employed that there has not been a breach of the peace. Although the higher courts, including Judge Rosalsky in General Sessions, have held that strikers have the right to employ pickets and call names, I personally differ from them. I think such conduct tends toward a breach of the peace.[52]

The strikers' response began a chain of developments that was to turn the tide of the strike toward labor. Rather than become intimidated by these developments, the strikers increased their picket and strike activity. As Mary, Malkiel's factious striker, recognized, "The judges and the police make the mistake of their lives if they hope to stop us by keeping up this jail business—every arrest makes a firm convert to the cause."[53] The strikers also raised money for a defense fund.[54] Then, in a critical move, they brought middle-class women onto the picket lines and made their presence the centerpiece of strike resistance. Before the direct engagement of the middle-class reform women on the side of labor, the manufacturers' association was clearly winning the strike. As long as they could keep the shops open with scab labor, they could hold out. Now the presence of middle-class women on the picket lines disarmed the association.[55]

On October 23, the police arrested Margaret Johnson, a middle-class "ally" and member of the WTUL, for picketing. With this, the activity of the WTUL increased. One incident, which sparked a sustained controversy, was the arrest of Mary Dreier on November 4. Working-class women had demanded that their allies in the WTUL fully participate in the strike by scheduling themselves for picket watches around the clock.[56] Dreier, a socially prominent woman and WTUL leader, had been persuaded to picket in an effort to protect the strikers. Many working-class members of the WTUL believed that the mere presence of the middle-class women would be enough to end the violence, or more specifically, to shield them. Picketing peacefully in front of the Triangle factory, Dreier tried to convince some of the scabs not to cross the lines. One of their escorts called her a "dirty liar." With that, Dreier approached a police officer and said, "You heard the language that man used to me. Am I not entitled to your protection?" The policeman replied that he could not be certain that she was not a liar. When a scab then accused her of assault, it was Dreier who was arrested. She was brought to the Mercer Street station, but when the police discovered who she was, they released her immediately. The arrest of Dreier brought heightened press coverage and a more intense WTUL effort to end police brutality and legal injustice.[57]

Dreier's arrest and immediate release, however, demonstrates the difference in perspective between the workers and the allies. Dreier, a woman of wealth and privilege, was accustomed to police protection. Workers, on the other hand, were accustomed to police abuse. Dreier found her treatment intolerable—upset by the simple fact that she was being treated like a common worker. The police were not just disrespectful of her as a "lady," they were disrespectful of her class privilege as well. Dreier and many other WTUL allies wanted the police and judges to treat the girl strikers with the same respectability accorded to women of the middle class. For Dreier, gender trumped class.

After Dreier's arrest, the WTUL began to investigate police abuse and the use of private detectives by the association. On December 4, Bertha Poole Weyl, WTUL member and wife of prominent liberal journalist Walter Weyl, issued a press release detailing her investigations of the use of criminal elements by the association to crush the strike. The WTUL traced the criminals to agencies that, for a fee, would provide strong-arm men for the association. These "special detectives" would move in and cause a disturbance on the picket line, knowing that the police would arrest everyone but would eventually let them go and jail only the strikers. Weyl suggested that the police were working with these criminal elements and called for an official investigation. I. B. Hyman, chair of the association, responded that it was the strikers who caused the violence. "I shouldn't blame the employers if they used toughs . . . these strikers do such things!" he argued. The employers, he suggested, were simply protecting themselves and the workers who were not on strike from danger.[58]

However, the abuse of strikers by management thugs and the police continued unabated, regardless of the WTUL's reports or protests. In late November, Judge Joseph Corrigan, in fining Jeanie Bloom ten dollars for disorderly conduct, announced that if any more strikers came before his bench he would send them straight to the poorhouse.[59] In late December, Corrigan kept his promise, sentencing shirtwaistmakers

Bessie Alperin and Rosa Rabinowits to Blackwell Island.[60] Actions such as this got women such as Anne Morgan and Alva Belmont, two of the richest and most prominent women in New York, involved. Belmont, of the Political Equity League, was an active suffragist, who saw in the Uprising an opportunity for building cross-class alliances for the suffrage movement. After spending countless hours observing trials at the Jefferson Market Courthouse, her suffrage hopes led her to conclude that women judges would solve the workers' problems:

> I have arrived at the conclusion that we would all be better off if we visited the night court more frequently. Conditions in the mismanaged social life of New York City are no where else so forcefully brought out.... There will be a different order of things when we have women judges on the bench.... During those six hours I spent in that police court I saw enough to convince me and all who were with me beyond the smallest doubt of the absolute necessity for woman suffrage.[61]

In an effort to connect the Uprising to the suffrage movement and forge a cross-class coalition, Belmont and her Political Equity League organized a massive public meeting at the Hippodrome on December 5 to protest police brutality, gain the support of strikers for suffrage, and gather middle-class support for the strike. Ministers, rabbis, and unionists addressed the crowd. But, it was noted socialist speakers such as Methodist preacher Dr. Anna Shaw, Rose Paster Stokers, and Leonora O'Reilly who were the stars of the evening. Each, in turn, addressed the large crowd in terms that connected the strike's class and gender components.[62]

Class cleavages, however, always threatened to dissolve this coalition. Moreover, this problem of class would be a critical one in the creation of Protocolism and industrial democracy. Workers needed their middle-class allies, but they constantly had to fight with them over who would control the process, who would speak for the workers, and what was the proper role for an ally of labor. Even before the formation of the first Protocol, in 1910, workers were constrained by the actions of their allies. On January 2, a huge meeting was held at Carnegie Hall to raise money for strikers and gather public support for the strike. While the event was paid for by Anne Morgan, Mrs. Nathan Strauss, and Mary Beard, among others, the event was an effort by the strikers and the union to take back the strike from their wealthy allies by redefining the issues. Here, they would redefine the issue of police involvement in the strike. It could be said that the police were a surrogate or metaphor for the state. Therefore, workers were trying to redefine the relationship between labor and the state. On the stage that night, in the first row, were twenty strikers who had served time in the workhouse. They wore signs declaring that they were "workhouse prisoners," or that they had been "arrested." Over their heads, behind the stage, was a sign that read: "The workhouse is no answer to a demand for justice." Behind those 20 girls stood 350 girls who had been arrested. To the workers who organized this display, then, the state was no friend to the working class, but a tool of capital. Morris Hillquit, Rabbi Stephen S. Wise, and Leonora O'Reilly gave impassioned speeches. O'Reilly led out Rosa Perr, a striker who had served a five-day sentence in the workhouse. Perr described in detail the abuse she suffered.[63] Many mainstream daily papers like the *World* and the *Evening Journal*, not to mention the socialist *Call* and the *Jewish Daily Forward*, spoke of the "innocent girls." In contrast, the *Times* scolded the WTUL for not curbing the passion, lawlessness, and what it saw as the "untrained impulses" of the strikers. The *Times* seemed to suggest that jail would not be required if only these girls were better behaved. The *Times* went on to call for more workhouses and prisons for those that did not.[64] The pageant forced the middle-class allies to look anew at the role of the state. They began to ask how it could be made neutral, or even better, how the state could be refashioned into a tool for reform.[65]

The next day, 10,000 strikers marched four abreast to City Hall. Led by WTUL leaders Mary Dreier and Helen Marot and, most importantly, by worker Rose Schneiderman—special East Side organizer for the WTUL and leader of the Triangle strikers—they marched to present Mayor McClellen with a petition calling for the city to end police abuse. Many of the marchers wore armbands that said, "We are not slaves" in Yiddish. The mayor met the marchers, took the petition, and told the group that he would have the police commissioner look into the matter.[66]

The workers' public actions made the police abuse visible to the middle class. Moreover, it was in this way that the strike was brought to the immediate attention of Progressive reformers in New York City. The unjust treatment of the strikers forced E.R.A. Seligman, professor at Columbia University and active member of the American Association for Labor Legislation (AALL), Mary K. Simkhovitch, social worker at the University Settlement, muckraking journalist Ida M. Tarbel, and social reformer Lillian D. Wald to write to the *New York Times* in protest "against the injustice displayed by the police in the case of the young shirtwaistmakers on strike." The *Times* responded that the police were just doing their duty; they were not partisans. Seligman and company responded with details of "shocking and offensive partisanship." This dialogue lasted for several days, and while neither side convinced the other, it provided readers with a detailed airing of police abuses. It also allowed the public a glimpse of what workers faced almost daily.[67]

In addition to providing public support, middle-class reformers aided the strikers in a number of important ways. The WTUL had sixty-five members on picket watch, raised $50,000 to $60,000 in fines and bail for strikers, coordinated press conferences, helped to edit special editions of both the *Call* and the *New York Journal*, and raised more than $20,000 for the strike fund. In exchange for this activity, the WTUL was given two seats on the union's Strike Committee.[68] The WTUL and the UHT also arranged for legal aid. During the course of the strike, eight lawyers aided the union and the strikers. These lawyers and the WTUL helped draft detailed rules for strikers to help minimize their legal danger and to aid in their defense.[69]

The attention gained through the police brutality incidents brought much needed support and assistance from reform groups, most notably the WTUL. Despite all this assistance, many of the strikers and their more radical allies chafed at the control the WTUL attempted to wield over day-to-day operations. Many strikers felt the allies were condescending. Bertha Weyl's characterization of dealing with the strikers as "like handling a vast kindergarten" was typical.[70] Also representative was the working girls' reaction to a December 19 luncheon at the Colony Club. A committee of society ladies (WTUL members all) invited women from New York's "400 families" to meet the strikers for lunch. Ten strikers met these women and, over lunch, told them of their plight. These women eventually gave $1,300 for the strike fund. Yet, many of the strikers and their working-class supporters, including Theresa Malkiel, felt they had been put on display, much like animals in the zoo. Like characters out of Malkiel's *The Diary of a Shirtwaistmaker*, these strikers were forced to perform for the money. Malkiel criticized the society women for never leaving their living rooms or social clubs to see the reality of workers' daily lives, instead preferring the fiction of a novel or the drama of recreation to the real thing. When, on December 12, Malkiel and a group of strikers unexpectedly showed up at Alva Belmont's front door for an impromptu discussion, Mrs. Belmont's secretary informed them that they would have to submit their questions in writing. Women like Malkiel, and O'Reilly for that matter, believed that while the support of middle-class women was necessary, workers should have little faith in their sincerity, or in the possibilities of a united front of women.[71] However, Malkiel realized, as the strike dragged on and interest began to wane, support of any kind was necessary. Some of these allies, especially the youngest of them, the college students, could be "the bravest of the brave, day in and day out shivering from cold and at time drenched to the skin."[72]

The WTUL was not alone in its support for the strike. Behind the scenes, the Socialist Party, the Workingman Circle, and the United Hebrew Trades (UHT) were all aiding the union and the strikers. They remained constant in their support throughout the strike. In late December and early January, when the strike was at its darkest days, the UHT's members helped raise money for the shirtwaist strike fund by assessing half of one day's wages from each member.[73] Newspapers like the *Call* and the *Forward* ran daily accounts of the strike, and almost daily calls for strike funds, especially from December through February. The *Evening Journal* and the *Call* printed special strike editions, edited by the union and allies, to publicize the strike and raise money. The strikers had many allies. But it was their union that took the lead as the strike dragged on. Public support could only go so far.[74]

NEGOTIATIONS

Central to almost any strike is the ability of the union to reach a successful settlement. The relationship between middle-class reformers and the ILGWU was both important and complex. However, the reformers' relationship was with the leadership of the ILGWU, not with the rank-and-file membership. The leaders of Local 25 and the ILGWU needed the reformers to put public pressure on the city administration to stop police abuses. In addition, they needed the reformers to pressure the shop owners to come to the bargaining table. Once there, however, the union leaders and their advisers would handle the process of negotiations. Even as early as 1910, workers, who created the union and the movement for change, were being slowly and surely pushed to the side by a team of union leaders, professional advisers, and reformers, all pushing for industrial democracy.

Negotiations to end the strike began as early as the strike's second month, but without much success. While much is known about the picketing, curiously little is known about the process of negotiation. What made this strike different from others was not just the number, age, and gender of the strikers, but the *style* of bargaining that developed. Early on, both sides created elaborate new organizational structures for collective bargaining. In addition, individuals and groups outside of the New York garment industry and union shaped the bargaining process. The forces behind the new structures were led by men from within the union and elite women and men from without. One reason given for the need for this new, more bureaucratic structure was the youth and gender of the strikers. The strikers' inability to overcome the biggest stumbling block, combined with the association's absolute refusal to deal with the union, led many to believe that the details of bargaining should be handled by professionals—union leaders and reformers. The shift in structure proved necessary to set the process in motion for transforming IR in the industry.[75]

On December 6, a break in the stalemate came in the form of John Mitchell, ex-president of the United Mine Workers, and Marcus M. Marks, president of the Clothiers' Association. Both of these men embodied a new spirit of industrial relations. They saw labor relations as involving more than just workers and managers. They argued for and used their collective influence to gain a position for "the public" at the bargaining table. Acting on behalf of the National Civic Federation (NCF), Mitchell and Marks offered their services to help break the deadlock and end the strike. Their solution called for a six-member Board of Arbitration, each side choosing two members and the four choosing the remaining two, who would represent the public's interest. They argued that the current situation would hurt both sides and "prove only which side is stronger, not which side is right."[76]

The union quickly responded to the NCF call and appointed socialist leader and union adviser Morris Hillquit and Mitchell as their chosen representatives. Hyman, speaking for management, on the other hand, refused the services of the NCF, announcing that he would have nothing to do with the union. Marks, trying to give the association an out, announced that Hyman spoke only for himself, that his statements were personal, not official.[77] Marks's strategy proved effective. On December 10, Hillquit and Mitchell met with Hyman and J. B. Flaherty of the association. But, after only a few hours, the meeting broke up.

The central issue that stalled the talks for the association was union recognition. The association issued a statement later that night which stated that "under no circumstances [would they allow for the] unionization of their shops . . . the waist and dress manufacturers would never sign any union agreement." At its heart, the disagreement was simple. The association would not submit the issue of a union shop or recognition for arbitration. For its part, the union would not discuss other matters until this central one was resolved.[78] The workers' strength lay in collective action, and by extension, industry-wide collective bargaining. But, to succeed, the union needed to be duly recognized as the sole bargaining agent for the workers. Recognition was therefore central. Speaking later in December, Hillquit reminded the union that the primary issue had to be an industry-wide collective agreement. Anything less would be a defeat. As he said:

> [C]ollectively the waistmakers are strong, individually they are helpless and defenseless. If the employers were today to concede all the demands of the strikers, but be allowed to destroy or even weaken the union, they could and would restore the old condition of servitude in the shops, with in a very few weeks or months.[79]

The union and its members saw union recognition as an emancipation proclamation to end years of servitude. It was something they were intent on holding out for as long as possible.

During the week following the breakdown in talks, Marks tried to get the association to reconsider its position, while Mitchell attacked them for backing out of a deal.[80] The association responded to these arguments by attempting to connect this strike with the open-shop drive. It also attempted to tarnish the ILGWU as a radical union, which it in fact was, and to sell the open shop as part of the American principles of individual liberty and democracy. Nevertheless, by 1909 and 1910, even the conservative *New York Times* had begun to argue that unions must provide class stability and, quite possibly, were a bulwark against revolution.[81]

In an effort to regain public support, the association invited elite women to investigate its shops and factories, which, it insisted, were some of the best in America. The WTUL's Alva Belmont led the investigation. However, after a few weeks she turned it over to the New York State Board of Arbitration and Mediation, stating that without subpoena power her report would be woefully inadequate. The effort to enlist the support of society women had backfired, and the association turned back to injunctions and lawsuits to stall a state investigation.[82]

In late December, Marks, Mitchell, and Mrs. Frederick Nathan, of the National Consumers' League, teamed up to push the association toward arbitration once again. For its part, the association was more inclined to negotiate as the strike spread to Philadelphia, cutting off its principal alternative supply of garments during the strike.[83] On December 27, the two sides met for several hours and hammered out an eight-point agreement that was submitted to the union for ratification. The points included a fifty-two-hour workweek, equalization of pay among all workers during slack seasons, four paid holidays, a program by which employers would supply employees with all the necessary items needed for production (thread, needles, and electricity included), and wages and piece-rates set jointly by shop committees of employers and employees. Management also agreed to hire back all strikers before hiring any new workers. But the recognition clause, which was most important to the union, was sidestepped. This agreement failed to discuss the issue of union recognition and the closed shop, and therefore the strikers rejected it.[84]

In a last-ditch effort to hold the meeting together, Marks and Miles Dawson, legal counsel for the union, created a substitute clause, which tried to open the door to the union. This new clause suggested that the union would be one of many possible parties in talks: "The Association will confer with employees and the representatives of the Ladies Waistmakers Union as to any differences, which may not be settled between the individual shop and its employees." Now it was the association's turn to reject the agreement.[85]

As negotiations failed and the strike wore on, many workers returned to work. Some signed the agreement with the second clause, some with the first. Some returned to their shops without any union contract at all. By early January, the morale of the strikers and their allies was low.[86] Sensing an opportunity, John Ludrigen and Michael Reagan of the New York State Board of Arbitration and Mediation offered their services. They believed that the open- versus closed-shop dilemma could be solved only if both sides defined what they meant by the terms. They believed that once both sides started talking, a settlement would follow. To begin, they suggested a new Board of Arbitration. While the union appointed three members, the association refused to cooperate, causing Ludrigen and Reagan to withdraw.[87] With the collapse of talks, some prominent New Yorkers called for Mayor Gaynor to mediate, but he refused.[88]

Some in the union considered increasing the stakes by calling out all the shirtwaist workers. Again, many of the shops that had settled were in fact subcontracting for shops still out on strike. Fearing another general strike, many more shops quickly began to settle.[89] During the first week of February, some of the larger shops, Rosen and Leiserson included, settled with the union. These agreements accepted the first seven points of the Mitchell-Marks agreement, but added three more: no union recognition of any kind, no nonunion workers would be fired, and union members would be (re)hired without prejudice.[90]

The Philadelphia strike ended on February 6, with a momentous new agreement that broke important new ground in IR. The features were very similar to the proposed Mitchell-Marks agreement. What was unique was the inclusion of a five-person Board of Arbitration, which would proceed throughout the contract's lifetime—from February 6, 1910 through May 1, 1911. This most important and permanent feature of the agreement would constitute the basis for a new IR model and would come to the New York ladies' garment industry the following year, in the wake of yet another strike.[91]

On February 15, the ILGWU called off the New York general strike. In reality, it had all but ended at least two weeks before. Yet, the union declared the strike a victory, and in many ways, it was. What was gained came from individual shop contracts with small and medium-sized shops, not the industry-wide agreement as was hoped for. Of the 320 contracts signed, 302 recognized the union. Membership in the local went from 500 members in August to over 20,000 by February. The union had also survived to fight another day. To be sure, without an industry-wide agreement, these shop agreements were weak. However, the strikers were able, at least for the present, to end the most noxious features of their servitude and begin to claim their rightful place as industrial citizens.

The victory of unionization, however, was accompanied by substantial bureaucratic developments, which limited workers' ability to mount militant protest in the future. Both union leaders and company bosses had come to see that the militancy of the workers and the sheer size of the union necessitated a more formal and bureaucratic organization. Simply said, the strike brought significant structural changes to the union. These changes became critical as the industry moved almost of its own will toward a new style of IR. As part of the changes, the union in New York divided itself into seven districts, with two divisions per district. A new Executive Board was created. Because of the nature of the settlements—individual shop agreements—delegates from each district were brought onto the Executive Board. They were usually older, skilled male workers, who recognized the localized nexus of power within the new ILGWU brought on by the new contract systems. The impact of this agreement was to bureaucratize the union structure and remove rank-and-file workers, particularly women, from the important process of industrial relations. The incorporation of local leadership tied the locals to the International in new and curious ways. Most important, the International gained authority in its claim to be the sole legitimate voice of all garment workers. To retain this legitimacy, it would expend much time and energy in keeping more radical workers in line. In some ways, then, the ILGWU would increasingly become a police force for regulating workers' militancy. Its ability to control workers and regulate the entire industry directly corresponded to its success with management.

The strike, however, also demonstrated the enormous support women workers had within reform circles, support that the union as a whole could tap for future contests. The strike also ultimately forced the industry to recognize the union as a stabilizing force in the industry. While management did not support the revolutionary socialism that the ILGWU espoused, it did recognize how a "regulated" industry could transform revolutionary socialism into a more palatable corporatist alternative. At first, bosses sought private regulation, or self-regulation; only later did they come to accept state regulation of industry.[92] The strike, in addition, had demonstrated the need to bring in supposedly neutral "experts" and outsiders to help arbitrate a settlement. These features would have lasting impact on the industry and the shape of the new IR. These outsiders, representing the "public," were at first concerned citizens; in time, such men and women would become agents of the state itself. But, we get ahead of ourselves. For now the ILG had won the right to claim a place at the bargaining table, but it remained to secure that place in the hearts and minds of the workers it represented. Similarly, the principle of arbitration did settle the procedure for choosing such representation. This system would not become firmly cemented in place until after the Great Revolt of cloakmakers in 1910, and it was transformed again by the Triangle Fire of 1911.

THE UNION PREPARES FOR ANOTHER STRIKE

The surprising success of the shirtwaist strike brought a renewed sense of possibility to workers and their union leaders in other sectors of the ladies' garment industry. The lessons learned were many; the most obvious was the power of the general strike as a constructive tool for IR. In an unrationalized industry such as the ladies' garment industry, the general strike seemed to have the *revolutionary* potential to organize the entire industry. Also, the 1909 strike, if anything, saved the ILGWU from possible extinction. In a period of several months, the union went from an ignored, moribund group to being *the* premier labor institution in the city, state, and possibly the nation. Another lesson, not lost on the ILGWU, was that under the right circumstances, public opinion could be mobilized to aid the union and win the battle. The Uprising elevated the union in the eyes of the public through the involvement of concerned public citizens and reform groups. Reformers began to see in the ILGWU an ally in reform efforts, especially those involving issues of injustice and poverty, which were central to the reform impulses of the Progressive Era.[93]

Many Lower East Side radicals saw unionization as a mere extension of socialist politics. Therefore, they were anxious for continuous, militant action: strikes. These socialists and radical intellectuals pressed the ILGWU's Joint Board of Cloak, Skirt, and Pressers Unions of New York (Joint Board)—the coordinating executive body in charge of the cloakmakers—to step up strike activity.[94]

Many on the Joint Board and in the leadership of the ILGWU cautioned patience. They argued that workers were not ready for a massive strike. Concerted efforts would need to be made, and plans laid, they argued. These more cautious unionists drew lessons from the Shirtwaist Uprising.[95] The Uprising, many argued, was not a total success because workers were not fully prepared for the strike. These "women" were too passionate, too irrational. If the cloakmakers were to avoid their fate, they would need to organize, plan, and orchestrate a general strike: in other words, act like rational *men*. All the strikers would have to act as a singular, well-oiled machine, or as an army following a singular directive. Another factor motivating the union leaders was the lack of union discipline among the rank and file. ILG leaders wanted to develop a more centralized, disciplined union movement. This was a central principle, whether they knew it or not, of industrial democracy. These workers were essentially building the foundation that others would use to erect the Protocol of Peace. They firmly believed that only through organization could success flow. This argument eventually won over the majority of the Joint Board, and soon plans were made for a coordinated general strike.[96] In its December 1909 Convention, the ILGWU passed a referendum with 90 percent of its cloakmakers voting for a strike tax.[97]

The cloakmakers had reasons to hope for success; their numbers were indeed growing. Local 1, a cutters local, for example, had a mere 200 members in 1908, and yet by 1910, it claimed to be 2,000 strong. Similarly, the Cloak Tailors, Local 9, was saved from the brink of collapse as thousands of Jewish and Italian male tailors filled its ranks. These locals' experiences were not alone—most of the cloakmakers' locals swelled. The result, as the unions recognized at the time, was great enthusiasm born for a general strike. The Uprising had convinced many garment workers that their day was near, that they could achieve industrial democracy in their lifetimes.[98]

Continuing deplorable conditions in the industry gave fuel for the strike call. Unsanitary conditions, long hours, inadequate pay, undemocratic work rules, seasonal employment, and many more grievances were the norm. Because of the nature of the industry, standards arose, not from the large shops, but rather from the small manufacturers. Cutthroat competition was the business norm. Profits came out of savings from labor; therefore, wages were driven lower and lower (sweated) to undercut prices in a contract. This system led to a "race to the bottom," which froze the industry into an early state of industrial development. This competitive nature left no room for strategic planning, and therefore the industry was thoroughly chaotic, operating on survival mode, day to day. Each shop operated as an atomized unit of production. Once one shop cut its labor rates, the others soon followed.[99]

The union blamed these conditions on the presence of nonunion workers and demanded that union members organize the industry. However, without a strong union to protect them, management held tremendous power. The industry was thoroughly antiunion. It was common for shops to fire union members and some even forbade their workers from joining unions. Many shops required workers to deposit "security," or took regular deductions from their pay. This security would be lost if workers joined unions. This technique kept the unions out and ensured shop owners that workers would stay on the job through the busy seasons. Most employers circulated a "blacklist" of union activists. Almost all regularly closed their shops—locking out workers—long enough to get rid of all the union members, and then reopened with nonunion workers.[100]

The ILGWU's Joint Board of Cloakmakers believed that elaborate plans had to be laid to succeed. Workers needed to be educated on the importance of working together for the collective whole of the union rather than individually for the shop. Their target was not to discipline a single shop, or even several shops, but rather to unionize and thereby discipline the entire industry. The Joint Board needed to stop the shop strikes and have workers prepare for a massive general strike. To prepare, early in 1910, the Joint Board established a new publication, the *New Post*. First a newsletter, then a weekly paper, the *New Post* was published in English, Yiddish, and Italian in order to reach all of the cloakmakers, and it became a direct line of communication between leaders and workers. Circulation was large. Shop committeemen and the writers for the paper tried to channel the restlessness among the workers into preparations for a general strike and away from "disastrous" shop strikes, which simply sidetracked the movement. Shop strikes were said to be a selfish diversion, and workers were told to try to avoid them and bide their time for the real thing.[101]

Starting in early spring, preparations were well underway for a general strike. Manufacturers obviously sensed what was happening. Most of the smaller shop owners lived in the same communities as the workers and often read the same newspapers. Normally April and May were reserved for production of cheaper styles, and the more expensive Fall lines were produced during the summer months. However, if a strike came before the fall lines were finished, manufacturers would lose their most valuable products. As news of an impending general strike spread across the industry, manufacturers attempted to speed up their fall production to fulfill their orders before the strike. In so doing, they shifted their production to outside contractors. Jobbing, the contracting system that the industry eventually evolved into, seriously threatened the ILGWU. Jobbing rates were normally low. In addition, this speed-up would provide the manufacturers with the fall lines early. This vast inventory would, in turn, allow the manufacturers to sit out the strike with little or no real loss to them.[102]

To combat this turn of events, the Joint Board began to experiment with a series of what it called "building strikes." These strikes were nothing more than modified shop strikes. However, the union, having spent weeks denouncing these job actions as useless, needed to differentiate these strikes. The main logic behind these strikes lay in the fact that these strikes were tightly controlled and orchestrated by the union leadership, and were designed to slow down jobbing and outside contracting in order to buy the ILGWU more time to launch a successful general strike. Rather than spontaneous rank-and-file actions, these strikes were controlled centrally by the union.[103]

By early June, the call for the general strike had reached a crescendo. The building strikes had some success in that they limited the production of jobber goods. In addition, there was a massive May Day Parade in which the cloakmakers and the ILGWU figured prominently. The ranks of the ILGWU, especially the cloakmakers' locals, grew exponentially with discontented and impatient workers. The ILGWU and the Joint Board continually cautioned the rank and file to wait until after the upcoming ILGWU Convention, when plans would be finalized. The union was also concerned that the bureaucracy would not be in order until then. It wanted to make sure that it was the union leaders who controlled this strike.[104] The leadership argued continuously that if the workers acted too soon, before they were prepared, the results would be disastrous. This planning and orchestration did not go unnoticed among the industrial democrats.[105]

When the ILGWU finally held its convention in Boston, on June 6–12, 1910, the central issue was the possibility of a cloakmakers' general strike. Numerous resolutions calling for the general strike were presented to President Abraham Rosenberg, so many in fact that on the first day of the convention he created a special committee to look into the matter. On June 10, the committee issued its report urging a general strike vote. John A. Dyche, secretary-treasurer of the ILGWU and the leading industrial democrat within the union, amended the resolution to give full power over the strike to the General Executive Board of the ILGWU. A five-hour debate erupted over who would control the strike—the rank and file or the union's leadership. The rank and file (opponents of Dyche) wanted control to rest with the cloakmakers' own Joint Board. However, Dyche pushed his amendment through by a vote of 55 to 10. The ILGWU was thus given the power to run the show. This is an important moment in the history of the new IR. From this point forward, it was the ILGWU leaders who would be in control of IR within the union—contested as it was. The Committee also passed a measure to strengthen the strike fund. Every male ILGWU member was taxed one dollar and female members fifty cents to augment the fund.[106] It further recommended that the General Executive Board (GEB) of the ILGWU collect monies weekly from nonstriking members. The GEB was further instructed to draw up a detailed list of grievances and present it publicly to the manufacturers. The Special Committee's report was approved, but as a nod to rank-and-file demands, the GEB ruled that all such strike taxes must first be approved by the membership in a July 1 vote. GEB representatives Rosenberg and Dyche appeared before the upcoming AFL Convention to ask for support for a general strike.[107] In an effort to retain rank-and-file support, the ILGWU planned to hold a massive public meeting at Madison Square Garden on June 28.

On June 20, Rosenberg and Dyche appeared before the AFL Convention, where they received pledges of support from the AFL Executive Council. The AFL, though, requested that its own treasurer, John B. Lennon, be placed on the ILGWU Strike Committee. AFL President Samuel Gompers and AFL Secretary Morrison promised to participate prominently at the Madison Square Garden rally.[108]

Following their Boston convention, the GEB and the Joint Board made enthusiastic preparations for the general strike. The failure of the shirtwaist strikers to turn a passionate strike into an industry-wide contract stayed with the ILG leadership. The key to the cloakmakers' success, they argued, was to get the largest manufacturers to recognize the union. Therefore, as plans were made, all agreed that this strike would not end with shop-by-shop contracts. Instead, they wanted only an industry-wide contract and would stay the course to get it.

The GEB and Joint Board created a General Strike Committee to coordinate the strike. From its inception, the organization of this strike was different from the 1909 strike as it was controlled from the top down. The Strike Committee consisted of five representatives from each of the nine locals affiliated with the Joint Board, with leaders from both the GEB and Joint Board playing decisive roles. This large committee was divided into separate subcommittees, each with special tasks. Abraham Rosenberg, Sol Polakoff, John Dyche, and the AFL's John Lennon played the role of coordinators between these subcommittees, giving them influence and control. In addition, Dyche, Lennon, and Rosenberg would determine the timing of the strike call.[109]

The Strike Committee wanted to demonstrate unity between the rank-and-file workers and the union leadership through a show of force to send a powerful message to the manufacturers and public alike. The committee thought that thousands of workers putting down their tools and leaving shop by shop at different times—as had happened in the Shirtwaist Strike—demonstrated chaos and weakness rather than strength and order. Therefore, the ILG leadership saw the Madison Square Garden rally on the twenty-eighth as paramount to their efforts. Rather than risk an open-air rally, which might send a message of radicalism, an indoor rally would build on planning, strategy, respectability, and efficiency. At the rally, the manufacturers would be confronted with a list of well-thought-out grievances and demands.[110]

The men standing at the podium at the Garden represented the cautious leadership of the ILGWU, the AFL, and the Lower East Side political establishment: Rosenberg, Dyche, Lennon, Hugh Fraye, Jacob Panken, Meyer London, Abraham Cahan, the AFL's Frank Morrison, and Gompers himself. The workers assembled to participate in this strike vote had promised to follow their lead and not leave their jobs until they were instructed to do so by a special strike edition of the *New Post*. Rosenberg reminded the rank and file to conduct themselves in an orderly and respectable fashion. Gompers reminded workers how important this strike would be. "This is more than a strike," he pleaded, "it is an industrial revolution." With that, 20,000 cloakmakers rose to thunderous applause. Gompers was giving voice to the growing belief that workers, through their unions, could shape industry in a democratic fashion. He was also right to see this strike as the first important step in that process.[111]

Five days after the Garden meeting, the strike vote took place at three locations. Of the 19,586 votes tallied, 18,771 voted for the general strike. What was important for the union was the manner in which the vote took place: the smooth efficiency of the vote, the organization of the tally, the publicity they received, and the simple fact that the ILGWU seemed to finally be in charge of its members. The vote demonstrated that the ILGWU was now dedicated to industrial democracy.[112]

Immediately after the vote, Rosenberg, Dyche, Lennon, and Polokoff called the strike for 2 P.M., July 7. They then requested a special meeting of the Strike Committee for July 6 to straighten out any last-minute snafus. By the meeting, the Strike Committee also found itself transformed into a neat bureaucratic structure. There were now nine recognizable subcommittees. The Hall Committee rented the various halls where the strikers would meet and gather during the strike. There would be one central strike headquarters, in addition to several subheadquarters. A Relief Committee would handle the strike fund. A Press Committee would put the union's demands to the public and coordinate the union's relationship to the public. The experience of the shirtwaist strike had taught the cloakmakers the value of good public relations. The shirtwaist workers had not actively pursued it; it had come to them naturally. The cloakmakers were not going to take that chance. As its first duty, the Press Committee published the strike issue of the *New Post*.

At the center of the organizational effort stood the Settlement Committee. This committee was responsible for negotiating and drafting model contracts. Its plan was that all individual shop contracts would be identical, creating a de facto industry agreement. Every aspect of the strike was to be controlled and regimented. Before a striker received strike benefits, he or she would have to meet the approval of the shop committee chair (the shop level), the hall chair (on the district level), and the local relief chair. Only then would the striker's claims go to the Relief Committee (on the International level).[113]

At 7 A.M. on the morning of July 7, the Press Committee began the distribution of the strike edition of the *New Post* in Yiddish, Italian, and English. With the "Red Post," as the *New York Times* called it, the Great Revolt began. By 2:30 in the afternoon, the cloak district was literally clogged with tens of thousands of idle workers. By the end of the afternoon, there were 75,000 workers on strike.[114]

The union leaders prided themselves on the fact that their strike was not visited with the same chaos and confusion as the shirtwaist strike just a few months before. The shirtwaist strikers, once they had finally figured out where to go and had arrived there, had found anarchy. There had been little or no clerical support, and no one seemed to be in charge. In contrast, the *New Post* told workers where they were to report. Once they arrived at the assigned hall, they were given their strike assignment—usually picket duty. The cloakmakers' halls were well staffed, each hall had staff members and clerical help to sign up workers and hand out their assignments. These offices ran with un-nerving efficiency.[115]

Large manufacturers, usually fiercely independent, responded to the strike with a call for the formation of a manufacturers' association. On July 8, an initial, select group of manufacturers met at the Broadway Hotel to draw up plans for a cloakmakers' association. Three days later, a few hundred manufacturers meet at the Hoffman House to form the Cloak, Suit, and Skirt Protective Association (association). There they elected their leaders: A. E. Lefcourt was chosen as chair, Max M. Schwarcz was elected treasurer, Max Meyer was made secretary, and most important, Julius Henry Cohen was named legal counsel.

Cohen proved to be the heart and soul of the association. Partner in the law firm of Cohen, Creevey, and Richter, Cohen had many years of experience representing cloak manufacturers. Moreover, he was a committed industrial democrat. As such, he shaped both the structure and program of the association. Each member of the association signed a pledge that he would adjust shop grievances—settle with the union—only with the aid of the Executive Committee of the association. In addition, members also pledged that they would not sign any documents or agreements that recognized the union. The strike and the ILG's efforts at organization forced leading manufacturers to organize themselves, if only defensively. Workers, it would seem, were organizing more than themselves; they were organizing the industry.[116]

The formation of the association broke open the concealed cleavages between small and large manufacturers. Smaller manufacturers were leery of, and downright hostile to, the association. They worried that an industry-wide standard, supported by the association, would raise labor costs and thereby jeopardize their existence. From the small shop owners' perspective, the association would, in essence, be using the union to drive the smaller manufacturers out of the industry, which was precisely Cohen's idea.[117]

As the strike began, a legion of reformers watched from the sidelines. They were eager to offer their advice and services. A small group, however, saw this strike as a unique opportunity to begin a larger experiment in industrial relations. These reformers and their experiment, the Protocol of Peace (described in the Chapter 2), would have enormous consequences for more than garment workers. Organized labor and organized management were now poised on the verge of a new day in IR.

The Cloakmakers' Strike of 1910, to use Samuel Gompers's apt phrase, was "more than a strike, [it was] . . . an industrial revolution" because it created a new system of IR, finishing what started in 1909.[118] "The signing of the Protocol," as the contract that ended the strike was called, as historian Louis Levine has noted, "ushered in a new period of constructive experimentation in collective bargaining."[119] Benjamin Stolberg, another earlier historian of the union, believed that "the Protocol of Peace marked a decisive turning point [in part because] . . . its basic idea was later copied by the other needle trades. . . . And in time its influence spread throughout American industry."[120]

To fully understand the Protocol and the new role of industrial democrats, we need to see the process through which the Protocol was born and evolved. The Protocol "introduced the notion," as garment industry expert Benjamin Stolberg observed in 1944, "that labor had a stake in efficient management, continuous prosperity and social responsibility. The Protocol," Stolberg continues, "assumed a benevolent partnership between capital and labor, a sort of joint industrial syndicate of boss and worker."[121] This is the subject of Chapter 2.

2 The Making of Industrial Democracy in the Ladies' Garment Industry
The Creation of the Protocols of Peace

INDUSTRIAL DEMOCRATS AND THE 1910 GREAT REVOLT

Reformers, such as those involved with the Protocol, saw industrial democracy as *the* answer to industrial anarchy. "A radical transformation of society might take place," write historians Nelson Lichtenstein and Howell John Harris in *Industrial Democracy in America*,

> [B]ut it would be achieved in gradual, peaceful fashion, by piecemeal activities of men or women of good will, of all social classes, sharing common concerns about injustice and wastefulness of the social order . . . it was a vision, a goal, an implicit ideal for focusing criticism of the existing order.[1]

Industrial democracy held out a promise to workers as well. There was, however, a built-in contradiction. The democracy reformers envisioned was not easily contained. The more self-involved workers became, the more democracy they demanded, and the more unruly the system became. Thus, the driving force behind the Protocol—industrial democracy—would also be a principal source of its demise. Indeed, many of the designers of the Protocol feared this problem from the start and sought to create institutional safeguards against it that were profoundly antidemocratic. The "peacemakers," as the creators of the Protocol were called, established rigid top-down systems of bureaucracy in industrial relations (IR).[2] To fully appreciate the problematic nature of these transformations, we must first understand how the Protocol came about and how widespread it became.

On July 7, 1910, the cloakmakers' "Great Revolt" began. As work ground to a halt throughout the city, diverse actors moved to reshape the future of industrial relations. Involvement came from many fronts. As soon as the strike started, Michael Reagan, industrial mediator of the New York State Board of Mediation and Arbitration, entered the fray.

Reagan, in a July 8 letter sent to both sides, offered his services and that of the Board to establish "a conference committee" to mediate the strike. While the union quickly jumped at the offer, management remained aloof. After a week of frantic efforts, Reagan's plan remained insufficient to convince the owners to come to the table. Finally, at the suggestion of John Lundrigan, chair of the State Board, Reagan scheduled a July 19 meeting in the hopes that management would reconsider. The most important issue, however—union recognition—continued to divide the two sides. The association refused to give in on recognition.[3]

Meyer Bloomfield, a prominent Boston social worker and industrial reformer, began another effort to end the strike on behalf of industrial democrat A. Lincoln Filene, owner of the Boston department store Filene's. Filene sent Bloomfield and J. R. Simpson, his merchandise manager, to New York for the talks. Bloomfield and Simpson were in immediate contact with both sides. In fact, Bloomfield's presence may have caused the state-sponsored talks to falter. Simpson wrote to Filene early on that the union had honest grievances. But, he worried whether the union had demonstrated its ability for self-government. Without it, he argued, collective bargaining would be useless. Simpson suggested that the union be pressured to give up recognition and instead focus on the most glaring bread-and-butter grievances; once the union had properly matured, recognition would come. If the manufacturers proved obstinate, as Simpson assumed they would, Filene should, according to Simpson, "bring together twenty-five or so of the leading merchants [retailers] of the country to get the manufacturers to do what is right."[4] Industrial democrats like Filene believed mature, responsible unions were important to stabilize the industry. In addition, as a large retailer, Filene could exert enormous economic pressure on garment manufacturers, forcing them to the bargaining table. According to historian Kim McQuaid, Filene understood something few others did at the time: America was fast becoming a consumers' republic. As such, providing goods and services to consumers was a form of public service. To deny the public access to consumer goods, as was happening under the strike, was against the public interest.[5]

Bloomfield, Filene, and others had been involved with "the labor question" for some time by 1910. Both had been active in the national and regional National Civic Federation. Both had experience with the ladies' garment industry and Jewish labor. Moreover, both were keenly interested in forging a new IR. It was from this involvement that the Protocol would spring. As historian Arthur Goren has observed, "From downtown social workers and uptown patricians came the peacemakers." Yet, while Filene's involvement was indeed important, his efforts, and those of his associates, were not solely responsible for the accord. Most accounts of the negotiations leading up to the Protocol depict the reformers as altruistic angels, sent to save the helpless working masses.[6] Yet, as we shall see, the story is much more ambiguous and complicated than that.[7]

On July 21, Bloomfield met with Lefcourt, of the association, to offer his services in settling the strike. The next day, Bloomfield met with Julius Henry Cohen, lawyer for the association, and addressed the Executive Board of the association. It was decided that if "a big man" made a call for a settlement conference, and if the union and Cohen could set certain preconditions, talks could begin. In a July 21 letter to famed Boston attorney Louis Brandeis, Bloomfield explained how he laid the foundation for talks:

> Said to [the union leaders John] Lennon and [John] Dyche that there was only one open door—to take a big man like Brandeis and empower him ... to confer with both sides and draw up a fair basis of negotiations. Both responded heartily and suggested that I invite Mr. B. and come with him for a private talk. Am convinced that in final conference fundamental injustices will be righted, the union not smashed, and the open shop prevail.[8]

In their initial vision, industrial democrats sought to walk a fine line between preserving both the union and the open shop.

That initial meeting set in motion a process that eventually led to the Protocol. Brandeis recalled in 1913 how he initially got involved. Filene had written him, "I think you had better come [to the cloakmakers' strike] too." Brandeis later recounted, "There and then, I told him that I would have nothing to do with any settlement of the strike involving the closed shop. That I did not believe in it, and that I thought it un-American and unfair to both sides."[9] This was not Brandeis's first experience with the ladies' garment industry. In 1907, he served as the lawyer for Boston's cloak manufacturers during a bitter strike. He at first tried to get the union to give up its demand for a closed shop, offering it instead what would later be recognized as the "preferential shop." When this effort failed, he filed and received an injunction barring picketing, hence crushing the strike.[10]

Brandeis left for New York on the twenty-third, writing his brother Alfred that "I was called to N.Y. Saturday P.M. to try to settle the N.Y. Garment Workers' strike."[11] He took with him a "draft of a proposed labor agreement." This draft included several ideas, the most important of which was the request that the union give up its demand for a closed or union shop. Brandeis, like Simpson, believed that the ILGWU was not yet ready to govern itself, let alone the industry.[12]

For the next two days, Brandeis met with leaders of the union and association. His main contacts with the union were through Dyche. Brandeis appears to have been a skillful negotiator. He removed the most disturbing issues for later discussion. Issues like the union shop could stall the talks before they even began.[13] In meeting with the union leaders, then, Brandeis urged that they put aside the demand for a closed shop and instead focus on bread-and-butter issues such as hours and wages. Together they drew up a revised list of grievances, including the reinstatement of all strikers. Brandeis wrote to Cohen that the "closed shop is not a subject which can be discussed at the conference." The issue of reinstatement was then placed on the table. When Brandeis stepped away that evening, it appeared that he was well on his way to a quick and peaceful settlement.

Two days later, as the details of the previous talks were publicly revealed, a major split arose in the union over Brandeis's known opposition to a closed shop. The socialist paper the *New York Call*, representative of rank-and-file sentiment, noted in a reprinted statement from the association that "his [Brandeis's] opposition to the closed-shop idea is well known, and in retaining him, the strikers tacitly waived their demand for the closed shop." Cohen further infuriated what would gel into an anti-Dyche faction of the ILGWU by stating, "It gratifies me beyond expression that Brandeis has consented to act as attorney for the unions in this strike. His presence in the situation expresses more emphatically than any words the complete elimination of the demand for the closed shop. This is no longer a matter for discussion."[14]

The union had not hired Brandeis. He was merely working as mediator. What concerned workers was that their union leader Dyche was apparently acting without consulting the Strike Committee or without rank-and-file knowledge. Dyche's decision to remove the closed shop from discussions was seen as a sellout. Rosenberg, ILG president, while trying to mediate between the two union camps, threatened publicly to boycott any talks unless the closed shop was reinstated and unless the union pledged to make a firm commitment to its attainment. In an article in the *Call*, he responded angrily,

> The [employer's] statement is a misstatement from top to bottom. In the first place, we have not retained Brandeis as our attorney. Brandeis was in New York...visited us, and asked if we were not willing to meet the manufacturers in conference. We told Brandeis that we were.... With this the matter ended. We have not asked Brandeis to act as our attorney, and we have not waived our demand our people will be out on strike twenty weeks yet, and then they will rather lose it then submit to such a compromise.[15]

The Strike Committee split evenly between the Dyche and the rank-and-file/Rosenberg factions, and with that, the hopes of settlement faded. It was at this moment that AFL President Samuel Gompers inserted himself into the process, most likely at Dyche's request. Gompers hoped to make peace between the two warring factions and get the talks back on track. To bolster union unity, Gompers suggested a new member be added to the Strike Committee that both sides would accept. This member would assure that the union's integrity be kept intact, Gompers stated, and it would restore rank-and-file faith in the leadership. And with that suggestion, Benjamin Schlesinger, a former ILGWU president and, at the time, business manager for the *Daily Forward*, joined the Committee and the talks resumed.[16] Cohen notified Brandeis that his proposal had been accepted and he believed "that the two organizations can together work out a constructive policy for the betterment of the industry."[17]

After a preliminary meeting between the principal negotiators, Meyer London for the union and Cohen for the association, a conference was scheduled for July 28.[18] At this first meeting were ten representatives from each side plus Brandeis and his staff. In writing about this meeting, *McClure's Magazine's* Edith Wyatt was struck by the similarities on both sides. Both groups were almost entirely Jewish. The union delegation included middle-aged unionists, radical workers, East Side intellectuals, and socialists. The management group contained some former ILGWU leaders, many who rose from the sweatshops and some who were involved with the Ethical Culture movement. The mood at that first meeting was hopeful.[19] Gompers was so confident that he returned to Washington on the twenty-ninth, telling the *New York Times* he was sure "that the garment workers' strike would be settled speedily."[20]

Brandeis set the mood for the conference. He told the twenty men assembled that they were witnessing an important moment in history, the birth of a new system of industrial relations. They would help shape the future. "Gentleman," Brandeis stated,

> [W]e have come together in a matter which we must all recognize is very serious, and an important business, not only to settle this strike, but to create a relation which will prevent similar strikes in the future. That work is one which it seems to me is approached in a spirit which makes the situation a very hopeful one and I am sure from my conferences with council of both parties, and with individual members whom they represent, that those who are here are all here with that desire.[21]

The first few days were well-orchestrated affairs as Brandeis, Cohen, and London had placed the most difficult issues last and started by tackling the most easily agreed-to issues first. Therefore, the first two days gave an impression that the strike would end quickly. The format provided Brandeis with a useful tool in pushing the talks along once they stalled. Also, in putting the more easily agreed-upon items first, when one party broke off talks, walking away meant giving up real gains. Thus, those first two days were critical in setting a pattern. Issues were either settled quickly or postponed—a method that, unfortunately, plagued the Protocol throughout its life, as we shall see.

On July 30, once all the easier topics were settled, the taboo issue of the closed shop arose. It was Lennon who brought up the issue. Cohen objected, stating that the union had previously agreed that this topic would not be discussed. Brandeis stated that the topic had indeed been ruled out in preconference arrangements, but sensing that to stop all talk on the subject would lead to the union members storming out, he tried to redirect the debate:

> I do not understand that Mr. Lennon is at all discussing a closed shop. . . . he refers to a union shop, to a shop that has reached that high degree of perfection in organization that everybody in it is a union man, and not by organization with the employer. . . . I think that that obviously is what Mr. Lennon means, because it would be a distinct breach of the terms on which our meeting and conference has proceeded if what we commonly refer to as the 'closed shop' were a subject before us.[22]

Instead, in a neat sleight of hand, sensing a back door to bring in the closed shop, London jumped in and asked "that the subject of the closed shop be taken under the subject of remedies." Brandeis, however, reminded London and the union that the closed shop "is one of the taboo subjects" and that it would not be discussed "under any circumstances." Brandeis, trying to regain control of the debate, would permit discussion only of the union shop. London pressed the issue. Knowing that it would split the union representatives and stop the conference, he suggested that the issue of the closed shop be used as a possible remedy, if no others suggested themselves. Brandeis ruled him out of order. London then asked and received an adjournment to confer with the union representatives.[23]

After a few tense moments, when it appeared that some union representatives would leave the talks, thereby ending the conference, Brandeis called the meeting back to order. He then made what must have been a stunning announcement. Sensing that the open versus closed shop was the rub, he offered the "preferential shop" as a solution:

> It seems to me . . . that aid could be effectively and properly given by providing that the manufacturers should, in the employment of labor hereafter, give the preference to union men, where the union men are equal in efficiency to any non-union applicants.[24]

For Brandeis, this plan would solve many problems. It was a compromise both groups could live with—what he believed to be a true middle ground. More importantly, it would prevent the ILGWU from creating a labor monopoly, which he believed would disrupt industry. His belief that the ILGWU would not be effective at policing its members drove much of his thinking. Only a "mature" union, one that would form a partnership with industry, could be trusted with the union shop. This Proto-Keynesian partnership would involve "scientific management," a no-strike pledge, and high wages to provide for leisure-time activities and consumer spending for workers. The ILGWU had not yet proven itself mature. But, in time it might. Thus, for Brandeis, unionism was for now a tool to rationalize industry, not "merely an instrument . . . [for] improving the condition of the working man." For workers, however, unionism was the vehicle for democratic reform, an end in itself.[25]

Cohen, speaking for the association, quickly agreed to the new shop, although personally, he had little immediate faith in the plan. The union, however, rejected it. Led by Lennon, the union wanted to terminate the conference, and it was all Brandeis could do to keep the participants in the room. He tried to return to other issues and tabled the preferential shop. But, the genie was out of the bottle. Dyche finally terminated the conference when he declared he had lost faith" in the current proceedings. He added, "For the sake of self-preservation, you would be committing suicide to go into an agreement where such a condition prevailed."[26] And with that, Brandeis adjourned. Before leaving, he suggested that London, Cohen, and he draw up an agreement consisting of all the settled issues of the past few days to be used as the basis for future talks.[27]

On August 1, Cohen sent Brandeis a written agreement that contained the clauses on which settlement had already been reached before the conference broke up. Included in this agreement were three Joint Boards, one each for Grievances, Arbitration, and Sanitary Control. Cohen reiterated his view that the association would accept the preferential shop. Brandeis, on receipt of this agreement, revised the language for the preferential shop to make it more acceptable to the union. It now read: "a shop in which union standards prevail and the union man is entitled to preference" over nonunion workers. Brandeis then forwarded the agreement to London without comment, and London forwarded it to the Strike Committee, also without comment.[28]

Opposition to the preferential shop united the deeply divided ILGWU in new and exciting ways. Rosenberg and Schlesinger were joined by Dyche in their public denunciation of the new agreement. Their public pronouncements spilled into the press as both the *Jewish Daily Forward* and the *Call* denounced it. The *Forward* called it "the scab shop with honey and a sugar coated poison pill."[29]

While the mainstream press denounced the union for breaking up constructive talks for what they viewed as selfish motives, the union tried to explain its actions. The *Call* reprinted a letter Meyer London wrote to Cohen rejecting the agreement. London explained that the real obstacle was decades of distrust combined with an overly ambitious agreement; by giving employers the right to judge a worker's "ability," the preferential shop simply gave the employer too much power. Employers could legally discriminate against the union and have the contract to back themselves up! How, London asked rhetorically, could the union, knowing this, be a party to such as agreement?[30]

With the publication of London's letter and any hope of reopening the talks disappearing, Brandeis returned to his summer cottage and Filene retreated back to Boston. Henry Moskowitz, a prominent New York social worker, was left to keep watch and report to Filene. Moskowitz, active in New York reform circles, attempted to reopen avenues of communication, but to little avail.[31]

In the meantime, with talks stalled, the union returned to concentrating on individual shops and contracts as attention once again returned to the rank and file. Each day was filled with massive demonstrations and fiery speeches, marches, and parades. These shows of strength were as much for the strikers as for the owners, as the union continued to sign up individual shops. Many smaller manufacturers, afraid to lose their whole season, waited and watched as the talks progressed, but when the talks stalled without any hint of restarting, they began to settle. In doing so, they recognized the union. It seemed as if it would be 1909 all over again—all but the big shops would hold out, and the smaller, settled shops would reap untold gains and profits at the expense of larger shops.[32]

As the strike entered mid-August, the painstaking plans that the ILGWU had laid began to unravel. This was most evident in the strike fund. The ILGWU had made enormous efforts to put the fund on the right track. While the fund was never much, it helped keep the workers on the picket lines. All too often, it meant the difference between starving and eating for the strikers. And because the fund covered the so-called orphan shops, the manufacturers had a harder time recruiting scab labor. By mid-August, this strategy was falling apart as the fund all but dried up.

The ILGWU responded quickly to restore the fund. August Began, spokesperson for the strike fund, announced a new round of calls for aid. The Strike Committee worked with many Lower East Side groups to raise money. The Workman's Circle, the United Hebrew Trades, the Socialist Party, and the Central Federated Union of New York, among others, joined the workers. The *Jewish Daily Forward* and the *Call* ran almost daily reports on the need to rebuild the fund. The papers kept the community abreast of the efforts, and by September—only a month later—reported that the fund stood at $246,403. That the ILGWU could raise this extraordinary sum of money as quickly as it did was a sign of just how integral it was to the Lower East Side community. The success of the fund-raising helped restore the morale of the strikers and renewed the faith of those bargaining on their behalf. It surely also sent a message to the manufacturers and their negotiators: the union could and would hold out.[33]

Yet, as the union was regrouping and demonstrating its resolve, liberal middle-class public opinion began to shift. When the union rejected "the Brandeis Compromise," as the preferential shop was now called, news coverage in the mainstream press shifted in favor of the association. The coverage in the *New York Times*, portraying the workers as selfish and greedy, was typical. The Brandeis "deal" was portrayed as more than adequate; what more did the workers want?

Hostile coverage worried the union. Possibly hoping to shift the coverage to open a wedge between workers and their union, the association stressed the increase in wages and improvement in conditions to which it had already agreed. On August 3, the *New York Times* reported "rumors" that many manufacturers were already making plans to restart production, regardless of a settlement, to save the fall season.[34] Then on August 5, the association dropped a bombshell announcement: it would recruit out-of-town replacement workers from Cleveland and Chicago. It also rented hotel rooms to house the replacement workers. Moreover, it announced that several shops had already reopened and were now beginning production. At the same time, the association hired 190 "special police" to protect the replacement workers and the manufacturers' shops.[35]

Violent outbursts erupted at several factories as workers fought with scabs and security guards to keep the shops closed. Running battles between strikers and the association's "guards" brought even closer media and public scrutiny. The union argued that workers were simply defending themselves against "hired thugs." The association argued that its security agents were defending themselves from "East Side gangs," apparently hired by the ILGWU to defend the strikers. The union leaders soon learned that, even if they were justified in responding, the popular press coverage and ensuing public perception did not concur. The press and public alike took the attitude of "a plague on both your houses." In addition, unlike the 1909 strike, the cloakmakers were predominately men, and not "helpless" women, so the cry of abuse typically fell on deaf ears. The cloakmakers, as men, did not elicit the same empathy from the public.[36]

Intent on positioning himself as an honest broker so as not alienate voters on either side, mayor John Purroy Mitchel called for an investigation. Mitchel wanted to avoid the charges of favoritism that had lost the Democratic Party many working-class voters in 1909. His findings told of abuses on both sides, as the press had duly reported. While he did not demand a "crackdown," on August 12, in a letter to Police Commissioner William F. Baker, Mitchel told Baker that the law must be equally applied to both parties. Furthermore, in an unprecedented action, the mayor told the police department that workers had a "right" to organize and to picket peacefully.[37] Mitchel also wanted to avoid the courtroom scenes of 1909. So, the next day, he wrote to the chief magistrates asking that they show tolerance and understanding in their dealings with arrested strikers. He demanded that the judges show patience and compassion toward many of the immigrant workers who had a poor knowledge of English, that they be guided by the law, not their prejudices.[38]

The union and association responded to the mayor's involvement in predictable ways. The Strike Committee applauded Mitchel's stand. The association was appalled. Manufacturer Paul Bonwit demanded that the police protect his property as well as his loyal (replacement) workers. To do otherwise, Bonwit argued, was to reduce the police to a "farce."[39] According to the association, the mayor's actions were tantamount to an endorsement of the union's activities and encouraged the spread of violence. Instead, the association called for a grand jury investigation into the cloak industry. The union's response was to remind the public that this strike was relatively peaceful. "Considering the number involved," the union stated, "the present strike is the quietest on record, and exaggerated statements by employers will not change the facts."[40]

Like many employer groups of the time, the association turned next to the courts, seeking an injunction. Cohen knew of the courts' general opposition to unions and strikes.[41] As mainstream press opinion shifted against the union, negotiations stalled, and a seemingly uncooperative city government, Cohen sprang into action. On August 16, Cohen filed for an injunction against the union with the Supreme Court of New York State before Justice Irving Lehman. Cohen's argument was, because the union would not settle for what appeared to all reasonable parties to be a good agreement, it must be a criminal conspiracy to gain the closed shop. Meyer London, representing the union, failed to convince the judge otherwise and Justice Lehman issued a temporary, limited injunction to Cohen and the association. This injunction restrained the union from coercing employees to leave work. The court ordered the union to show cause as to why this injunction should not be made more sweeping and permanent. The case was then assigned to Justice Goff for a later hearing.[42]

In the interim before the hearing, Cohen tried to get Brandeis to use his great influence to help with the injunction. Cohen argued that the union had authorized Brandeis to act on its behalf and in doing so had waived the closed shop during the first preliminary meetings. Once the talks stopped progressing in ways favorable to the union, they had reintroduced the closed shop issue. Cohen requested the correspondence between Brandeis and the union to use in court in order to prove a criminal conspiracy case.

Brandeis was leery that any actions on Cohen's behalf could permanently stall the talks, destroy whatever trust the union had established in him, and indefinitely prolong the strike. So, rather than make a hasty decision, he asked Filene, Moskowitz, and Bloomfield to look over the papers and decide which, if any, should be turned over to Cohen. Filene told Brandeis that he should refuse all such requests unless London and the union consented. If the papers were turned over, Filene warned, Brandeis's neutrality would be thrown into question and his usefulness as a skilled arbitrator forever ruined.[43]

Yet, Cohen persisted. He claimed that these documents showed the union leaders had lied to the public and their members. He noted that they gave up the demand for a closed shop as a precondition to the first round of talks. The union had been quite vocal in insisting that it was only postponing discussions on the closed shop; they only temporarily tabled *that* discussion. But the correspondence could be read otherwise, and Cohen was an able enough attorney to present the evidence to support his claim. Brandeis, Filene, and company knew this. More important, however, was their need to stay—or at best to appear—neutral. Handing over these documents would be seen as cooperating with Cohen.[44]

Filene, Moskowitz, Bloomfield, and Brandeis agreed that it was critical that they, as a team, remain removed from the courtroom. "The theme which ran through the correspondence which passed between the peacemakers," writes historian Hyman Berman, "was that their position of neutrality not be disturbed." Filene wrote to Moskowitz further to tell him not to accept an assignment to write a piece about the strike for the *Outlook* and chastised all of them, including and especially Brandeis, for speaking publicly about the strike. Only if they retained the veneer of impartiality and worked quietly behind the scenes would their efforts be effective. While they might have personal opinions on the strike, they should remain personal.[45]

By this time, the team of "peacemakers" saw two major obstacles to a peaceful settlement: the injunction and the ILG radicals who would not accept the deal being offered them. The radicals were spurred on by the *Jewish Daily Forward*. By radicals, the Protocolists were referring to the rank-and-file workers who resented the increasing bureaucracy and centralization of authority within the ILG. These workers sought a more direct form of industrial democracy. The second and equally problematic obstacle was Cohen himself. By bringing labor relations into the courts, Cohen had made them contested and removed them from the more conciliatory ambiance of a joint conference. Cohen was attempting, in Moskowitz's opinion, to make "a lawyers' scrap" out of the proceedings. Moreover, he was dividing the association. Worrying that the radicals had too much influence on the union, he wrote to Moskowitz urging him to find more "conservative" Jewish leaders to be added to the Strike Committee to counterbalance and moderate the radicals.[46]

The effort to place more conservatives on the Strike Committee was part of an ongoing obsession within the city's German-Jewish community with the public's image of Jews. There was concern that the strike fed an already pugnacious anti-Semitic stereotype of Jews as radical workers and money-grubbing shop owners. This racism helped Moskowitz and Filene to persuade Louis Marshall and Jacob Schiff, leading Jewish bankers, to take a leadership role in ending the strike. The press, both mainstream and labor, applauded these efforts. They praised these men for taking the initiative.[47]

Marshall first met with Brandeis and his associates to work out the details on the preferential shop, which both men considered the central element of the agreement. Then, on August 22, Marshall met with both sides. At first, Cohen, in the flush of the injunction and the positive press, resisted these overtures. When Cohen rejected the new preferential shop language, Marshall brought in banker Jacob Schiff and Joseph S. Marcus, president of Public Bank on the Lower East Side, to pressure the manufacturers to settle, as many manufacturers did business with these bankers. This pressure worked: by August 25, Cohen had agreed to meet with London and Marshall and reopen talks. Meeting late into the night at Marshall's office, they returned to the original Brandeis agreement. But, once again, the issue of union recognition threatened to stall the talks.[48]

When the meeting adjourned, Marshall, Brandeis, Filene, and Benjamin Schlesinger, future ILG president, continued to work out language acceptable to both sides. The crux of the matter was that both sides wanted to claim victory. Finally, after several drafts, a revised "Marshall Compromise" was sent to London and Cohen.

The evolution of the language of the preferential shop demonstrates how central language was to the deal. In the original, Brandeis had stated that the preferential shop would be defined as follows: "preference to union men, where the union men are equal in efficiency to any non-union applicant." Labor had rejected this wording because it allowed the employers to judge "efficiency" and therefore allowed them to discriminate against the union. Filene attempted to solve the dilemma with a redraft that recognized the union and added language to seemingly favor employment of union men and women:

> The preferential union shop is one which the manufacturers recognized the union and declare in appropriate term their sympathy with the union, and their agreement that as between union and non-union men of equal ability to do the job, they will employ union men as long as union men are obtainable.[49]

But, Filene's wording had the opposite affect on the association. It saw his change as a form of union recognition and therefore rejected it. In response, Schlesinger compromised with a third version that spoke more of working conditions: "a union shop by which they mean a shop in which union standards prevail and union men are given the preference in employment." But, to the association, Schlesinger's version also smacked of recognition. Marshall's final version of the draft worked out the differences:

> The manufacturers agree that as between union men and non-union men of equal ability to do the job, they will employ the union men . . . the preferential union shop is a shop in which union standards prevail and the union man is entitled to the preference. This preference shall consist in giving employment to union men as long as they are obtainable.[50]

Marshall's wording allowed both to claim victory. The union claimed it had won because the employers would not be able to judge the worth of their employees. As long as the union could supply workers, the union would receive preference. In this way, the union got the union shop as long as it could continue to recruit qualified workers. The union also got the "union standard" for the entire industry. But, the association could also claim victory: it did not formally have to recognize the union, nor did it have to share responsibility for managing the industry. Furthermore, the union could be called upon to help police workers and the industry.

With the language worked out, the settlement went to the union and association. The association quickly accepted the settlement. The union had a more difficult time. Deeply split, the Strike Committee sent the agreement to the workers for a vote without a recommendation. Confusion reigned and tensions ran high at the various meeting halls where the vote took place. Mainstream press announcements that the strike was over only added to the confusion. Like their leaders, the strikers appeared to be divided. Some saw the settlement as a realistic victory. Many, however, saw anything short of full and complete union recognition as defeat. When the leaders of the Strike Committee, who supported the settlement, tried to speak at meeting halls, they were often met with hoots, rotten fruit, and threats of violence. Crowds chased Lennon from one hall, and Block needed bodyguards for a few days. Many saw the settlement, done behind closed doors, as a sellout. Workers at shops that had already settled had their own complaints, as some of them had better agreements than the industry-wide agreement now being voted on. They worried that this would supersede their own gains. The striking workers roundly rejected the settlement. The union might have remained divided and the strike might have continued had not legal matters infringed on the parties involved.[51]

Judge Goff ruled the strike an illegal action by the union: "a common law, civil conspiracy having been shown by overt unlawful acts, done in pursuance of an unlawful object." While the court "can not compel the workmen to return to work," Goff asserted, it could "restrain all picketing and patrolling, though lawful where not accompanied by violence and intimidation, are unlawful where in aid of an unlawful act." Goff took away the one weapon the union had: the picket. Speaking for the association, a jubilant Cohen told the *New York*

Times that it was "the strongest [decision]... ever handed down in an American court against trade unionism." He believed that it would end the strike once and for all and provide an immediate victory to the association.[52]

Even the press, which had criticized the union after each of its rejections of the agreement, took a new sympathetic turn. Goff's decision threatened to upset the delicate balance between labor and capital that many felt minimized the worst abuses of industrialization and kept labor peace. To the *New York Evening Post*, it "was strange law and certainly very poor policy ... which would seriously cripple such defensive powers as legitimately belong to organized labor." Traditional critics of labor now complained that the injunction's sweep would further radicalize labor and diminish the authority of the more responsible leaders of the movement.[53]

The injunction also compromised mayor Mitchel's pro-labor policies. On August 30, he wrote to the police commissioner revoking his directive of August 12 ordering police neutrality. He stated that because the police were an administrative agency, they must carry out the injunction and arrest peaceful picketers. The ILGWU tried to test his resolve and sent out eighty-five picketers. They were immediately arrested and fined for contempt of court.[54]

The injunction had a devastating effect on the strike, but incredibly, it helped to both unify labor and mobilize the community to rebuild the framework for IR. The news of the injunction unified the ILGWU as the Dyche versus rank-and-file split was temporarily forgotten and the union announced its intention to appeal to a higher court. Samuel Gompers, who had kept a low profile up to this point, remarked that Judge Goff had stepped on the constitutional rights of the strikers and he was sure the ILGWU would win on appeal.[55]

While the union was planning an appeal of the injunction and the association was celebrating, Filene and company were quietly working to get the union to accept the "Protocol of Peace," as the Marshall Compromise was now known.[56]

The injunction, coupled with the activities of Filene and Moskowitz, forced the ILGWU's General Executive Board to rethink the strike. The union finally officially dropped its demand for the closed shop. London wrote the mayor that the union only wanted a "union shop," therefore signaling that the union was moving toward the Protocol. This letter was also sent to Filene and was used as the basis for another meeting between London and Cohen. On September 2, the two lawyers met with Marshall to draw up a settlement.[57]

Meeting on September 2, Cohen and London worked out a compromise that was only mildly different from the one the union had previously rejected. The language was rewritten to remove terms such as "non-union men" and "equal ability." In addition, wage and hour issues were compromised to avoid the settlement bogging down in arbitration. All that was needed was for the union to ratify the agreement.[58]

At this point, in an effort to avoid the confusion and riots of the earlier vote and to assure a positive outcome, the ILGWU's General Executive Committee stepped in. In a decision that would foreshadow the increasing bureaucratization of a top-down labor movement removed from the rank and file, the ILGWU took control of the strike away from the Strike Committee. Ratification would not come through a massive rank-and-file voting campaign. Instead, only the shop chairmen (200 in all) would vote, at 6 P.M. at the general strike headquarters. With only a few moments of debate, at the appointed time, the shop chairmen voted to accept the agreement, ending the Great Revolt and signaling the birth of the Protocol of Peace.[59]

As word of the settlement spread, both sides quickly claimed victory. Cohen told the *New York Times* that the Protocol provided "a great opportunity to build up a strong working relation between the unions and the manufacturers." The union and the strikers declared victory and, what is more, a new day in labor relations. All sides thanked Marshall, Filene, Moskowitz, and Bloomfield. Brandeis was hailed as a true hero.[60] The celebrations lasted for well over a week.[61]

The Protocol established "a kind of industrial self-government" that Brandeis had been trying to establish for some time. There were three parts to the Protocol. First were the normal labor contract issues of hours, wages, and paid holidays. In this regard, the Protocol was better than most contracts of the day, clearly better than garment workers ever saw. The second part involved features unique to the garment industry: abolition of charges for electricity and supplies; the establishment of shop committees to establish a just piece rate; and, most revolutionary, a Joint Board of Sanitary Control—a committee made up of representatives of both the union and the association who would oversee working conditions. The third and most important part of the Protocol was the implementation of Brandeis's conceptions of efficiency and industrial democracy.

The centerpiece of Brandeis's program for industrial democracy was clearly the preferential shop, the ban on all strikes and lockouts, and the establishment of grievance and arbitration mechanisms. Crucial was the last clause and agreement, on the preferential shop, which, in effect, recognized the union shop indirectly. It read in part:

> Each member of the manufacturers is to maintain a union shop, a "union shop" being understood to refer to a shop where union standards as to working conditions, hours of labor, and rates to wages as herein stipulated shall prevail, and where, when hiring help, union men are preferred, it being recognized that, since there are differences in skill among those employed in the trade, employers shall have freedom of selection as between one union man from another, and shall not be confined to any list, nor bound to follow any prescribed order whatever.[62]

As garment industry expert Benjamin Stolberg states, "The clause was as effective, for the union's purpose, as if the full closed shop had been adopted" because the union could always supply workers.[63]

A central aspect of the Protocol, and one most often missed by scholars was the attempt to rationalize, standardize, and Taylorize the garment industry. All work stoppages would be eliminated. Work would continue as grievances were arbitrated. As a tripartite agreement between labor, management, and the public, the Protocol steered the industry into the modernity of an industrial consumer society. In exchange for giving union leadership some authority, the Protocol mandated industrial self-management. In essence, the association expected the ILGWU to police its own members for the benefit of the industry. The union was to supply "efficient" workers and ensure continuous and rational production. If the union could do this effectively, workers would benefit.[64]

Julius Henry Cohen, chief counsel for the employers throughout the life of the Protocol, recognized the substantial benefit management had reaped. Writing in 1916, he explained how the ILGWU helped make the ladies' garment industry a modern industry:

> Into this industry came a union. Another nuisance to add to the plagues of the manufacturer. Is it any wonder that at first it was ignored, then fought, and only with reluctance accepted as a factor. Then, if, through the union, some order could be brought out of this chaos, hailed with

hope! If all paid the same price for the same labor, as all paid for merchandise, efficiency as manufacturers would count for something against
unscrupulous competitors.[65]

By controlling its own members, the union brought to industry what
the manufacturers could not: stability and rationality.[66]

One measure for the Protocol's success could be seen in both the
unionization that followed and by the new role for union leaders and
outside arbitrators. Union leaders could be cheered by swelling membership rolls, as with the increased authority and respectability the
Protocol vested in them. In 1910, the New York City cloakmakers represented three-fourths of the entire ILGWU membership. The agreement
covered 1,796 out of a possible 1,829 shops. By 1912, 90 percent of all
cloakmakers were in the union. Manufacturers could take a measure of
hope that the anarchy and chaos of the seasonal wildcat strikes were
over as all garment workers were being brought into a disciplined and
maturing labor union.[67]

The signing of the Protocol of Peace finally institutionalized for the
cloakmakers, and then for the whole industry, some of the major features
that the shirtwaist workers had struggled for in 1909. But, creating the
Protocol, as we will see, proved to be an easier task than making it work.

To "Commence the Campaign of Education": Selling the Protocol

Even before the ink had dried on the cloakmakers' Protocol, reformers
were heralding it as *the* solution to "industrial war." Noted reform journals, such as the *North American Review*, *Forum*, *Atlantic Monthly*, and
the *Outlook*, as well as the scholarly *Annals of the American Academy*,
published feature articles on the historic settlement. These essays, taken
as a whole, were fawning in their praise. They extolled the Protocol—
the *idea* of the Protocol—as the embodiment of industrial democracy
and the savior of American democracy in an age of excessive industrialism. They also gave full credit to Louis Brandeis, whom they called
the father of the idea. What they neglected to discuss was the role of
workers. Read carefully, the press coverage of the Protocol depicts the
distrust that most affluent Americans had for labor. What made the Protocol unique was that it placed an organizational structure above the

shop floor, one that was principally designed to control workers. The Protocol set up a paternalistic top-down bureaucracy more interested in rationalizing industry and controlling workers than in "true" democracy. Workers, male and female, soon chafed at the centralizing features. They demanded quick action to their grievances. They soon rejected the notion of conciliation (a slow process of negotiation between equals) in favor of binding arbitration. And when private arbitration proved untenable, they would turn to the state as broker.

The Protocol was a collectively bargained contract that was meant to solve the problems in a particular trade at a particular time. It was therefore designed to be flexible. But Protocolists treated it as the Holy Grail, making it static and untouchable. The original flexibility was quickly abandoned, and as demands were placed on it, it simply snapped under the pressure. Yet, scholars can learn much from this process. First and foremost is the fact that by ignoring rank-and-file workers and refusing to cooperate with them, the arrangement was doomed to failure. Second, rank-and-file garment workers were able to shape the Protocol in ways Brandeis and company never expected. Workers forced the Protocol leaders to address issues they would have rather left unaddressed.[68]

Journalists and writers had not fabricated the public image of the Protocol out of whole cloth; they were simply following the design of the Protocol founders. Brandeis, and those around him, had envisioned the agreement as nothing short of revolutionary. They argued that past labor problems (Homestead especially), which all too often resulted in violence, necessitated a new approach. Brandeis believed the Protocol was such a new approach. And to ensure its success, as well as gain public support for it, Brandeis publicly argued:

> The advance of unionism demands...some relation between the employer and the employee other than either the closed or open shop, and I feel confident that we have found a solution in the preferential union shop...and although introduced under conditions in some respects unfavorable [a strike], it has worked admirably.[69]

Brandeis insisted that this new approach would transform the American industrial landscape, fulfilling America's democratic promise. He wrote to the leading journal and newspaper editors of the day urging their support. "This seems to be the time," he wrote to Ray Stanndard Baker in 1912, "to commence the campaign of education."[70]

Brandeis firmly believed that the root causes of "the present [industrial] difficulty" belonged to the rise of big business and cutthroat competition.[71] "Is there not a causal connection between the development of the huge, indomitable trusts and the horrible crimes now under investigation," he wrote to Paul Kellogg in 1911. Because of their sheer size, he saw these large corporations as able to exert undue influence on the market and society, creating an economic jungle. The nature of the economy and the newly arrived immigrant groups jointly threatened American society. The Protocol, therefore, could be a tool of corrective "civilizing" action by bringing industry and labor in line with the forces of democracy.[72] Brandeis did not favor unionism per se; it was for him a useful means to an end. The Protocol, he proposed to Lawrence Fraser Abbott, "seems to offer a solution consistent with American spirit and traditions as well as with justice." Through it, he believed he could preserve democracy.[73]

Brandeis was not alone in his beliefs. Julius Henry Cohen, the association's leading intellectual and prime mover, also came to believe that the Protocol offered unlimited solutions to industrial problems.[74] Cutthroat competition, industrial self-regulation, and combative class warfare had failed.[75] The Protocol system offered a new path: tripartite industrial regulation. The Protocol brought the vested interests—labor, management, and the public—together into a unitary framework, in efficiency, profitability, and production. The agreement could rationalize and stabilize the industry. Once rationalized, they believed profits would flow at increasing levels.

The Protocolists were not alone in their "search for order."[76] Other models were being discussed at the time. One such approach, which vested complete faith in objective social science to solve industrial problems, was developed by University of Wisconsin political economist John R. Commons, and his students. Commons believed that labor and management were incapable of solving their own problems. Only objective social science could solve these complex socioeconomic problems. The Protocol, while finding social science useful, left the main issues to the parties directly involved. Commons's model called for the training of thousands of autonomous IR experts. But, the Protocol's use of private conciliation made the Protocol unique.[77] Cohen and others spent the next thirty years preaching the new religion of Protocolism. They made three appeals. First, Protocolism avoided the extremes of socialism by ushering workers into "constructive" unions. Second, it avoided the anarchy of laissez-faire capitalism by rationalizing industry through associationalism.[78] Lastly, by establishing a quasi-private system of labor relations, it excluded the state.[79] Cohen argued for a quasi form of tripartitism. He went on to argue that

> [T]he enlightened employer needs his organization. The worker needs his union. The public needs both, and each needs each other. If we can substitute rational methods for physical warfare and contests of reason for contests of physical endurance, we may approach a truer American democracy and realize a higher standard of living for all.[80]

Cohen's faith in the Protocol rested in its structure, which he saw as built on social scientific foundations, not inflamed passions. The Protocol would work because it was rational and efficient and, more importantly, because it was based on what he believed to be the common interests of employee and employer.

The structure of the Protocol intended to impose efficiency and rationality on a chaotic industry. Bringing industrial hygienists, reformers, shop owners, and workers together, it sought to contribute to the larger discourse on the role of work in the newly forming consumer society and on the rights of management and workers in an industrial society. Most shared the opinion that the current situation was chaotic. The Protocol's answer was the principle of layered bureaucracy, which Protocolists envisioned as an industrial version of our nation's constitutional checks and balances.

At the top of this system stood the Board of Arbitration, which consisted of three members: one from management, one from labor, and Brandeis, who represented the public. All decisions of the Board were binding. Below it was the Committee on Grievances, which consisted of four members, two from each side, which acted as a conciliation agency. This committee heard all grievances filed by either side. A majority vote brought settlement, meaning at least one member from the other side had to switch. Only if a deadlock occurred—which happened, as we will see, all too often—would it go to the Board of Arbitration.[81]

Another remarkable feature of the Protocol was the Board of Sanitary Control. This was a prototypical Progressive Era reform effort. This Board consisted of seven members, two from the union, two from management and the remainder chosen by the four to represent the public. Its first order of business was a systematic investigation into the sanitary conditions of the cloak, suit, and skirt industry. This was one of the first full-scale public health surveys of the industry. The Sanitary Board did not, at first, have enforcement powers. Its power lay in its ability to marshal public outrage against unsanitary conditions. Members of this board had great faith in the public at large, believing that if they only knew the true conditions they would become outraged and demand action. The board members saw themselves as illuminating the dark spaces of industrialism, bringing them to the light of justice. When this failed, as it often did, they intended to develop new sources of illumination.

The most dramatic of these new sources was the authorizing of "sanitation strikes." Under the sanitation provisions of the Protocol, workers would be allowed to strike over unsanitary conditions authorized by the Sanitation Board. In addition, the Board developed a sanitary certificate that shop owners had to hang in their shops to show they were in complete compliance with the sanitary features of the Protocol. Funding for the board came jointly from the ILG and the association.

The Board's heart and soul was Dr. George M. Price, a pioneering industrial hygienist. Originally an ILG Board member, Price quickly assumed the role of public representative. The other public members were William Jay Schieffelin, social worker Lillian Wald, and Brandeis confidant Henry Moskowitz. Moskowitz also served as secretary for the Board of Arbitration and as a sometime Grievance Committee member.[82]

While the machinery of the Protocol was being put into place, Protocolists began to spread the agreement to other sectors of the ladies' garment industry in New York City. To prove their thesis about the Protocol's revolutionary potential, they needed to demonstrate its potential to bring peace to an entire industry. Thus, even before the bugs were worked out of the initial settlement, Brandeis and company were seeking to implement the Protocol in new sectors of the ladies' garment industry.

WORKERS ORGANIZING MANUFACTURERS IN THE LADIES' GARMENT INDUSTRY

The success of the cloakmakers' strike convinced many reformers that labor-management cooperation strategies, such as the Protocol, were the wave of the future.[83] Yet, for all of its success, the great Protocol of Peace covered fewer than 50,000 workers, as it applied solely to the cloak trade.[84]

The Protocolists were assisted in their movement to spread the co-operative model of the agreement by a tragic event, the Triangle Fire of 1911. As we will see in Chapter 4, the Triangle Fire ignited the spark for governmental action, but it also propelled the union and its allies into action. In an effort to protect those outside of the cloak industry, especially women garment workers, the ILGWU dedicated itself to spread the Protocol to the entire ladies' garment industry.

The women's trades were the natural place to turn after the fire. This trade included dresses, waists, underwear, kimonos, and children's wear. The vast majority of the workforce consisted of young women, very much like those who struck in 1909 and died in the Triangle Factory in 1911. Over 80 percent of the workers were female, and the majority between the ages of 16 and 22. By 1913 in New York City, there were 36,858 workers in 707 shops with $55 million of profit. Of the women in the workforce, approximately half were Jewish and a third were Italian. More than three-fourths of the workforce were under twenty-five years of age, 50 percent were under twenty.[85] If the Triangle Fire taught the union anything, it was the need of a strong union to protect these young, innocent women.[86]

Within several months of the Uprising of 1909, the waistmakers' union (Local 25) had lost most of the new members it had gained during the strike. The Uprising was settled shop by shop, and one by one, the shops refused to bargain once their initial contracts had expired. Without contracts, union membership plummeted. By 1911, the local was a shell of its former self.

To the male leadership of the ILGWU, the lessons of the 1909 Uprising and the 1910 Great Revolt were clear. One had been successful, the other a failure, due in large part to the gender of the waist strikers. The men of Local 10 had created for themselves a "revolution" in industrial relations, the women of Local 25, while passionate strikers, had not. Women needed to be "brought along" and educated. Men needed to step in to teach as well as to protect. The paternalism of male union leaders partly explains why they were able to force powerful alliances with maternalistic women reformers, as we will see.

The ILGWU placed the four women's trades locals into what amounted to a quasi-receivership. Vice-presidents Abe Mitchell and Saul Elstein took control of the locals and hired three women organizers. These three—Rose Schneiderman, Gertrude Barum, and Josephine Casey—were seen as unique by the male ILG leadership. They had, even at their young ages, distinguished themselves as union activists and rank-and-file leaders. Therefore, they were perfect role models. In a phrase, they had somehow transcended gender.[87]

The ILG spent most of 1912 educating and organizing the women in these trades. Support for this project was enlisted from the Socialist Party, the Women's Trade Union League (WTUL), and the United Hebrew Trades (UHT), as well as other ethnic fraternal orders from the Lower East Side. By the 1912 ILGWU Convention in Toronto, the union was ready for action, authorizing a general strike in all women's trades.[88]

Early in 1912, while the union was making strike plans, A. Lincoln Filene and several other reformers involved in the previous cloak strike approached Samuel Floersheimer, a leading manufacturer of women's clothes in New York City, to sell the idea of Protocolism. With Filene and company's advice and prodding, Floersheimer revived the moribund Dress and Waist Manufacturers' Association. Julius Henry Cohen was appointed as chief counsel. (He remained counsel to the cloakmakers' association as well.) Walter Bartholomew resigned from his position as manager of the Ladies' Tailors Association to head up this reborn group.[89]

Filene and his allies believed that if both workers and owners were organized collectively into strong organizations, Protocolism could succeed. To this effect, Cohen and Bartholomew tried to move manufacturers into the Protocol camp. It was not an easy sell. The waist manufacturers were one of the most antiunion groups of manufacturers. To help the effort, Cohen enlisted several noted industrial relations experts to speak to the manufacturers. George M. Price, of both the Cloak Industry's Joint Board of Sanitary Control and the New York Factory Investigating Commission (FIC), and Charles H. Winslow, of both the U.S. Department of Commerce and Labor and the FIC, spoke on numerous occasions to the manufacturers. They presented powerful arguments for cooperation.[90]

As Cohen was preparing the manufacturers for organization, the ILGWU was preparing the workers for a strike. Early in the fall of 1912, the two camps opened secret talks. In November, at the American Federation of Labor Convention, Bartholomew and Floersheimer met with the ILG's Dyche and Rosenberg, with Samuel Gompers, president of the AFL, as host. At Gompers's suggestion, it was agreed to hold more formal "conversations" under the guidance of the AFL on December 13.[91]

These secret conversations lasted through January 11. Delegates from the ILGWU, Locals 25 and 10, the AFL, and the association met and agreed to follow the model of the cloakmakers' settlement (the Protocol). They suggested several slight modifications, however. Unlike the cloak trade, which was predominately in New York City, the waist and dress trades—partly as a result of the Uprising—had centers in Philadelphia and Chicago as well as New York. Organizing the New York industry might give manufacturers outside of the city an unfair advantage. To compensate for this unfair advantage, it was suggested that the industry adopt a "white label," or union label. The delegates also redesigned the wage-scale system. To come up with a fair piece-rate, a joint board would first create an hourly rate. Another committee would develop a fair average number of garments produced per hour per worker, and then a fair and just piece-rate would be created from this. This would be done shop by shop with an industry-wide Wage Board—sixteen members, eight per side—as final arbiter.[92]

The union and the association hit on a novel way to organize the industry: an orchestrated general strike. Both sides embarked upon a co-ordinated effort to quickly and painlessly rationalize the industry. First, the association provided the union with a list of all member shops. The union, in turn, pledged to pressure all nonmember shops to join the association. Lastly, both agreed to a general strike to organize both workers and employers in the industry. The association stated that "unless the union . . . as a result of the 'general strike' enroll[ed] in its membership the bulk of the workers in the industry" the agreement would certainly fail. It was clear, then, that this strike was, from its inception, a tool to organize not just the workforce, but the entire industry as well.[93] Both sides agreed that the strike would last only seventy-two hours at member shops. Then member shops would settle en masse, announcing a

Protocol. This would leave the nonmember shops most vulnerable. The hope was they would scramble to settle quickly.[94]

Before the call for the strike, a two-member joint committee (one each from the union and association) was formed to draft the language for a Protocol. To encourage as many new members as possible, the union lowered its dues by half. On December 20, the General Executive Board of the ILG (GEB), meeting in closed-door session, authorized strikes in kimono, white goods, waist, and dress trades. In addition, they endorsed the then still-secret negotiations. The main goal remained the organization of the waist and dress trades. The strikes in the kimono and white goods were secondary: they were designed to prevent waist and dress manufacturers from shifting production to these other shops during the strike. Organizing the strike across all these boundaries of the trade, however, also removed the threat of possible scab labor. As ILG Vice-President Mitchel stated, "By calling a strike at the same time [in these secondary trades] . . . I am more than certain that the strike [in the waist and dress sectors] will terminate more speedily and that it will be more successful."[95]

This strike was indeed different. First, there was the matter of secret negotiations. Second, the ever-present International was overseeing every detail. Lastly, rank-and-file workers were totally uninformed, as manufacturers knew more about the strike than workers. At no time were workers involved in the call to arms. The GEB authorized a strike vote, and from December 23 through January 5, the union held a series of mass meetings that were organized to serve two purposes: to give the impression of a groundswell of support for the strike and, more importantly, to make sure the workers would actually follow the union's call. It was at the January 5 meeting, held at the Hippodrome, that the workers in the women's garment industry were informed of the general strike vote to be held in two days. At the same time as this strike vote was called, 100,000 men's garment workers were already on strike in New York City.[96] The ILG saw this as an opportunity too big to pass up, as the presence of over 150,000 strikers would surely put the fear of god into the manufacturers.[97]

The process by which the strike vote was obtained is interesting. The women's trades' vote was long and orchestrated, lasting four days. Results were not announced until January 13: a landslide in favor of the general strike. One reason for the delay in tallying the vote was to buy more time for negotiations with the association. The union and the association, not so coincidentally, reached agreement the same day as the strike vote ended.[98]

At 7:00 A.M. on January 15, the strike call went out. At the same time, the ILG dispatched a delegation to Philadelphia to organize the women's trades there. By organizing preemptively in Philadelphia, it hoped to prevent New York shop owners from outsourcing work during the strike. Philadelphia was never truly a primary concern, but organized, again, defensively to protect New York.[99]

At first glance, the strike was a success. Three-fourths of the workforce walked off their jobs, demonstrating that the ILG could control and marshal the workers. Over 30,000 strikers were meeting at thirty union halls throughout the city. By the end of the day, only 3,000 workers remained on the job.[100]

On the second day of the strike, the employers' association announced a settlement—the same settlement that they had worked out with the ILG before the strike vote. The association urged all of its employees to join the union and publicly spoke of the stabilizing effect this settlement would have on the industry. In the wake of the 1909 Uprising and the Triangle Fire, this was something that reformers loudly and publicly applauded. Only the International Workers of the World (IWW) and Daniel DeLeon's Socialist Worker Party (SWP) criticized the settlement.[101]

The employers' association and the ILG adopted a Protocol on January 18, covering approximately 50 percent of all shops in the city. To avoid the confusion after the 1909 strike, the union decided not to settle with the other shops individually. Instead, all nonassociation shops that wanted to settle with the ILG were directed by the union to join the association and thereby fall under the umbrella of the Protocol. The goal was, after all, to organize the industry by organizing both workers and manufacturers. It was a successful strategy. On January 18, the first day of the strike, the association consisted of only sixty-one shops. Within two weeks, its membership had grown to 292.[102]

While the association grew, not all manufacturers were happy. Small manufacturers opposed the new arrangements because the association was dominated by the industry's larger shops. Some manufacturers were so antiunion that they wanted nothing to do with the Protocol. The Triangle factory owners, Harris and Blanck, were the most vocal members of this camp. They called the Protocol a "conspiracy between some manufacturers and the union" to drive them out of business. And they had a point. The Protocol was so successful in terms of the number of shops covered that nonassociation shops could easily be driven out. The union targeted them for special strikes, and while they were fending off the union, association shops took their business. These owners saw the Protocol exactly for what it was: a team effort to rationalize a chaotic industry and drive inefficient small producers out of business. So successful was this combined effort in the women's trades that by January 25, only a handful of shops remained outside of the Protocol system.[103]

The ILG's hyperorchestrated effort to mobilize support for the Protocol appears to have only increased worker skepticism. Workers did go on strike, and after the first day, they exhibited the typical garment worker's zeal for striking. But, when the union called off the strike after the third day, workers were slow to return. The ILG implored workers to return to their jobs. These pleas continued for at least three days after the strike "officially" ended. In an effort to regain control over the workers, the ILG held a vote of confidence in the union's leadership. The leaders easily won that vote, but the fact that they had to have one at all suggests that they feared growing rank-and-file discontent.[104]

As the ILG struck the waist and dress manufacturers, it also simultaneously struck the white goods and kimono trades. This industry was not heavily organized before this strike. Nor did the manufacturers have a trade association. Shop owners continued business as usual, ignoring strike talk, as they always had. On January 9 and 10, workers went out— Local 41 (white goods), Local 62 (kimono), and Local 10 (cutters) joined them.[105]

As the workers were walking out, a small group of manufacturers invited Julius Henry Cohen to a meeting. Cohen told those assembled that the workers were organized and the owners were not. The new calculus of IR demanded organization, which provided a tool of great leverage at the bargaining table. Hence, the shop owners were in a perilous position. He urged the manufacturers to organize and to negotiate with the union as quickly as possible, to settle the strike before serious damage was done to their trade.[106]

The manufacturers heeded Cohen's advice, to a point. On January 15 and 16, the two trades organized manufacturers' associations. But they stopped short of union recognition. Unlike the other women's trades, the kimono and white goods trades were not centered in New York. Therefore, a settlement like the one in the waist trades would put the city's manufacturers at a distinct disadvantage.[107]

Unwilling to agree to any settlement that even hinted at union recognition, even the preferential shop, shop owners turned to tried-and-tested antilabor activities: the use of violence, toughs, and prostitutes. In response, learning from its experiences in the Uprising, the ILG quickly recruited middle-class women reformers to its side. The union argued that the prostitutes who the bosses hired to beat the pickets were in fact there to recruit these honest, hard-working "girls" into the white slave trade. It was tried-and-true garment trade practice for shop owners to hire prostitutes to attack women strikers. In addition to intimidating the pickets, the prostitutes would cause a public commotion, and the police would arrest all for solicitation. Rose Schneiderman quickly requested that Mayor Gaynor deputize male strikers to protect the honor of these noble striking women.[108]

By depicting the strikers as innocents needing protection, the union was again able to win broad public support throughout the city and across the nation. Socialist Congressman Victor Berger and U.S. Senator Robert LaFollette began a campaign calling for a congressional investigation of the New York garment industry. On January 21, because of the activities of middle-class reformers such as Grace Barnum, Theodore Roosevelt met with the strikers. During an impromptu press conference, he announced that "this [strike] was crushing the future motherhood of the country. It must be stopped." The manufacturers were losing the public relations war as the paternalism of the union leaders and middle-class reformers converged.[109]

Henry Moskowitz, long an advocate of the Protocol idea, further enlisted Roosevelt to use his influence to end the strike. Moskowitz and Roosevelt met with Harry Gordon of the Cotton Garment Manufacturers' Association and urged the association to settle. But Gordon remained obstinate. After the meeting, Roosevelt wrote to State Assemblyman Michael Schaap suggesting that the assembly investigate the industry, for the heat of a government investigation might speed settlement. He further suggested, after visiting with the workers, that the assembly should also consider enacting minimum wage legislation to aid workers.[110]

Roosevelt's presence brought increased public pressure, the possibility of government activity, and disunion among manufacturers. Many contractors in the kimono trade seceded from the association to create their own organization: the East Side Kimono and Petticoat Manufacturers' Association. They quickly accepted the assistance of the New York State Board of Mediation and the New York Child Labor Committee to help broker a deal with the ILG. On January 30, they signed a one-year contract that included provisions for a fifty-hour workweek, wage increases, sanitary conditions, and the promise that manufacturers would supply all materials for work.[111] Under continued public pressure from the new contractors' agreement, the Association of Wrapper, Kimono, and House Dress Manufacturers' Association signed an agreement on February 4 ending the strike.[112]

The ILG leadership was split on the new agreements. For one, because they were not industry wide, they were not Protocols in the true sense. Yet, they were the best that could be hoped for. Even a strong Protocolist such as Dyche supported them in spite of their shortcomings. Abraham Rosenberg, ILG president, however, argued for their rejection. His complaint was that the new wage increases would be a great benefit to unskilled workers but would hurt skilled workers. Rosenberg suggested that the contractors' association renegotiate the wage ceiling, which it refused on principle. The contractors attempted to resume production without much success. On February 11, they signed a Protocol with Locals 41 and 10.[113]

With the strike in the kimono trades settled, all attention focused on the white goods manufacturers. Henry Moskowitz, working with Louis Brandeis, was able to bring the two sides together for a conference, which Brandeis chaired.[114] The negotiations in the kimono trades took ten days to hammer out. Modeled after the cloakmakers' agreement, this Protocol had an even weaker system of enforcement. Local 62 organizers, Samuel Shore and Rose Schneiderman, realized this shortcoming, but believed that it was the best that could be achieved at the time. They were chosen by the ILG leadership to sell the agreement to the membership. On February 10, the Local rented Cooper Union for a mass meeting. Rank-and-file opposition to the Protocol was strong, stronger than the ILG had expected. The main concern was that the Protocol did not do enough to protect workers. The opposition in this industry among rank-and-file workers was well organized. They were able to force a vote that enabled each shop committee to vote on the agreement. On February 11, two-thirds of the shop committees rejected the Protocol.[115]

Even as Brandeis and company worked behind the scenes to salvage the talks, the strike erupted into violence as manufacturers hired African American workers as strikebreakers and the union pickets responded with violence.[116] On February 15, the largest manufacturer, Puritan Underwear Company, withdrew from the association and signed a contract. With that, the association relented and began talks. Once again, the smaller manufacturers were worried that larger firms, such as Puritan, would settle early and gobble up larger shares of the trade, leaving nothing but crumbs when they resumed production. After two days of talks, the strike finally ended. The kimono Protocol, in its final embodiment, called for a wage board, as well as boards of arbitration and grievances. There were two differences with the cloakmakers' strike, however. First, this Protocol had a time limit of two years. Second, and most importantly, this Protocol did not include the preferential shop; it included instead the closed shop.[117] With this settlement, only one sector of the ladies' garment trade remained unProtocoled: the children's dress trade. On March 8, with the combined weight of public opinion and union-management accord leaning down upon them, the process of negotiations began in this trade. The union declared an organizational strike on March 10, and three days later announced the Protocol.[118]

By the end of March, the Protocol had come to encompass the entirety of the ladies' garment industry. Reformers and the press heralded these events, but few anticipated the problems that would soon arise. To many outside of the rank and file, the Protocol was a magic bullet, an inoculation against class disruption and an "uncivilized" economy. Blind to the realities of the day-to-day functioning of Protocolism, the public soon moved on to other concerns.

PROBLEMS ARISE

While on the surface the Protocol seemed to be functioning as planned, problems were smoldering beneath. One of the first problems to arise revolved around the issue of wages. The Protocol had promised the equalization of the piece-rate system. To speed this process along, the agreement called for the establishment of shop committees where shop stewards and management representatives would jointly set the rates.

This proved to be a contentious issue. Between December of 1910 and September of 1911, 28 percent of all recorded disputes were over piece-rates.[119] In an effort to avoid this confusion as the Protocol spread to other trades, the setting of the piece-rates became more centralized. In the waist trades, for instance, one board set the entire piece-rate for the industry.[120]

The increase in grievance filings recast the Protocol framework itself. As originally formulated by Brandeis, the Protocol was to be based upon conciliation and compromise. He believed that both labor and management had a common interest. Therefore, under his plan, the industrial court (Committee on Grievances), and not the supreme court (Board of Arbitration), would be more important. The original language of the Protocol spelled out the role of the Board of Arbitration in great detail, but left the role of the Committee on Grievances ambiguous at best. This was done because Brandeis wanted to leave the Committee on Grievances flexibility to maneuver around the thornier issues he expected to come before it. The unexpected number of grievances, as well as the seriousness of these charges, placed the Committee on Grievances at the center of an industrial volcano.[121] By late 1912, it was generally recognized by the parties involved that the Committee on Grievances held the major responsibility for the Protocol. As it went, so would go the Protocolism. And, to some, that board appeared ill equipped for the job.[122]

The committee's inability to deal with the rapidly growing backlog of cases compounded the matter. When the union charged that the manufacturers were using the slack season to lay off active union members while keeping nonunion workers, the Committee was slow to respond. Workers, tired of waiting for the Committee, took matters into their own hands and struck the offending shops. Once the workers walked out, the shops would file charges of unauthorized strike activity with the Committee. The increasing frequency and number of these work stoppages brought the work of the Committee to almost a complete standstill.[123] Sensing that the Committee's inability to settle the large backlog of grievances might jeopardize the life of the agreement, Henry Moskowitz began meeting with both sides. He hoped to at worse ease some of the tensions, let some of the steam vent before the pot boiled over. At best, he hoped to convince both sides that it was in their better interests to preserve the agreement.[124]

By the beginning of 1911, the wildcat strikes were so numerous that some were calling for the end of the Protocol. Cohen, writing A. Lincoln Filene in mid-January, demanded that the Arbitration Board step in, claiming that if it failed to act, "There is plenty of cause for the manufacturers to declare the Protocol off." He accused the ILG for failing to stop unauthorized strikes and, therefore, of acting in bad faith. Finally, Cohen filed formal charges against the union on January 17.[125]

While the Arbitration Board was envisioned as an industrial supreme court, until these charges were filed, it had not met. After the union filed its countercharges, the Board held its first meeting on March 4, 1911. The Board was designed so as to give Brandeis complete control. Composed of three members, one each from the union and manufacturers, Brandeis always possessed the winning vote.[126]

During the first meeting, it became clear that the central question was the role and responsibility of both Board and Committee. If the Committee on Grievances was constituted as an industrial court, as indeed Brandeis expected, and the Board of Arbitration as a supreme industrial court, then any meeting of the Board of Arbitration meant that the grievance mechanisms had failed. Moskowitz and others soon argued that the grievance procedures needed a major overhaul.[127]

After listening to testimony for three days, the Board adjourned to render its decision. The Board chose Hillquit, the labor representative, who agreed with Brandeis on many issues, to draft the final report, if only to make the decision more tolerable to the union.[128] On March 14, the Board, in recognition of the importance of the Committee of Grievance's central role, changed its name to the Board of Grievances. To speed up the decision process, the number of Board members was increased to ten. The report created "Rules and Plan[s] of Procedure" for hearings in order to streamline the grievance process. The union was required to recognize all new association members. And on the issue of out-of-town shops, the Board ruled that the agreement applied to all association shops regardless of location—ending, on paper at least, the runaway shop issue. The Board also argued for Protocol imperialism, arguing that "the salvation [of the garment industry, and by extension, industry in general] . . . lies in the ever greater extension of such fair and humane arrangements as are embodied in the Protocol."[129]

THE PROTOCOL SYSTEM OF GRIEVANCE SETTLEMENT

The Protocol mechanisms were bureaucracy embodied. The Arbitration Board's decision of March 1911 sped up the centralizing mission of the new IR system that the Protocol had unleashed. It took almost all authority from workers and the shop floor and placed it in centralized and regulated bodies dominated by industrial experts. Often forgotten, however, is that this decision was rendered the same month as the Triangle Fire.[130]

The grievance process was a complex one. If a problem arose in a given shop, the worker was to inform the shop steward. The shop steward was to inform management's representative in the shop to try to settle the issue. If no settlement could be reached, the shop steward informed the union's Joint Board, the federation of the various locals. At this level, a formal complaint was issued and sent to the Board of Grievances for investigation and a hearing. All the while, the worker(s) was to remain at work. Failure to do so could result in management replacing the offending worker with another union worker and rendering the grievance moot. If the complaint made it to the Board, two clerks (one from each side) were dispatched to investigate. Once both were satisfied with their findings, they attempted to settle the matter themselves. If they failed to do so, which was almost always the case, the grievance went to the two chief clerks. If they failed to solve it, a formal hearing of the board was called.[131]

The newly reformulated Board of Grievances was required to hold weekly meetings to hear all pending petitions and review weekly reports of the chief clerks filed before it. If the Board could not solve an issue outright, it created a subcommittee to provide a recommendation for the next meeting. If the Board failed to issue a decision because of a deadlock, or if one side appealed such a decision, the case went to the Arbitration Board. Under the new rules, no petitions would be acted on if a strike or lockout existed. A key modification for the new Board was to allow itself the flexibility to change. Modeled on the U.S. Constitution, its creators saw the Protocol as a "machine that would go of itself." The new Board was also given the authority to call joint conferences to revise the agreement when it seemed necessary, as long as the Board of Arbitration approved. In addition, two alternating chairs were appointed (one from each side) to keep the Board running smoothly.[132]

The Board of Grievances was charged with the seemingly impossible task of settling all disputes. Yet, for a time, the new board functioned smoothly and quickly. From April 1911 to October 1913, 7,956 grievances were filed with the Board. Of these, 7,477 were handled or settled by the clerks. Only 179 went to the Board of Grievances, and only 20 continued on to the Board of Arbitration. The pace of grievance filing, however, escalated with each passing month. From early in 1911 to April 1912, there were an average of 150 petitions filed per month. But, by spring of 1913, the number mushroomed to 384. Because of this pattern, by as early as 1912, the real power of the Protocol machinery seemed to rest in the offices of the chief clerks.[133]

The grievances that were filed and that eventually went to the full Board reveal a pattern. Of the 179 cases brought forward, 122 came from the union. A significant number of these, forty-eight in all, involved some form of discrimination against union members by shop owners. Of the petitions brought by the association, the vast majority dealt with wildcat strikes, often resulting from workers' perceived discrimination by owners. As early as 1912, it appears that workers increasingly took matters into their own hands rather than wait for the Protocol's machinery of justice. This shop-floor militancy, which was so much of a tradition among the ladies' garment workers, was increasingly becoming the principal obstacle to the proper functioning of the Protocol.[134]

By 1912, a critical issue emerged as the wrongful dismissal of union activists began to challenge the usefulness of the Protocol. Under the Protocol's preferential shop agreement, the worker had to prove wrongful dismissal. As Brandeis explained it to Moskowitz in 1912, "The burden of proof should be on the employee in all cases to show that the employer acted without just cause." Because few discharged workers found the "smoking guns" that the legalist Board of Grievances required, few got reinstated. Because shop owners seemed able to dismiss workers indiscriminately without fear of retaliation from the machinery of the Protocol, they did so with increasing frequency. At each occurrence, the union blamed the Protocol, and the rank and file became more activist as ill will increased. Furthermore, wildcat striking got results: many shop owners, desperate to fill orders, settled with their wildcatting workers quickly.[135]

In an effort to win back rank-and-file workers and renew interest in the agreement, Brandeis conducted a successful one-man public relations blitz. The troubles of the Board of Grievances centered on the key element of the Protocol: the meaning of the preferential shop. Trying to convince America that this element would "be a way out of our current difficulty," he tried to revive interest in his idea, writing to over a dozen major magazines and writers. Writing to muckraking journalist Ray Stanndard Baker in February 1912, he argued that "this could be made into a great human story. Would it not be possible for you to take it up?"[136]

Brandeis's efforts paid off. Almost all the major journals and reform magazines of the era produced feature articles on the Protocol that served to reinvest public confidence in it that it did not possess of its own accord. But again, as public interest seemed to revive in Protocolism, critical events were brewing that would have dire consequences for the future of IR in the ladies' garment industry.

The Protocol, from this moment forward, never fully recovered nor did it live up to its promises. Partly, as we have seen, the reason for the Protocol's weakness laid in its inability to allow a voice or a place for rank-and-file workers. Unlike the 1909 strike, rank-and-file cloakmakers were denied a visible public forum to discuss their grievances. Building on the 1909 strike, union leader and middle-class reformers and experts paternalistically bargained on behalf of the rank and file. When confronted with a problem, as we will also see, these Protocolists tried to settle it with more bureaucracy. The second reason, which will become clear in the next chapter, was the insufficient powers of the Protocol's Board of Arbitration. Workers were willing, it seemed, to trade some voice for a speedy and fair adjudication of their grievances. This is seen in their demands for a system of binding arbitration. But, the Board of Arbitration was not designed to function this way. It was clear, then, that if Protocolism were to survive, a stronger role would have to be played by the public members. That the state would eventually step into the arena of IR only seemed a natural progression to the parties involved in the Protocol.

3   The Shifting Ground of Protocolism
Struggling for the Soul of Industrial Democracy

THE PROTOCOL offered a vision of industrial democracy that made little room for rank-and-file or shop-floor voices. It attempted to provide efficiency before democracy and have the former pay for the latter. Yet, workers did not passively accept the Protocol as created; workers shaped and contoured the developing industrial relations (IR) system. At the heart of these struggles was representation. Who spoke for the workers? Who represented their interests in the IR process?

Three episodes, revolving around the issues of local versus (inter)national union control, highlight the persistent question of who spoke for the rank-and-file workers at the Protocol table. By 1912, the ILG leadership had invested a great deal in the Protocol. The locals, and for that matter the rank-and-file workers, were leery of the International's influence and wanted more direct democracy. They resisted the loss of autonomy and the push toward centralization that came from the ILG leadership. And, they wanted arbitration over conciliation.

PART I: LOCAL 38

The first of these tests involved Local 38, the Ladies' Tailors. The workers in this local were unique: they produced custom-made clothing, were better paid, and worked in small shops. A small local, at no time more than 3,000 members, it had a strong tradition of collectivism and direct democracy.[1]

Local 38 was chartered in 1909, following the upsurge in union activity brought about by the Uprising. In the spring of that year, Julius Henry Cohen was appointed chief counsel to the Merchant's Society of Ladies' Tailors, a trade group. Cohen, together with the union leadership, commenced the selling of Protocolism to this sector of the industry. At the

Cleveland ILGWU Convention in 1911, the General Executive Board (GEB) authorized a general strike for the ladies' tailors. Within days, the ladies' tailors walked off their jobs. On September 18, a Protocol was signed and the strike ended.[2]

The ladies tailors' Protocol shared many features of the original Protocol. Like the others, it too was negotiated in secret by what had become the Protocol team—Julius Henry Cohen, Henry Moskowitz, Meyer London, and Morris Hillquit, with A. Lincoln Filene and Louis Brandeis playing supporting roles. Like the other Protocols, it was handed down to the rank and file from above. Yet, for all its outward similarities, two significant differences reflected the unique work culture of these workers. First, the agreement eliminated all piecework and Sunday work. More significant, however, was the arrangement for work sharing. In slack seasons, all work was to be equally divided among the workers in an effort to prevent lay offs, and in boom times, all overtime was to be shared as well. The new arrangement outlawed the giving of overtime to some workers and laying off of others.[3]

Industrial war erupted within three months of the beginning of the Protocol as the industry was hit with a wave of unauthorized shop strikes. Cohen wrote Brandeis that "the situation is very tense ... although we have peace on paper we really have a condition of war."[4]

Almost immediately, the Protocolists blamed the local's leaders for the troubles. Moskowitz summed it up in a letter to Brandeis in early December when he blamed the "weak unstable, [and] incompetent" leaders of Local 38 for the difficulties. The ILG's John Dyche weighed in, calling the rank and file of the local a "syndicalist membership," and threatening the local with expulsion if it did not stop the wildcat strikes. Again, demonstrating full faith in Tayloristic social science and notions of efficiency, Moskowitz suggested the solution rested in applying scientific management principles to the industry. To this end, he suggested the establishment of an investigative board and expert report to examine the trade thoroughly.[5]

The true cause of the wildcats was the clash of conflicting cultures: the bureaucratic Protocolist versus the rank-and-file collectivist cultures that coexisted within the union. This conflict played itself out over discussions of overtime. The rank and file refused to accept overtime, forcing shops to hire more workers. This tactic also allowed the rank and file to protect their own members: shop owners could not fire some workers and use overtime for the remainder to continue production. This behavior, for obvious reasons, directly challenged the rights of management. Lockouts and wildcats, by early December, became the norm in the trade. At this point, the Trade Association, and Protocolists Moskowitz and Brandeis, teamed up with the ILG leadership of Rosenberg and Dyche to correct the problem and "manage" the workers. Moskowitz, reporting to Brandeis, recounted how the ILG would discipline the rank and file: the ILG's Rosenberg was "disgruntled with Local 38, and contends that the only way to discipline that body is to have it whipped into some fashion.... Dyche will attempt to club them into line." By January 1912, Dyche had become the most significant agent of the Protocol within the ILG. In the process, however, the rank and file began to see him as a class traitor and enemy. By late January, the Arbitration Board was called together and asked to rule on issues of overtime and holidays, but more importantly, over control of production. Cohen argued that management had the right to fire workers for poor workmanship. To do this, he argued, management had to institute time and motion studies in their shops. The union countered that the "equal distribution of work" clause meant that once hired, workers could not be fired by management. The owners countered that the local leadership was confrontational and did not support the spirit of the agreement and therefore should be replaced by the ILG itself.[6]

On February 27, the Board handed down its decision. Overtime rates were set at 1.6 times normal wages, and holiday pay was set at double time. On the control issue, however, the local was dealt a crushing blow. The Board ruled that management could hire as many workers as it wanted, and it could hire only those it deemed suitable. Labor lost the right to challenge management on issues other than hours, wages, and conditions. Bread-and-butter unionism won out.[7]

Local 38 leaders did the unimaginable. They simply refused to accept the Board's ruling. Local 38 leader Sol Rossman claimed only the rank and file had the right to decide overtime and could decide who worked and who did not. Then the rank and file refused all overtime requests outright. The stage was now set for a showdown between Rossman and Dyche, between two contesting cultures, and the meaning of industrial democracy.[8]

Moskowitz watched from the sidelines, wanting to see how the ILG handled this "affair." The Protocol, to be a successful instrument of IR, required that the union control its members. Would the ILG demonstrate maturity? As Moskowitz wrote to Brandeis, "This Local 38 situation . . . is a chaos, and unless the International steps in firmly, the Protocol will not work here. I do not know whether it will work at all."[9]

Here was a local taking the promise of industrial democracy seriously. The rank and file had the advantage of having engaged in this contest during the rush session. By refusing to accept overtime during the busiest season of the year, the rank and file forced many firms simply to hire more workers to fill their orders. At the shop of Steine and Blain, for example, when the shop filled its orders and attempted to lay off the newly hired workers, the shop committee refused. They argued that once hired, the only justification to fire a worker was for incompetence. Because shops could not usually prove incompetence, the union claimed it had to keep the new workers on the payroll. Then the rank and file conducted a slowdown. The shop owners, backed against a wall, kept the new workers on and filed a grievance. When the shop suggested a return to the piece-rate system, the local declared a violation of the Protocol and ordered the workers to strike.[10]

With the strike, the battle of words and ideologies between Rossman and Dyche heated up into a battle of control over the rank and file. Dyche called the strike unauthorized and anarchistic, demanding that the local follow the letter of the law of the Protocol: order the workers back and if they refused, replace them. Rossman attacked Dyche, calling him a "class traitor" and "tool of the capitalists."[11] When the shop owners demanded that the International union replace the strikers with union labor, Rossman prepared for a general strike in the industry.

Word of a possible general strike reached Dyche and the ILG. To prevent this, the GEB placed the local into a three-person receivership and quickly settled the strike at Steine and Blain. While Rossman accepted the strike's settlement, he would not accept the receivership. He refused to give up control of the local to representatives of the International. He argued that the local was sovereign and the ILG had no authority to mess in its affairs.[12]

By April 1912, the grievances finally reached the Board of Arbitration. "Perceiv[ing] . . . a lack of fixed determination on either side to cooperate with the other in carrying out provisions of the Peace Treaty," the Board called for a total reorganization of the local by then newly renamed Board of Grievances, demanding that both sides only elect men who truly believed in Protocolism. In trying to preserve the fragile peace, Brandeis tried to offer each side something it wanted. The Board ruled that the overtime and holiday scales were retroactive. This was an issue because the strike was settled months before the scales were worked out. Next, it granted the shop owners virtual freedom to fire workers at will by granting them the ability to interpret the incompetence-in-employment clause of the agreement.

Again, Local 38 refused to abide by the Board's decision. Speaking for the ILG, Dyche issued assurances that if the local persisted, it would be thrown out of the ILG and replaced with more responsible leadership.[13] Purchasing an ad in the *Jewish Daily Forward*, Dyche denounced the strike and the local. Rossman responded with an ad of his own denouncing the dictatorial actions of the International and Dyche. Finally, the ILG gave Rossman an ultimatum to return to work immediately or else suffer the consequences. When Rossman refused, the ILG expelled the local on July 12 as promised. While the International finally triumphed over an unruly local, it lost the support of many rank and filers. While other locals accepted the International's new expanded role, they still quietly upheld the ideals of local sovereignty. Dyche declared the Protocol saved by the actions of the "responsible" leadership of the ILG. But, the problems with the Protocol that arose in the "Local 38 situation" were not solved with the union's expulsion.

PART II: THE BISNO AFFAIR

The events of Local 38 sparked discussion among the locals of the ILG. Local autonomy, and the increasing presence of the International, remained an issue. By January 1912, Local 10 (cloakmakers), the largest and most powerful of the locals, realized that it needed to become more active in the Protocol, rather than sit on the sidelines. The solution? The Joint Board, the federation of the New York cloakmakers' locals, would take control of the machinery of the Protocol. The logic being the closer the machinery was to the locals, the more democratic it would be. The linchpin for this effort, therefore, would be the office of the chief clerk. This office became increasingly important after 1912. The locals believed that what they needed was a more committed representative within the Protocol machinery. The Joint Board quickly removed Sol Polakoff as labor's clerk. An unlikely man, Abraham Bisno, replaced him. Bisno was an outsider, a spokesperson for Chicago garment workers. Rather than having rank-and-file credentials, he had cultivated relationships with reformers in Chicago and New York.[14]

The ILG leadership acceded to the Joint Board's choice. Dyche and Rosenberg believed that because Bisno was an outsider, he would not have strong ties to rank and filers. He might even be more responsible and more willing to work with ILG leaders within the Protocol system. At first, the ILG had every reason to rejoice. Bisno's first order of business was the complete reorganization of the Joint Board. Up until then, the Board had been composed of all local leadership (forty-five locals). Bisno created a fifteen-member Executive Board, with himself as chair, to run day-to-day activities. Duly installed as Joint Board chair and labor's chief clerk, Bisno ran the labor side of the Protocol in the cloak trade almost single-handedly from January through September 1912.[15]

Once the unions were brought under his domain, Bisno searched for the causes of rank-and-file discontent. After a series of investigations and meetings with local representatives, he reached a conclusion: non-Protocol shops were placing huge burdens on Protocol shops to reduce expenses in order to remain competitive. The Protocol's plan had been to drive small shops to either modernize or go out of business. Many, however, continued to operate as sweatshops or small contract shops—moving frequently to avoid detection. The result was increased pressure on larger shops to resort to outsourcing to compete with the lower labor costs of the small shops. In addition, many association shop owners shifted production to out-of-town shops or to in-town nonassociation shops to avoid the Protocol.[16]

In an effort to end the practice of subcontracting and jobbing, Bisno called for a Joint Conference between labor and management and demanded seven reforms. The demands were sweeping: an "expert" price committee, made up of social workers and industrial experts; a true enforcement mechanism for subcontracting violations; provisions to denounce and discipline association members who outsourced orders to avoid the agreement; the creation of the Protocol "white label"; a demand that anything that an association shop buy or sell meet all Protocol standards—effectively ending the advantage outsourcing provided; and lastly, to have every shop in the city fall under the Joint Board of Sanitary Control, a requirement that only shops that were duly certified by the Board could do business with association shops.[17]

Having marshaled his forces and presented his case, Bisno was a force to be reckoned with. On April 12, 1912, Bisno claimed a victory as the Joint Conference announced its decisions. The Conference agreed to place all out-of-town shops owned by association members under the Protocol agreement. It agreed, in principle, to the idea of an "expert" price committee. And in May, the Board of Grievances made mandatory the registration and inspection of all contractors by the Joint Board of Sanitary Control.[18]

All seemed well, then on May 2, the shop of Carl Bonwit fired all the workers in one department, claiming a slump in economy and the slack season had cut business. Bisno declared this a lockout and filed a petition with the Board of Grievances. The association, speaking through its chief clerk, Dr. Paul Abelson, responded that there was no basis to Bisno's charge. Bonwit was simply responding to market conditions. Bisno demanded that Bonwit open his books; if economics was the cause, he had better prove it. Up until this episode, Dyche had remained a quiet observer on the sidelines. Now he entered the fray. Sensing the possibility of another round of wildcat strikes, and the inability of the Board of Grievances to act effectively, he suggested that Bisno contact Brandeis.

Both Dyche and Bisno traveled to Boston to meet with the lawyer on May 9.[19] Bisno went in the hopes that the "great man" could mediate and offer a solution to the present problem. But, Bisno was sadly mistaken. Dyche had taken Bisno to Brandeis for a stern reprimand. As Brandeis recalled the meeting to Moskowitz, he "convinced them that the discharge of the men, although wholesale, was not a lockout." He went on to state that "I made it clear to them . . . [that the problem] . . . ought to be met by a further invention of machinery and legislation." On the issue of mediation, one that would resurface again, Brandeis flatly rejected Bisno's claims. "Bisno," Brandeis claimed, "urged strenuously that there should be an immediate referee . . . I told him . . . I was loath to substitute the decision of an umpire for the resulting agreement between two opposing parties; that, to my mind, one of the valuable parts of the Protocol was the forcing of a decision between the parties."[20]

In the conflict with Dyche, Bisno found himself surrounded by unlikely allies. By opposing Dyche, Bisno became the patron saint for rank and filers and radicals, who never forgave Dyche's actions in the Local 38 affair. This was disconcerting for Bisno, whose politics were actually much closer to Dyche's and Rosenberg's than to the union's radical wing.

Yet, in Dyche's eyes, Bisno had shown his true colors. What started as a dispute over the issue of "third-party mediation" soon revived the older dispute over local autonomy. Bisno, whether knowing it or not, was moving the debate on industrial democracy into new directions and in the process he was providing voice for the rank and file.[21]

As the dispute escalated, lines were drawn. Dyche responded to Bisno's open rejection of his advice by calling Bisno a "syndicalist" and "a dreamer and a settlement worker." In July, Bisno overwhelmingly won reelection to both the office of chief clerk and chair of the Joint Board. Furthermore, he received approval to decrease the number on the Joint Board's Board of Directors from fifteen to twelve. The three members removed from the Board were ILG representatives, including Dyche and Rosenberg. Bisno then created an official organ for the Joint Board, rejecting Dyche's *Ladies' Garment Worker*. He hired Dr. B. Hoffman to edit the *New Post*.[22]

Hoffman used the pages of the *New Post* to give voice to rank-and-file grievances against the centralizing and bureaucratizing affects of the Protocol. Hoffman and others denounced the central tenant of Protocolism—conciliation—as a sham. He denounced Dyche for selling out the rank and file, and in an editorial on August 24, he openly attacked the association. Dyche responded by formally apologizing to the association in the pages of the *Ladies' Garment Worker* and called both Bisno and Hoffman "ignorant and dogmatic."[23]

During the political infighting of the summer of 1912, Moskowitz reported every action and reaction to Brandeis. In July, Moskowitz recognized the rank and file's frustration with the agreement. He wrote Brandeis that the workers "look upon the Protocol as a farce." His suggestions were twofold: first, something should be done to settle down the rank and file and second, the issue of outsourcing—which Moskowitz believed was the root of the evil—needed to be addressed by the Arbitration Board.[24]

Bisno, realizing that Dyche, the association, and Brandeis were now counseling against him, began plotting to circumvent the association. In July, he opened negotiations with smaller cloak shops, which organized themselves into a separate protective association, later entering into an agreement with the Joint Board that covered all of the reforms Bisno had demanded of the larger association. To many—Dyche, Moskowitz, and Cohen at least—it seemed that Bisno was planning to force the association to accept his reforms by organizing their opponents in the industry.[25]

Cohen (with Dyche's and Rosenberg's approval) wrote to Brandeis asking the Arbitration Board to remove Bisno for the sake of the agreement. While Cohen was pressuring Brandeis, Dyche was working behind the scenes on the Joint Board. Many of the local leaders questioned the functioning of the Protocol, but many still thought they were better off with it than without it. By October, Dyche had orchestrated a coup. The Joint Board removed Bisno as chief clerk, replacing him with Dyche himself, while Bisno remained chair of the Board of Directors.[26]

Upon assuming his new role as labor's chief clerk of the Protocol, Dyche proclaimed a new day, a rebirth of Protocolism. "I thought," he wrote of this period,

I could demonstrate to our people [rank-and-file workers] that by using tact and diplomacy—by using the ordinary trade union methods [pure-and-simple unionism]—I could make more progress than by keeping the threat of a general strike over the heads of the . . . Association.[27]

Part of the problem Dyche faced in winning rank-and-file support, however, emerged from his notion of efficiency, values he shared with Cohen, Brandeis, and Moskowitz. In the name of "efficiency," Dyche removed the rank and file from the entire process of IR. The measure of efficiency for the Protocolists, then, was the expeditious handling of cases. This myopic vision led to increased bureaucracy. This in turn, led to a great chasm between union leaders and union members.[28]

A problem at the Stratton shop in October of 1912 demonstrates Dyche's total lack of understanding of rank-and-file realities as well as the limits of pure-and-simple unionism. After difficult negotiations over piece-rates were settled, a walkout occurred. The strike was not over any of the bread-and-butter issues that were familiar to Dyche. It was, harkening back to the Uprising, over humane treatment. When a foreman "called out" a female worker, her fellow workers walked out in protest, demanding that he be fined and fired for his inappropriate actions. While the workers were out, the associate clerks refused to conduct Protocol business until the Stratton dispute was settled. Dyche was called in. He had hoped to gain advantages over the association at the bargaining table by offering the employers what they seemed to want most: the ILG's crackdown on unauthorized shop strikes. Dyche called a meeting of the strikers and read them sections of the ILGWU constitution and Protocol agreement, which made unauthorized strikes illegal. He then ordered the workers back to work. If they did not return within fifteen minutes, he threatened they would be dismissed and replaced by union members.[29]

When they did not return to work, Dyche fired the mostly Italian workers, replacing them with mainly Jewish workers—further widening the union's ethnic divisions. Dyche's handling of the Stratton strike further deepened the rift between himself and the rank and file. The rank and file responded by calling Dyche a tool of the association and no friend of labor. Many workers were angered by Dyche's refusal to handle individual grievance cases, preferring shopwide disputes. Individual workers who expected their union's support filed the bulk of grievances. When Dyche failed to act on these cases, many questioned his motives as well as the purpose of the International.[30]

On December 11, a Joint Conference was held to discuss the Stratton strike and other issues; it resulted in a changing of the guard. Again, the association demanded that that the ILG act to hold the Protocol together. Rosenberg, sensing the seriousness of the association's veiled threats, went so far as to depict the Bisno group as "merely . . . a few idiots and fools." The ILG did step in, and within a few weeks, Bisno's role was diminished to the point that he resigned and returned to Chicago. Dyche's responsibilities also changed. Drafted to lead the ILG's organizing effort in other sectors of the trade, he stepped aside as chief clerk.[31]

PART III: THE HOURWICH AFFAIR

With a momentary leadership vacuum in the Joint Board, another outsider came on board: Dr. Isaac Hourwich. Hourwich originally had been offered a new position heading the new statistical department of the Joint Board. Before he had even accepted this position, he was offered the job of chief clerk. Not a garment worker, he had been a statistician for the United States Census Bureau. Dyche and Rosenberg had wanted an ILG insider and would have surely blocked anyone they saw as too closely associated with the rank and file. Hourwich was an outsider and therefore he offended no one. Each side hoped to be able to win him over to its cause. On January 15, 1913, he accepted and signed a one-year contract.[32]

Hourwich was an odd choice. A lawyer and Ph.D., he had no shop-floor experience and only limited experience in New York's garment industry. In the 1890s, he infrequently represented Local 10 as legal counsel. Well known on the Lower East Side as the "Professor," he was seen as a friend to immigrants. An intellectual socialist who studied the political economy of immigrant life in urban America, he seemed to have more in common with the reformers and Protocolists than with the average rank-and-file worker he was now to represent.[33]

No sooner had Hourwich assumed his new position when Goldfield and Lachman, a medium-sized shop within the association, refused to let the "price committee" set prices. The workers walked out. The association promptly ordered all of its clerks to pull out of the grievance machinery, bringing the entire Protocol to a halt. Twice before, when the association had done this, Dyche had caved in. Hourwich, rather than order the strikers back to work, attacked the employers for provoking the workers.[34]

Hourwich took the mantle of chief clerk and headed into battle. Proclaiming himself "secretary of war" for the army of rank and filers, he proclaimed that he would protect, at all costs, the rights of his members from the abuses of the association. He saw his role as legal advocate for the locals and their members, a "lawyer for the oppressed."[35] He told the association, just after his appointment, that it had no right to stop the Protocol unilaterally: "You have no right to strike. You have no right to stop the machinery of the Protocol in 499 shops, which are in no way involved and whose employees are in no way responsible for the transgression of the people in that one shop."[36]

At the Board of Grievance hearings for this shop strike, Cohen and Hourwich came head to head. Cohen argued, for the first time in public, that the Protocol was an agreement that the association had with the ILGWU, not with the Joint Board. In an effort to circumvent the local entirely, Cohen sought to make the ILG the sole partner to the agreement. Cohen added that the association need not have any dealings, formal or informal, with the locals. Any contact with the locals on the association's part was strictly voluntary and done out of a sense of courtesy. Playing on the growing rift between the locals and the International, Cohen hoped to force the ILG leadership to take over the labor half of the Protocol. However, Cohen had met his match. Hourwich argued that if the association wanted to, it could meet with the ILG. However, the International did not speak for rank-and-file garment workers. He argued that if the association "desired to deal with the shadow instead of the body it is your privilege."[37]

Hourwich raised fundamental questions about industrial democracy: who was responsible for the Protocol? Who had authority to bargain for the rank-and-file union members? The locals, represented by the Joint Board? Or, the International? While always a hidden issue within IR, Hourwich brought it out front and center. Before this, both labor bodies could claim co-authority. Now a showdown was set. When news of Hourwich's calling the ILG a "shadow body" reached Dyche, who was never one to hold back, he readied to send the "professor" back to Washington. Only Meyer London restrained him. London, aware that an open split in labor's camp would only benefit the association, argued that Dyche should bide his time and remain quiet. By claiming to be the sole representative of labor to the Protocol, Hourwich put enormous pressure on the ILG. Because he had the ILG on the ropes, Hourwich presented Dyche with a letter and requested that he sign it. The letter stated that the ILG was *not* a signatory body to the Protocol, only a legal adviser to the Joint Board.[38]

Hourwich had been able to do in a matter of weeks what Bisno had not done in months: demonstrate the authority and supremacy of the locals over the International in matters of the Protocol. Because of this, Hourwich became the instantaneous hero of the rank and file, who rejoiced in his victory over both Dyche and the centralization and bureaucratization of the Protocol. Hourwich was shifting the terms of debate on industrial democracy.

Sensing that Dyche was losing control, Moskowitz contacted Brandeis and urged him to "interpret the instrument [agreement] so as to make the International the responsible body with the Joint Board as agent or the Joint Board as a party with the International as guarantor." He went on to state that "Personally, I prefer the former [option]."[39]

At the February 3 meeting of the Board of Arbitration, Brandeis ruled that the association could not stop the machinery of the entire Protocol over one shop strike. On the larger matter of who had authority for the agreement, he ruled that the "agreement was made by the Joint Board," making the ILG merely a guarantor to the Protocol, as Moskowitz had suggested. In one fell swoop, Hourwich was triumphant: the association was found in violation of the agreement, the integrity of the Joint Board was upheld, localism won over the forces of centralization, and Dyche was defeated.[40]

Hourwich was convinced that he had discovered a successful strategy for settling disputes: a purely legalistic approach. Hourwich, therefore, began to see the industrial relations of the Protocol as a complete legal system and began acting accordingly. He studied past decisions to discover "a case law" of the Protocol based on precedent. To aid him, he hired George Wishnak as his assistant, and he demanded that a better record-keeping system be established. Wishnak was a radical cloakmaker who was exceptionally popular with the rank and file.[41]

In contrast, the ILG and association leadership were not at all happy with Hourwich. He had turned what they saw as a system of conciliation with a centralized role for the ILG working to control shop-floor insurgency into a political battleground with less predictable rank-and-file grievants. The ILG leadership, along with the association, spoke of the Protocol's unique flexibility for the art of compromise and, indeed, its removal from direct contact with the rank and file. Hourwich turned everything into a contest, undermining the power and authority of the ILG at the same time. Hourwich's strident stands, on the other hand, were paying off as he gained increased rank-and-file support.[42]

One of Hourwich's strongest supporters and a direct link to the rank and file was *New Post* editor B. Hoffman. Under Hoffman's guidance, the pages of the *New Post* consistently attacked the association, the ILG, and the idea of the Protocol itself, all the while heaping abundant praise on Hourwich as a knight in shining armor. Dyche, obviously goaded, replied in kind in the pages of the *Ladies' Garment Worker*. But the more Dyche attacked Hourwich, the more unpopular he became with the rank and file.[43]

The rift between rank and filers and the union leaders continued to grow until April, when another crisis over union power erupted that ultimately put the ILG in the position of bringing in unionized scabs to replace wildcatting union garment workers. Twenty-three operators at the shop of Jaffee and Katz walked out. Hourwich ordered the workers back to work pending a formal investigation by the Joint Board of Sanitary Control. But when the workers returned, they found they had been permanently replaced. At this, Hourwich called an emergency meeting of the Board of Grievances.[44]

At the April 18 special meeting of the Board, Hourwich dominated the discussion. He shifted the entire issue onto the association's shoulders. "It looks very much as if they [association] were trying to irritate their employees into an act of insubordination which would justify their discharge," he argued. "When the employees complained that the place assigned to them is unfit for the work they are required to perform, it is a misinterpretation of the Protocol, to demand that they should go to work in that place.... We [speaking for the Joint Board] hold the discharge of the whole department by the firm entirely unwarranted and contrary to the provisions of sections XVII and XVIII of the Rules of the Board of Grievances. [Which stated only the union could discipline workers.]"[45]

While Hourwich waited for the meeting of the Arbitration Board, union men replaced the shop strikers at Jaffe and Katz. As the rank-and-filers' impatience grew, Hourwich began a campaign of intimidation against the replacement workers. Labeling them "scabs with union books," he called the ILG a "sort of scab agency." Moreover, in a veiled threat, he announced that workers were losing patience and faith in the Protocol.[46]

Hourwich was beginning to see that the problem was larger than arbitration, binding or otherwise. The problem was the constitution of the Protocol itself. In part, the problem was the power given to the "public" members of the Board of Arbitration. There was simply no way for the rank and file to influence these members. Hourwich was moving toward a new system. He believed in the idea of the Protocol, but was seeking an overhaul that would make it more malleable to rank and file preasure. That overhaul would eventually come as Protocolism was changed as the state replaced the quasi-public figures such as Brandeis. Hourwich, therefore, began to disagree openly with Brandeis. Demanding quick action, he tried to convince Brandeis to call the Arbitration Board into a special emergency session. Brandeis put him off, telling him that they could not meet until later in the summer. Instead, Brandeis suggested the Joint Board meet and draft recommendations for a Joint Conference. Privately, Brandeis wrote to Moskowitz to "get him [Hourwich] into line."[47]

Hourwich did exactly as Brandeis suggested. Soon after he had returned to New York from his May 9 meeting with Brandeis in Washington, Hourwich and the Board of Directors of the Joint Board appointed an eleven-man committee to redraft the Protocol. In keeping with Brandeis's wishes, Dyche and other ILG leaders joined this effort. The Committee took a week to draft a fifteen-point program, which the Joint Board endorsed on May 17.[48]

The proposed changes to the Protocol were overwhelming in scope. The tenth proposed change was the most important feature, however. It called for a fundamental reorganization of the Board of Arbitration through the addition of a new set of public representatives:

> The Board of Arbitration shall be increased by the addition of a sufficient number of representatives of the public, to be named in the manner provided in Section 19 of the Protocol. The manufacturers' Association or the unions shall be at liberty to call upon any such representative to render a decision in all cases when the clerks of the Board of Grievances disagree. The decision shall be rendered within 48 hours after the submission of all evidence and shall be final.[49]

The Joint Board asked for an immediate conference with the Arbitration Board to discuss this matter. The association refused. "I fear this dilatory policy may lead to serious complications," Hourwich wrote Brandeis. "It is our contention," he continued that if the association continued, it risked destroying the Protocol. Hourwich tried to explain to Brandeis that the union was acting responsibly, while the association was the irresponsible party. If the association continued, he foretold an abrupt end of the Protocol. The union hoped, he argued,

> [T]o open negotiations early in June, while the factories are practically idle, so that we might reach an understanding before the beginning of the new season. This delay will bring the Association face to face with the unions at about the same time as in the memorable Summer of 1910. If the Association will persist in its unyielding attitude, I do not want to foretell the consequences.[50]

With Hourwich's closing words, the threats were no longer veiled. Moskowitz gave too much credit to Hourwich and Hoffman. He believed that they were responsible for the anti-Protocol "rumblings" from below. Closer to the truth was that Hourwich and Hoffman gave voice and visibility to these rumblings; they offered the frustrated rank and file a direction. That direction was to modify the Protocol or face its extinction.[51]

By mid-June, Brandeis and Moskowitz feared for the future of their "instrument," as they called the Protocol. They demanded unsuccessfully that Meyer London intervene. He refused. Stating that while he was philosophically opposed to "Hourwichism," he did not want to interfere in what he saw as an internal union affair. As Moskowitz wrote Brandeis, "London is straddling." But he continued, "I am hoping he will come to the rescue [at the appropriate time]." For London, the time was not yet right.[52]

When the Arbitration Board finally met in early August, Brandeis unilaterally rejected the bulk of Hourwich's and the Joint Board's recommendations. Instead, he recommended a detailed study of the industry. He selected Dr. Walter Weyl, a current Board member, to oversee it. Weyl, in turn, hired Dr. Charles H. Winslow of the U.S. Department of Labor to lead the study.[53]

Hourwich was infuriated by this. He called the study nothing but an "eggheaded" stalling tactic. He saved his strongest venom for Brandeis, calling him a dictator. When questioned later before the U.S. Commission on Industrial Relations, Hourwich stated, "Have you ever heard of arbitrators interfering when the parties have agreed? It is the duty of arbitrators to arbitrate disputes; it is not their duty to create disputes; and that is what Brandeis has done."[54]

Unable to get what he wanted from the Board of Arbitration, Hourwich made plans to get it himself through direct action. As he saw it, the biggest problem was the submanufacturers, who could be brought down with a series of strikes. Therefore, he began a massive organizational drive to bring them under the Protocol umbrella. In August, 7,000 workers walked off their jobs. The strike, however, was poorly planned. The submanufacturers, strongly antiunion, proved to be harder to organize than Hourwich had thought.[55]

Unable to defeat Hourwich in direct battle, Dyche began formulating alternatives to remove him. He urged Brandeis to use his influence to help get Hourwich the job of chief statistician for the U.S. Commission on Industrial Relations, which was just then hiring staff. Rather than take the new job when offered, Hourwich used it as leverage with the Joint Board, who not only reappointed him for one more year but also gave him a raise.[56]

The August strike was followed by a new season of wildcat strikes throughout the industry. At one strike, the local leadership actually walked the picket line with the wildcatters. The association brought formal charges against the union, and a special meeting of the Arbitration

Board was held on October 3–4. At this meeting, Cohen again called for Hourwich's removal. By now, the Protocolists blamed everything on Hourwich and truly believed that only if he was removed and replaced with a more sensible unionist would the Protocol be safe. "The Protocol can not go on," Cohen argued, "unless there is mutual respect":

> It cannot go on when he [Hourwich] defends picketing as he has done here ... our complaint not only charges the Joint Board with failing to uphold the Protocol, but we also bring to the attention of the Board the fact that the International has been unable to control the situation.[57]

Cohen was again beginning to build the case for replacing the Joint Board with the ILG. And this time, Brandeis did not disappoint him. He found that Hourwich was "absolutely wrong" and called his behavior "an act of insurrection and rebellion against the Protocol." He censured the *New Post* and ordered it not to print any anti-Protocol items. But, most importantly, he finally made the ILGWU a full and equal partner to the Protocol.[58]

Aware that the Arbitration Board was siding with ILG, rejecting his reforms, and censuring the *New Post*, Hourwich began to contemplate his future. In the fall of 1913, he announced he was running in a special off-year election for Congress on the Progressive Party ticket. If he had won, which he did not, he would have had a graceful exit from the Joint Board.[59]

While Hourwich was off campaigning for Congress, London stepped in to bridge the gap between the ILG and the Joint Board and provide the Board a dignified way out of its association with Hourwich. By blaming everything on Hourwich, the Joint Board had a way to both give in to the ILG and keep its principles—at least on paper. Rosenberg wrote a letter to the Joint Board asking it to remove Hourwich for running for public office on a "bourgeois party" ticket.[60]

The same day that Rosenberg's letter arrived, the Joint Board also received a letter from Local 1 formally requesting Hourwich's reappointment as chief clerk for 1914. The Board appointed a committee. Hourwich, however, had certain conditions: a salary of $6,000, a declaration in support of free press in support of his stance against ILG, and a referendum vote of the membership on his leadership. When some locals of operators threatened to secede from the Joint Board if Hourwich was not reappointed, the committee reversed its earlier stand and agreed to submit the issue of reappointment to a membership referendum on December 13–14, 1913.[61]

Seeing an opening even before the election, Moskowitz, together with Dyche and Cohen, devised a new way to terminate Hourwich. Using diplomatic language, the association could simply refuse to recognize Hourwich and request another ambassador. "If Hourwich is elected," Moskowitz wrote before the election,

> [T]he Association can say to the union [the ILGWU] that this particular ambassador is persona-non-grata; that the Association is not quarreling with the Protocol, but like any foreign government, it has the right under the circumstances to say that this particular "minister" is persona-non-grata without breaking relations. Mr. Cohen is partial as you know, to diplomatic analogies. He talked with Deitch [Dyche] of this in confidence. He thought it was a good plan. However, I think he had better wait developments before the plan is introduced.[62]

Following the vote, Moskowitz enlisted London in his planned coup. Hourwich, through membership vote, was named chief legal representative for the rank and file, in essence, formally replacing London. On December 16, then, London resigned as the Joint Board's chief counsel, in protest over Hourwich's actions. On the day of London's resignation, Cohen set the plan in motion with his letter from the association to the ILG requesting Hourwich's removal.[63]

Hourwich refused to step down without a fight. "I had been elected by the whole of the membership," he later told the U.S. Commission on Industrial Relations, and the the current ILG's efforts were an undemocratic efforts by the International's officers:

> [I]f we live in a democratic country the will of the people, after it has been spoken, is the law. If our union is a self-governing body, the International officers were within their rights in objecting to me before I was elected. After I had been elected this whole agitation . . . to unseat me . . . is defying the will of the membership. [The ILG] officers have no right to defy the will of the membership.[64]

Hourwich further argued that the ILG was simply caving into pressures from the manufacturers' association. "Outsiders can not interfere," he argued, in internal labor matters. "When a demand is made to this organization [Arbitration Board] that I shall be removed, it is a demand absolutely beyond the scope of the Protocol."[65]

Hourwich's actions placed the ILG in a bind. If it refused to endorse the election and removed Hourwich, it risked a massive strike wave that might destroy the Protocol. If it endorsed the election, it risked having the association destroy the agreement. Rosenberg devised an unusual solution. He called a special conference of the AFL leadership—of International union leaders like themselves—to advise the ILG. Gompers chaired the conference. After hearing testimony, John Mitchell, United Mine Workers president and National Civic Federation activist, wrote the report. Gompers and Mitchell gave the ILG a solution. Gompers recommended that Hourwich be removed: "We feel that Dr. Hourwich does not possess the necessary qualifications which would enable him to perform properly the function of the office . . . we recommend that your Joint Board request Dr. Hourwich to tender his resignation." Yet, the report endorsed Hourwich's proposal that a third party, representing neither labor nor management but the "public," be appointed chair the Board of Grievances: "a disinterested person . . . to decide only disputes that have not been or cannot be decided by the Board of Grievances itself." Gompers gave everybody a partial victory. The ILG and Protocolists got rid of Hourwich, and the rank and file got binding arbitration. The ILG quickly endorsed this report and gave the Joint Board thirteen days to act.[66]

At first, the Joint Board refused to back down. It claimed only a referendum of the membership could remove Hourwich. The Operators' and Tailors' Locals recalled their representatives to the GEB in protest. The ILG, however, still seeking to circumvent a rank-and-file election, asked that the whole matter be brought before the Board of Arbitration. Rather than adapting the Protocol to the workers, the Protocol persisted in trying to force workers to adapt to the Protocol.[67]

Sensing that this might be the end to the Protocol, Filene and Bloomfield came in from Boston, and Bisno returned from Chicago. All three, together with Abraham Cahan, editor of the *Jewish Daily Forward*, offered to mediate. Cahan suggested that Hourwich be forced out. He also suggested that Dyche, "the pure and simpleton instigator," be tossed out with him.[68]

At this, Brandeis stepped in and offered an alternative to the Board of Arbitration. He convinced Mrs. J. Borden Harriman, a member of the U.S. Commission on Industrial Relations, to hold a public hearing on the "Hourwich affair" in mid-January. Brandeis had two motives:

first, to buy time to mediate a settlement, and second, to take the sole responsibility for the Protocol off of his shoulders and place it on others, such as the Commission on Industrial Relations. The Commission, after a lengthy investigation, found the conflict of personalities, subcontracting, piece-rates, and slowness of machinery to be at the root of the problems.[69]

The Board next met on January 18–19, and things were no better. "While the manufacturers have no right to compel his [Hourwich's] withdrawal," Brandeis said, he did believe the ILG had the right to remove him. But, the best solution would be if "he himself ... [would] withdraw" from the chief clerk's position. Sensing that nothing would be solved, Brandeis adjourned until January 26, getting from both sides the promise that they would do nothing until then.[70]

Hourwich, sensing that his days were numbered, began bargaining for his withdrawal. He made the central principle for which he had fought the one condition of his resignation: the appointment of an impartial chair to the Grievance Board. On this, Brandeis agreed, and at a January 19 meeting of the Joint Board, Hourwich offered his resignation. But after several tense moments—in part caused by the presence of ILG leaders at this meeting—the Joint Board took no action and postponed the decision until a future meeting.[71]

When the news that Hourwich had offered his resignation reached the rank and file, several hundred Hourwich followers led a number of noisy and vocal demonstrations against the Protocol. They sacked the Joint Board offices. They marched on the ILG headquarters, but were stopped by police. While these workers took to the street, the Joint Board met again. In a nonstop meeting that lasted two full days, the Joint Board voted 28 to 14 to accept Hourwich's resignation. At 7 A.M. on January 22, the Hourwich affair ended.[72]

In an effort to curtail the protests and to fulfill his promise to Hourwich, Brandeis announced the creation of the Committee on Immediate Action, a three-member committee made up of the two chief clerks and one impartial chair. Any matter that deadlocked at the Board of Grievances, which did not involve larger issues of Protocol policy, would go to this committee for immediate arbitration.[73]

No sooner had Hourwich resigned then major personnel changes rocked the Protocol. On February 2, Sydney Hillman was named as the union's chief clerk. Hillman was the leader of the men's garment workers union in Chicago. Famous for creating a Protocol-type settlement with the largest firm in the industry, he was just the type the ILG wanted to lead the New York City Protocol, a bureaucrat's bureaucrat with little connection to New York's rank-and-file ladies garment workers.[74] Hillman brought in John E. Williams to become chair of the Committee on Immediate Action. Williams had been the "impartial arbitrator" in the Chicago Hart, Shaffner, and Marx Protocol. And Morris Hillquit became chief legal counsel for the Joint Board. There were changes in the association as well. Paul Abelson, the chief clerk, resigned. He did not like the victory of arbitration over conciliation. The hard-nosed Eugene Lezinsky, a cloak manufacturer, replaced him.[75]

The changes in the New York Protocol reverberated throughout the ILG. At its Cleveland Convention, Dyche and Rosenberg—while renominated—refused to seek reelection. This predetermined withdrawal was designed so that both could save face. Benjamin Schlesinger assumed the presidency, and Morris Sigman took on Dyche's old position. These new men were more in line with the rank and file's socialist philosophy. Plus they carried no previous baggage. Their election stopped the ILG's drift toward pure-and-simple unionism and publicly reaffirmed the socialism and militancy of the old ILG. This would be necessary, as arbitration became the norm in industrial relations.[76]

While Hourwich disappeared from the Protocol, he left a lasting legacy. He both recognized and foretold the growing legalization of industrial relations, which the Protocol set in motion. More importantly, however, was his recognition that the public members of the Protocol held enormous power and could not be easily trusted. The only way the Protocol would work effectively would be if the public members followed a purely legal framework or if they could be manipulated through political pressure. After the Triangle Fire and the failure of a volunteeristic and private Protocol, as we will see, the state seemed the only likely solution to the vexing role of the "public" role in labor relations. Lastly, these three episodes demonstrate how fluid industrial democracy was. They provide insight into the process of IR and more importantly into issues of union democracy. They show how the rank and file placed real limits on IR and provided shape for the developing industrial regime.

The removal of both Dyche and Hourwich signaled a new phase for the Protocol. It also signaled a new sense of cooperation between the ILG and the rank and file. For the first time in the history of the Protocol, both were on the same side. That unity would be necessary, as the Protocol became a more confrontational test of wills. By the summer of 1914, the spirit of conciliation, the hope that Brandeis held for industrial relations, was dead: in its place stood raw power and confrontation. The test for the Protocol was if it could channel this into something constructive. Could it really offer something new for IR?

The Failure of the Protocol

Problems besieged the Protocol almost from its inception. While it was limping along in the cloak trades, as we have seen, it was disintegrating in the dress and waist industry. The problems were both similar and unique even though the workforces were quite different: workers in the dress and waist trade were predominately female, while those in the cloak trades were mostly male. The workers in both industries complained of the slowness of the grievance machinery. Like their "fellow" workers in the cloak trades, dress and waist workers took matters into their own hands. Shop strikes nearly brought the dress and waist trade to a standstill during 1911. Rather than make things smoother, the Protocol increased worker unrest. A critical issue, as we have seen, was the role of the "public" in the Protocol that was in a state of flux. When Brandeis resigned to become a Supreme Court Justice, a Board replaced him. This new Board did not have the same authority that Brandeis had. The result was that from 1914 on, the Protocol did not function effectively because it did not have a serious "public" presence.

Ironically, Brandeis's departure produced a new heightened sense of cooperation between the union and association. In an effort to replace Brandeis, the two sides created a Board of Protocol Standards, along with a new system to set and administer piece-rates. This new Board was an effort to take the larger, more confrontational issues away from the Arbitration Board, allowing it to focus solely on mediation and conciliation. The new Board, therefore, tied the two sides more closely to the Protocol at a time when they knew it to be most vulnerable.[77]

The new Board was given wide powers of investigation and inspection. It had enforcement powers in wages, hours, conditions, and terms of employment. Issues of health and safety remained under the Joint Board of Sanitary Control, charged with creating one uniform wage scale schedule for the industry. In an effort to develop a fair wage schedule, the Board hired "price adjusters" to investigate the industry. These experts were to use the methods of scientific management to measure time and subdivide work, creating a base rate per hour across the entire industry.[78]

One sign of this newfound cooperation was the agreement the association made to support a 1916 general strike in the industry in hopes of helping the union regain its membership and stabilize the trade. The union could not act unilaterally because the language of the Protocol outlawed strikes. Therefore, the strike needed to be a Protocol activity. Thus, with the association's accord, on February 9, the union issued a call for a general strike.

The strike was a success. Union membership climbed to nearly 30,000 by the end of February—an all-time high. It had agreements with 829 shops, although only 211 of these shops were association members; the vast majority of the workers were covered by agreements with individual shops. While these shops used the Protocol as a baseline, they were distinctly separate from it. The Board of Protocol Standards finally tried to address this.[79]

Robert G. Valentine, a former U.S. Commissioner on Indian Affairs, chair of the Massachusetts Minimum Wage Board, a respected reformer, and a politically astute activist, headed the new Board of Protocol Standards. In an effort to settle a piece-rate controversy, he established a model workroom for time and motion studies. These studies were to be used to set the piece-rates. Conducted as "scientific studies," but without input from or consultation with workers or manufacturers, both sides thought them suspect from the start. Many workers believed that this was at best a waste of time, and at worst a stalling tactic, because the initial studies were similar to the one the Wage Board had conducted three years before.[80]

Valentine's report validated the workers' complaints. His study showed that workers faired better in nonassociation shops. Not only were their grievances settled faster, but also on the average, they were paid more. He argued that manufacturers kept poor records and competed with each other at the expense of workers. In short, the report concluded that the industry was in such disarray that it needed an impartial body to regulate it. Valentine argued that the Board should be broadened to fulfill this function.[81]

After a two-week comment period, the dress association rejected the report. Criticizing Valentine for exceeding his authority, the association also forbid him from publishing his report. As a result, Belle Moskowitz and Bartholomew resigned from the association. With their resignation, the spirit of the Protocol essentially died.[82]

In contrast to the slow suffocation of the Dress Protocol, the Cloak Protocol died quickly. The Bisno and Hourwich affairs were never truly settled. These were merely episodes in larger struggles within the ILG. In addition, the association—having lost Dyche as an ally—became more legalistic and formal in its dealing with the union.

The new ILG leadership was indeed more militant than Rosenberg and Dyche. Benjamin Schlesinger, the new president, had a long and complicated history with the ILG. A Chicago cloakmaker, in 1903 he became ILG president for one year. Starting in 1904, he was both leader of the Chicago Joint Board and regional manager for the *Daily Forward*. Within a few years, he had left the union to assume the editorship of the *Forward* in New York. Schlesinger, as an older former leader of the ILG, commanded a certain respect from conservatives. As the general manager for the *Jewish Daily Forward*, the more militant rank-and-file workers respected him. He was the natural choice for president of the divided union. Morris Sigman, Dyche's replacement as ILG secretary-treasurer, had been the leader of the Presser's Local of the Industrial Workers of the World (IWW). In 1909, he became an organizer for the Joint Board.[83]

Similar changes had occurred in the Cloak Association. Militant leaders replaced more moderate leaders. More important was the fact that, after 1914, the leaders had less of a sense of cooperation. Especially important was the resignation of Paul Abelson as association chief clerk. Abelson, a committed Protocolist, resigned in 1914.[84]

The new leadership of the Protocol, created after the Hourwich affair, Sidney Hillman, Eugene Lezinsky, association chief clerk, and John Williams, chair of Committee on Immediate Action, worked hard to bring the two sides together for talks surrounding the piece-rate system. When they were finally able to bring the two camps together, Hillman was no longer a part of the team. He left in the summer of 1914 to head a dissident group of the United Garment Workers that would eventually become the Amalgamated Clothing Workers Union. While Hillman was not around long enough to gain support among the rank and file, he did win the respect of both the union and association. His departure set back the talks.[85]

Without Belle Moskowitz, Paul Abelson, Brandeis, and popular union representatives who were willing to try to settle disputes, the new team passively sent all matters straight to the Board of Arbitration. From September through November, both sides met in formal and informal conferences as well as corresponded through the mail. The issue that divided them, an old one, was the right of employment versus the right of management to hire and fire at will. While both parties were discussing abstract philosophical issues, reality interceded. In early November, the firm of Schuss and Company dismissed over forty workers in a reorganization. It hired back less than half. The union called this a lockout, and the manager, Nathan Schuss, did just that and locked out the workers. He claimed the supreme right to hire, fire, and rehire workers. Morris Sigman, acting in the immediate aftermath of Hillman's withdrawal as chief clerk, filed a formal complaint with the Grievance Board. John Williams, chair of the Committee on Immediate Action, refused to take action on the case and sent it directly to the Grievance Board.[86]

Meeting in late November, the Board of Grievances heard the case. Morris Hillquit, representing the union, presented an impassioned plea, stating that under the agreement managers had the right to hire from among union members. He insisted that management alone had the right to test competency. Once workers passed this test, they had the right to work until it could be proven that they were incompetent. Julius Henry Cohen, speaking for the association, argued that the association never gave up these rights. The Board of Grievances deadlocked and the case went to the Arbitration Board.[87]

The Arbitration Board did not meet until late January 1915, nearly ninety days after the union's initial complaint. Again, the Board refused to offer a definitive decision. Instead, it argued that through the spirit of mutual understanding and respect, industrial democracy would arise. The Board tried to offer something to everyone. It stated that workers' desire for stability and security was an important right, but it also recognized the right of management to reorganize production. No longer would this type of conciliation be sufficient.

Finally, a joint conference in mid-February heard the association offer a detailed plan. Cohen, speaking for the association, called for the division of workers into four categories: regulars, seasonal, casuals, and apprentices. Each group would have a set system of regulation. This four-tier system promised full employment for the "regulars." Workers were able to move up the ladder. In addition, the proposal created a Seasonal Employee's Unemployment Insurance Fund, funded by joint contributions from employers and regulars.[88]

The conference adjourned for a month to give the union time to respond adequately. On March 16, the union presented its claims. The union's alternative plan called for a three-tier system: regulars, casuals, and apprentices. Regulars were defined as "full fledged and competent workers in any branch ... during any part of the year ... who have passed through a full course of apprenticeship." The union rejected the distinction of seasonal worker, believing it would eventually lead to the creation of a two-tier labor system, with the seasonal worker in a perpetual subservient relationship. Instead of the unemployment fund, it called for a plan to regulate the labor supply and strict wage-scale systems. In addition, the union called for the creation and use of a Protocol label.[89]

Failure by both sides to agree on a definition of "regular" stalemated negotiations once again. Hillquit demanded an immediate hearing before the Arbitration Board. The association, losing interest in the Protocol, fired Lezinsky and did not replace him with another chief clerk. Without a chief clerk, the machinery ground to a halt. Thus, souring on the Protocol, the association opened negotiations with its archrival, the United Association, to form a "defensive and offensive alliance against the unreasonable Union demands."[90]

The union, sensing that its gains were in jeopardy, tried to regain rank-and-file support. It announced that it planned to prevent the association from "getting back all that we forced them to yield to us." Furthermore, the union complained that the association had directly violated the Protocol by refusing to aid the union in collection of dues. Brandeis announced, yet again, that both sides should meet together and work out their difficulties themselves. If no compromise could be reached, he announced, a meeting of the Board of Arbitration would be held in May.[91]

In May, the association announced its alliance with its longtime rival, the United Association. Having joined together, the two associations now assaulted the union and the Protocol. Henry Gordon, writing in the pages of *Women's Wear Daily*, the industry paper, signaled a new spirit among the manufacturers, one that had no place for either the Protocol or the Protocolists:

> The relationship between the employers and the employees in the cloak industry has been built upon sophistry, casuistry and ethereal concepts . . . all this because certain settlement workers, social uplifters, and reformers have been tolerated to formulate the rules . . . because the relationship between employer and employee has been controlled, not by economics and business principles, but by theoretical precepts which were often communicated over the long distance telephone [an obvious dig at Brandeis]. . . . The time has come to banish these alleged conciliators, legislators, and industrial Napoleons . . . and to revert to a natural and rational relationship between employer and employee.[92]

While Henry Moskowitz was pleading with Brandeis to convene a meeting of the Arbitration Board, the association announced on May 17 that it had withdrawn from the Protocol.[93]

The union, sensing this moment was nearby, had begun preparations for this break months earlier. The ILG believed that if it could flex its muscle in a general strike, which would cripple the industry, it could force the employers back into the Protocol. As part of this effort, and to gain public sympathy, the ILG held a massive public meeting at Madison Square Garden on June 12. Gompers, speaking to the assembled workers, pledged nothing less than the entire support of "labor" to the cause of the ILG to "preserve peace with honor." While the ILG was rallying the rank and file, Hillquit was working behind the scenes with the forces of mediation. It was during this meeting in June that the Protocolists learned that the union was no longer interested in "experiments." It wanted a simple two-year contract, not some social contract.[94]

The reform community entered the fray and sided with the workers, blaming the employers for this crisis. Reformers demanded that employers meet and negotiate with the union in good faith. The *New Republic* and the *Independent*, among others, assailed the shop owners. Leading Jewish American businessmen Jacob Schiff, Louis Marshall, and Oscar Strauss demanded compromise. Filene came down from Boston and personally intervened to get both sides talking again. The union, in 1915, had what it had not had in some time: solid public support. For the first time, a core group of citizens came to believe that they had more to gain from the labor movement than to fear. This partnership between labor and concerned citizen reformers who occupied a central political space as the voice of the public would find clearer expression during the New Deal.[95]

The public pressure of reformers on labor's side placed new pressure on the association to compromise. Felix Adler, a well-known reformer, met with Mayor Mitchel to urge his intervention.[96] On July 9, the mayor appointed a six-person Council of Conciliation: Brandeis, Henry Bruere, George W. Kirchwey, Charles Bernheimer, Judge Walter Noyes, and Felix Adler as chair. This distinguished panel of reformers and leading urban citizens began its work four days later and continued for ten straight days. The Council asked many of the original men involved in the Protocol to submit recommendations on how best to settle the issues at hand. The statement the Council issued on July 23 dealt with the central issue of industrial democracy. How do you reconcile democracy in the workplace with the rights of owners to a profit in a capitalist society? It required a "delicate balance." As the Council stated:

> That the principle of industrial efficiency and that of respect for the essential human rights of the worker should always be applied jointly, priority being assigned to neither. Industrial efficiency may not be sacrificed to the interest of the workers, for how can it be to their interest to destroy the business on which they depend for a living, nor may efficiency be declared paramount to the human rights of the workers; for how in the long run can the industrial efficiency of a country be maintained if the human values of the workers are diminished or destroyed. The delicate adjustment required to reconcile the two principles named, must be made. Peace and progress depend upon complete loyalty to reconcile them.[97]

Calling for a system of two clerks, the Council reconstituted the now defunct Protocol, replacing the Board of Grievances with a Joint Board of Supervision and Enforcement of Standards. In addition, the Council itself was to function as the Board of Arbitration did, as a high court. Aside from these changes, all other articles of the Protocol were revived.[98]

The union jumped at the Council's plans—even if it still had all the problems of the Protocol—but the association was divided between two factions, one led by Gordon, the other by Cohen, and remained deadlocked. Schlesinger, with little recourse, called for a strike vote (it carried by 39,337 to 751), and announced that on August 5 a general strike would occur in the industry. Only then, the day before the strike, did the association agree to the plan. With the announcement that the Council's agreement would be accepted by the association, the reformers and press rejoiced.[99]

While the press was celebrating the triumph of industrial democracy over the forces of chaos, the seeds of the agreement's failure were firmly planted. Many manufacturers blamed Cohen and his allies for the "forced deal." They believed it hampered their economic freedom and immediately planned to undermine it. They immediately elected E. J. Wile as chair of the association. Wile was one of the leaders of the Gordon faction, an outspoken opponent of the Protocol and this new agreement. Even more telling, the association dismissed Cohen, arguing he was guilty of having "social uplift tendencies." Cohen's replacement was none other than Henry Gordon. Many union leaders and reformers saw this move as proof that the association had no plans to follow the agreement. In fact, Henry Moskowitz, among others, believed the association was already planning to ignore the agreement in its entirety.[100]

Only days after the ink on the agreement was dry, a crisis erupted. Wile and the new leadership refused to honor an arrangement made by the previous leadership that would have honored shop wage agreements negotiated between May and August. Hillquit protested to Adler and the Council, claiming that the association had acted in bad faith. Adler, to the shock of the union, announced that because these agreements occurred before the Council's agreement they were beyond the jurisdiction of the current agreement. Fearing that this position would signal an open war on individual shop agreements, the union announced a new policy to strictly enforce shop agreements. It would be hypervigilant in protecting its turf. By mid-August, the garment industry resembled the Wild West before the gunfight: both shooters ready on the draw.[101]

Strikes and lockouts besieged the garment industry in the first six months, but by far the biggest challenge for the Council was the interpretation of the preferential rule.[102] The union claimed that the preferential shop clause not only operated in securing a job, but also by implication gave workers more security in slack times: union members were to be the last ones fired. When, in February 1916, the union filed a grievance over both aspects of the preference system, the issue was formally engaged. First, Adler and the Council sided against the union but did agree to a formal definition of the preferential clause. Adler defined it as giving preference in employment to union workers in good standing and he demanded that shop owners allow stewards to collect dues at the factory. Because many manufacturers undermined the union's membership by not allowing such activity, Adler's pronouncement was a union victory. Adler's decision meant, in effect, that the union could chase after workers in the factory, and management could not stop it. To both the union and employers, Adler's decision portended the end to the decline in union membership.[103]

The association refused to accept the unanimous decision of the Council. Wile, speaking for the association, insisted "the principle of the closed shop . . . is an issue that is non-arbitrable and cannot under any circumstances be submitted . . . [for] adjustment." "For us," he continued, "to grant this would permit the Union to dictate terms and conditions in the factory and place our plants in their hands and absolutely abrogate our rights to operate our factories on the basis of efficiency."[104]

When news of the association's refusal to abide by the Council's decision reached the union, Schlesinger and Wishnak—Hillman's replacement as chief clerk—announced to Adler on March 7 that the union would no longer have any dealings with the association. As shop strikes escalated, the Joint Board and the ILG did little to stop them. At the same time, the number of lockouts increased as shops used the impasse to fire the most active unionists in their employ. Again, the association watched idly by. By spring, most involved believed a showdown was coming.[105]

Last-minute efforts to avoid a crippling general strike proved futile. To no avail, Moskowitz again rounded up leading Jewish American businessmen to use their influence. Mayor Mitchel also invited both sides to a Gracie Mansion meeting on April 26. While the union eagerly attended, the association refused to submit anything to arbitration. Two days after that meeting, the union declared a lockout of 25,000 workers in its 409 shops of the association.[106]

The ILG and the Joint Board declared a general strike for May 3, spreading the conflict to the entire industry in an effort to regain control of the situation. In the days leading up to the strike, several groups tried to intervene. The mayor again offered his services. Several members of the political science faculty of Columbia University also offered to mediate. Reformers, social workers, and a host of others waited on the sidelines to be put into the game. Yet, the association adamantly refused to allow what it called "outside interference."[107]

The ensuing strike was one of the largest in New York history as 60,000 cloakmakers struck for fourteen weeks. The strike was so large it brought immediate national attention. Eventually, Secretary of Labor Wilson and Commerce Secretary Redfield intervened to end the strike. This strike provided an opportunity for rank and filers to vent their frustration with the IR system of the Protocol. Massive public displays, street-corner rallies, and direct action signaled an end to the spirit of cooperation. Local newspaper coverage and national reform journals heralded the end of the Protocol.[108]

The agreement signed on August 4, 1916, formally ended the Protocol. The manufacturers retained the rights to hire and fire. Workers retained the right to strike. All the machinery of the Protocol, save the Joint Board of Sanitary Control, was eliminated. Workers received a reduction in hours, from fifty to forty-nine a week, as well as a small increase in wages. The agreement was to last for a two-year period. When the workers returned to work three days later, the experiment in industrial democracy that was the Protocol had ended.[109]

Protocolism failed for a number of reasons that were not entirely clear at the time. Topping the list was its inflexible legalistic structure. Based on the legal world that Louis Brandeis knew well, the Protocol proved incapable of adjusting to the day-to-day world of the ladies' garment industry. Brandeis could not recognize this incomparability, because before the Protocol there was no other model available. The Protocol also was unable to provide the new day that Brandeis and company had promised manufacturers and workers. It simply lacked the enforcement powers necessary. In addition, it could not provide the uniform codes over wages, hours, and conditions that would create an industrial standard. The Protocol could never standardize the industry because it was based on privatism and voluntary association. Most crucial for the workers, it also lacked a principle of social justice. Yet, the main reason for its failure was that it could never cover the entire industry. Therefore, it could not level the playing field as envisioned. Sweatshops, runaway shops, jobbing, and outsourcing all remained essential problems in the industry, placing downward pressures on unionized firms to race to the bottom.

Fortunately, another institutionalized form of tripartite Protocolism was developing alongside the garment industry's Protocol at the state level. The Factory Investigating Committee (FIC), created in 1911 after

the Triangle Fire, offered to provide the enforcement powers that the
volunteeristic Protocol simply could not. In fact, the two shared key
personnel. The Protocol taught labor that it needed a political base with
power to enforce equality. It also taught the ILG that it was simply not
strong enough by itself to provide industrial democracy for its members. It needed a partner. The Protocol promised such a partner in the
amorphous "public." But it did not fulfill this promise. The FIC offered
hope because it replaced the amorphous public within the state. At this
historical moment, it was possible that labor and its middle-class reform allies within the state could improve the position of workers in
society better than the purely voluntary Protocol. Because of the size of
the working-class vote in New York City, it was possible that the state
could be more receptive to labor's desires than the concerned citizens
who served on Boards. As workers and their union were losing faith
in the Protocol, they began to place more and more faith in the FIC.
This faith, as we will see, was equally misplaced. For in the end, the FIC
also failed to deliver industrial democracy. In order to understand the
role the FIC played in the new industrial relations we must return to
1911, the first year of the FIC. This parallel development, the FIC, which
embodied key elements of the Protocol, would prove to have greater
staying power.

"Identifying the Dead." In the hours after the fire, tens of thousands of New Yorkers walked past the coffins of the Triangle dead: some to identify relatives, some to witness the tragedy, and some to mourn. By the sixth day, seven victims remained unidentified burned beyond recognition.

II PUBLIC PROTOCOLISM: THE TRIANGLE FIRE AND THE TRANSFORMATION OF INDUSTRIAL DEMOCRACY

PROTOCOLISM WAS a complex industrial regime that brought together labor, management, and "the concerned public." It was an important attempt to start a new day for industrial relations. And, it was not without its problems, as we have seen. But it took an event in 1911 to highlight the limitations of Protocolism, as it then existed.

On March 25, 1911, the Triangle Factory was the sight of one of the worst industrial fires in American history. One hundred and forty-six, mostly young, immigrant women died. What is central is that Triangle, though one of the largest manufacturers in the industry and a central actor in the 1909 strike, remained outside of Protocolism at the time of the fire. Triangle had successfully resisted both the union and the association. The fire brought home to many the limits of Protocolism. Immediately after the fire, reformers, workers, and industrial democrats attempted to harness the public's outrage to the Protocolist reform agenda. To many, the fire, though obviously tragic, offered a unique opportunity. It demonstrated that the union alone could not protect workers if it could not organize the entire industry. Industrial democrats came to rethink the role of the state in labor reform. Protocolists harnessed the growing police powers of the state to the industrial democracy agenda. Within months, people who had worked within the Protocol headed key components of the newly formed New York State Factory Investigating Commission (FIC).

The FIC, in a few short years, transformed New York into one of the most progressive states in terms of labor reform. In the process, "the state" slowly supplanted the notions of "concerned citizens" involved in industrial relations. With this, the state became a partner in industrial democracy. Part II of this book traces this development. Chapter 4 retells the story of the Triangle Fire through the lens of Protocolism. Chapter 5 discusses the political transformations that empowered the FIC. Chapters 6 and 7 trace the development and evolution of the FIC's vision of industrial democracy. In the end, New York got a form of industrial democracy that empowered reformers and experts at the expense of rank-and-file workers. In short, the FIC replicates the forms and functions of the Protocol that made it less democratic and less connected to the lives of New York's workers. Rather than becoming active participants in the reform efforts, workers morphed into clients of political factions, using their numbers and political clout to influence policy outcomes. This proved a highly successful strategy when friends of workers were in positions of power. However, as we know when the political climate shifted, workers were left with a "barren marriage."[1]

4 "The Burning Building at 23 Washington Place"[1]
The Triangle Fire and the Transformation of Industrial Democracy

THE FIRE

The Triangle factory was one of only a handful of firms that had not settled with the International Ladies' Garment Workers Union (ILGWU) after the 1909 Uprising, remaining a nonunion shop. Triangle's sheer size and power in the industry enabled it to resist the union. Garment manufacturers were usually small; Triangle, however, was a vast economic enterprise. Its ability to pay prevailing union wages, import strikebreakers and thugs, and contract out gave it the strength to beat the union.

The Triangle factory occupied the top three floors of the modern Asch Building on the corner of Washington Place and Greene Street in New York City's fashionable Greenwich Village. Constructed in 1900, the Asch Building was thoroughly modern in design and safety. For maximum productivity, Triangle utilized every available square inch. Cramped working conditions resulted in workers performing their jobs literally on top of one another.[2]

Saturday March 25, 1911, began as a typical Saturday at the Triangle factory. At 4:00 P.M., workers on the eighth floor (the factory occupied the eighth, ninth, and tenth floors) heard the watchman ring the bell, signaling quitting time. The girls raced for their pay envelopes and then off to the dressing rooms to begin what was left of their weekend.[3]

Five minutes after the bell rang, a fire was discovered under worktable 2 near the Greene Street windows, and it spread rapidly. The fire most likely started as the result of a discarded cigarette thrown carelessly on a pile of "cut-aways"—scraps of cloth that were saved and sold to scrap cloth dealers. It was common for Triangle to accumulate over a ton of scrap before it was carted away, creating a serious fire hazard. While it is impossible to know the exact amount of cloth on

129

hand, there had not been a pick-up for nearly three months. It is likely that over a ton of scrap cloth, plus much more uncut cloth was on hand.[4] The presence of that amount of cloth caused the factory to go up in flames within minutes.

The fire was first discovered by Eva Harris, the sister of Isaac Harris, one of the two owners of the Triangle factory. Harris smelled smoke and saw flames on the eighth floor. She ran to tell Samuel Bernstein, the production manager for the factory, who was also related through marriage to Harris. As Bernstein later told a court, he "heard a cry . . . it was Eva Harris. She was running toward me from the middle of the shop. She was hollering, 'there is a fire Mr. Bernstein.' I turned around. I saw a blaze and some smoke at the second table from the Greene Street windows. As I ran across the shop toward the fire, some cutters were throwing pails of water."[5] Like many firms that employed immigrants, Triangle relied on family connections for recruitment.[6] Brothers screamed out sisters' names; everywhere family members searched for their kin.[7] Celio Saltz, an eighth-floor survivor, was typical of Triangle's employees in that both she and her fourteen-year-old sister worked together. Saltz recalled that women rushed to the elevators because the "door to the staircase wouldn't open." It was later discovered that the door to the stairs was chained shut. Saltz explained how she and others "rushed to the passenger elevators. Everyone was pushing and screaming. When the car stopped at our floor I was pushed into it by the crowd. I began to scream for my sister. I had lost her, I had lost my sister." Saltz was one of the fortunate few who were reunited with loved ones after the fire.[8]

A panicked communication was received in the executive offices located on the tenth floor. While the fire raged on the eighth floor, management escaped from the tenth floor, never bothering to notify the 260 workers on the ninth floor. These workers collected their pay envelopes and went to the changing rooms, completely unaware of the impending disaster. "We didn't have a chance," Rose Grantz, one of the few surviving workers from the ninth floor, later complained. "[T]he people on the eighth floor must have seen the fire start and grow. The people on the tenth floor got the warning. . . . But with us on the ninth, all of a sudden the fire was all around. The flames were coming in through many of the windows."[9]

One of the first to arrive on the scene was Patrolman Meehan of the New York City Police Department. Meehan was patrolling in fashionable Washington Square Park, one block west of the factory. He heard an explosion and raced to the site. He heard a bystander saying, "someone's up there alright [*sic*]. He's trying to save the best cloth," as what appeared to be bundles of cloth were flung from the windows to the streets below. To the shock of the onlookers, the bundles opened in the wind halfway through their descent to the street revealing the bodies of young girls. One of the spectators broke ranks from the crowd and called in the first fire alarm at 4:45 P.M., ten minutes after the fire had started.[10]

Many of the young workers on the ninth floor jumped out the windows rather than burn. The vision of young women jumping to their death was a sight many New Yorkers would never forget.[11] The *New York Times* reported that "girls rushed to the window and looked down at Greene Street 100 feet below them. Then one poor, little creature jumped. There was a plate of glass protection over part of the sidewalk, but she crashed through it, wrecking it and breaking her body into a thousand pieces. The crowd yelled 'DON'T JUMP!' But it was jump or be burned—the proof of which is found in the fact that fifty burned bodies were taken from the ninth floor alone." The *Times* went on to tell of five girls on the Greene Street side of the building who jumped at once, "clinging to each other."[12]

Helpless spectators witnessed dozens of workers falling to their deaths, and they vowed never to be that helpless again. The fire brought in a total of five alarms, and 150 police officers were called to the scene to keep order. Ten doctors and ambulances from at least three area hospitals were pressed into service.[13] All those at the scene were greatly moved. Captain Dominick Henry of Mercer Street's Eighth Precinct recalled that he saw "a scene I hope never to see again. Dozens of girls were hanging from the ledges. Others were leaping from the windows." Mrs. Lena Goldman, owner of a small restaurant near the factory that was frequented by workers, recalled, "I could see them falling. I could see them falling." These accounts convey both horror and helplessness. Doctors, firemen, friends, and the police could do nothing to aid the workers.

Hundreds of people, of all social stations, gathered in front of the factory. Rookie fireman Frank Rubino recalled the scene:

[W]e came tearing down Washington Square East [the east block of the nearby park] and made a turn into [*sic*] Washington Place. The first thing I saw was a man's body come crashing down through the sidewalk shed of the school building [New York University occupied an adjacent building]. We kept going. We turned into [*sic*] Greene Street, began to stretch . . . our hoses. The bodies were hitting all around us . . . we had to lift them off [the hoses] before we could get to work.[14]

Rubino reported that the firemen had to turn their hoses on the bodies lying on the sidewalk because they were aflame.[15] As Dr. D. E. Keefe of St. Vincent's Hospital arrived at the scene, a woman's body landed so close to the ambulance that he realized "if we drove up to the curb it would be possible for some persons to strike the top of the ambulance and so break their fall."[16]

Many of the spectators knew the factory well, for it was infamous from the 1909 strike. Middle-class reformers watching the blaze knew the workers who had been involved in the 1909 strike. Martha Bensely Bruere, of the Women's Trade Union League (WTUL), was with them in 1909 on the picket line. When the strike was lost at Triangle—and won just about everywhere else—these workers had been forced to return to work without a contract or recognition. Bruere remembered walking down Fifth Avenue the day of the fire when two distressed working-class women ran up to her. They told her of the fire and that "fifty of thems [*sic*] jumped already and just think how many there must be left inside." The women led the way as they rushed to the scene. It was a sight Bruere never forgot.[17]

Many of the workers who gathered that afternoon in Greenwich Village did not overlook the Triangle factory's critical role in the 1909–1910 waistmakers' strike. "I was one of the pickets and was arrested and fined several times," Rose Sabran, a Triangle worker, recalled. She added:

The union paid my fines. Our bosses won and we went back to work as an open shop having nothing to do with the union. But the strikers who were taken back stayed in the union [secretly], for it is our friend. If the union had won we would have been safe. Two of our demands were for adequate fire escapes and for open doors from the factories to the streets. But the bosses defeated us and we didn't get the open doors or better fire escapes. So our friends are dead.[18]

Clara Lemlich, veteran strike leader, agreed with Sabran: "If Triangle had been a union shop there would not have been any locked doors, and the girls would have been on the street almost an hour before the fire started."[19] Later that May, Martha Bensely Bruere wrote in the pages of the WTUL paper what must have been on the minds of other observers of the fire:

I[I]t was these same policemen who had clubbed and beaten them back into submission, who kept the thousands in Washington Square from trampling upon . . . the bodies, [who] sent for the ambulance to carry them away, and lifted them one by one into the receiving coffins which the Board of Charities send down in wagonfulls.[20]

Bruere noted the irony; if only these policemen had not done their jobs so effectively during the strike they would not have had to perform the grisly tasks of March 25. Bill Sheperd, a United Press International reporter and the first newsman at the fire, reported the horror:

Floods of water from the firemen's hoses that ran into the gutter were actually red with blood. I looked upon the heaps of dead bodies and I remembered *these* were the shirtwaist makers. I remembered their great strike of last year in which these same girls had demanded more sanitary conditions and more safety precautions in the shops. These dead bodies were the[ir] answer.[21]

The city was thoroughly unprepared to cope with a fire of this magnitude. The *New York Times* stated, "Mostly all there was to do was to determine if life was extinct in the bodies on the pavement and cover them over."[22] At the time of the fire, New York's Fire Department had at its disposal the latest in firefighting technologies. It had one of the nation's first fully motorized units—still in an experimental stage. The Asch Building was located in one of the city's few new high-water-pressure areas. The Fire Department dispatched to the scene one of its newest pump engines, as well as the new hook and ladder companies. When Fire Company 20 arrived with the city's largest hook and ladder, witnesses recalled that the crowd screamed for them to "raise the ladder!" But "the ladder had been raised . . . it was raised to its fullest point. It reached only to the sixth floor."[23] "The [fire]men did the best they could," according to Battalion Chief Worth, "but there was no apparatus in the department to cope with this kind of fire."[24]

The firemen made valiant efforts to save the women who jumped to avoid certain death in the flames. They brought out life nets and horse blankets to try to catch the girls as they fell. "One girl jumped into a horse blanket held by firemen and policemen. The blanket ripped like cheesecloth, and her body was mangled almost beyond recognition. Another dropped into a tarpaulin held by three men. Her weight tore it from their grasp and she struck the street breaking almost every bone in her body."[25] The *New York Daily Tribune* stated that "in the death dealing scramble for possible safety the girls did not wait to jump by ones or twos; they leaped five and six at a time, and the result was that the fire nets were torn from the grasps of the firemen and the women were dashed to death."[26] Life nets were useless. "[L]ife nets? what good were life nets—the little ones went right through the nets, pavement and all. The nets are good for the low tenements," according to Battalion Chief Worth, "but nobody could hold life nets when those girls from the ninth floor came down."[27] The *Tribune* stated, "The sight of their fellow workers making the fatal leap seemed to fill the other women with horror. They stood for a while though fascinated then plunged down to their own death."[28] A few women did survive their leaps from the top floors. In the process of interviewing survivors for an investigation, Leonora O'Reilly of the WTUL noted that Mary Bucelli jumped from a sixth- or seventh-story window and Daisy Fritze apparently jumped from the ninth floor.[29]

Over 500 workers escaped by the elevator from the eighth floor. The two elevator operators, Joseph Zitto and Joseph Gaspos, never got above the eighth floor, because by then, their cars were filled. Many women on the ninth floor realized the problem and jumped down the elevator shafts onto the roofs of the cars. Zitto reported that he could hear the thud of bodies and the sound of silver from pay envelopes on the roof of the elevator car.[30] Sarah Friedman was one of those who jumped onto Zitto's car. "I slid all the way down [on the cables] and ended up on top of the car where I lost consciousness. One of my hands was burned by the friction. When I opened my eyes I was lying in the street—among the dead."[31] When one of the operators, Zitto, gave up hope of saving more women and abandoned his car, a spectator jumped in and made upwards of ten more trips, saving an additional 100 workers. He only stopped when the heat of the fire welded the cables—making the car inoperable. Then he slid back into the crowd, never to be identified.[32]

Workers and management on the tenth floor had escaped via the only means available to them, the roof. According to newspaper accounts, the idea to run to the roof was that of Isaac Harris, one of the two owners of the factory. The Asch Building's roof adjoined the roof of a New York

University building, and law students in the school building assisted in the rescue.[33] Some had tried to escape down the Greene Street stairway, but, Anna Gullo recalled, "At the vestibule door there was a big barrel of oil. I went through the staircase door. As I was going out the door, I heard a loud noise. Maybe the barrel exploded."[34] Lucy Wesselofsky recalled that all but one of the seventy odd workers who were on the tenth floor that day survived. According to Wesselofsky, Clotila Tedanova panicked and jumped to her death.[35]

The Aftermath: Urban Liberals Respond

What would be done? In the fire's aftermath, emotions in the city's working-class communities ran high. To middle-class guardians of law and order, however, the scene at the fire's site was that of a mob. All the city's major newspapers reported that police pushed the extremely large crowds gathered in front of the building into nearby Washington Square Park. Police reinforcements were needed to "hold back" the crowds, which gathered for many reasons: some were morbidly curious for the grisly details of the fire, others were searching for family and friends, and many were simply shocked.

"As fast as bodies had been looked over for identification and tags fastened to them," the New York Times reported, "coffins were brought from the supply depot established in East Washington Place. In these wooden boxes . . . the bodies were placed in patrol wagons and driven away."[36] By the end of the night, 133 bodies had been sent to the morgue at the Twenty-Sixth Street Pier, and the process of identification began.[37] By 8:00 P.M., a large crowd had gathered on the pier. When the doors opened and viewing began, "everywhere burst anguished cries," reported the Times, "names in Italian and Yiddish rising in shrill agony above the deeper moan of the throng."[38] The New York American stated that the East River, where the pier was located, "was thronged with shrieking, struggling men and women, crying in Russian and Italian, tearing their hair and rendering their clothes."[39] By 11:30 P.M., on the night of the fire, the police had identified 136 bodies.[40] Twenty-six hours after the fire, the police reported that 200,000 people had come to view the victims of the fire. Monday's crowd was only slightly smaller.[41]

While the crowds seemed too numb for action, the police, however, called out reinforcements, just in case. On the night of the fire, the crowd began to overflow from the site into the nearby park and police barriers were erected to hold them there. "They pleaded, demanded and stormed to be let through."[42] As time passed and a more definitive knowledge of the "horror's proportion spread," according to the *World*, "the pressure on the police grew greater. The lines were reinforced but the frantic beating upon them outweighed every precaution of the authorities." On several occasions, the crowd broke past the police lines. "Men and women had rushed the tarpaulin-covered mounds [under which were the victims' remains]." "Here and there," the *World* reported, "a woman caught up a hat or a slipper or a fragment of a burned skirt, grabbed it wildly and ran to a fireman or a policeman, begging them to throw the light of their lanterns on the things." The *World* added, "In more than one instance before the women gave way before them, the police were compelled to use their clubs."[43]

For days after the fire, hundreds of workers came to the site of the Triangle factory on their way home from work, and silently prayed.[44] Some vowed to avenge the death of their loved ones. Max Hochfield, who lost his sister in the fire, recalled his emotional response: "I began to plan how to get a gun. I would go to collect the wages they [Triangle factory owners Isaac Harris and Isaac Blanck] owed me—and my sister. The bosses would be there. I would come in and ask for the money. I would kill them." However, like many other immigrants, Hochfield did not have the money for the gun. He believed he could borrow the money from the union. He went to the union's relief committee, and when a union delegate began to suspect what he wanted the money for, he told Hochfield that killing Harris and Blanck would not bring his sister back, nor improve working conditions. It would only land him in jail and cause further hardships for his family. The thing to do, he was told, was to build the union. The delegate argued that the union would be the best and strongest weapon against the greed of capitalists and the helplessness of workers. Years later, Hochfield recalled that from that moment on he became a dedicated unionist—many others responded similarly.[45]

In the immediate wake of the fire, a small vanguard of industrial democrats organized to raise the collective consciousness of the city. The fire became a rallying cry, a clarion call. One of the first public statements issued by this collective of urban liberals was a call for relief. Two such relief committees were formed with conflicting agendas. The Relief

Fund Committee, formed by the Ladies Waist and Dress Makers' Union, Local 25 of the ILGWU, ran notices in almost all labor and left papers.[46] The union's committee mirrored its political orientation: first, aid the families, then establish the labor and socialist movements to prevent future such disasters. The union did not see the fire as an isolated disaster, but as a symptom of a larger problem. The monies raised by the union came from many sources: unions, various socialist and reform-minded groups, philanthropists, theater groups, and reform organizations.[47] These groups all shared the union's political vision of building a new world order based on social justice and working-class politics.

Within hours of the fire, the Charities Organization Society (COS) of New York, in connection with the Red Cross of New York, organized the second relief group. This group saw the fire as a "natural disaster," an isolated tragedy. Its solution was simply to aid the families and then move on to the next disaster. Both Robert DeForest, a leading force within the COS, and Mayor Gaynor wrote requests for funds that appeared in all major papers. The Red Cross Committee was aided in its efforts by most of the city's major charities and some businesses. The Metropolitan Life Insurance Company, for example, donated office space. By the morning after the fire, the committee had a staff of ten, most of whom were volunteers from the New York Society for Improving the Condition of the Poor. On March 28, Jacob Schiff, a prominent German Jewish philanthropist and banker, recommended the appointment of Italians and Jews to counter the heavy "native, Protestant" tinge to the Red Cross Committee.[48]

The ILGWU's committee mapped out its turf, however. While the union's committee was thankful for the financial support, it was leery of charities unduly influenced by business interests. The ILGWU had staked its claim as protector of the immigrant garment workers and wanted to protect its place in that community. The union was decidedly secular and socialist and played a prominent role in the garment workers' communities.[49] It hoped to act as the conduit of charity—it wanted the Red Cross to raise the money that the union would distribute.[50] The union alone would handle all matters dealing with members. The union's committee raised over $17,000, of which over $15,000 went directly to union members.[51]

The Red Cross Committee took a different approach. Operating within the ideological framework of the COS, the guardians of morality, it used "scientific" perspectives to allot aid. The Committee asked, would aid interfere with the work ethic or promote dependence?[52] The Monday after the fire, an army of "friendly visitors," most volunteers from the Society for Improving the Condition of the Poor, went out to interview the victims' families and survivors. These visitors handled 166 cases. While the Committee raised almost $104,000, it doled out less than $81,000. Few of these dollars went to the families of survivors or victims; the Red Cross Committee, in assessing the families' needs, reported that their standards of living had not been changed drastically by the loss. Red Cross and COS reformers feared charity would be a luxury and would spoil them, cutting off their work drive. Instead, the Red Cross argued, what was needed was the establishment of permanent programs to improve the conditions of these workers—education and vocational programs.[53] The *New York Times* reported that while hundreds of people besieged the union with requests for aid, few visited the Red Cross Committee. Workers were leery of charity, preferring the helping hand of the labor movement that they themselves had had a hand in building.[54]

The Aftermath II: The Workers Respond

The families of the victims spent most of the week following the fire arranging for burials. As is common in tragedies with a social subtext, these funerals became a catalyst for protest. The WTUL and the ILGWU made most of the burial arrangements.[55] The cloakmakers' union announced that its members would symbolically work only a half day on the day of the mass funeral for the remaining unidentified victims and turn out in mass for the service. Other unions declared similar intentions.[56] The 146 young women who died in the blaze (one died a few days after the fire) were honored in one of the largest displays of class solidarity the city had ever experienced.

While families buried their kin separately, the union planned a mass service for the final seven victims who were not claimed by family because they could not be positively identified. The union wanted to bury them together. The women shirtwaistmakers in Local 25 of the ILGWU insisted on making all funeral arrangements, refusing to have male unionists control what they saw as a funeral for their sisters. The local held back on finalizing its plans until all of the bodies were released from the morgue. At the morgue, seven victims remained. Their numbers only identified them: 46, 50, 95, 103, and 127. Number 127, marked "Fragments from the Fire," contained body parts.[57] Four days after the fire, the city announced that it would hold the remaining coffins for ten additional days to aid in identification. Most of the families of those girls saw no point; the bodies were so badly burned that no one could tell them apart. They preferred to bury them together, as they had died. The *Call* found, it believed, that the city's motivation in holding the bodies was to cool the tensions of the workers planning the funeral.[58]

While the union was struggling over the release of the remains, mass meetings were taking place throughout the city. At two meetings held on April 2, it became obvious to those at the *Call* that the grief had inspired a new agenda: "It could almost be supposed that the great army of workers crowded in the building[s] were paying tribute to the living rather than mourning the dead."[59] The cloakmakers held a mass meeting early in the afternoon of that day in the Grand Central Palace at 43rd Street. A crowd of 5,000 gathered inside the hall, and thousands more stood outside. While many of the speakers spoke in Yiddish, a Mr. Brady, representative of the Allied Printing Trades Council, arose to address the audience in English. He told those assembled that only if they elected "honest men" could tragedies like this be prevented. At this, a man from the galleries asked, "Why shouldn't the working class elect its own candidates?"[60] Only through a concerted, collective, working-class effort, he suggested, would this type of tragedy be avoided. There was some speculation that workers needed their own political party and that maybe the ILGWU could become a political base. It was, after all, the largest union in the city. That evening thousands more gathered, not in silent prayer, but to protest. Mourning was over.

New York's middle class unsuccessfully attempted to supplant the voices of the masses with their own more tempered voices at the second meeting, held at the Metropolitan Opera House. Anne Morgan, WTUL faithful and niece of capitalist J. P. Morgan, had rented it for the occasion. The seating for the evening's events is illustrative of the class divisions in the emerging reform efforts. The Opera House meeting had been called to present a unified cry that something had to be done. But exactly what was to be done? At the Opera House, almost to ensure their silence, the mass of workers were seated high in the galleries—as if they were merely spectators to the ongoing drama. The participants—all middle-class reformers—sat up front. After several speakers argued for reform to the applause of those in the orchestra seats, Rabbi Stephen Wise rose to speak. Rejecting the advice of those who spoke before him, he declared that the lesson of the fire was clear: human greed had caused the tragedy. "It is not the action of God but the inaction of man that is responsible. The disaster was not the deed of God [a natural disaster] but the greed of man [systematic]." His solutions were better laws to protect workers and enforcement of these laws:

> We have laws that in a crisis we find are no laws and we have enforcement that when the hour of trial comes we find is no enforcement. Let us lift up the industrial standards until they will bear inspection. And when we go before the legislatures let us not allow them to put us off forever with the old answer 'We have no money.' If we have no money for necessary enforcement of laws which safeguard the lives of workers it is because so much of our money is wasted and squandered and stolen.[61]

Wise's comments reflected a split at the meeting over strategy. While many in the middle-class audience attended merely to provide charity for the victims, Wise politicized the event. When the meetings' sponsors attempted to start a debate on resolutions, wild hissing broke out from the galleries where the workers were packed in. The meeting threatened to implode until Rose Schneiderman rose to speak. Schneiderman had been sitting quietly on the platform, representing both the WTUL and the ILGWU. Many seated in the orchestra might not have known this small woman, but to the workers in the galleries she was instantly recognizable. She was one of them, an immigrant factory girl—the woman who led the workers out of the Triangle factory during the 1909 "Uprising of Twenty Thousand."

Schneiderman is symbolic of the centrality of gender to all these events. A veteran of the WTUL, Schneiderman was possibly one of only a handful of people who, with angry words, could have quieted the crowd. For her, the issue was not *a* law, but the character of *the* law. Workers, she stated, were tired and disgusted with reformers' efforts to aid them by passing more laws. Her own experience on the picket line taught her that no matter how progressive the legislature, the law was always used against workers. The answer for Schneiderman was a revolutionary, rank-and-file working-class movement that would demand social justice, and achieve it, evolutionary socialism embodied. The irony, of course, as we will see in later chapters, is that Schneiderman would join reformers, politicians, and male unionists in redefining IR in a more bureaucratic manner.

Schneiderman's speech and the enthusiastic worker response to it reflected a changing political consciousness within the working-class community. In moving beyond working conditions, wages, and hours, workers were beginning to set political agendas. Schneiderman's call for action challenged the reformers' usage of the "public." She demanded that workers engage in the public discourse that surrounded and affected them. When she rose that night to speak, she was speaking for a whole class of workers, long ignored and forgotten. She served notice to the City of New York that things could never be the same; the fire had changed too much. "I would be a traitor to these poor burned bodies," she proclaimed:

> [I]f I came here to talk good fellowship. We [the working class] have found the good people of the public and we have found you wanting . . . We have tried you, citizens: we are trying you now, and you have a couple of dollars for the sorrowing mothers and daughters and sisters by way of a charity gift. But every time the workers come out in the only way they know to protest against conditions which are unbearable, the strong hand of the law is allowed to press down heavy upon us. I can't talk fellowship to you who are gathered here. Too much blood has been spilled. I know from my experience it is up to the working people to save themselves. The only way they can save themselves is by a strong working-class movement.[62]

Schneiderman's words spoke to the heart of the anger and frustration in the working-class community. She felt that unless workers acted on behalf of themselves, nothing positive and long-lasting would be done for them. The reformers would simply dole out charity and slightly modify a few laws, while the repressive structure and lack of enforcement would remain. Schneiderman knew that unless workers themselves engaged in the public debate, as equals, nothing would change. She was announcing that garment workers were uncloaking themselves and becoming visible.[63]

Becoming Visible

One aspect of becoming visible involved the planning of a public funeral. Theresa Malkiel, a committed socialist who enlisted the aid of unions and other radical groups, chaired the Joint Funeral Committee of Local 25 and the WTUL. In addition to the garment unions, socialist groups, and the United Hebrew Trades, the Committee included locals of carpenters, plasterers, cigar makers, printers, typographical workers, stenographers, hatters, and woodworkers.[64] The funeral plans morphed into a planned general strike in the garment industry on the day of the funeral to display class solidarity.[65] The *Call* and the *Jewish Daily Forward* issued calls for a general strike. Headlines asked workers to "Be Ready" and "Arise Working Men and Women of This Great City." The *Call* incited workers to "lay down your tools, shake the dust of the mills and factories from your feet and come to answer our call."[66]

Workers concluded that the funeral would have political meaning. The union planned to bury the unidentified bodies in the Workingmen's Circle cemetery and devised a mass political demonstration to coincide with the funeral.[67] Both were set for April 5. This strategy divided the workers' committee from its reformist allies. Middle-class reformers saw the fire as simply a natural disaster; fire escapes and fire safety were the desired cure. But for the workers, this was the beginning of a larger effort. The fire symbolized the workers' powerlessness, and they did not want the voices of their fallen comrades to be silenced. Fire safety, for workers, was part—and only a small part—of the larger movement for industrial democracy. They did not separate public and private issues the way the reformers did all too easily. They recognized the importance of the public in industrial relations (IR), already having been well schooled in Protocolism. Unlike the skilled workers that made up the majority of the American Federation of Labor (AFL), the ILGWU did not rely on the same strategy of private bargaining of shop locals and employees. It relied on massive public displays, general strikes, and the quasi-public protocol. Its method would be an organizational strike, not to organize the industry, but to organize the state politically. On the day of the planned protest, the ILGWU declared: "Workers should lay down their tools and refuse to work until the fire escapes are installed. [They should] strike for the wiping out of death-trapping shops."[68]

A rift occurred early on between middle-class Jewish reformers, mainly of German origin, and the more numerous Eastern European Jews, of whom many were socialists and working class. The rift was most obvious in the debates surrounding the "proper" burial site between the Hebrew Free Burial Society, a middle-class German-Jewish charity, and the more radical and secular ILGWU and the Workmen's

Circle, a fraternal Jewish sickness-and-death fund with a radical orientation. The Burial Society aided the victims of the fire by providing free burial plots for all victims. It declared, however, that it would not participate in a public event, nor would it sanction such action. Speaking for the Society, H. E. Adelman stated that a display such as the one the union had planned would be both "unJewish" and "un-American."[69] For Adelman, and other German-Jewish businessmen, a funeral was no place for politics. Privately, Adelman wrote to Mayor Gaynor that this demonstration was an attempt by "loudmouthed agitators . . . to denounce and array class against class."[70] Adelman and the middle class of New York opposed any public display for the working class. Adelman saw this as a funeral; workers saw it as a political call to action. It was their chance to push the issue of industrial democracy to the forefront of New York politics and beyond the ladies' garment industry. This effort was something the *Call* understood well. The socialist paper declared that the state and the laws it made did not provide safe workplaces; workers, by becoming active at the polls and in their shops, would.[71] Nor did Adelman understand how the workers defined themselves as both working class and Jews, and with an emerging sense of rights borne to them as citizens.[72] Democracy for them sprang from everyday lived existence. It meant respect and fair treatment on the job and in the dominant culture. Workers wanted freedom where they lived and worked. But few found it. One fire survivor, in an oral history interview, stated that her parents believed that "in America they don't let you burn."[73] Many had learned the hard way the limits of citizenship and strove to expand them.[74] All the protests of Adelman and the middle class proved ineffective; as the *Times* wrote: "Plans to make the funeral service as an occasion for a labor demonstration on a large scale were perfected."[75] The union announced that only ILGWU banners and black flags would be used in the demonstration that would be "one of the most impressive spectacles of sorrow New York has ever known." In short, workers were expanding the Protocol, without consciously knowing it.[76]

City officials, however, still refused to release the bodies. Officials believed that the demonstration would be canceled without the bodies to bury. The Joint Committee of the ILGWU and WTUL requested that Morris Hillquit, noted lawyer, socialist, and adviser to the union, take whatever legal action was necessary to get the bodies. Hillquit knew his task would not be easy. Commissioner of Charities Michael Drummond stated that the presence of the unknown dead would cause "riotous demonstrations." Drummond believed it was his responsibility to spare the City these events.[77] Mayor Gaynor, worried about public safety, announced that the City would bury the unknown in a plot it owned in the Evergreen Cemetery in Greenpoint, Brooklyn on April 5, the day before the scheduled public funeral. The *Call* editorialized that "many of the eager working men and women declared that the refusal of Coroner Holthauser to turn over the unidentified bodies [was based solely on the fact that the City] fear[ed] that if the demonstration were to be held this week a million people would join it. And their protest would echo throughout the world."[78]

Without bodies to bury or a permit to assemble, the Committee decided that the masses of participants would march behind empty hearses in what the *Call* declared would be the "greatest demonstration of workers ever seen here . . . when the Triangle's victims are laid to rest."[79] The Joint Committee released hundreds of thousands of leaflets calling for a march beginning at 1:00 P.M. on the fifth. They were going to bury their own, at least symbolically. "There would be a general strike," the Committee announced, "rain or shine stay away from your shop."[80] Hundreds of thousands of workers lined the march's route. Back in Manhattan, after the ferries left for Brooklyn, the crowds gathered uptown for a mass memorial service held at the Metropolitan Opera House. Over 30,000 marchers followed the empty hearses under the Washington Square Arch in Greenwich Village, just two blocks from the site of the fire. They followed the carriages to the Twenty-Third Street Pier where they watched the bodies as they were ferried across to Brooklyn. A crowd of nearly 10,000 met the ferries in Brooklyn.[81]

At the head of the workers' procession was Rose Schneiderman. The papers reported that, leading the crowds through the rain, she was "hatless and without a raincoat" (very unladylike). As a tireless fighter for both workers' and women's rights, she found the fire was a pivotal moment in her life, as it must have been with others. Having spent a good many years working in these factories with these women, she was all too well aware of the problems they faced. As a leader of the 1909 strike, she also knew their frustration. The fire was a turning point because it led women just like Schneiderman to see the limits of male-dominated labor unions and to look increasingly to cross-class, gender-based organizations like the WTUL and politics. Moreover, it moved her and others to see partnership with urban liberals as the only practical means to aid workers.[82] Others that day "tried to trudge along in the dripping procession," wrote the *Times*, "but long before it [the crowd] reached its uptown destination, [Schneiderman] began to falter." Mary Dreier, WTUL president, and Helen Marot, also of the League, "each took her under an arm and the three leaned into the wind supporting each other." One could see this scene as a larger metaphor. The fire marked a critical shift in unionism from a system of rank-and-file activism to a system in which the union functioned more and more as a vehicle representing workers' demands before the newly created activist state. Schneiderman, walking arm in arm with industrial democrats, represented the new partnership between reformers and labor as lobbyists. It was the two groups, reformers and workers, who collectively "leaned into the wind supporting each other." But it was the industrial democrats who led labor along this new path to create the new industrial relations. Schneiderman stated that day that "this parade has been the only thing that will demonstrate to the people of the enormous responsibility resting on them to see to it that fire protection is given these thousands and thousands of factory workers." Only one banner was carried that day: "We Demand Fire Protection." Yet, the workers saw this demand as part of a larger agenda: industrial democracy.[83]

From Industrial Democracy to Industrial Paternalism

As workers sought their own answers, city agencies began the process of assessing responsibility for the disaster. There appeared to be a frenzy of administrative activity following the fire. The *Times* noticed that "scores of city officials busied themselves . . . seeking to explain and fix responsibility for the fire of Saturday afternoon."[84] One of the first to make a statement was Coroner Holthauser, who, the *Times* reported, "sobbing like a child," held the Building Department directly responsible for not being "insistent enough" in the enforcement of laws and building code violations. He continued, "They are as guilty as any."[85] But this was only the opening salvo in what would be a long series of accusations and investigations. After the fire, the Fire Department, Building Department, Office of the Mayor, Coroner's Office, and District Attorney all announced investigations, as did the New York State Assembly and Senate.[86]

From the evidence at hand, it appears that most of the investigating agencies were only trying to clear their departments of responsibility, and thus blame some other agency. One of the first of these investigations, a coroner's inquest, established the forum for shifting the blame. It declared that it was "going to find out who is responsible . . . and put the blame where it belongs."[87]

The coroner's office called all parties involved before it. The two most significant agencies involved were the Fire and Building Departments. Almost immediately, after the embers from the fire cooled, the two agencies traded accusations. The battle spilled into the pages of the city's major papers, and the newspapers exploited this opportunity to sell more papers. The *American* assembled a panel of "experts" to investigate the fire. They appointed Fire Chief Croker to the panel, and in a series of essays published in the *American*, Croker attempted to clear his department of responsibility. He argued that the city was legally exempt from state fire codes, pointing out that state codes at the time were much stricter than the city's. According to Fire Commissioner Rhinelander Waldo, however, part of the problem was divided responsibility: the Building Department was in charge of fire escapes. Croker added that six different city agencies had jurisdiction over various aspects of fire safety. His solution was to reorganize the city's agencies and concentrate power over fire safety within an expanded fire department. New laws and a stronger fire department with more money would prevent a recurrence of a disaster of this type, according to Waldo and Croker.[88]

Believing the problem of fire safety was a limited one, Croker advocated new laws requiring fire escapes. He argued, "This calamity is just what I have been predicting. . . . I have been advocating and agitating that fire escapes be put on buildings such as this. This large loss of life is due to this neglect."[89] However, for Croker, the blame lay at the feet of the Building Department, as it had failed to live up to its responsibility. Croker noted that his department had reported the Asch Building for fire code violations and, following procedure, had notified the Building Department to enforce the code. The result, Croker argued, was plain to see.[90]

The intra-agency squabbling brought forward the arcane nature of Tammany Hall political appointments. Eventually the Manhattan Borough president, McAneny, became involved. He was the person who had originally appointed Building Superintendent Miller, and the Asch

Building had fallen under Miller's domain. Croker's attacks on Miller soiled the reputation of McAneny as well.[91] The *American*, with which Croker was affiliated, brought the matter to a boiling point with its banner headline: "Who Is Responsible for This, Mr. McAneny?"[92] Even the tepid *New York Times* editorialized, "Controversy between officials should be avoided. There is no time to waste."[93]

Squabbling between reformers seeking to place blame elsewhere continued nonetheless. Chief Croker used the pages of the *American* to accuse the Manufacturers' Association and the "City Beautiful" people of blocking all previous attempts at fire protections. He warned them that now they could not stop such legislation because the city was united in its quest.[94] Croker berated the Building Department for its utter lack of professionalism. He noted how, on countless occasions, his department had cited the Asch Building for lack of fire escapes, as recently as one week before the blaze. Yet the Building Department did nothing.[95] In response to Croker's allegations, Assistant Building Superintendent Alfred Ludwig noted that while the building should have had three fire exits, it only had two. The design had been approved nevertheless. He also noted that he had not heard of any violations on the Asch Building, and he assured the public that his department would thoroughly investigate the fire and reform all necessary building codes to prevent another disaster.[96] Indeed, in the days following the fire, no city agency accepted responsibility for the fire, nor did any agency appear ready to take the lead in preventing future disasters. Only Croker came forward. And his forum on fire escapes was more of the same. The problem went beyond just fire escapes and antiquated building codes.

The working class did not wait quietly for an "official" verdict. The strikes of previous years had taught them not to rely on city bureaucracy. They had learned the value of independent action and knew the importance of their own ties with middle-class reformers.[97] The WTUL created a Committee of Twenty-Five to lead its own investigation and recommend appropriate remedies, legislative and otherwise. Rabbi Stephen Wise, a member of the Committee, stated that he did not "trust public officials to determine [responsibility] for us; it is our task as citizens to do that for ourselves."[98] Wise's reference to "we" referred only to the middle class, the "better sorts." Yet, the garment strikes of 1909 and 1910 with their resulting IR system should be seen as an attempt by workers to expand past this myopic notion of "we" the public to include workers—workers were seeking a new place in the polity. Wise did not easily recognize this distinction. The Committee of Twenty-Five did not include workers. The call Wise made that day was for distinguished people, men and women of the "first order," who had recognized public experience:

> New York ought to be able to obtain a committee of 25 men and women who can get the facts. Then we should frame legislation.... We don't want this to create a great panic of charity and then [the public] would forget the whole thing.... No public investigation should satisfy us. We must have a large citizens committee and should ask the *first* men and women of the city to serve on it.[99]

For middle-class reformers, such as Wise, however, citizenship was decidedly elitist.

Leonora O'Reilly and New York WTUL President Mary Dreier felt the most effective role for the WTUL would be that of shaping public opinion. Dreier wrote to O'Reilly shortly after the fire declaring that she "was swept into action by that meeting Sunday afternoon after the fire." She declared that the proper role for the WTUL was to get "together a representative citizens committee, so as not only to help us focus public thought, but get the great stupid unconcerned public to take action, so that our struggling sisters [efforts would] be reinforced by public opinion in our work." This "call to action," she added, "might wake the sleeping public."[100] The WTUL also had to make sure that the "sleeping public," the mass of apathetic middle-class Americans as yet unaffected by the progressive reform movements, heard from them.

Yet, within the WTUL there was some division. Leonora O'Reilly developed a more activist, worker-orientated policy. O'Reilly was a rough-and-tumble Irish immigrant who had spent much of her life in factories and shops and was a former member of the Knights of Labor. As a member of the WTUL, and later as an official, she tried to temper the more middle-class reformers' impulse to control workers with a nuanced approach that employed a democratic partnership between the classes. She felt middle-class "allies" (as workers called the middle-class reformers in the WTUL) provided a vital source of funds and political advantage in workers' struggles, especially in the struggles of women workers, who could not expect support from traditional sources of working-class action: unions. Yet, she also knew that she had to guard against these allies. If workers were not careful, these "allies" would control them. This concern, however, seemed to bother only the working-class members of the WTUL.

Working-class members of the WTUL experienced something of a duality of existence. Not quite one, nor the other, working-class women straddled both worlds, living what Audre Lorde has called the "simultaneity of oppression."[101] As members of the working class, they strove continuously to aid their sisters and brothers. In their struggles, they made many allies. Eventually a few of these "girls" left the shop floor and became paid staff at either the ILGWU or the WTUL. At all times, they felt the pull of a divided identity. Which would be greater, the ties of class in the union or those of sisterhood in the WTUL? In their hearts, they knew neither place was perfect.[102]

O'Reilly forged her primary allegiances in the communities of workers where she organized them to demonstrate. Often these mass rallies were designed to put pressure on elected officials. One such meeting, planned nearly a year after the fire on March 22, is illustrative. Organized to take place in state Senator Robert F. Wagner's district, O'Reilly wrote that this "public meeting" was to demonstrate the community's anger at the fire.[103] O'Reilly also worked on the WTUL's efforts to pressure agencies to enforce existing laws. While she knew this was at best only a short-term solution, it could prevent another disaster, and more importantly, it would keep the issue alive until a report she was working on could be finished. O'Reilly and the WTUL collected data on "fire traps," sending this confidential information to both the Fire and Building Departments.

O'Reilly helped inundate these agencies with lists of buildings in violation of codes. The Committee received 1,000 responses in three days[104] and over 4,500 replies to a questionnaire that appeared in many newspapers. With only a limited staff, the WTUL was still able to investigate 223 factories.[105] O'Reilly chided Fire Commissioner Waldo that "perhaps out of all of this sacrifice of life, we may get some better laws for the protection of lives in the community." The Fire Department, with limited staffing and intra-agency squabbles, moved slowly on these matters. O'Reilly wrote back to Waldo, "does your letter [where he tells her of the problems with staffing] mean that it is useless to send you any more lists, as we have lists coming in continuously?" O'Reilly shrewdly used the press to pressure the city agency. When the department went too slowly on a matter, she simply went public with the information and shamed the department into action.[106] Still, O'Reilly's efforts met with limited success. For instance, she and the WTUL wrote to the State Labor Department complaining of numerous firetraps in the city. In his reply, Commissioner William Street stated that he "was aware that many of these buildings were a fire menace but under present law I have no authority to rectify these conditions."[107] O'Reilly did have some success. On May 9, Rudolph Miller, Manhattan superintendent of buildings, wrote her that 31 of the 223 factories had been ordered to be brought up to code or be closed. Nearly two weeks later, he wrote: "Dear Madams . . . an order has therefore been filled calling for the erecting of fire escapes on the front of each building, and automatic fire doors between two buildings."[108] While these few gains were symbolically important, most of the city's workers still toiled in unsafe conditions.

The WTUL did not fight alone. The Socialist Party's Central Committee instructed New York City's Executive Committee to connect the growing fire prevention movement to the larger political issues and to increase the political and economic awareness of workers.[109] Hundreds of workers gathered each evening before the Asch Building, putting their voices behind the protest movement. At a mass meeting called by Local 25, the Waist and Dressmaker's Union, audience calls for a militant response interrupted the moderate speech of Abraham Cahan, editor of the *Jewish Daily Forward*. Speakers such as O'Reilly, Meyer London, and Morris Hillquit reminded workers that only a strong independent union could protect them and their interests.[110]

While various city agencies denied any responsibility for the tragedy that had occurred, politicians and the daily press alike began to look for someone to blame. The *Tribune* ran front-page boxes declaring, "Try to Fix Responsibility" and "What Are You Going to Do?"[111] Miriam F. Scott, writing in the *Outlook*, expressed the one thought all could agree upon: the tragic and needless loss of life. She declared that all New Yorkers and Americans, whether they were "conservatives, liberals and radicals of all shades and intensity," were outraged at this senseless loss of life.[112] The *Tribune*, typical of its coverage, began to carry a box on its front page demanding "Justice." The *Evening Journal* carried a drawing of a gallows with the caption: "This ought to fit someone: Who is He?"[113] Eventually all eyes looked to the owners of the Triangle factory.

The trial of Harris and Blanck, the owners of the Triangle factory, got underway on December 4, 1912. They were charged with manslaughter for the deaths of several of the girls. In only eighteen days of trial, 155 witnesses were called, 103 of them by the state. The state's case, argued by Assistant District Attorney J. Robert Rubin and Charles S. Bostwick, rested on the simple fact that the owners had knowingly locked the door on the ninth floor in violation of city and state codes and that the locked doors prevented the girls from escaping death.

Max D. Steuer handled Harris and Blanck's defense. Steuer was a native of the Lower East Side and in an earlier career was a noted labor lawyer.[114] His strategy was to show that the owners did not know the doors were locked, nor did they order them to be so. Playing to middle-class conceptions of womanhood, Steuer tried to discredit the state's witnesses, mainly the young immigrant women who worked in the factory. In this view, women were either Madonnas or whores. And because these women did not model themselves on the middle-class standard, he presented them as the latter.[115] He attacked them for being young and impressionable. For instance, when sixteen-year-old Ethel Monick proved an uncooperative witness, Steuer retorted, "you like to argue some now little girl." Questioning the survivors on how they escaped the fire, he tried to prove that the girls had panicked and that the panic had caused their deaths. His line of questioning sought to present the girls as irresponsible. Imputing their immorality, he asked one girl, "was your skirt about as tight as the skirt you've got on now?"[116] Because they were young women and independent working girls at that, Steuer implied they had acted irresponsibly and that was in part why their friends had died.

Steuer's tactics were based on both class and gender biases. He attacked the honesty of all the state's witnesses as "people who come here [before the courts]—most of them with law suits. Many of them because they lost their dearest relatives, are not telling the truth." For Steuer, commoners litigated solely to seek monetary reward. Indeed, many of the witnesses also had civil suits pending against Harris and Blanck, and a guilty verdict here would aid their cases. But that verdict could never bring back the 146 dead.[117] In response, the state brought forth evidence showing that men in the employ of Triangle had attempted earlier to coerce witnesses.[118] In the end, though, Steuer's defense had created sufficient doubt for the jury about who was telling the truth, and the jury acquitted Harris and Blanck on all charges. Ultimately, as historian Leon Stein so ably put it, "The jury had been given the impossible task of determining whether Harris and Blanck knew the door was locked at a specific time."[119]

On March 21, 1912, Harris and Blanck were back in court. The district attorney, bowing to political pressure from workers' organizations—who voted in large numbers—brought another set of manslaughter charges. This time, Judge Samuel Seabury intervened on the manufacturers' behalf. Seabury, who later was instrumental in destroying Tammany Hall,[120] addressed the jury, telling them that he thought it unfair that these men were being charged again for a crime of which they had already been acquitted. The jury returned a verdict of innocence after only minutes of deliberation.[121] Three years later, Harris and Blanck settled the twenty-three civil suits filed against them by the victims' families. The settlement was $75 per victim.[122]

"Who is responsible?" the editors of the socialist *Call* had asked after the fire. Because the trial had been so unrewarding, the paper warned that workers should set their sights higher. Individuals were certainly at fault, but it was the economic and political system that permitted them to do what they did and get away with it. The same court system had allowed the State Court of Appeals to overturn the state's workmen's compensation laws as infringing on the rights of corporations. In the *Call's* words, that system told the industrial classes "you may go on murdering as many working men and women and children as you find necessary in order to extract the last possible dollar of profit out of your respective businesses." The socialist paper also blamed the working class for failing to mobilize effectively before this. Lacking "self-consciousness," their leaders, complained the *Call*, were "Civic Federationized," co-opted by the corporate liberalism of the National Civic Federation, of which Samuel Gompers was a member. Only when workers acted collectively in their own best interests, according to the *Call*, would this wholesale killing end.[123] The fire added a new dimension to the emerging IR, the state. In the years following the fire, the state would come to play an important role in IR. At first, the workers' political mobilization suggested a new direction. If workers could use their political muscle to push the state, they could influence IR. But, as we will see, the workers' middle-class allies also looked to the state. And they were in a better position to guide the state in its new role.

THE FIRE'S MEANING FOR IR

The Triangle Fire, in the most dramatic way possible, brought to the attention of New Yorkers the horrible working conditions of factory labor. Industrial democrats responded with efforts to enforce codes and broaden laws. City managers attempted to shift blame and broaden their own bureaucracies, but ultimately focused on what they saw as the basic flaws in the political system. Young Tammany upstarts such as Alfred E. Young and Robert F. Wagner emphasized the need for changes in the urban environment and new opportunities for political realignment, reforms that would serve Tammany for a generation or more.

In contrast to these views, workers interpreted the fire as yet another example of the abuses of a repressive economic and political system.[124] The true key to understanding the fire had to be gender. Central to the emotional response, which the fire engendered on all sides, was the image of its victims as 146 helpless, vulnerable young women. Gender was a double-edged sword though. It had empowered the immigrant women in 1909, causing the middle class to support them, and, with the creation in 1911 of the Factory Investigating Committee (FIC) as we will see, brought the state into industrial relations. Paternalism built bridges among male progressive employers, male industrial experts, male and female middle-class reformers, and male-dominated trade unions. The real meaning of the fire rested not in class, which was the foundation of Protocolist industrial democracy, but rather in the view of "innocent" victims needing a strong state to protect them. Gender, a missing component of Protocolism, became an important political and policy issue. In the process of protecting women workers, the state remade itself, as we will see in the seceding chapters, with the creation of new policies and laws. The fire, in addition, brought a renewed determination to the Protocol. It was seen as connected to the problems the Protocol was dealing with. The FIC, therefore, should be viewed as a continuation and adaptation of Protocolism, rather than something completely separate.[125]

5   Politics

Setting the Stage for Industrial Democracy in Progressive Era New York

The Triangle Fire set into motion a series of events that transformed New York's "governing system," to use historian Alan Dawley's apt phrase, including a state apparatus (courts and legislatures), linkage institutions (parties, unions, or any other institutions that link voters to the state apparatus), and a dominant worldview or ideology.[1] New York's governing system was reinvented during the years of Protocolism.[2] In the process, it forged an important relationship with workers and their unions. Protocolism also awoke a new element within the placid Democratic Party, and it cemented a new political coalition around issues of workers' welfare.[3]

These transformations were situated around one institution: the New York Factory Investigating Commission (FIC), a legislative body that marked the high point of New York's reform efforts during the Progressive Era and embodied Protocolist ideas of industrial democracy. The FIC transcended the Protocol by establishing a "base" for reform that rested on the state rather than on private efforts. This base was forged in a partnership between industrial workers—especially those in the International Ladies' Garment Workers Union (ILGWU or ILG)—and Tammany Hall, the machine of the Democratic Party of New York City. This coalition was joined by and mediated through industrial democrats.[4]

The Triangle Fire provided an opportunity for the state's Democratic Party to seize the reigns of power from Republicans. Too often historians have seen the Progressive Era urban machine as either a foe or a spearhead of reform. Such binary thinking, however, clouds important issues. It portrays urban machine politicians as either reacting against reform or using it for their own selfish purposes. It makes more sense to see reform, first, as a process with many actors, and second, as a process in

154

which politicians are themselves changed. So, Tammany Hall politicians entered reform and were transformed by it.[5]

After the fire, as we have seen, passions in the working-class communities of New York ran high. The language of socialists writing in the *Call* and workers speaking on street corners convinced many reformers that something "dangerous" would happen unless they acted quickly. Appreciating what workers would do if left to their own devices, reformers hoped to channel these emotions into "constructive" action.[6] Carl Smith, an American Studies scholar, argues convincingly that reformers used dramatic events, such as tragedies, to help shape "belief" or worldviews of progress and modernity. In just this way, this chapter argues that the Triangle Fire provided industrial democrats with an enormous opportunity to reshape their urban, political landscape.[7]

Workers, too, had good reason to look for legislative help. By 1912, they chafed at the more bureaucratic aspects of the Protocol. The "agreement," as we have seen, had great limitations as a private instrument. It also was limited in whom it protected. In contrast, the FIC could be a vehicle to spread industrial democracy throughout New York's many industries. At the same time, in the FIC, workers could ally themselves with the very same reform groups who had aided them in forming the Protocol. But here, their sheer numbers could influence outcomes, as this was a political contest of sorts.

At the forefront of these reform groups was the Women's Trade Union League (WTUL). The WTUL was a natural agency for this activity. It had been active in New York labor circles and was an original supporter of the Protocol. Its actions in 1909 and 1910 also gave it solid credentials in working-class communities.[8]

The Sunday following the fire, the WTUL held a meeting where it learned just how divided Protocolists were politically. Socialists associated with the WTUL—Morris Hillquit, Meyer London, and most importantly, Leonora O'Reilly—labeled the fire "industrial warfare" and demanded workers respond appropriately. While London went on to call the fire the result of a system of "greed," O'Reilly and Hillquit created a Committee of Five to fully investigate fire hazards in the city. Chaired by O'Reilly, the Committee received over 1,000 complaints of fire safety violations.[9] At that very same meeting, another group emerged: the so-called Committee of Twenty-Five. Made up of prominent reformers, social workers, academics, philanthropists, and religious leaders, this was the group that had staged the larger April 2, 1911 meeting at the Metropolitan Opera House. This group, which slowly took control of the growing protest movement around working conditions, directed it toward a legislative outcome.[10]

Meanwhile, the Committee of Twenty-Five quickly metamorphosed into the Committee on Safety. While funded by R. Fulton Cutting, a wealthy civic leader, the force behind the Committee was John Kingsbury, leader of the Association for Improving the Condition of the Poor (AICP). As one of the oldest and most venerable social welfare organizations in the city, the AICP gave the new body instant access to the city's social welfare forces.[11]

The impressive names of supporters immediately made the Committee's activities newsworthy. The Committee transformed the public outcries about the fire by giving them direction. It focused solely on issues of fire safety, partly because this was the easiest issue around which to build a reform consensus. As important, though, was the myopia of the elite leadership of the Committee's leaders, who could not see the connections between fire safety and the current industrial regime. They focused the Committee's attention on a limited legislative agenda. As Committee member Henry Morgenthau put it, we focused on "what laws could be passed." Thus, the Committee helped to transform the protest movement into a lobbying group within the conventional political arena.[12]

A legislative response such as the FIC was familiar to New York reformers. The New York State legislature had, by 1911, been active in investigating utilities, life insurance, immigration, labor, and workmen's compensation. It had, in short, a history of responding to organized citizens' groups.[13]

With pressure mounting, happenstance aided the reformers' cause: a fire that destroyed part of the state capital on March 29 broke Tammany Hall's resistance to reform and fire legislation. Frances Perkins, a well-known industrial democrat, used this opportunity to work tirelessly to educate Robert Wagner and Al Smith, then young Tammany Turks, in matters of reform. Perkins recognized something others had not: Smith and Wagner were not traditional Tammany Hall types. Most reformers had written off "Murphy's boys" or the "Tammany Twins," as they were collectively known, as mere party hacks. Not Perkins. She made the case that reform would be good for all: the city, their party, and their constituents—the workers. By late spring, her efforts began to pay off. In May, both houses of the legislature passed bills creating the FIC. Governor Dix signed it into law on June 30.[14]

The FIC had more investigative authority than any other previous committee in the state, labor or otherwise. The reason was simple: Tammany Hall. Wagner and Smith, as both chair and vice-chair of the FIC and leaders of their party, made it a tool for Tammany. As party leaders, Wagner and Smith were also in a position to marshal its resources. The FIC had powers to appoint commissioners, subpoena witnesses and records, employ a staff of experts, and change its governing rules. While it only had a small budget of $10,000 for 1912, it was able to rely on a vast army of volunteers.[15]

The FIC was directly responsible for the future eminence of Wagner and Smith in New York and national politics. Joining them in the FIC coalition were Republican Senator Charles Hamilton, State Representative Cyrus Philips, and Democratic Assemblyman Edward Jackson. The governor appointed the four public members: industrial democrat Mary Dreier, AFL President Samuel Gompers, businessman Simon Brentano, and realtor Robert Dowling. The two Tammany leaders, worked with reformers to help fill out the FIC staff and overcome their limited budget. Henry Morgenthau, acting as president of the Committee on Safety, offered to help. Morgenthau, once convinced that Smith and Wagner were serious about investigation, wrote to them: "I can get you a first-class lawyer who will not demand any fee, and he will be satisfactory to everyone concerned, including Tammany Hall." That lawyer, Abram Elkus, became FIC chief counsel and brought his assistant Bernard Shientag with him. Elkus and Shientag ran most of the public hearings and became a leading force on the Committee.[16] Frank Tierney, a prominent journalist with strong connections to the Democratic Party, was appointed secretary by Wager and Smith. George Price and H.F.J. Porter headed the investigation. Price and Elkus, who were collectively the heart and brains of the FIC, together pushed Wagner and Smith into new areas of reform. By 1915, Tammany Hall's leaders were attempting the creation of a quasi-welfare state.[17]

In line with the Progressive Era's infatuation with "expertise," Smith and Wagner brought in a cache of social scientists to assist them. Both men relied heavily on industrial democrats: for Smith it was Belle

Moskowitz; for Wagner it was Frances Perkins. Moskowitz, married to Protocolist Henry Moskowitz and herself a chief clerk for one of the associations, in turn brought in George Price, the pioneering industrial hygienist who was head of the Protocol's Joint Board of Sanitary Control, to the FIC. Price took with him into the FIC a score of industrial researchers who had worked with him on the Joint Board. For example, Price hired Clara Lemlich, 1909 strike leader, as an FIC investigator. Perkins brought a team of social workers, investigators, and women garment workers such as Rose Schneiderman and others from the WTUL. These were an interesting assortment of experts for Smith and Wagner to associate with. There was a complete and transparent mixing of personnel from the FIC and the Protocol. These people, mainly the experts and reformers, I collectively refer to as Protocolists. Lawrence Arnold Tanzer and Clarence King of Columbia University's Bill Drafting Bureau arrived to help write FIC legislation. Ironically, Tanzer had come to this work through the Citizen's Union—long a foe of Tammany Hall. Yet now they were all part of the same reform team.[18]

The creation of the FIC came at a particularly auspicious moment in New York State politics. A political vacuum existed in the state, and Wagner, Smith and Tammany Hall soon realized that they could ride the Triangle hobbyhorse to great political advantage. The Republican Party had disintegrated amid scandal. The state GOP had been built on a firm base by Charles Evans Hughes's reform efforts. In 1906, the party had turned to him to defeat the reform-minded ticket of newspaper mogul William Randolph Hearst. Rather than working through traditional party machinery, Hughes built an alternative party of reformers. By 1909, he forced his party's more conservative wing to accept reforms in banking, utility regulation, insurance, election procedures, and for pure water, food, and drugs. He also pushed for labor legislation: curbing hours worked by minors as well as reforming employers' liability legislation. By 1910, GOP conservatives joined Tammany Hall bosses to defeat Hughes's agenda. He soon was appointed to a position on the U.S. Supreme Court—there was a long tradition within the state GOP of promoting troublemakers up and out. With Hughes gone, the conservative anti-reform wing of the GOP began to take full control, leaving progressives who still constituted a significant percentage of the party helplessly on the sidelines.[19]

With no place else to go, many reform-minded Republicans drifted to the Progressive or Bull Moose Party. Nationally, this was a shell of an organization solely designed to elect Theodore Roosevelt president. But in New York, it became an active and substantial party. Others mobilized at the GOP State Convention held in Saratoga Springs in upstate New York and retook control of the party chairmanship, electing Roosevelt as chair. With Roosevelt firmly entrenched, the Progressives nominated Henry L. Stimson for governor.[20]

Meanwhile, the Progressive Party, having obtained a modicum of independence from Roosevelt, nominated Oscar S. Straus for governor. Straus was an outsider, a Jew, and a Gothamite. Active in reform efforts and a minor player in the Protocol events, he had little political experience but great name recognition in New York City. Politicians believed he would surely out-poll Stimson downstate. This meant that for the first time in many years the Democratic Party had a chance at the governor's mansion because progressives were divided between Stimson and Straus, and the conservatives were homeless.[21]

The undisputed boss of Tammany Hall, Charles Francis Murphy, saw the division within the progressive ranks as an opportunity to further consolidate his power and reunify his party.[22] The 1911 legislative session was rocky for Tammany Hall. An alliance with upstate Democrats had proved temporary as Tammany Hall fought with them over the selection of a U.S. senator. After months of infighting and struggling over a third candidate with whom both groups could live, the party had lost control of the state's lower house. The Democrats' 83 (of the 150) seats in the lower house fell, after the 1911 election, to only 48. The cause of the party's defeat was simple. As the *Knickerbocker Press* pointed out: "The defeat of Murphy was the great issue of the campaign." Ironically though, in defeat statewide, Murphy's control of the party actually increased. The heavy losses for the Democrats came in upstate and suburban districts. Lower New York remained solidly Democratic and, therefore, solidly Tammany.[23]

Tammany Hall was nonetheless in deep trouble. The major issue in the 1911 campaign was the fire, and playing to it, socialists made heavy gains in New York City and throughout the state. They gained around 27 percent more voters than they had in 1910. In addition, they ran a full ticket for the first time. Socialists voiced the concerns that many,

many workers felt. The Socialist Party was now seriously challenging Tammany Hall for working-class urban votes.[24]

The FIC thus provided an opportunity for Tammany Hall to demonstrate its commitment to workers who had been drawn closer to the socialists. In this regard, the FIC created a coalition that won the active participation of spokespersons from all sides of the issue. Most importantly, the FIC was able to win over both reformers and rank-and-file workers to its cause. Mary Dreier had connections to New York's reform community; Smith and Wagner had ties to Tammany Hall's immigrant base; Samuel Gompers and State Assemblyman Edward Jackson had avenues to the skilled workers; Dr. George Price bridged the forces of Protocolism; and lawyers Abraham I. Elkus and Bernard Shientag had connections to New York's middle-class Jewish community. Rural voters, real estate, and business interests as well as Republicans all had their representatives in this coalition (in minority standing, of course): Robert E. Dowling, Simon Brentano, Charles Hamilton, and Cyrus Phillips. Yet, of all these groups, Tammany Hall was critical to the success of the FIC, providing the glue which held it together. The spokesmen for Tammany on the FIC were now Wagner and Smith, and it was now their show.[25]

Historians studying New York have paid too little attention to the critical importance of the FIC in shaping—indeed, transforming—the Democratic Party. In New York, the independent voter (today called swing voters) held the reigns of power during the early Progressive Era. To gain power, parties courted these voters through new forms of outreach: newspapers and reformist magazines. But historian Paula Baker has demonstrated that parties also sought out alliances with interest groups. The critical role of the FIC in this process, however, remains underappreciated. The FIC brought all of these forces together. It allowed the Democratic Party to attract reformers and independent voters through its relationship with reform organizations and the media, all without losing its working-class base.[26]

So successful was Tammany Hall that the tarnish of bossism was quickly forgotten, as Smith and Wagner became "liberal" heroes in New York. Smith and Wagner knew the value of the language of reform. Throughout the life of the FIC, they constantly talked of morality, efficiency, social justice, and the "duty" of the state. Smith and Wagner were *the* politicians of their time. Progressivism for them was more than the means to power and elections. It was a tool to truly help those that got them elected: urban, immigrant workers. They never forgot that and constantly "delivered the goods." Long after Protocolism failed, Wagner and Smith advanced a vision of labor reform that picked up the failed mantle of Protocolism and grafted it onto modern liberalism.

Wagner and Smith's thinking on reform was proto-Keynesian. In 1912, they stated that it made simple business sense to be *for* workers. "It has been proven," one report stated, "that it means dollars and cents not only in the pocket of the manufacturer, but in the pocket of the working man to improve the conditions under which he works, because it . . . enables him to do more" to work more efficiently and purchase more goods and services. In 1915, the year of the final FIC report, the message was much the same: "Improvement of the working condition is real economy." These are words Brandeis and other Protocolists would have approved.[27]

The FIC had an ambitious program during its limited four-year span. It progressively took on more and more "liberal" causes. During its first two years, it limited its scope to issues of safety and health. Legislatively, it was limited to the nine largest cities in the state. Yet, the FIC was a blur of activity. In 1911, it only operated for a few months that year. Its staff visited 1,836 firms in twenty different industries. They held twenty-two public hearings, questioned 222 witnesses, and took 3,409 pages of testimony. The result was proposed legislative changes in eight areas: fire hazards, factory inspection, sanitation, employment of women and children, disease, and special legislation protecting consumers in the baking industry and workers in iron foundries. Of the fifteen proposed bills sent to the legislature, the FIC was able to deliver on eight of them.[28]

With the success of 1911, the FIC moved forward. The next year its jurisdiction increased to forty-five cities. It investigated 1,338 firms, including 211 of the largest dry-goods stores. It held thirty-seven public hearings, grilled 250 witnesses, and took over 3,500 pages of testimony.[29]

By 1912, the FIC had become the adopted child of New York reformers. FIC members freely maneuvered between it and the staffs of the major reform organizations and the Protocol itself. The WTUL publicly called attention to its connection to the FIC. The Consumers' League offered assistance. Members of the American Association for Labor Legislation—the product of John R. Commons's students—directed FIC investigations and endorsed the FIC legislative agenda. Groups as diverse as the American Institute of Architects and the *Nation* supported it, as did the *New York Times* and the Republican Club of New York. None were more supportive than the city's social workers. In fact, the reform social-work journal the *Survey* was practically the public relations arm of the FIC.[30]

The principal group among the coalition remained labor, especially the ILG (both the locals and the international). The most visible labor support, however, came from FIC Commissioner Samuel Gompers. Gompers's FIC experience demonstrates historian Julia Greene's contention that the AFL's policy of volunteerism—avoidance of political entanglements—was more complicated than generally thought.[31]

Riding the crest of the FIC social reform, Tammany Hall remade itself in 1912. The FIC also won the Democrats some unlikely support. Henry R. Seager, Columbia University political scientist and president of the AALL (American Association for Labor Legislation), wrote to Jane Addams that the Democrats were the best hope for reform in New York. Rabbi Stephen S. Wise likewise endorsed the Democrats. Republican Henry Morgenthau, chair of the Committee on Safety, also stayed with Wagner and Smith. Most surprising, however, was Lillian Wald, social worker and socialist activist, who had remained neutral during the election season, but publicly endorsed the Democrats after November.[32]

To be sure, some FIC activists remained active in the Progressive and Socialist Parties. But the access to real political power that the FIC brought reformers was hard to miss. "Just think," wrote Mary Dreier, "of having all the world listen to our story of social and industrial injustice, and have them told it can be righted. We are going to have the biggest educational campaign that country has ever seen." Henry Moskowitz, who straddled both the FIC and Protocol, also believed in this "educational" activity. Neither of them talked of the possibility of their party winning election. In New York, the Progressive Party endorsed the work of the FIC, calling for legislation to protect workers, improve working conditions, restrict women's and children's labor, and for support of the eight-hour workday, workmen's compensation, unemployment and health insurance, and the right of labor to organize.[33]

Republican progressive forces hoped to save their party by co-opting the Progressive Party candidate, Oscar Straus. They claimed Straus would unite what they saw as the two wings of the divided party: stalwarts and reformers. In addition, they believed, he would deliver the Jewish vote in New York and the combination would spell victory. This hope faded quickly when Straus told reform Republicans that he would only accept their party's nomination if the GOP accepted the entire Progressive Party platform. GOP boss William Barnes refused and forced an old-guard candidate on the party, Job Hedges.[34]

The clearest sign that Tammany Hall had been transformed was its platform. Traditionally, it was the old guard who wrote such an important document. In 1912, Murphy entrusted the young upstarts, as Robert Wagner drafted the party's platform. The document expressed his spirit and the reform principles of the FIC, so that, in 1912, through Wagner, the FIC and the Democratic Party became one. The Democrats claimed the FIC as theirs, declaring that through it they had provided the most progressive legislative record in America protecting workers, eliminating fire and other safety hazards workers faced, and passing workmen's compensation.[35]

Not all Democrats were so happy. Upstate independents, led by Thomas Mott Osborne and a young Franklin Roosevelt, demanded a more moralist reform movement. They were not at all happy about the labor coalition that Smith and Wagner had forged.[36]

The election was a masterful event, thoroughly orchestrated by Tammany Hall. Using every opportunity to connect themselves to the work of the FIC, Democrats held the workers and immigrants in urban areas to the cause. The margin of victory was created in the state's twelve most industrial districts. These districts accounted for 65.6 percent of the entire statewide vote. Democratic candidate William Sulzer won a resounding 68.5 percent of his votes there. But the statewide victory was total. When all votes were counted, Democrats controlled 34 of the 51 state senate seats and 103 of the 150 seats in the lower house. They were now back in charge of state politics.[37]

The year 1913 was therefore a turning point in New York political history. The FIC coalition was in power throughout the state. Robert Wagner and Al Smith headed their respective legislative bodies (senate and assembly). From these seats of power, they guided FIC legislation into law. They reformed the state the Tammany Hall way—by sheer force. Sensing that the FIC would create a solid coalition for the Democratic Party, Smith and Wagner steadily increased its activities after the first year. Its 1913 agenda included an investigation of prison labor, mutual benefit societies, a fire in Binghamton, and a survey of fire safety in department stores. Most important, however, was a detailed minimum wage investigation. Conducted by City College political scientist Howard Woolston, the minimum wage investigation involved most of the principal reform groups in the state in a sustained study of one of the larger issues of the day. Smith and Wagner also created a series of "Advisory Committees" empowered to study certain areas where "expert" advice would be needed.[38] The team of Wagner-Smith pushed through twenty-five FIC bills in the early part of 1913, recreating the state labor code in one fell swoop. In addition to improving fire protection and inspection, they increased sanitation and safety, limited at-home work, reorganized the state's Department of Labor, and passed special legislation for women, children, bakeries, foundries, and canneries. They also funded the FIC for one more year and dramatically expanded its scope and budget.[39]

So connected had the FIC coalition become to the Democratic Party that newly elected Governor William Sulzer claimed labor as "the spirit of all progress." He insisted he wanted to elevate the condition "of men and women" through FIC-type legislation. He quickly signed FIC bills into law. Wagner signaled the meaning of the FIC: "The Democratic Legislature," the *New York Times* quoted him as saying, "has surpassed in progressive legislation the record by any Legislature in the history of the State."[40]

Wagner and Smith, through their FIC actions, were able to cement the Democrats' new alliance with the state's workers. Both the state labor federation and the AFL singled out the Democrats on the FIC for special praise. "No Legislature in the history of the State Federation surpassed the session of 1913 in the passage of so many important remedial measures for wage-earners," stated a state federation resolution. It continued, "We doubt if any state in the Union can now compare with our Empire State in its present code of labor laws."[41]

Reformers were as supportive as labor. Most reform organizations singled out the work of the FIC as a positive example, often naming Wagner and Smith for extraordinary actions. Mass meetings were held to support specific bills. And several prominent organizations gave their full endorsement: the Consumer's League for City of New York, the American Association for Labor Legislation, and the Child Labor Committee, to name a few. Activist Florence Kelley called FIC action "extraordinarily radical for an Eastern State."[42]

Groups as diverse as the National Civic Federation and the Socialist Party supported the work of the FIC. The *New York Times* proclaimed that it had "done very good work." The *Call*, usually suspicious of government action, stated that the FIC "has done more for humanity than any commission in the history of this great state of New York."[43] Things were going almost too well.

Yet, in the summer of 1913, old Tammany Hall ways returned and threatened to derail the FIC. Tammany Hall led an effort to impeach its own carefully chosen governor. At issue was Sulzer himself. Sulzer was close to Tammany Hall before the election. But after his ascendancy, he tried to build his own independent political power base. At the center of Sulzer's power play was the FIC coalition. Sulzer openly courted the anti-Tammany Hall upstate Democrats—often moral reformers— by supporting liquor reform and the direct primary. He also clashed with Murphy over political appointments.[44]

Sulzer simply miscalculated. While he did gain the support of up-state Democrats, he met a roadblock in William Barnes, the Republican boss. The direct primary would also hurt his power base. So on this issue the two bosses joined forces. When the state legislature adjourned on May 3, without moving on his bills—the direct primary bill and one to investigate Murphy's government contracts—Sulzer called a special session. Tammany Hall fought back. Murphy pressed his troops into action. Tammany Hall legislators verbally attacked the governor. Some began to call for his impeachment over a charge of inappropriate use of campaign contributions—something for which Tammany Hall was in-famous. Finally, under pressure from Murphy, an eight-count impeach-ment charge was brought forth.[45]

Sulzer sealed his fate by trying to build his own support base to fight the charges. "Instead of facing his accusers," Henry Morgenthau claimed, Sulzer, "spent his time in a frantic but futile effort to make polit-ical combination that would save him." His supporters, including men who had been essential parts of the FIC coalition such as Morgenthau, Jacob Schiff, and Abram Elkus, claimed they made unrestricted contri-butions to the governor's campaign fund. Sulzer was breaking apart the FIC coalition and therefore he had to go.[46]

By mid-October, with a party-line vote of 39 to 18, Sulzer had been impeached. It was a pure power play on Murphy's part. On October 17, Martin Glynn, a former Albany newspaperman and the present lieu-tenant governor, became governor. According to the *New York Times*, many reformers saw the impeachment as "a travesty, the defendant a petty misdemeanant, and the purpose of the trial a spiteful vengeance on a rebellious henchman." Many realized that Sulzer was no choirboy, but removing him from office over a minor offense demonstrated to reformers that Tammany Hall had not changed that much after all.[47]

Reformers were disgusted by Tammany Hall's actions. Trade unionists such as Gompers stuck by Sulzer. Sulzer became a cause celébre to them. Gompers was appalled that men he had worked with so closely would go after Sulzer so personally and viciously. Theodore Roosevelt spoke on his behalf. William Randolph Hearst and his Independent League openly discussed the possibility of supporting Sulzer in an upcoming election.[48]

In the wake of this internecine party warfare, the 1913 elections were a disaster for Tammany Hall. In New York City, the heart of its power base, Independent Democrat John Purroy Mitchel won the mayoralty on a fusion ticket. Mitchel's keenest supporters, however, were the very reformers and social workers that the FIC coalition had earlier brought together behind Tammany. Reformers would prove the key to Democratic Party success. Therefore, in the next few years Tammany Hall moved closer and closer to reformers to forge their alliance. They viewed reformers as a conduit to working-class voters. However, in the process they abandoned any desire to develop a direct relationship with workers themselves. Voters also repudiated Tammany Hall candidates across the city. Republicans and Progressives endorsed the same candidates in an effort to win in urban districts. In the Sixth District, Progressives nominated Sulzer for the Assembly.[49]

The election results told the story: Democrats lost fifty assembly seats. They lost forty-one seats in the twelve most industrialized districts—where they had previously made the most gains. Four New York Progressives won with a major party endorsement. It was a terrible defeat for the new reform forces within Tammany Hall.[50] Even more to the point, of the seventy-nine assemblymen who voted for impeachment, only forty-six won their party's nomination. Of these forty-six, only seventeen won reelection. With such dismal results, a cry for Murphy's resignation was heard in every corner of New York.[51]

Signs of the collapse of the FIC coalition came in the loss of two of its stalwart members. Seeking to capture the high praise from his FIC work, Abram Elkus ran as the Democratic candidate for a seat on the state's Court of Appeals. He lost to a traditional Republican. As importantly, Edward Jackson lost his Assembly seat. If not dead politically, the FIC was badly wounded, and Smith and Wagner would need to revive it, or better yet, reinvent another coalition.[52]

By the end of 1912, the FIC had already turned in a new direction to regain middle-class reformers to its coalition. It had finished with some of its less controversial issues—fire safety and sanitation. Now it moved into the realm of social welfare, as epitomized by the minimum wage investigation. Without a strong coalition to reinforce its action, the FIC would find itself in a hopeless battle with the state's united business and real estate interests.

Buffalo and other upstate cities became the center of opposition to the FIC's new efforts. Upstate critics argued that FIC laws were drafted to deal with New York City problems and did not fit the their situation. A Buffalo business organization, Associated Industries, led the assault. Upstate newspapers openly lambasted the FIC's new direction.[53]

The business assault brought some revitalized support for the FIC, but many reform organizations had moved on to new areas. The WTUL had turned its attention to suffrage; the American Association for Labor Legislation (AALL) now focused on health and unemployment insurance. So, Wagner and Smith needed to move the FIC in the direction of their interests to keep them involved.[54] At the same time, many of the earliest supporters of the FIC, including several staffers, moved on to new endeavors. Mary Dreier became part of the mayor's administration. George Price left to create the ILG's Union Health Center. Samuel Gompers, disenchanted with the "professional or so-called social worker" dominance on the FIC, by 1914 openly began to oppose its new direction. Finally, labor unions became sidetracked in disputes surrounding immigration, which many inevitably saw as undercutting wage scales.[55]

Governor Glynn tried to aid Wagner and Smith. He endorsed the FIC program, calling for increased labor legislation as a sign of "political humanitarianism." The legislature passed his reforms and FIC programs such as the direct primary, workmen's compensation, and a widow's pension. Glynn then passed them quickly in the last days of the Democratic-controlled government. He also consulted with Murphy for appointments.[56]

But in the wake of the Sulzer fiasco, the Republicans further consolidated their control of both houses. When Barnes, the old-stalwart boss, stepped down as GOP boss, the Republicans went into the 1914 elections with a unity they had not seen in decades. Progressive and independent Republicans reentered the "brotherhood" of the GOP, but they did so without embracing the Democratic reform agenda. Except for a plank endorsing workmen's compensation, the GOP platform ignored FIC labor and social welfare issues.[57]

The election, part of a larger political and electoral realignment, taught Wagner and Smith valuable lessons. In 1914, 74.6 percent of the vote for Glynn, the Democratic candidate for governor, came from the twelve largest industrialized districts, most of which were downstate. All of these districts were the sites of FIC investigations. The party was hemorrhaging rural votes but holding on to working-class urban votes. The reason was clear: the FIC. Yet, even in these districts the GOP, now reunited and reconstructed, gave Democrats a run for their money. The GOP won, by a narrow margin, in nine of these districts. Democrats carried only Kings, Queens, and New York counties. When all votes were counted, Democrats, once with a considerable advance in the Assembly, now had only fifty-one seats, while the GOP controlled ninety-nine. In the end, however, new voting patterns had emerged. Most of the new seats that the GOP gained were from upstate, suburban, and rural districts. Democrats still held considerable pull in large urban centers. Gotham was quickly becoming an urban state, as its cities' populations grew. It would be only a matter of time before Tammany returned to power with the election of Al Smith as governor. What they needed to do was reinvent a coalition and build for that future. At the same time, they needed a program that would protect them against the charges of bossism. And to do so, they needed to get rid of bossism itself.[58]

In the 1914 election, the FIC also lost its Socialist and Progressive Party allies. The Progressive Party, once a force in New York politics, received only 45,486 votes. In most districts, the Socialist Party also polled behind at least one of the major parties. The one exception was the state's twelfth district, the Lower East Side, where voters sent Meyer London to Congress. While many scholars have seen this as a victory for socialism, London, by 1914, was in many ways a mainstream political reformer, an "acceptable" radical.[59]

While these political changes were in the air, the FIC moved forward steadily. It conducted a remarkable minimum wage investigation. Led by Dr. Howard Woolston, it employed a staff of forty-one investigators, coming mostly from the Protocol machinery itself. In the end, they conducted research on 577 firms employing 104,561 workers in several leading industries.[60] Sensing a sea change, the FIC presented the legislature and the Republican governor with only four bills: one dealing with sanitary conditions in mercantile shops, two others limiting hours of employment for women and children, and a fourth extending the FIC for one more year. The FIC did not send them recommendations on minimum wages for fear it would spell its own political suicide. The legislature rejected only one of the FIC bills, a proposal to recodify the state labor code. Opposition from business groups and Republican fear that it was "too radical" blocked it.[61] Still, 1915 was the most radical year for the FIC. In that year, it pressed for labor law reform, establishment of labor exchanges for the unemployed, and old age and disability insurance. But rather than advancing reform, New York's legislature, now run by the GOP, attempted to repeal previous FIC reforms. GOP opposition put the coalition on the defensive, but in the end, it had a major positive impact in their reform coalition: reuniting the Democrats with reformers who, once again, were on the same side. Together, reformers and their Democratic allies moved toward the creation of the welfare state. In the process, the FIC remade industrial democracy, grafting it onto urban liberalism.

6   The Politics of Administrative Reform
The Factory Investigating Commission, 1911–1913

THE FACTORY Investigating Commission (FIC) incorporated much from the Protocol. In addition to personnel, the FIC adopted the language of industrial democracy. The Protocols' chief goal was to modernize industry and thus gain profits through efficiencies rather than from sweating labor. The Protocol, therefore, needed to cover all shops within the industry to be effective. This proved an impossible task. Consequently, many began to realize that the state might be able to do what the Protocol could not: effectively regulate all industry. This would go a long way toward the transformation of industrial democracy that originally saw unions as the policing agents of industry. Yet, at its heart, it reveals the political dimension of industrial democracy that American reformers such as Brandeis sought to ignore. Through the state, industrial democracy became a political contest mediated by the very industrial democrats who helped create it.

The FIC, which existed from 1911 to 1915, had two distinct and separate phases. The early phase, 1911–1913, the subject of this chapter, concerned itself with issues of fire safety, hygiene, sanitation, and industrial accidents and disease. It operated with two powerful interlocking Progressive Era premises. The first was the belief that ignorance permitted the present miserable conditions under which workers toiled. The plain fact was Progressives believed that the public's ignorance of economic and social injustices allowed these injustices to become ingrained in American life. The solution to the problem, therefore, was to shed light on the dark crevices of industrial life. The second premise, which drove the FIC until 1913, was its weapon of choice to attack this "ignorance": social science. The FIC, in its early years, relied on social scientists to investigate the social ills of industrial America and offer "objective" solutions. While social science was important to the Protocol, its place was

170

always in a supporting role. With the FIC, it became much more central and in doing so provided the vehicle that helped shift the balance of power to industrial democrats.[1]

The second stage of the FIC, after 1913, saw reform efforts become more concerned with what we would now commonly call social welfare issues; this is the subject of the next chapter. A proto-Keynesian logic, which got stronger and more pronounced in 1914, drove the FIC. FIC staff justified early safety and sanitation reforms in monetary terms, echoing the Protocol's Tayloristic language. Arguing that in the long run it was cheaper to have safe and clean workplaces, FIC reports increasingly spoke of fewer workmen's compensation claims, fewer instances of industrial unrest, and higher real estate values and profits. We have to "convince some people [opposed to reform]," FIC counsel Abram Elkus told his fellow reformers, "that it is dollars and cents in their pockets to do the sort of things you are doing." And dollars and cents in workers' pockets, too, they were quick to point out.[2]

On fire safety, the FIC had unprecedented public support. Various civic and business groups cooperated with the FIC through the Civic Organization's Conference on Public Safety. The Conference on Public Safety included members of the City Club and the Citizens' Union, engineers, real estate interests, insurance people, and a host of other business leaders who supplied the FIC with detailed evidence and testimony supporting fire safety reform.[3] These business leaders were joined in their call for reform by a host of reform agencies, including the American Association for Labor Legislation (AALL), the Women's Trade Union League (WTUL), the Consumers' League, and organized labor. Together, the FIC united business, labor, and reformers under its umbrella, making it the single most important instrument of reform in the state at the time. The fire's sheer horror propelled fire safety reform. The charred remains of the Triangle workers and the pictures of their dead burned bodies were carried by every major newspaper in the state. The *New York Times* reported that "no one has dared oppose" fire safety reform.[4]

The FIC followed the lead of several of the reform organizations in the area of fire hazards. The Committee of Safety, the WTUL, and the Joint Board of Sanitary Control all investigated fire hazards. Leonora O'Reilly of the WTUL and Dr. George Price of the Joint Board had argued for reform long before the fire. Now people listened. Price, and other reformers, found an audience in the FIC; eventually, he joined the FIC and brought with him to the agency many, if not most, of the Joint Board staff.[5]

Reformers such as Price were able to cite state reports detailing the hazards workers faced. In 1911, two-thirds of all factories were multiple-story buildings such as the Asch Building. Only 1,500 of the thousands of buildings in the state were considered "modern" and designated as "fireproof." The Asch Building was one of those. Still, some doubted the investigative authority of the state or the economic system that favored property over people. "Fireproof buildings," wrote the *Call*, "bear a remarkable resemblance to our courts.... They have been devised for the sole purpose of protecting, not human life, and least of all the lives of workers, but property."[6]

The city's factory codes were also vague and full of holes. More significant, it was never fully clear which agency was in charge of enforcement. Were fire safety and fire codes the charge of the Fire Department, local building departments, or the state Building Department? This confusion permitted most owners to ignore existing laws, allowing the historic disregard for fire safety to continue.[7]

Yet, reformers who gathered at the Metropolitan Opera House on April 2, 1911, did recognize the opportunity for reform that the Triangle fire presented. Their demands that night were limited to fire drills, fireproof exits, alarms, sprinklers, inspections, and fire doors that were fire doors. It took the public and vocal pressure of workers and their allies— notably Protocolists like Price and garment worker and WTUL activist Rose Schneiderman—to broaden their horizons and prompt them to further action.[8]

Following the fire, H.F.J. Porter, an insurance expert, together with the Citizens' Union, proposed remedial legislation to the state lawmakers. In May, the state passed the Sullivan-Hoey laws, which paralleled these demands. Principal among the laws was the creation of a fire prevention bureau to investigate all buildings, new and old.

Beginning work in 1911, the FIC quickly set up shop to investigate the "fire problem," first in New York City and then statewide. Porter began an exhaustive investigation of 159 buildings. In 1912, another engineer, James Whiskeman, was brought in to examine an additional 200 factories. The FIC also utilized the WTUL and Committee on Safety reports, which covered more than 450 buildings. FIC staffers created a detailed questionnaire that they sent to reformers, politicians, fire experts, labor leaders, and manufacturers.[9]

The results of these efforts showed that New York was a tinderbox awaiting disaster. Most manufacturing took place in buildings originally designed as tenements. They were poorly designed, dark, wooden, six to seven stories high, with little to offer in the way of fire safety. Even the newer buildings, as the Asch Building so painfully demonstrated, were less fireproof than advertised. Too often, owners, upon hearing that the building was fireproof, proved apathetic to further, even minor, fire prevention measures. In addition, as the case of the Asch Building again illustrated, the highly flammable contents of many of these buildings created desperate situations.[10]

Therefore, the FIC repeatedly called for reduced occupancy on upper floors of factory buildings. Occupancy of upper floors, it argued, should be based on the fire safety of the individual factory or building, and vigorously enforced. Investigators, reformers, and a stream of expert witnesses all called for firewalls, fireproof stairwells, fire towers, and general structural fireproofing changes.[11]

Fire escapes were another matter the FIC looked into carefully. While many buildings had them, they were often insufficient in number. Protocolist Henry Moskowitz reported to the FIC that in a Joint Board of Sanitary Control investigation, 80 percent of buildings had just one fire escape, and most of these ended a floor before the ground, or led into blind alleys—as was the case with the Asch Building. Many also went past open windows and were too narrow and flimsy to handle the necessary weight. Unionists and Protocolists like Moskowitz were successful in lobbying on this issue. Porter's plan, again in 1911, forbade increased occupancy without additional fire escapes, and in 1912, Whiskeman reported that new fire escapes should have to meet new, tougher standards. Similarly, other FIC recommendations led to laws dealing with inward-opening doors, locked doors, blocked exits and aisles, fire drills, storage of combustibles in fireproof containers, and timely removal of waste.[12]

The FIC extended these early investigations of fire safety from factories into mercantile shops, demonstrating it was to use the occasion of the fire to press labor reforms across workplaces. Frances Perkins, of the Consumers' League and Committee on Safety, led the investigation of mercantile shops. During the process, Perkins educated the "Tammany

Twins," as Al Smith and Robert Wagner were known, on working conditions. "We used to make it our business," remembered Perkins,

> [T]o take Al Smith . . . to see the women, thousands of them, coming off the ten-hour nightshift on the rope walks in Auburn [New York]. We made sure Robert Wagner personally crawled through the tiny hole in the wall that gave exit to a step ladder covered with ice and ending twelve feet from the ground, which was euphemistically labeled "Fire Escape" in many factories. We saw to it that the austere legislative members of the Commission got up at dawn and drove with us for an unannounced visit to a Cattaraugus County cannery and that they saw with their own eyes the little children, not adolescents, but five-, six-, and seven-year-olds, snipping and shelling peas. We made sure that they saw the machinery that would scalp a girl or cut off a man's arm. Hours so long that both men and women were depleted and exhausted became realities to them through seeing for themselves the dirty little factories. . . . [These experiences convinced] members of the Commission that conditions in industry were frequently bad for the workers; that they were correctable by practical means; and that correction by lawful process would benefit industries as well as workers. Production and business would increase and the whole state would profit.[13]

In its first report, the FIC declared that 75 percent of industrial fires could be prevented if the state adopted the FIC's plan. Wagner and Smith were eventually able to get six of their proposed bills through the legislature by early 1913. By mid-1912, however, business and real estate opposition to proposed FIC fire remodification matured. Many business leaders began to see that changes in fire codes would mean higher rents for buildings that needed to be retrofitted to meet the new codes. Governor Dix, responding to political pressure from business interests, vetoed two of the bills.[14]

One of the bills passed required factory owners to provide fireproof containers for flammable waste and to remove them twice a day. It regulated lighting and gas jets as well as prohibited smoking on shop floors. It also divided enforcement between agencies (two state and one local): the local fire commissioner, the state labor commissioner, and the state fire marshal.[15] Another of the bills required fire drills in shops employing more than twenty-five workers.[16] A third required sprinklers in buildings over seven stories high and in factories that employed 200 or more workers. The final bills dealt with tracking, reporting, and enforcing fire inspections between the various state agencies.[17]

Three bills failed to pass, two bills vetoed by Governor Dix, and one that called for the fireproofing of walls, floors, and partitions in new factories with over two stories that died in committee. Of the two vetoed bills, one dealt with fire escapes and the other with occupancy of upper floors in factories with narrow stairs and improper "fire apparatus." The governor claimed that these measures caused jurisdictional conflicts and that the fire escape bill did not go far enough. While the FIC could claim victory, it was at best incomplete.[18]

In 1913, the FIC started where it had left off: trying to strengthen the 1912 provisions on fire safety. The FIC submitted stronger versions of the failed laws of 1912 and several amendments, which tightened enforcement to the governor in 1913. In this case, the new governor, Sulzer, signed the bills, giving New York the most technically advanced set of fire codes in the nation.[19]

Industrial democrats rejoiced in the FIC achievements. The reform journal the *Survey* held a symposium on the changes in state law. Frances Perkins and George Price declared that the FIC had given New York "a skeleton of a complete program of fire prevention," and reformers needed to redouble their efforts to complete the revolution. While some reformers basked in the light of their success, others followed the lead of labor and began to chart a new course for the FIC in the fields of sanitary conditions and industrial accidents. "A fire, such as led immediately to the creation of the Commission, is fortunately of rare occurrence," proclaimed the FIC. "On the other hand, industrial accidents, poisonings, and diseases maim or disable in the state and nation tens of thousands every year. Insufficient ventilation, bad sanitation, and long hours of labor also work their deadly effects."[20]

SANITATION

The FIC's achievement in sanitary reforms demonstrated that it could extend Protocolism. Building on its success in the areas of fire safety, the FIC in 1913 adopted the Protocol's program of the Joint Board of Sanitary Control as its own, making what was a private system of industrial relations (IR) into a public system.

The FIC built on a solid foundation. Reform groups such as the WTUL, Consumers' League, and especially the AALL had already championed sanitary reform, as reforms demanding improved working conditions were called. John B. Andrews, secretary of the AALL, was a leading pioneer in industrial sanitary reform efforts. He had gathered a well-known group of intellectuals, academics, and activists around the AALL. But before the FIC's involvement, the AALL was only able to make recommendations, issue reports, and publish its data. It had little impact outside of academic debate. All that changed in 1913, when the FIC embraced sanitary reform.[21]

Heading the FIC's effort was the nation's leading expert on industrial sanitation: the Protocol's own George M. Price. As director of the Joint Board of Sanitary Control, he had led the nation's largest sustained investigation of worker safety and health since 1910. While other states investigated industry, none took on the scope of the Joint Board. In 1910, his agency had investigated 1,243 shops and, by 1911, that number was 1,738. He quickly assessed the problems in 1911. He was "struck not only with the paucity of measures and enactments relating to safety and sanitation, but especially with the lack of standards, and with the vague, meaningless, and too general language of the various statutes." His broad survey method soon became standard in the growing field of industrial health. Price and the Joint Board were now submerged within the FIC framework. The claim of Thomas Kerr, an FIC historian, that the Joint Board "stood as a prototype for the FIC" underappreciates the way Price co-opted the FIC to carry on the Protocol's agenda.[22]

Price set to work quickly at the FIC, realizing that the FIC could do what the Protocol only dreamed of: create a labor code through law rather than through a system of privately enforced contracts, and it could cover all workers in all industries. In a two-month period in late 1911, Price led his team of ten, borrowed from the Joint Board, in an investigation of 1,838 factories in twenty industries. In addition to this mind-numbing workload, Price and his team physically examined over 800 New York bakeries. Price pushed the FIC in an activist direction from the start. It took two years for the FIC to catch up to this research.[23]

In 1912, Price expanded his research to the entire state. The 1911 mandate bound the FIC in its first year to New York City and issues of fire safety. In the FIC's second year, Price's team investigated 1,338 firms across the state. Within a two-year period, according to the FIC's own statistics, it had investigated 7.1 percent of all businesses in New York State, employing 18.8 percent of all workers in forty-five cities and in over eighty industries.[24]

Widening the focus and meaning of workplace safety, sanitation was Price's mantra. Sanitation included ventilation and heating, as well as working conditions. Price brought in researchers from the AALL who had vast experience with these issues. "There is a tendency on the many employers," wrote Price, "to economize not only in matters of legitimate expense, but also in space, light, air, and certain other safeguards to the health and lives of workers." Price, using the social science research of reform groups, was advancing two important points: workers deserved decent conditions and the state was responsible for ensuring them. Price was pushing industrial democracy past the voluntarism of the Protocol and, in the process, he moved the FIC one step closer to the welfare state and modern liberalism.[25] The bosses "must be shown," he argued, "that the health of the workers is of paramount importance to the state, which not only has the right but is bound to take measures that workers be properly safeguarded in the course of their employment." For Price, the state *was* responsible for maintaining and protecting human life.[26]

Price also orchestrated many of the FIC's public hearings. Witness after witness told of the horrors of working conditions, especially the filth. In the problem of dirty workshops, Price found an issue, a wedge, to win public support for his program. These hearings, as public performances, provided enlightenment as well as entertainment. In many ways, they served much the same purpose as the nineteenth-century lyceums. The public learned the horrors and then was supposed to spring into action. What Price expected Americans, especially the middle class, to learn was that management had such contempt for workers that it let them toil in subhuman conditions. Price and others were resorting to a tried and true American reform tradition: moral swaysion and a sense of moral outrage. By playing on the public's heartstrings, Price believed the FIC could position public acceptance for a revolution in governance: the acceptance that the state was responsible for people's welfare.[27]

Price's investigations were convincing. The numbers made clear that too many factories were clearly unsanitary—but what to do about them? The FIC recognized that merely passing new laws would do little unless there was a comprehensive enforcement mechanism. To this end, the researchers recommended that factories register for licenses with the State Labor Department, and that the Department have authority to investigate any factory. If a factory were found in violation of the sanitary codes, the Department would then revoke its license, putting it out of business. This was essentially how the Protocol's Joint Board of Sanitary Control functioned. Now he proposed it as a state policy. Price had originally proposed this for bakeries and other food industries, but the idea soon spread. This was a variation—clearly a much larger one—on the union label campaign that Price ran as part of the Joint Board of Sanitary Control under the Protocol.[28]

Enforcement soon became an important issue. Licensing might help, but only if the laws were clearly defined and enforced. Existing laws were often so vague as to be meaningless. Often they referred to "adequate," "sufficient," or "proper" conditions, but rarely did they explain what these terms meant. Some FIC policy makers argued that the Labor Department should be allowed to create rules. Price, for one, urged that the Department be given such rule-making authority, in essence, giving it the power to evaluate and apply laws on a case-by-case basis. Price also offered an entire set of sanitation proposals dealing with washrooms, dressing rooms, and toilets. Price, taking with him his Joint Board experience, knew that independence and rule-making authority were important. Because on the surface, sanitation did not appear to be a controversial issue, Price was able to keep the issues of working conditions front and center for the FIC. And in doing so, he helped keep the rank and filers in the FIC coalition.[29]

THE "DANGEROUS TRADES"

Another area that the FIC tackled during its first period was the so-called dangerous trades. Work was dangerous, often deadly, in America.[30] The FIC moved to investigate safety and health in part because of the obvious connections between sanitation and health. But it also did so because of the unrelenting pressure from industrial democrats. Price, along with Columbia University political economist and the leading light behind the New York AALL, Henry Seager, and social worker Josephine Goldmark, besieged the FIC to move quickly in this area.[31]

Price enlisted a small army of industrial hygienists to testify about industrial disease and poisoning. Experts testified to the problems of lung disease and lead poisoning, among others. The FIC paid particular attention to the growing use of chemicals in industry, and it found overall that the hazards were both "terrifying and unnecessarily numerous." To further highlight the scientific evidence, the FIC paraded legions of injured workers before the public, putting human faces on the numbers. This testimony established a rationale for the FIC recommendations regarding remedial legislation to protect workers.[32]

The FIC focused on lead poisoning. Dr. Edward E. Pratt, of the School for Philanthropy in New York City, led a team of thirteen students and investigated 376 cases of reported lead poisoning among workers. Fifty percent of these workers were under forty-five years of age. They were so injured that they could never work again. None of them recalled ever being warned of the dangers they faced at the workplace. They spoke of eating at the same tables on which they worked. All the while, employers refused to take responsibility, claiming that the workers assumed all the risk.[33]

Building on his work under the Protocol, Price demanded a legislative response to industries that were dangerous to workers' health. He demanded periodical medical investigations and detailed reports. Price's demands raised more questions than answers. Where would the line be drawn and by whom? What would the politics of industrial democracy look like when it included health? Unable to win sweeping reforms, Price moved cautiously toward reforming certain notorious industries.[34]

One industry that received FIC attention was the baking industry. As early as 1896, mostly to improve sanitary conditions, the legislature in New York mandated that work in bakeries be limited to a ten-hour day and a sixty-hour workweek. But the U.S. Supreme Court had declared the law unconstitutional in a famous 1905 case, *Lochner v. New York*, arguing that the state had exceeded its police powers.[35]

Price and Pauline Goldmark of the Consumers' League provided the FIC with a new line of argument and scientific ammunition. Starting in 1911 and continuing through 1912, Price investigated 625 bakeries and hundreds of workers. At the same time, Goldmark, through the Consumers' League, conducted an independent investigation of the industry. The evidence was overwhelming and horrific. The FIC reported that a large number of bakeries were in cellars, lacking lighting, ventilation, plumbing, and many other necessities. Sewer pipes, puddles of stagnant water, and rats abounded. Dust, animal droppings, and everything else fell into the dough. Only 22 percent of the bakeries had toilets and most of these were found to be unsanitary. To the Commission and public, it was clear that unsanitary bakeries endangered both workers and consumers.[36] New Yorkers reacted to these reports in ways that resembled how Americans reacted to Upton Sinclair's *The Jungle*. To paraphrase Sinclair, Price and company were aiming for the hearts of New York, but instead hit them in the stomachs.[37]

In contrast to his early successes, though, Price soon found a strong vocal opposition on this issue. Real estate interests, bakers, and the flour industry protested. They argued that licenses, medical examinations, and inspections would eventually lead to higher bread prices and would drive small businessmen out of business. Opponents could not, however, deny the evidence: bakeries were unsanitary. So instead, they ignored it.[38]

Price and the FIC met the opposition head-on, arguing for the prohibition of new cellar bakeries and stronger enforcement powers for the Labor Department. In New York, Price demanded that enforcement be handled by the Health Department and also called for licenses for bakers and medical examinations for employees. The FIC went along with his requests, and in both 1911 and 1912 included specific legislation regarding bakeries.[39] Price and others on the FIC staff saw bakery regulation as a model for regulation that could be expanded to all industries.

Through investigations of foundries, department stores, and a host of other industries, the FIC developed a case for government intervention in the workplace to protect and preserve human life, or, as Dr. Charles R. Graham-Rogers put it, "conservation of life."[40] "Our system of industrial production," argued Dr. Price,

> [H]as taken gigantic strides in the progressive utilization of natural resources and the exploitation of the inventive genius of the human mind, but has at the same time shown terrible waste of human resources, of human health and life.[41]

FIC investigations of sanitary conditions and workers' health revealed the underlying economic policies that drove its reforms. Wagner stated the FIC's fundamental principle: laws were needed to provide that "the working man may be preserved in health" from the abuses of industrialism.[42]

The FIC marked a distinct change in government policy away from the laissez-faire philosophy of the day. To be sure, many business attitudes remained unchanged. "I don't believe we are under any obligation," said one manufacturer, "to work and force spiritual and mental improvement on the men because they work for us." Another simply said: "This is not a charitable business."[43] But the three bills dealing with sanitation and health, which became law in 1912, brought a new set of responsibilities to the state. The first law amended a 1909 tenement act, which allowed the labor commissioner to inspect tenement shops. If filthy workrooms were discovered, the items (mostly garments) would be marked as unsanitary and could not be sold. Only if a future inspection revealed changes would these tags be removed. This clearly was an aid to the Protocol's very own efforts. The second act amended a 1910 law requiring employers to provide drinking water, washrooms, and toilets. It required that if poisons or gases were used in production, hot water had to be provided. As ineffective as this law was, it was the first to deal with dangerous trades. It also forbid employees from eating in workrooms; employers had to provide separate, sanitary eating areas. Finally, the third new measure required all businesses to register with the Labor Department. This law was designed to allow further investigation and the collection of statistics.[44]

While the FIC never lost complete interest in sanitation and industrial disease, after 1913, its focus shifted to other areas. Sensing that their demands for the protection of all workers were falling on deaf ears, the FIC shifted to the issue of protection of women and children, which will be discussed in Chapter 7.

ADMINISTRATIVE REFORMS

Another area in which reformers focused their attention during the first phase of the FIC was in the administration of labor law. These experiences with safety, sanitation, and industrial accidents taught them the need to refine enforcement of labor laws and code. "Labor laws," argued Price, "stand below all other laws [in their]... lack of Scientific Standards." This spirit was evident in the working-class community. When Rabbi Stephen Wise rose to address the assembled crowd at the Metropolitan Opera House after the fire, he said as much: "We have laws that in a time of crisis we find are no laws and we have enforcement that when the hour of trial comes we find is no enforcement."[45]

Many agreed that it was nearly impossible to measure the effectiveness of the current labor laws.[46] "The laws are perfect," stated John

Coleman, an upstate labor council president. But, he added, "the trouble is they are not enforced." Other labor spokesmen and reform women voiced a similar understanding of the problem. They suggested the need for more inspectors, stiffer penalties, and licensing and registration for better record keeping. Some argued for giving more power to labor inspectors and for the reorganization and centralization of labor law enforcement. In sum, reformers directed the FIC toward greater enforcement in this complicated area.[47]

For their part, bureaucrats laboring within the developing labyrinth of state and local agencies charged with administering the labor laws admitted their frustration with the limited and inadequate nature of the current system. They paraded before the FIC at public hearings and spoke of the enormous task presented them, the limited budgets, and the even more limited personnel available for their Herculean tasks. Many also told of confusing legal structures. They were only able to inspect workplaces after receiving complaints. They could merely issue warnings, but could not return to the offending factory for follow-up inspections until the following year. In fact, one inspector mentioned that factory owners regularly prepared for inspection.[48]

Like the labor spokespersons, these low-level government bureaucrats lacked a clear solution to what they saw as a major dilemma. They too demanded increased budgets for inspection and personnel, increased and clearer powers, and greater guidelines. Some argued for more centralization, for one body that would oversee all labor law. Others demanded a more localized solution; giving power to the localities, they argued, would eliminate confusion, streamline inspection, eliminate red tape, and clarify lines of authority.

In the end, then, government inspectors failed to give the FIC a unified program of reform, and without a strong mandate, FIC leaders were free to create their own.[49] They sent out a detailed questionnaire to labor, business, and reform leaders. The survey looked at four areas: enforcement, research, executive authority of state agencies, and conflicts over jurisdiction. Responses demonstrated wide support for enhancing and expanding labor-law enforcement efforts. Some demanded that labor commissioners be given greater authority. Others argued for the establishment of an "expert panel" to assist commissioners. Half the respondents, however, did not endorse the idea of a permanent labor commission to replace the commissioner.[50]

In the years between the creation of the Labor Department in 1901 and the FIC, reform groups, especially the AALL, the Consumer's League, and the WTUL, as well as work by unions, had convinced the state legislature to expand the 1901 statute. The legislature authorized the addition of inspectors. It then authorized the Department to inspect mercantile establishments, which originally were exempted from the 1901 law. Finally, new departments were added in immigration and research.

These new amendments aimed to improve factory inspection, but the effect was to create a growing bureaucracy without a clear sense of direction. Even with a staff of 203, by 1912, the piecemeal efforts of these amendments never allowed the Labor Department to keep pace with the explosion of new industrial sites. The lack of a department-wide administrative policy complicated the Department's problems. The Department was divided into eight districts, with an autonomous head for each. Within their own districts, these directors interpreted the statutes as they saw fit. Therefore, each district, in effect, had a different set of rules, with different standards of enforcement. Reformers, especially those surrounding the FIC, saw the "Wisconsin Model" of an independent industrial commission as a solution to these problems. Wisconsin provided for the establishment of boards with broad enforcement power.[51]

The FIC's ties to Tammany Hall, however, compelled it to offer its own modified version of the Wisconsin plan. It objected to giving power to an independent "expert" body. It wanted to make any expert accountable to political forces. Rather than recommending the appointment of an independent, expert panel with rule-making powers, the FIC recommended two changes. In an effort to control reform, it recommended the establishment of an Industrial Board and the retention of the labor commissioner. The Board would include several (later five) experts and be granted limited rule-making authority, much like the Protocol's Arbitration Board. Unlike the Wisconsin model, the New York Board would be less autonomous and operate under legislative guidelines. The second recommendation was the establishment of the labor commissioner as a labor czar of sorts. This political appointee would be granted great powers to apply standards, enforce laws, and implement the Board's decisions. However, the commissioner would not be granted powers to make rules him/herself. In this, the legislature refused to give up its authority.[52]

Wagner and Smith took the lead in selling the modified plan to the various members of the coalition. Labor had deep reservations about the creation of an expert panel. Many worried about settlement workers taking over labor regulation. They were also concerned about the division between the Board and the czar. Could enforcement be achieved? Manufacturers, who also objected to the rise of independent experts, were satisfied with the diminished role they would play in New York.[53]

Wagner and Smith knew which way the political winds were blowing on this issue. During the election of 1912, the ineptitude of the Labor Department had become a campaign issue for all three major parties. Both Democrats and Republicans called for reorganization of the Department in their platforms. Bullmoose Progressives had not given up hope of a Wisconsin-type settlement in New York and demanded a Labor Department that had "authority to make and enforce regulations." Thus, after the election, Governor William Sulzer made reorganization one of his priorities. Wagner and Smith, in this atmosphere, could count on support for their plan that did not exist a year before.[54]

Empowered with their new legislative authority, in its 1913 report, the FIC included a new bill to revamp the state Labor Department. It again increased the staff of inspectors and raised the salaries to help attract more professionals to the positions. To replace the one medical inspector for the state, the FIC bill proposed the creation of a Division of Industrial Hygiene. Modeled after the Protocol's Joint Board of Sanitary Control, this new Division would be headed by a chief medical inspector, who would be a licensed physician. In addition, the Division would hire a mechanical engineer, a civil engineer, and a chemical engineer. This Division would serve as a research and educational arm for the Industrial Board. Also, the Department of Labor Statistics became a full-fledged bureau with separate divisions: statistics, industrial and manufacturing directory, industrial accidents and disease, and special investigations.[55]

At the center of the FIC's 1913 reorganization plans stood the Industrial Board. The Board was to be the institutionalization of something new to New York, but with early precedents in the federal Bureau of Labor Statistics: the labor expert as legislative actor. It drew on the Protocol idea of a public interest in labor relations but provided for enforcement power by locating the expert's authority in a state-regulated agency. The state would take on, in limited form at first, the reins of labor relations to

"harmonize the interests of both worker and employer." The Industrial
Board was, in short, the fulfillment of the Protocolist idea of industrial
democracy. Like the Protocol, the State Industrial Board would "act as
an educational agency." But, most importantly, the Board would install
"into general practice the best methods of production now in use in
establishments of the highest scientific efficiency." The Board would replace a system that was "arbitrary in character" with one with "reasonable elasticity and flexibility . . . [in dealing with] the progress of industry
and its varying conditions." The Board would embody "reasonable authority" to make rules "too great to entrust to any one individual [or
class]."[56]

In many ways, the Board was the culmination of the Protocol, but it
also marked the subsuming of the Protocol within the FIC. After 1913,
as the Protocol was dying, its seeds were planted firmly within the state
through the FIC. In the bill authorizing the Board, the FIC declared
its overall policy: "All factories, factory buildings, mercantile establishments and other places, shall be constructed, equipped, arranged, operated and conducted . . . to provide . . . adequate protection to the lives,
health and safety of all persons employed therein." The Board, to implement this policy, would "make, alter, amend and repeal rules." The FIC
gave the Board substantial powers to interpret and enforce laws. Yet, in
the end, it was not granted the power to enact legislation.[57]

The FIC act would grant the Board some legislative powers. It could
investigate, and, more importantly, it could subpoena witnesses and
request records. Also, its decisions would receive "the force and effect
of law." To prevent secretive meetings, the Board would have to hold
public hearings and would need the majority of Board members to make
decisions. In addition to the commissioners, four other members would
be nominated by the governor and would need senate approval. Thus,
mixing labor, business, and expert/reformer representatives among its
appointees, the Board became the state embodiment of the Protocol's
tripartite ideal.[58]

The composition of the Board reveals the drafters' true intentions.
While the FIC recommended a labor appointee, none was made. The
leading light of the Board was Pauline Goldmark, social worker, reformer, and executive secretary of the Consumers' League. Goldmark,
appointed Board secretary, played a central role in how the newly reconstituted Labor Department would function. Goldmark would, through

her efforts to professionalize the Department, further remove labor from the higher and more important levels of the Department, making the Department the bastion of the "neutral" liberal expert.[59]

Wagner and Smith tried to stop this winnowing of labor representation that developed within the Department. They blocked various attempts by Sulzer to appoint a reformer to the position of labor commissioner. They were holding out for someone more acceptable to labor. For months, the position lay vacant. And without anyone in the key position, the reorganization stagnated. Goldmark tried to take charge, but without the powers of commissioner, her efforts stalled. When a terrible factory fire that was reminiscent of the Triangle Fire occurred in Binghamton, reformers blamed Tammany Hall. Sulzer publicly denounced the Hall for holding up the Department's reorganization and declared that if Tammany had not blocked the nominations, the fire would have been prevented and thus lives saved. This episode reinforced in the minds of reformers the need to keep politics out of labor enforcement.[60]

The episode over the appointment of a labor commissioner strapped the hands of Wagner and Smith. The dispute between Goldmark and Tammany fed into the growing battle between Sulzer and Tammany Hall, which alternatively led to Sulzer's impeachment. This process diverted the attention of Smith and Wagner—who, as Tammany Hall leaders, led the charge against Sulzer. Labor legislation, therefore, was put on the back burner until the beginning of 1914. After the disposal of Sulzer, Wagner and Smith returned to the FIC with a renewed sense of urgency and tackled the issue of the administration of the law itself. To redraft the state's laws, the FIC appointed a special advisory panel of legal experts and hired the Bill Drafting Bureau of Columbia University. Of special concern to Wagner and FIC staffers was the constitutionality of these new laws.[61]

The recodification project was an effort to achieve greater efficiency in labor law administration. This streamlining effort placed all labor laws under general headings and, more importantly, consolidated and rationalized the state's laws dealing with labor. The goal of this effort was "to preserve the policies of the present substantive law, but to state those policies more clearly, more briefly, and more consistently with each other." At the end of its work in 1914, the FIC submitted its massive efforts to the legislature in a series of bills.[62]

Because the FIC came to address recodification late in the legislative season, public hearings were out of the question. While the FIC received wide support from reformers, labor was at best lukewarm to this idea. Gompers, the voice of the conservative, skilled sector of labor, slowed down the move for recodification. The FIC drafted the bill, but Smith and Wagner did not maneuver for its passage. They took a slower approach. Not giving up on the effort, but hoping to bring labor along, they postponed until 1915 their efforts in this area.[63]

As the 1914 legislative season ended, FIC staff and allies began the siege for labor law reform. The FIC, in an effort to build support in a time when it was not formally in session and therefore could not hold public hearings, sought the opinions of reformers, labor, and management leaders. In addition, the FIC appointed two panels to advise it on this issue, one was for New York City and the other for upstate.[64]

In 1915, the FIC presented a more refined version of recodification closely resembling the plan first presented in 1914. The 1915 bill, unlike the now dead 1914 bill, clearly delineated the legal differences between shops and factories (important because different laws applied to each). The new bill also would allow the Industrial Board to grant variances in individual cases. Aside from these "improvements," the 1915 bill closely resembled the 1914 bill.[65]

As with the derailed 1914 bill, the FIC again failed to "educate" the key members of the coalition. People such as George Price, who consistently voiced the concern of workers, was unconvinced that this new 1915 bill could prevent abuses by manufacturers. In short, Price and other labor spokesmen failed to see the issue of recodification as the magic bullet reformers had. The FIC's insistence on this as one of its main concerns in 1915 essentially pushed labor out of the coalition. Samuel Gompers threatened to resign from the FIC over this and other issues. With a deeply divided coalition and the growing strength of the Republican Party in 1915, the FIC had more to worry about than recodification. Republicans used this and other issues to strip the FIC of funds and eventually kill it. The FIC spent the last months of its life trying desperately to cling to life and protect its past agenda.[66]

Another rift that developed over the issue of appointments also weakened the FIC coalition. Reformers demanded the strict enforcement of civil service examinations and the appointment of only "qualified" experts to the Labor Department. Seeking to make room for their own members to hold these positions, labor union representatives demanded that appointees have "practical knowledge" of the issues. Tammany Hall supported labor in this battle. As Smith and Wagner pushed through labor appointees, reformers attacked them as unqualified and as a detriment to labor law reform. The reform-minded *Survey* reported that "the Tammany Tiger's paw [was] on labor laws in New York State." And, it was right.[67]

In subsequent years, as the state became the forum for labor relations in New York after 1915, both labor and management would learn to adjust. Labor would also learn to live with liberal reformers. Unions, recognizing the need to remain close politically to these reformers, would form a marriage of sorts with them. And workers, while gaining materially from this relationship, slowly would see the prize of industrial democracy slip away.

7   Industrial Democracy Meets the Welfare State in Progressive Era New York

"My Fingers is Broke": Women and Children First[1]

The Factory Investigating Commission (FIC) transformed Protocolism and industrial democracy by bringing in the state. The state took responsibility for policing industry, ensuring humane working conditions, and setting up standard industry practices—all part of the Protocol's agenda for industrial democracy. Having achieved a limited success with this agenda, the FIC moved beyond "standard" labor issues into the realm of social welfare reform. Too often, scholars fail to see welfare reforms as part of a larger labor reform program. In many ways, the FIC's turn to welfare was a natural and logical outgrowth of its evolving understanding of industrial democracy.

Having moved from reform successes in safety, sanitation, and health to the failures of recodification, by 1912 the FIC took up social welfare. By then, the FIC had begun efforts to curb child labor and "protect" women workers in New York. Industrial democrats, having failed to find that wedge with sanitation and health that they wanted, turned to New York's immigrant, working-class women and children to provide a successful doorway to the welfare state. In the process, they forever transformed industrial democracy. This transformation in industrial democracy is pivotal in the evolution and development of modern liberalism. In the end, as we shall see, this effort further removed labor from the picture and exalted reformers into penultimate positions of power, transforming workers from partners in industrial democracy to mere clients.

The FIC laws for women and children used a moral and racialized language of conservation to argue for "protective" legislation. The FIC's most effective arguments demanded state intervention to protect the nation's "natural resources." This was effective precisely because

189

Progressives within the FIC coalition saw childhood and motherhood as sacred.[2]

Reformers associated with the FIC believed that most workers, especially women and children, were in weak economic positions. They did not have power to ameliorate their condition, nor could they get a fair bargain with employers. No Protocol would aid them. To many progressives, the plight of children was complicated by the failure of mothers to come to the aid of children, even if they worked alongside them. For such reformers, there was little alternative but to step in and "save" both the oppressed children and their mothers, who were seen as simultaneously negligent and exploited. It was with this moral mission that the FIC tread new ground in Progressive Era America. Using the arguments of conservation, tinged with Darwinian discourse, the FIC argued that the state had a sacred duty to "conserve their [women and children's] physical . . . interests." Robert Wagner, FIC chair, summed up the new philosophy this way: "The girl of to-day is the mother of to-morrow . . . we have to preserve her a little better if we are going to have good future citizens."[3]

The FIC's moralisms incorporated into legislation a new emerging conception of civilization informed by colonial adventures and the "ordering" of immigrants at home. As historian Gail Bederman argues, changing definitions of manhood at the time led to new theories about civilization, whereby the "enlightened" had a responsibility to protect the weak to prove their superiority, and to guide the uncivilized masses into civilization. Bederman argues that Progressives believed in a system of biological and environmental determinism in which degenerate conditions could produce degenerate races. Reform could "raise" the immigrants, making them Americans, all the while protecting our biological stock.[4]

For many FIC reformers, trade unions were the best vehicle to reform the abuses workers faced. But the unions' failures in organizing women workers, and the lack of union efforts around child labor issues, forced many FIC reformers to search for a more immediate means to protect these special workers. In doing so, they slowly abandoned their union allies to pursue an independent legislative strategy of their own devising. The case of FIC reformer Frances Perkins is illustrative. Recalling years later in an oral history interview her actions and motivations during this period, she straightforwardly stated: "I'd rather pass a law than organize a union." The Triangle Fire had demonstrated just how weak unions and women workers were. She continued:

> We could drag Rosie Schneiderman up and say, "See, she's the President of a union." But it was a pretty weak union back of her . . . we took the lead and made the battle to get a law limiting the hours of labor of women. That, I think, was much more important than organization—much more important. They would never have had their hours reduced, if we hadn't gotten the legislation first.[5]

The FIC marks a sea change in the relationship between labor—unorganized as well as organized workers—and the state. Starting in 1912, reform demonstrated that the state had the capability and capacity to alter for the better the physical conditions of work: it could reduce hours, end deplorable conditions, and raise pay. The Protocol had promised such improvements, but by 1915, it still had not delivered them to the vast army of labor.[6]

Using the research of previous reformers, the FIC detailed the particular strains that industrialism placed on women workers. Standing at work for long hours, for instance, put undue stress on a woman's reproductive organs, and, reformers concluded, such regimes should be avoided. Therefore, starting in 1912, the FIC drafted a bill that required workplaces be fitted with seats with a back angle of no more than 100 degrees. When the legislation was amended the next year to require seats with backs but no defined angles, the bill passed and became law.[7]

During the first year of investigation, the FIC received numerous proposals to exclude women from a host of dangerous trades, to limit their exposure to hazards, and thus, to protect them. This movement was pioneered by the Consumer's League. Led by the actions of Frances Perkins, FIC staffer and League secretary, the FIC sent out a questionnaire to reformers on this issue. Overwhelmingly, the respondents suggested removing women from all strenuous activities. But the FIC rejected this position. Instead, it decided to focus on the work of women in one particularly onerous heavy industry—foundries—as an example of the problems women faced in industry. The FIC focused in on the core-room workers, where fewer than 300 women worked statewide.[8]

In choosing a heavy, skilled trade like foundry work as a test case, the FIC reformers chose wisely. The choice gave them a powerful ally in American Federation of Labor (AFL) President and FIC Commissioner Samuel Gompers. Gompers, as the representative of skilled, male workers, understood the issue. Molders argued that the presence of women in the core rooms undercut their wages and made it difficult for men to support their families. The Molders' Union had presented a bill excluding women from core making to the legislature in 1910, but it had failed to pass. Now, with Gompers as a commission member, it was revived and readdressed. The molders now replaced this family wage argument with a protective one: in 1912, they argued that core rooms had hidden dangers for women and, for their own protection, women should be excluded. "The foundry," argued one union leader "is no place for females, because of the brutal character of the work and the unhealthy and unhygienic conditions surrounding such employment." This argument played well with the FIC reformers, whose own maternalistic ideology said that women belonged at home with their children. Equally important, however, this position demonstrates just how closely linked materialistic protection and paternalism were for the FIC.[9]

Employers, of course, challenged the union's claims. At first, they argued that the union was using this claim simply as a way to increase its member's wages. When they sensed that this argument was not winning favor with the commissioners, foundry owners began to defend the women's right to work. Arguing that "light core making, under proper conditions, is entirely fitting work for women ... [and] gives them an opportunity to work," they described the terrible hardships women would face if denied this opportunity.[10]

After hearing from both sides and conducting an intense survey of the industry, the FIC recommended removal of the women. "Instincts of chivalry and decency," the commission stated, "as well as concern for the preservation of the race, demand that we should not permit women to engage in work detrimental to their health, that overtaxes their strength, and impaired their vitality as wives and mothers."[11] The law as passed in 1913 prohibited women from core making in oven rooms. It also authorized the Industrial Board to limit the work of women in core rooms based on the "health and safety of women."[12]

The issue of pregnant and postpartum women workers furthered the FIC's paternalistic protective campaign. As early as 1909, state factory medical inspectors had urged post-birth restrictions. Dr. C. T. Graham-Rogers wrote claiming a relationship extended between infant mortality and post-childbirth employment of mothers. In 1911, the Consumers' League added its voice to this campaign. Soon, it was joined by the

American Association for Labor Legislation (AALL), the Women's Trade Union League (WTUL), the *Survey*, and the United Garment Workers (UGW). Some reformers demanded a total ban on the employment of these workers, but most requested a four- to six-week ban before and after birth. Reformers couched their demands in the language of health. Relying on the model of a Massachusetts law that restricted itself to post-childbirth restrictions, the FIC-initiated law forbid the hiring of women for four weeks after childbirth.[13]

The FIC's approach to protecting the health and safety of women workers next focused on reducing the hours of their labor. There was a strong tradition in New York of restricting women's hours. In 1886, a law prohibited women under twenty-one from working more than sixty hours a week. In 1899, the law was expanded to cover all women. A 1906 law forbid the employment of women for more than twelve hours a day. The basis of these laws, as legal historian Melvin Urofsky has argued, was the special need to protect women workers. By arguing for a special category, the laws' framers were able to expand the powers of the state's police powers.[14]

The campaign for shorter hours legislation for New York's women workers was spearheaded by Mary Dreier, FIC commissioner, industrial democrat, and New York WTUL president. A parade of workers were called to testify about the harm of long hours on women workers. Doctors, public health officials, union leaders, and workers themselves pleaded their case before an understanding Commission. The chorus was clear. "Long hours," as one expert testified, "are the cause of all the ills woman's flesh is heir to." In many ways, the FIC came to see shorter hours as a magic bullet to solve all the problems women faced at the workplace. The bill that the FIC drafted and that became law soon after, established a fifty-four-hour week for women. In addition, it provided for a nine-hour day. It did provide a stipulation that as long as the hours did not exceed fifty-four, women could work three days of up to ten hours per day. Significantly, none of these efforts applied to male workers. Dreier, a tireless advocate for hours legislation, immediately began to demand a forty-eight-hour law and an eight-hour day. But, employer resistance and an onslaught of bills in the legislature exempting industries put the FIC on the defense.[15]

Undaunted, Dreier redoubled her efforts by focusing on women mercantile workers. Again, there was historical antecedent. An 1896 law provided for a sixty-hour week and ten-hour day maximum for women mercantile workers under twenty-one. Exemptions were made for a two-week period surrounding Christmas and for municipalities whose populations were under 3,000. These laws were administered by local health departments.[16] Now responding to pressure from reform groups, notably the Consumer's League, in 1912 the FIC received authorization from the state legislature to study mercantile establishments. Frances Perkins, FIC staffer and League stalwart, directed the research. The New York Consumer's League and the New York State Child Labor Committee staffed and conducted the study.[17]

Pauline Goldmark and George A. Hall, under the direction of Perkins, studied 216 mercantile establishments in the nine largest cities of the state. Of the 61,717 employees, women constituted over 60 percent. The average workweek was more than fifty-four hours. Many worked eighty- to ninety-hour weeks during busy seasons. They complained of "extreme fatigue." Almost everywhere, merchants openly violated local laws, or simply ignored them because of lack of enforcement.[18]

Based upon the 1912 study, the FIC in 1913 recommended that factory standards be applied to stores. Legislators agreed, but only in part: legislation applied the nine-hour day, fifty-four-hour week to women mercantile workers in six second-class cities with populations of 50,000 to 175,000. Larger cities were uncovered, in part due to the strength of the opposition of these cities' merchant classes.[19]

Sensing an opportunity, the Consumer's League demanded that the laws be expanded to all cities. In 1914, through Frances Perkins, the expansion of mercantile laws became a major concern for the FIC. Without further hearings or research, because of Perkins's influence and Dreier's ministrations, the FIC proposed a bill that applied the nine-hour day and fifty-four-hour week to all towns with a population above 3,000.[20]

One issue united reformers' concern for health and their obsession with women's morality: night work for women. Again, this had received legislative attention before 1911. In 1889, the state legislature forbade the employment of women under twenty-one in factory employment between the hours of 9:00 P.M. and 6:00 A.M. An amendment in 1899 extended this law to mercantile establishments. Another law, again in 1899, extended the night prohibition to *all* women workers, but excluded department store workers over twenty-one.[21]

In 1907, however, the state handed reformers a setback when the New York State Court of Appeals declared the 1899 law unconstitutional.

There was an unseen benefit, as reformers quickly noted. While the court declared that the 1899 law violated women's right to contract, it did not agree that the state had a compelling interest or reason to extend its police powers. It suggested that the state, however, could extend such powers for "the purpose of promoting health." Soon after the New York State decision, the Supreme Court handed down its famous *Muller v. Oregon* decision. What convinced the Court in *Muller* was the sociological evidence that none other than Louis Brandeis reported in his argument before the Court that there were links between long hours and women's poor health. So, armed with *Muller* and the State Appeals Court decision, New York reformers pushed forward. By 1911, they made restrictions in night work for women part of the FIC's agenda.[22]

Before the first meeting of the FIC, then, reformers in New York had gravitated to the issue of prohibition of night work for women workers. This was part and parcel of the larger movement to shorten hours for all workers. By piggybacking their reforms on women workers, they sought to develop a powerful wedge for larger reforms that would deal with all workers—male as well as female. As we will see, many of these reformers used gender "difference" to make their case for special protection.[23]

During the first year, the FIC simply studied the issue. Witnesses argued for night-work prohibition. The FIC distributed questionnaires. Researchers were careful to demonstrate the negative impact night work had on women's health, in keeping with the court's recent decisions. Investigators studied more than 250 individual female night workers. The testimony of the findings and researchers were clear: night work physically harmed women. The testimony documented that women, in addition to working in factories, still had domestic responsibilities. They spent their days cleaning, cooking, and tending to husbands and children, and then they worked nine hours. Women night workers, the FIC reported, got by with as little as four-and-a-half hours of sleep per night. These overworked women were more susceptible to disease and illnesses. Dr. Price, who led one of the teams of investigators, argued that night work was "the greatest evil of modern industrial life." It sapped women's strength and caused harm to the race.[24]

To further bolster their claims, reformers also stressed the immorality of night work. Their pronouncements suggested that "moral" women would not be out "on the streets" at night. So-called expert testimony told of the danger of being alone at night. Social workers testified that women working at night might not be able to find a "responsible" boarding house in which to live. Most of these houses had rules about entry after certain times. These women would be forced to live in indecent housing surrounded by "public women." They could easily be led astray. "It has universally been found," said one FIC commissioner, "that such work renders women liable to unusual moral dangers and temptations." Restrictions, therefore, were necessary for "the health and public welfare."[25] One 1910 study, which mirrored the FIC in its findings, argued that industrial work was counter to the natural role women should play in society that of wife and mother. The report stated:

> [T]he prime function of women in society is not 'speeding up' on a machine; it is not turning out so many dozen gross of buttons . . . in a day. . . . The prime function of women must ever be the perpetuation of the race. If these other activities render her physically or morally unfit for the discharge of this larger social duty, then woe to the generations that not only permit but encourage such wanton prostitution of function. The woman is worth more to society in dollars and cents as the mother of healthy children than as the swiftest labeler of cans.[26]

Reformers coupled the argument of physical and moral harm with an economic argument. One commissioner argued that these laws would not hurt "legitimate industry," an argument Protocolists would agree with. By removing women workers, greater efficiency in the workplace would follow and profits would rise. Writing in 1919, labor economist Don Lescohier, harkening back to earlier notions of industrial democracy, explained this argument as one of rationality. "Short hours of labor," Lescohier argued, "are practical only when employees have physical and nervous vigor so that they can work hard and fast. They inevitably make unemployable the slow and the weak." The FIC, like the Protocol, was focused on efficiency in work, seeing women as slow and weak. Social welfare historian Michael Katz explains the larger process as an adjustment of the labor supply, or as "policies that cleared the labor market of workers newly made unproductive by technological development." "Anxious to rid their factories and offices of workers insufficiently speedy and productive," Katz explains, "yet afraid of the impact on the work ethic and labor relations of a large, demoralized class of casual labor, management looked for ways to eliminate unwanted workers not only from their workplaces but, as well, from the workforce." Prohibition and other restrictive labor laws fit the bill.[27]

Building on social scientific as well as moral arguments, then, the FIC, in 1913, presented a bill that called for the elimination of all night work for women between the hours of 10:00 P.M. and 6:00 A.M. To ensure its constitutionality, the bill argued that the measure was designed "to protect the health and morals of females" in the state of New York. The bill became law soon after it was introduced.[28] In turn, the legislature, with FIC prodding, enacted a law that extended the FIC statute to mercantile workers.[29]

The FIC used protective precedents to extend its labor reform efforts. Combining arguments of physical need and moral reform, the FIC next moved for a statutory weekly rest day for the state's workers, regardless of gender. The AALL and John Fitch, author of the authoritative industrial study of the day, *The Pittsburgh Survey*, pressed the FIC to recommend one day of rest for the state's workers regardless of gender. Fitch blended arguments of "moral health" and "physical health" in making the case. This gender-free case, however, was an exception to the FIC's increasing reliance on protective legislation for women. FIC reformers rarely made such open distinctions between moral and physical arguments. For Fitch, however, the same arguments used to convince the legislature to protect women could be used to protect men. The two were not necessarily mutually exclusive.[30]

Fitch, the AALL, and the WTUL were joined by a variety of religious groups in calling for one day in seven as a rest day for the state's workers. While they remained opposed to protective legislation around public health issues, the Day of Rest Conference and the New York Sabbath Committee supported a Sabbath closing law on high moral grounds. Yet, despite the combined efforts of reformers and religious leaders, the FIC as a whole remained cautious about initiating legislation that was not clearly tied to health concerns and thereby moved slowly on this issue. Still, while the FIC did not specifically endorse a Sabbath bill, Wagner and Smith were active in the law's passage. In 1913, working outside the normal FIC channels, reformers, with the AALL, drafted a bill providing one day in seven for rest. It permitted each worker to receive a twenty-four-hour rest period after seven days of work. It exempted janitors and watchmen, who of course were usually men, and provided that the Industrial Board could expand the exemptions as needed.[31]

SAVING THE CHILDREN

The human conservation focus of the FIC demonstrates the centrality of a paternalistic ideology to its leaders. Nothing more clearly illustrates this than the FIC's efforts involving children. The employment of children in industry was an age-old concern for reformers.[32] During the first decade of the twentieth century, the number of children working for wages increased dramatically. In 1907, localities issued 16,032 work permits for children under sixteen. Four years later, the number of permits rose to 40,037. And without valid statistics, one could only guess the large number working without permits. Reformers and labor unions joined forces in an attempt to end this problem.[33]

By 1911, the leading advocates of work-permit reform had united in the New York Child Labor Committee. Here, the AALL, WTUL, Consumer's League, AFL, and other reform and labor groups united around a common legislative agenda. The Child Labor Committee coordinated research and publication of their findings. So forceful were these groups that the FIC authorized no further research, accepting the Committee's research as its own.[34]

New York had enacted child labor laws as early as 1886. There was a pattern that one can see from the early child labor laws in New York: the focus was on age. These laws prevented, or were at least designed to prevent, the employment of children under the age of fourteen (later sixteen), from working in "dangerous trades." The FIC shifted this focus on age to issues of health and safety, where it thought itself to be on firmer constitutional ground. In 1913, the FIC-sponsored law forbade the employment of children—defined as minors under the age of eighteen—from employment, which would be injurious to their health and well-being. In the development of this vague statute, the FIC was empowering the Industrial Board to set flexible and realistic standards.[35]

The FIC continued and furthered the medicalization of child labor that was encoded in previous regulations. Children under eighteen needed to go to local health boards to get work permits. The boards would examine them for the type of employment they were seeking and then grade them on a sliding scale of health. In 1912, reformers demanded and won passage of a law requiring that a medical certificate become part of the work-permit process. Testimony before the Commission from medical experts, public health officials, and members of reform groups such as the AALL, WTUL, Consumer's League, Charity Organization Society, and Child Labor Committee insisted that stiff medical certification for work permits with a thorough system of inspection and enforcement was a necessary health procedure.[36]

Further evidence of the medicalization of child labor was the demand by reformers, in 1913, of periodic, random medical examinations for all work-permit holders. Any worker who failed the physical would have his or her permit revoked. This new demand was drafted by the FIC. It placed the medical examination under the Department of Labor's medical inspector. If the child refused the examination, proved unfit, or if the employer interfered, the inspector was authorized to take corrective action.[37]

As in the past, each time the state enacted a child labor law it also revisited compulsory education. What was the proper education for America's working population? The FIC, working again with the Child Labor Committee and now with educational reformers as well, won passage of a law mandating a sixth-grade education for all applicants of work permits. Another FIC-sponsored law also required that each school district investigate "continuation schooling" for workers.[38]

Connected to all of these issues concerning child labor were the hours and conditions of labor. Starting in 1886, New York had limited and circumscribed the hours of children's work. First, the legislature limited work to ten-hour days and sixty-hour weeks; then it eliminated night work; then it extended restrictions to department store labor. Eventually, the state limited children to eight-hour days and forty-eight-hour weeks. These efforts were spearheaded by the Consumer's League working with other reform groups. Even before the FIC was formed, these groups were demanding a single standard for all legislation dealing with children's hours.[39]

By 1911, the FIC had drafted and the state had enacted a law that extended the prohibitions of child labor to stores in the state. Children working in mercantile establishments were not covered by the eight-hour law. Consumer's League activists, led by FIC staffer Frances Perkins, proposed the extension of the eight-hour day to all children workers. Investigations of department stores showed that 6.1 percent of the workforce were children and that the conditions of their labor demanded a reduction of hours to preserve their health and vitality.

Again, reformers made their case and won passage of a law covering commercial stores.[40]

HOME WORK AND CANNERY WORK

Two areas, home work and canneries, received considerable attention from the FIC and led to further gendering of the state in labor regulation. Both employed significant numbers of women and children under deplorable conditions. Both had been the targets of previous reform efforts, and both were the scourge of labor unions. These two industries were notorious for their miserable working conditions, poor wages, long hours, and their disruption of "home life."

In the fluid economy of New York City, home work had a long tradition dating back to at least the early nineteenth century and was most often associated with the garment industry.[41] Reformers made early efforts to prohibit or limit this form of sweated labor. In 1883, New York passed a law prohibiting cigar manufacturing in tenements. But a Court of Appeals overturned the law. In 1892, the legislature tried a new approach. Arguing health, the state passed a law that prohibited all but the immediate family from manufacturing goods from a proscribed list of forty-one items. In such cases, workers still needed to obtain a permit and the building needed to pass health and labor codes. In 1912, the Labor Department inspected 12,755 tenements and licensed 11,795. But with only ten inspectors statewide, this effort was futile. Countless thousands of illegal shops operated throughout the state.[42]

Reformers in New York had been leading the nationwide charge to curb these abuses. Lawrence Veiller, of the New York City Tenement House Committee and National Housing Association, had led several investigations and, together with Mary Van Kleeck of the Russell Sage Foundation, surveyed child labor in tenement shops. Their findings called for a total ban on tenement production. Veiller, Kleeck, the WTUL, the AALL, and various labor unions pressured the FIC to address this issue.[43]

The FIC's work on tenement labor underscores the "cooperative project" of the FIC. Throughout its history, the FIC was both the product of and vehicle for reformers. The FIC incorporated photographs of sweated labor taken by Lillian Wald and supplied by Perkins, reviewed the work of Violet Pike on women workers, responded to Pauline

Goldmark's study of industry in New York City, and used George Price's sanitary studies. In the end, the FIC incorporated into its own report an independent study of tenement child labor conducted by Owen Lovejoy and Elizabeth Watson of the Nation Child Welfare Committee.[44]

Collectively, reformers denounced the "parasitic industry" of home work. "The cost to the community under the present system," argued one FIC staffer, "in life and health of the little army of young children and mothers employed in this branch of industry is entirely too great to justify." Reformers, however, knew that home work was often not a choice, but a necessity for working-class families. FIC commissioners, therefore, moved carefully on this issue, concerned that their efforts to help might in fact hurt the families of New York. Smith and Wagner were particularly concerned with this matter because of their complicated political connections to the workers of New York.[45]

In 1912, commissioners expanded their investigations into home work. The FIC's anti-home-work campaign was directly connected to the Protocol. At bottom, one could read it as an anti-sweatshop campaign. FIC staff visited fifteen upstate cities and inspected 148 homes. In addition, they investigated 350 tenements and over 1,000 apartments in New York City. These investigations uncovered what the FIC and reformers already knew: disease, overwork, child labor, poor conditions, and low wages typified home work. As many as 125,000 tenement workers worked on unlicensed goods in unsanitary conditions.[46]

Appalled at what they found, reformers fought to preserve the split between home and work. In 1911, and again in 1912, reformers paraded workers and reports before the Commission. Slowly, they unveiled the evils of home work: rampant tuberculosis, sleep-deprived small children, a lack of education, and countless workers whose health was ruined by this system of labor. Whole families toiled all day for as little as $2. Reformers called the home-work system "absolute slavery." "We are a civilized community," noted social worker Lillian Wald, "and would not have . . . children pay the price of their food and shelter at the cost of their education and childhood." Home work, such reformers suggested, undermined American values and mores. Most home workers were recent immigrants. In keeping their children home in desperate poverty, keeping them from schools, they prevented their children from the only tool they could use to pull themselves up out of poverty: education.[47]

FIC commissioners, mainly Wagner, engaged in proto-Keynian and Protocolist economic arguments around the issue of home work. The removal of home work, they argued would benefit workers in general by removing a system that undercut their wages and kept the wage scale artificially low. Workers would see their standard of living increase. Manufacturers would replace inefficient home workers with a combination of technology and highly efficient factory workers. And taxpayers would gain. Inspection and the elimination of tenement labor would increase the living conditions in tenements, lessening disease and the need for public spending on public health. Also, increases in wages would cause a reduction in the charity rolls. More importantly, however, through increasing wages, workers would be better able to participate fully in the economy.[48]

Reformers were joined in their public outcry for an end of tenement labor by many of the state's newspapers. The *New York Tribune* ran a headline that said: "Babies on Fight to Survive Life in Tenements." A host of other papers ran similar stories and headlines. The massive evidence reformers assembled and that the FIC presented muted any immediate opposition.[49]

The opposition that did arise was limited and overwhelmed by the massive evidence the reformers gathered. In its second year, the FIC proposed and won passage of a law that prohibited children under fourteen from home work. Owners of tenements where tenants performed work would need to obtain permits. Manufacturers who used home work would have to receive a permit and would have to label goods with their name and address for inspection. This would aid the Protocol, as it regulated one of most notorious forms of sweated labor.[50]

The other industry that relied on child labor to a large degree was the canning industry located in rural upstate. The FIC estimated that the industry's more than 14,000 workers received little protection. The workforce was migratory, rural, and immigrant. The officials of the small villages and towns were overwhelmed with the burdens of enforcement. More importantly, according to the FIC, the canners openly ignored the law.[51]

Canners had continuously demanded exemptions from state labor laws since as early as 1903. They claimed that the seasonality of the business, the presence of perishable crops, and the presence of the work in rural, healthy settings all demanded that women workers be exempted from the hours legislation. When legislators ignored their pleas, canners openly ignored the law. In 1905, the industry had convinced the state attorney general that children working in sheds adjacent to factories were exempt from state law. The attorney general ruled that the law did not apply to these children workers because, technically, the sheds were not factories. In 1912, they were able to pressure their local representatives to amend the state's hours law to exclude cannery workers between June 15 and October 15, the peak season for the industry.[52]

Again, reformers coordinated efforts. Led by the Consumer's League, and together with the AALL, Child Labor Committee, Russell Sage Foundation, WTUL, and the state's unions, reformers countered the manufacturers' statements. They published reports, presented the FIC with expert testimony, and led commissioners through cannery factories so they could see firsthand the horrific conditions. More importantly, however, they presented the FIC with legislation to correct the problems encountered.[53]

In 1912, the FIC conducted its own investigation of the canneries. Zenos Potter, of the National Child Labor Committee, directed the FIC's research. Together with a team of nine researchers, Potter investigated over 120 factories and sent several investigators "undercover" as workers. These undercover investigators observed over 1,300 minors working in the factories. The average age of these children was fourteen: thirty were between three and six years of age. Work began at 4:00 A.M. and continued until well after 10:00 P.M. Some children simply collapsed of exhaustion at their workstations. Many of these children did not attend school regularly. "There can be no question," observed one commissioner, "that the mental development of these children is very seriously arrested by their going to the canneries." The FIC reports noted that some canneries operated without child labor, and did so with a profit. Therefore, the FIC declared, child labor was not necessary for the profitability of the cannery industry.[54]

In addition to child labor, FIC staffers documented over 7,000 women workers working under the same conditions. During the rush season, many women worked 18-hour days and nearly 120-hour weeks. During normal times, eighty-five-hour weeks were often the norm. The FIC, reiterating its special emphasis on protecting women and home life, noted that the pace of machine labor and the lack of time to care for their families put enormous strain on these women and disrupted their home life.[55]

Women working under these conditions were unusually susceptible to moral temptation, the FIC contended. The meager pay forced long hours. "You can't make enough money up here to pay your board," said one worker. But, she was told by her superior, "I will give you a chance to make two or three dollars on the side any time." Again, reformers raised the specter of a moral threat to womanhood and hinted at "white slavery" in their efforts to demonstrate the need for reform.[56]

Wagner, usually given to unemotional economic arguments, confessed that the dismal portrait of this form of rural labor shocked even him. "I used to have the beautiful pictures painted to me of the wonderful advantage it was for children... to work in the open air... but I saw it, and it is quite a different thing."[57] Years later, writing in his autobiography, Al Smith recalled:

> Probably nowhere were there more shocking revelations than in the factory commission's investigation of the canneries, where women and small children worked as many as sixteen hours a day.[58]

Samuel Gompers, president of the AFL and a commissioner, described the industry "with horror and inhumanity." Not surprisingly, then, the FIC dismissed the canners' objections as "entirely without foundation."[59]

The FIC's activities around child and women labor in the canneries produced positive publicity for protective legislation regulating working conditions.[60] Building on this momentum, the FIC proposed several bills dealing directly with cannery labor. The first bill, meant to ensure full coverage, declared sheds as part of factories. In a concession to canners, another bill permitted the employment of women over eighteen years of age for no more than ten hours a day and sixty hours a week during the peak season of June 15 to October 15. If demand were necessary, the Industrial Board could raise the hours to sixty-six for the week during June 25 to August 5. At the same time, though, night work was prohibited for women under twenty-one, and the nine-hour day and fifty-four-hour week were declared the norm for girls fourteen to eighteen and boys fourteen to sixteen. Finally, employers who provided living quarters for seasonal workers were required to keep them in "sanitary condition." When the bills passed in 1913, they empowered the Industrial Board to make additional rules as the need arose and gave enforcement powers to the state labor commissioner.[61]

Success with protective legislation for women and children led the FIC to larger issues after 1913. In doing so, the FIC moved from a gender-based paternalism to a class-based paternalism, only briefly returning to these issues to protect what it had already accomplished. Between 1913 and 1915, bills were presented to repeal several aspects of FIC reform. Smith and Wagner used the tireless techniques of Tammany Hall to quell these efforts. At one time, Smith used the recall in the assembly to teach an assemblyman a lesson. He asked, "will humanity and civilization" survive these anti-labor strike bills? Only one bill managed to squeak through, a seventy-two-hour week for cannery workers during the peak season, but following concerted pressure from reformers, the governor announced he would veto the bill. With that, the GOP recalled the bill and it died on committee. While the FIC did eventually lose one measure on mercantile establishments—a law dealing with legal exemptions— most of the FIC laws survived these challenges.[62]

"THE NEXT LOGICAL STEP": THE MOVEMENT FOR MINIMUM WAGE LEGISLATION IN NEW YORK[63]

The FIC's move to gender-neutral issues in 1914 focused on minimum wage legislation—a major concern for Protocolists. Reformers approached minimum wage legislation for workers, male and female, in much the same way they approached protective legislation for women workers: through the language of race uplift. "To maintain a race that is to be made up of capable, efficient, and independent individuals," was how one reforming social scientist put it. Another saw it as "the logical step" in "human conservation."[64]

Many reformers, such as Paul Kellogg, invoked the image of an anarchistic economy, which would radicalize underpaid immigrants. They saw minimum wages as a preventative measure to protect the weak. By extending the paternalistic arm of the state further, New York's reformers hoped to equalize what they saw as an unjust system. Florence Kelley, writing in 1914, believed that wage boards, such as the ones created under the Protocol, should be extended to all workers.[65]

As historian Michael Katz and sociologist Harry Braverman have pointed out, minimum wage legislation was part of the larger effort to create a welfare state by rationalizing the economy. This was a prime motivation for industrial democrats. In this vein, labor laws such as those sponsored by the FIC eliminated inefficient workers from the workforce. This was the first stage in rationization. The next logical step was to raise the minimum wages workers were paid. This would put pressure on manufacturers to become more competitive through efficiencies, technologies, and rationalization of the labor process (Taylorism) by taking away the ability of employers to gain an advantage by paying the lowest wages. By equalizing the wage structure, employers would continually be forced to seek higher stages of rationalization or go out of business. It was no surprise that these reformers celebrated scientific management as the next panacea. In this context, then, the minimum wage effort was more an effort at rationalizing the economy than a humanitarian effort. In this regard, we can see just how much the FIC incorporated the Protocolists notion of industrial democracy.[66]

Reformers did not deny that the minimum wage program would hurt some employers. They argued, echoing the Protocol, however, that only parasitic employers who preyed off low wages would be hurt. The goal was to remove these inefficient firms and replace them with efficient ones. Part of this effort called for the support of labor unions. While the state could establish a floor with minimum wages, it would require unions to raise productivity, making firms more efficient. As early as 1910, then, reformers clearly saw unions as tools of rationalization. Minimum wages would, in one fell swoop, raise the standards of workers, eliminate poverty, reduce the threat of socialism, and make American firms more competitive and modern.[67]

New York's efforts for minimum wage were spearheaded by two organizations: the Consumers' League and the AALL. Through the League's Florence Kelley and the AALL's John B. Andrews and his wife and fellow reformer, Irene Osgood Andrews, a plethora of reform organizations were drawn to this issue. Working together, Kelley and the Andrews welded a core of dedicated reformers who vaulted minimum wages onto the FIC stage at a critical moment. Significantly, they also presented the issue in such a way that it appealed to Wagner and Smith, who took up the cause as their own.[68]

By 1913, these reformers had convinced nine states to investigate minimum wages and pass statutes. These laws varied greatly in their scope and substance. But, one model stood out above others—the

Massachusetts plan. Under this plan, advanced by Kelley and others for New York, a Wage Commission would set rates with the aid of a committee of workers and management, much as the Protocol's wage boards functioned. Most states that enacted minimum wage laws used the Massachusetts model or the "commission" variant that Kelley was advocating.[69]

The FIC was a natural location for taking up the minimum wage discussion. Public health activists used every opportunity to draw connections between low wages and disease. Labor officials continuously discussed the plague of low wages, which affected honest working-men. They drew particular attention to the correspondence of women in a trade and low wages. Labor officials demanded a distinct minimum wage for women's trades to provide a floor in the labor market. However, they opposed minimum wage reform in male-dominated industries. In industrial unions such as the ILGWU, there was acceptance for minimum wage legislation. After all, at least some of the industry was already operating under some sort of universal minimum through the Protocol. Social workers, social scientists, and some union members joined the call for inclusion of minimum wage efforts in the FIC's work.[70]

The steward of this effort within the FIC was Mary Dreier. After viewing preliminary data gathered from the 1912 cannery and mercantile investigations, she declared that "the inadequacy of wages [paid women] is an evil." She pressed Wagner, Smith, and the other commissioners for a full-scale investigation and received the governor's public endorsement. To expand its efforts into this area, the FIC first needed approval from the state legislature.[71]

When a Joint Committee of the Assembly and Senate met on February 19, 1913 to discuss expanding the FIC's jurisdiction to include wage legislation, the outcome was a foregone conclusion. With the governor publicly on board, reformers vocally supportive, and Tammany Hall's young Turks, Wagner and Smith, leading the charge, the Committee quickly endorsed the new project. The reformers were not able to get everything they wanted. The law, which authorized an FIC wage study, was limited to women and children. Ironically, by 1913, reformers, while still adhering to gender-specific reforms in other areas such as night work, had begun to abandon their gender-specific demands for minimum wages and began to advocate across-the-board minimums regardless of gender or age. But the state legislature was not so convinced. There were three forces working against the reformers' new gender-neutral reform efforts. First, as noted earlier, the Supreme Court struck down gender-neutral minimum hour legislation for bakers, but upheld such legislation when it was for women alone. By logical extension, legislators argued the courts would strike down laws that regulated male labor. The state, the courts had declared, had an interest in protecting women workers. That interest did not extend to male workers. Second, the official labor movement, embodied in the FIC by Commissioner Samuel Gompers, opposed legislation for male workers. Gompers argued that male workers were best protected by unions. Women workers, who were for the most part unorganized, however, needed state protection. Third, and subtler, the FIC had already established a precedent in legislation and a set of attitudes that were deeply gendered.[72]

In this contested arena, the FIC's task was immense. The first task before the FIC was hiring staff and giving direction to the investigation. The commissioners hired Professor Howard Woolston of City College. To assist Woolston, the FIC appointed Albert Baron of the U.S. Department of Labor as assistant director of the wage study. Woolston and Baron would be assisted by a staff of forty-one.[73]

While the researchers combed previously collected data for their wage study and began to gather information on New York City, by 1914 it was clear to them that the task was too large to be completed adequately in the time frame. They requested that the study be extended for one more year. The legislature granted the extension, and in 1914, the study began to research upstate wages.[74]

As the FIC moved into unchartered ground, it relied more heavily on the reformers in its coalition. This cemented the relationship between reformers and politicians, but distanced both those groups from labor. The FIC's wage study was dominated by the AALL. Working through Mary Dreier, Irene Osgood Andrews and John Andrews were able to influence almost every aspect of the study. Irene Osgood Andrews served as a staff researcher. The FIC and the wage study staff relied heavily on an Advisory Board, which was dominated by John Andrews. This "expert board" did more than advise, they supervised the hiring of staff, drafted laws, coordinated outside research, and, most of all, they lobbied for minimum wages. The Andrews inundated the research staff with reports and independent research. They suggested which industries needed study and which ones were already studied and by whom.[75]

The Wage Study staff provided the FIC with dramatic data to demonstrate the need for minimum wage laws. They chose industries to study that were un- or under-unionized and where the workforce was predominately young, and because of the legislature's restrictions, the study focused only on women workers. These FIC wage studies were in no way comprehensive. They focused on four already widely studied industries: shirt manufacturing, department stores, box making, and confection making. They studied 104,516 workers in 577 firms, over 78,000 of whom were from New York City. They eventually extended their study to additional industries and workers. By 1914, they had studied over 150,000 workers. Woolston supplemented these studies with reports conducted by private groups. In this way, studies by the Russell Sage Foundation, Consumers' League, Charity Organization Society, Association for Improving the Condition of the Poor, and other groups were incorporated into the final FIC reports. These "scientific reports" were given maximum publicity through six FIC public hearings and one symposium where reformers testified. The *Survey* called this FIC effort "the most formidable array of facts ever brought together by a minimum wage inquiry."[76]

The findings and presentation of the data presented a compelling picture: women workers did not make a living wage, and they had no hope of achieving such a wage without state intervention. By presenting overwhelming evidence, the FIC was making a strong case for the expansion of the state. The FIC reported that in retail work, an industry that was deemed by the public as one of the best, workers were deeply abused. The FIC reported that 40 percent of all retail workers were under twenty-one and that more than 50 percent made less than $7.50 per week. Between 11 and 15 percent made less than $5.00. A system of fines predominated in the industry, so that actual wages were dramatically less than reported wages. In sum, 61 percent of women workers were reported as making less than $4.00 per week.[77]

The FIC study of wages for retail workers brought forward a simple fact that many tried hard to deny: most of the women who worked in this trade relied on the income as their sole source of support. These workers were not toiling for "pin money." They were working for sheer survival. Furthermore, the FIC declared that most of these workers needed to supplement their income in some way. They could not survive on the wages they earned from shop work alone. The most common alternative to supplementing wages was to take cheaper and cheaper lodgings; a solution that, the FIC decried, placed young women in great moral harm.[78]

In industry after industry, the picture was the same: women toiling in poverty. Women often earned less than $7.00 per week, and few earned as much as $500 per year. These low wages reduced these young women to a condition of poverty. The FIC played on the immorality of this situation. Reformers feared that the impoverished conditions and wages would force a life of dependency on working women. "It is obvious," argued Woolston, "that . . . a self-supporting and self-respecting girl can save nothing." Again, the FIC claimed, "No woman can live properly on $5 of $6 or even $7 a week."[79]

The studies conducted by Irene Osgood Andrews provided two important frames of reference for the public. First, she provided the FIC with a massive comparative study of minimum wages in an international perspective. But more importantly, Andrews documented widespread underemployment of women: most worked seasonally and were out of work approximately 20 percent of the year. Thus, for most women, simply measuring the full-time average weekly wages did not provide a true account of their hardship.

A second framework, provided by FIC researcher Dr. Frank Streightoff of Depauw University, compounded this grisly picture. Streightoff conducted the FIC's cost-of-living studies. He reported that many women workers were "habitually going without meals because they were too poor to purchase food." Estimating that survival in New York required a weekly wage of $9 ($8.20 upstate), he noted that the fact that most women earned less than that made a compelling case for the need for government action.[80]

The FIC staff conducted two additional cost-of-living studies of New York City working-class women in which they attempted to personalize the data. Scheightoff's reports were based on raw data. These new reports, conducted by Ester Packard and Marie Orenstein, were based on personal interviews and were concerned with the "quality" of the life these women lived. Both studies had a kind of "day in the life of a worker" feel to them, examining how the workers lived and on what items they spent money. Again, issues of morality arose in workers' values and the reformers' commentary. For instance, one worker, Orenstein reported, wondered "whether there is any difference selling yourself for $6 a week or $5 per night." The comparison made vivid for reformers the relationship between poor conditions, constant sacrifice, and chronic poverty and one grave alternative: prostitution.[81]

Many in the reform community saw the problem of low wages as genderless, despite their legislative mandate for only protective regulations. Questionnaires, which the FIC sent to scores of social workers, reformers, and labor leaders, revealed that many in the reform community supported minimum wage legislation that went beyond female protectionist support.[82] Social workers and reformers presented two arguments at the public hearings in support of universal minimum wage legislation. The first expressed humanitarian reasons. Reformers such as Felix Adler declared minimum wages to be an "expression of social conscience." The other argument was based on a concept of social efficiency. Reformers argued that minimum wage legislation was a cheaper and more efficient way of preventing poverty: it raised living standards, increased purchasing power, prevented radicalism, and promoted competition in the free market.[83]

But as reformers refocused the minimum wage push of the FIC around a universal provision, they failed—possibly out of sheer arrogance—to pay attention to their allies' opposition. Labor was, in fact, deeply divided on the issue. Most union leaders supported minimum wages for workers under eighteen years of age, and many supported laws for women workers. Samuel Gompers, however, had become disenchanted with any minimum wage laws, vehemently opposing all minimum wages on principle, believing that the minimum would become the ceiling rather than the floor for wage reform. He also took reformers at their word when they declared that minimum wage legislation for women was a wedge to win minimum wages for all workers. Rather than try to bring Gompers around to their side, FIC reformers attacked him. Reformers also pushed the FIC politicians, Wagner and Smith, beyond gender-based protective legislation. Reformers moved forward on this issue so quickly they forced the FIC to choose between its allies: labor, who was at best divided on minimum wage reform, and the reformers, who supported a gender-neutral policy. In the end, the FIC chose the reformers, killing the coalition in the process.[84]

The zealousness of industrial democrats and the hesitancy of labor split the FIC coalition. Sensing a vital opportunity, business groups moved quickly into opposition to the FIC. They presented their own "detached" research to disprove the FIC reports, thus undermining the demands for minimum wage legislation. They did this at the critical movement when the reformers were consumed trying to pacify their labor allies and slow to respond to their reports.[85] Thus, in 1914, when the FIC handed down its recommendations for minimum wages, its coalition became hopelessly divided. As the Republicans gained control of the legislature, minimum wage prospects dimmed.[86]

The FIC's recommendations show how the FIC and the struggle for industrial democracy had parted. Formed during the heat of the great strikes in 1909 and 1910, the movement for industrial democracy had been hatched by workers. Reformers sought to shape it during the Protocol period. With the final stages of the FIC, reformers had completely pushed their labor allies to the side. They pursued minimum wage reform to the exclusion of worker representatives.

The FIC created industrial boards that it treated as the embodiment of industrial democracy: the boards depended on "voluntary mutual action of those most directly concerned, aided by an enlightened public opinion." But, the boards that were established privileged the reformers who controlled the research on which the wage board would base its decision. In addition, they further removed a critical issue facing workers, wages, from the shop floor, disempowering workers in the process. The FIC had come to embody the more bureaucratic model of industrial democracy.[87]

In a last-ditch effort to salvage minimum wage legislation, reformers mounted a public relations assault. This effort is important. For the first time, reformers acted without organized labor. The WTUL, AALL, Russell Sage Foundation, *Survey*, *New Republic*, and others issued statements of support for a minimum wage. Absent from this roster was labor. Weakened by the Republican ascendancy and hopelessly divided, the efforts of reformers were all for naught. The law failed to pass, and in the wake of the loss, the FIC collapsed.[88]

In seeking to understand the failure and the disintegration of the FIC in 1915, historians have blamed the political shift in the New York legislature from Tammany Hall to a coalition of Republicans and upstate Democrats in 1914. While this obviously played an important role, it alone cannot explain the demise of reform. In the last years of the FIC (the same years as the collapse of the Protocol), 1913–1915, industrial democrats lost faith in rank-and-file workers as full partners in reform. Instead, they gained faith in their own ability to reform. Frances Perkins, FIC staffer and future secretary of labor, recalled this shift in her Columbia University oral history. She recalled her experiences with the FIC, years after the New Deal. The FIC taught her and others that reformers and a positive state could improve working conditions and enhance labor relations by themselves. "I'd rather pass a law," she stated proudly, "than organize a union." While Perkins was certainly an ally of labor and the working person, in a brief sentence she revealed her biases and the important shift in industrial democracy. Unions were good, but meaningful reform now came from a state dominated by industrial democrats such as herself. In the shift, workers went from partners and active shapers of policy, to clients of the state and constituents of a new political elite: liberals.[89]

Conclusion
The Historical Legacy of Industrial Democracy: From Protocolism to the New Deal

PROTOCOLISM, THE form industrial democracy took in Progressive Era New York, proved a radical departure from the past and an important answer to "the labor question" of the day. Collective bargaining, coupled with government regulation and a welfare state's safety net, was an important marker for the twentieth century. Protocolism provided better wages and conditions for workers, it revitalized the labor movement (making it legitimate in the process), and it reorganized the state's politics. Yet, for all its successes, Protocolism left unanswered key questions about the political economy of shop-floor democracy and the role of workers and unions in politics and the nation's economic life. While these experiments did not solve the labor problem, what is important is that Protocolism placed the question on the table of public discourse and set the debate for a generation.

At its height, Protocolism seemed to contain the promise to remake the industrial world. Many scholars as well as participants tended to view these events as the opening act of the New Deal. On the surface, this makes some sense as the two movements shared an impulse and concern for labor as well as shared personnel. However, careful study reveals that Protocolism was not the opening act of the New Deal, but rather that its rise and decline set the parameters for future discussions. It would be more correct to say that New Deal labor policy took place within the shadow of Protocolism.

Protocolism, I have argued, developed in two stages. It involved both private and public spheres. It included workers, unions, reformers, and politicians, and it changed all those involved in significant ways. Only through close study can we see the critical stages in the development of this model and truly understand how it worked.

214

The first stage of Protocolism had its origins in the massive wave of strikes that hit the New York ladies' garment industry starting in 1909. It was an effort to settle these strikes as well as an opportunity to test new ideals about labor relations. What marked these early negotiations as distinct was the direct involvement of middle-class reformers, in addition to the high level of organization between workers and manufacturers.

The cloakmakers' strike of 1910, which quickly followed on the heels of the Uprising, was, to use Samuel Gompers's apt phrase, "more than a strike, [it was] ... an industrial revolution" because it created a new system of industrial relations (IR).[1] "The signing of the Protocol," ending the strike, as historian Louis Levine has noted, "ushered in a new period of constructive experimentation in collective bargaining."[2] Benjamin Stolberg, another earlier historian of the union, believed that "the Protocol of Peace marked a decisive turning point [in part because] ... its basic idea was later copied by the other needle trades.... And in time its influence spread throughout American Industry."[3] More recently, Gus Tyler, a retired union official, asserted that the Protocol "was the beginning of a process that started in the cloak industry ... and that has continued in America into the closing years [of our century]."[4] In this way, the Protocol has been viewed as *the* watershed event in collective bargaining during the Progressive Era.[5]

Its creators also heralded its significance. As Louis Brandeis, father of the Protocol stated at the time, "It may prove to be a new epic [in labor relations, in keeping] ... with American Spirit and traditions as well as with justice."[6] And they were all right. The Protocol ushered in a new day for labor relations. In exploring the origins of these events, this book argued that the Protocol set the agenda for labor policy and industrial relations for years to come. But its influence was not because of its success, as scholars have long assumed, but because of its failure.

To be sure, the Protocol did go beyond hours and wages to the heart of the problems facing industrial America. The settlement rationalized and stabilized an industry known for just the opposite. By standardizing wages, hours, and working conditions, it took away the ability of the smaller manufacturers to undercut the larger ones. In this way, the Protocol created a new labor-management accord. "It introduced the notion," as Benjamin Stolberg observed in 1944, "that labor had a stake in efficient management, continuous prosperity and social responsibility. The Protocol," Stolberg continues, "assumed a benevolent partnership between capital and labor, a sort of joint industrial syndicate of boss and worker."[7] In essence, the Protocol helped introduce "regulatory unionism" to a larger America. This new form, really an added function to industrial unionism, as David Brody and others have previously noted, was finally accepted by management because it had an added benefit in that it could achieve what the manufacturers were unable to by themselves: industrial stability, efficiency, and enhanced profitability.[8] Manufacturers agreed to seemingly large gains for previously underpaid workers (hours, wages, improved working conditions, and other new benefits) because they gained in productivity. A rationalized industry with efficient production and distribution systems, without periodic work stoppages, was simply more profitable than what had gone before. A rationalized industry—with standards of production, wages, and other costs—undercut the smaller manufacturer. These small shops, often referred to as "moths of Division Street," lost the flexibility that made them so competitive. And the enforcement agency would not be market forces—that never worked—or the industry organization—that too was ineffective—but rather, it would be the union itself. Simply by enforcing the Protocol, the International Ladies' Garment Workers' Union (ILGWU) transformed the industry and increased corporate profits. In fact, larger manufacturers were willing to share a limited portion of these new profits with workers. Workers received more because they produced more.[9] Jesse Thomas Carpenter, a scholar of industrial relations, has noted how the Protocol rationalized the industry in a short time:

> Since 1910, collective bargaining in the needle trades has been the medium through which the substantial "legitimate" manufacturers, organized into employers associations, have joined hands with their more "reputable" plant workers, organized into labor unions, for the purpose of protecting their mutual interests from the small-scale, irresponsible, unorganized fringe elements (workers and employers), who, with their reduced wage scales and lower price tags, create unbearable competition. In so far as this new alignment of industry's organized forces has prevented the undermining of "decent" labor standards and of "fair" trade practices, collective bargaining has produced more business and more profits for organized

manufacturers, while providing more jobs and higher standards of living for the organized workers. At the same time, by stabilizing their industries against the disruptive influences of the unorganized factions, the parties to collective agreements have promoted industry welfare and fostered industrial peace.[10]

The Protocol in the ladies' garment industry proved somewhat successful. Conditions of labor and wages improved. More important, however, was the promise of the Protocol to usher in a new day of industrial democracy. While the Protocol could deliver on the bread-and-butter issues, it stumbled on the issues of democracy in the workplace. The strengths of the Protocol were also its weaknesses. The high level of organization and bureaucracy needed to orchestrate the agreement's machinery removed workers on the shop floor from leadership and replaced them with national labor leaders. For the promise of democracy to work, therefore, the union needed to become less democratic. What tore at the Protocol and was responsible for its eventual collapse was the tension between direct shop-floor democracy and the institutional variant that was Protocolism. As the agreement began to flounder, those most active in it began to seek new ways to spread this system beyond the garment industry.

Yet, what made the Protocol so effective also sowed the seeds of its ruin. By recognizing that labor—"responsible" labor that is—had an interest in the management of the industry, the Protocol unleashed a conservative notion of industrial democracy.[11]

A tragic fire in 1911 provided the Protocolists with an opportunity. The public and cross-class outrage that followed the Triangle Fire opened the way for a governmental response. Rather than a simple investigation, the political circumstances in New York permitted the empowerment of a unique body, the Factory Investigating Commission (FIC). The FIC not only had investigatory powers, but, because of its makeup, it had de facto legislative powers as well, making it unique among state industrial commissions.

The FIC became the embodiment of Protocolism. Part 2 of this book examined the evolution of the FIC from a fact-finding to a law-making body. I have argued that throughout the FIC's tenure, 1911 to 1915, it had a significant impact on the state of working-class New York. By 1915, New York had one of the most progressive labor codes in the nation. The

FIC moved quickly from issues of sanitation, industrial accidents, and disease to issues of protection and welfare. In the process, the FIC articulated a new political philosophy building on industrial democracy: modern liberalism. It claimed that the state had a legal and moral responsibility to protect its citizens. Extending the role of paternalism, in one swoosh it cast aside laissez-faire economic policies. The FIC moved from protecting women and children to demanding minimum wage laws and maximum hour codes for all workers despite gender. In short, by 1915, the FIC made the leap from industrial relations to the welfare state.

The deaths of 146 young working women in the Triangle Fire of March 25, 1911, is one of those rare, tragic events that alters the paths of history. The fire was pivotal for a number of reasons. First and foremost, the disaster highlighted just how vulnerable women workers were. Second, it established the debate as to what should be "done" about these workers. In doing so, the Triangle Fire provoked a discussion that led to a rethinking of the state and the creation of a gendered welfare policy. This horrific episode alerted both a city and a nation to the daily problems women workers faced. This book traced the fire and the various responses to it. It retraced historical evidence to put the fire into its larger political, social, and national contexts. The fire proved to be a catalyst between the new emerging industrial relations system and the new bureaucratic state. The massive uprisings of the garment industry had created the first stage of this system, Protocolism. Occurring just a short time after these events, the fire set the stage and ushered in a new phase, state involvement.

The Triangle Fire has become part of the mythology of American labor history. Often the fire is simply viewed through the lens of industrial disaster and violence, as an example of the helplessness of workers, the greed of corporations, and the inability of the progressives to prevent disaster.[12]

Other, newer works have attempted to explore such tragedies as the Triangle Fire as harbingers of change.[13] The major difference between Ludlow, Homestead, and the Triangle Fire, in addition to timing, is the active role workers play in policy formation in the latter. The fire signaled a new governmental style and expression—an élan—that some have called "urban liberalism."[14] The new impetus, whether a new liberalism or an older progressivism, provided the necessary governmental support for the Protocols of Peace and the new style of IR that grew out of the garment strikes of 1909 and 1910. As I have suggested, the developing IR system had two parts: one private and the other public. The private portion involved the Protocol. The public half was the Factory Investigating Commission that was created in the wake of the fire. The strikes and the fire together taught New York that private and public issues were inextricably linked, what was private was public. In their struggles for industrial democracy, some workers began to rely increasingly on the active paternalism of reformers for protection and support. And these reformers found a place in the state. In the process of seeking refuge in the arms of the state, many workers began to see the resulting policies as rights—hard won and not easily taken back. And in New York, the welfare state was born. The victory was not without its limitations though; while male workers accepted women in the workforce, they did so not as equals, but as secondary, temporary workers. Male workers and their unions accepted the state's maternalistic policies, dividing the working class by gender.[15]

The events that followed the fire were crucial to the formation of a new industrial relations paradigm. The fire provided both the state and a new governmental elite with a raison d'etre: to protect the working classes, especially working women. The state response to the fire, the FIC, was an important marker in the genesis of the welfare state.[16]

The fire also led to a reorientation of the electorate and a revitalization of the Democratic Party machine: Tammany Hall.[17] Thousands of workers in New York City began to recognize certain Democratic politicians as legitimately their own. Robert Wagner and Al Smith, then obscure Tammany Hall hacks, seized the event and its aftermath, thrusting themselves from smoke-filled rooms toward the upper echelons of the party and power. In the process, Smith and Wagner were transformed into a new political type, the urban liberal. Social workers and political reformers, the most obvious being Frances Perkins, received advanced on-the-job training in Progressive Era New York. These experiences they later brought with them to Washington during the New Deal. Trade unionist and socialist Rose Schneiderman, a leader of the new unionism movement in the garment industry, became a national labor leader and prominent Democratic Party member in New York State and later in Washington.[18] In short, the fire connected separate progressive forces and melded them into a new coherent political force.

Eventually this force would develop again during Franklin Roosevelt's New Deal.

This book, then, is an attempt to look at the connections between labor and welfare policy, the relationships between workers and the state, the position of reformers and professionals in the process of policy formation, and the connections between the modern concept of liberalism and progressive reform.

Protocolism was not simply the first stage of the New Deal. But like the New Deal, it was the creation of a rationalized government bureaucracy to handle labor problems as well as a new political outlook. Years later, in her Columbia University Oral History, Frances Perkins was asked where the New Deal impulse came from. On what was it based? Perkins outlined the relation of the Triangle Fire and the resulting government agency to the creation of this liberal agenda:

> We had in the election of Franklin Roosevelt the beginning of what has come to be known as the New Deal for the United States. But it [the New Deal] was based really upon the experiences that we [Perkins, Wagner and others] had had in New York State and upon the sacrifices of those who, we faithfully remember with affection and respect, died in that terrible fire [the Triangle Fire of March 25, 1911]... they did not die in vain and we will never forget them.[19]

What she is referring to was a new liberal mind-set that grew out of Protocolists' vision of industrial democracy. But, it would be a mistake to see it formed full cloth in the 1910s. It was shaped by the events of the Great Depression, worker radicalism, and economic conditions of the 1930s as much as by the events of Progressive Era New York. Protocolism, if anything, limited and shaped what was thought of as possible reform efforts for the future.

While the role of reformers and politicians is important, such thinking ignores the equally important influence of workers in the creation of the welfare state. Often workers are seen as mere recipients of the liberal state. But, if the lessons of social history have taught us anything it is that workers were not passive, they were active agents of history. Herbert Gutman reminds us of the existential nature of social history. In a 1980 essay he quotes Jean-Paul Sartre as follows: "The essential is not what 'one' has done to man... but what man has done with what 'one' has done to him." Gutman goes on to state that "studying the choices working men and women made and how their behavior affected important historical processes enlarges our understanding."[20] Gutman's assertion compels an explanation of the role workers played in shaping this state-centered response. If the fire, to use Theda Skocpol's term, brought the state back into historical events, did workers have a role in shaping both the state and its resulting policies? My reading of history shows how workers were pushed out of the process of policy formation. The irony is, of course, this was a process they initiated and saw co-opted.

Writing during the Progressive Era, the editors of the *New Republic* argued that democracy was now subject to "tests of unprecedented severity" and lamented that our nation's future "depends...upon the capacity of employers and workers to harmonize democratic ideals of freedom with the voluntary self-discipline essential to efficient production."[21] Reformers, such as those involved with the Protocol, saw industrial democracy as an answer to tyranny, socialism, or anarchy. Society could be saved in a peaceful and logical fashion. "A radical transformation of society might take place," write historians Nelson Lichtenstein and Howell John Harris in *Industrial Democracy in America*,

> [B]ut it would be achieved in gradual, peaceful fashion, by piecemeal activities of men of women of good will, of all social classes, sharing common concerns about injustice and wastefulness of the social order. Many hard questions were left unanswered, but that was part of the attractiveness of the idea: it was a vision, a goal, an implicit ideal for focusing criticism of the existing order.[22]

In addition, industrial democracy held out a promise to workers of a new day. There was a built-in contradiction, however. The democracy reformers envisioned could not be easily contained. The more self-involved workers became, the more democracy they demanded, and the more unruly the system became. Thus, ironically, the driving force behind the Protocol—industrial democracy—was also the source of its tension. Indeed, many of the designers of the Protocol feared this problem from the start and sought to create institutional safeguards against it that were profoundly antidemocratic. For instance, the "peacemakers," as the creators of the Protocol were called, established rigid top-down systems of bureaucracy in IR. When this proved ineffective, the state would be called in to enforce a systemization of IR.[23]

In the end, Protocolism did not answer the contradiction inherent within the form of industrial democracy that developed in America. It merely pointed it out. Protocolism unleashed a set of questions that informed future policy makers, unionists, workers, politicians, and business leaders. It created the format of future debate and led certain principles to the table, privileging some in the process. In short, it helped set the terms of discourse around labor for the remainder of the twentieth century.

Notes

INTRODUCTION

1. Nelson Lichtenstein and Howell John Harris, eds., *Industrial Democracy in America: The Ambiguous Promise* (Cambridge, UK: Cambridge University Press, 1993), 2. On the earlier efforts to redefine a new political economy, see Barbara H. Fried, *The Progressive Assault on Laissez Faire: Robert Hale and the First Law and Economics Movement* (Cambridge: Harvard University Press, 1998). The principal advocate for debating democracy in the Progressive Era was the philosopher John Dewey. On Dewey, see Kevin Mattson, *Creating a Democratic Public: The Struggle for Urban Participatory Democracy during the Progressive Era* (University Park: Pennsylvania State University Press, 1998); Robert B. Westbrook, *John Dewey and American Democracy* (Ithaca, NY: Cornell University Press, 1991). On changes with in the field of economic thought, see Lowell Gallaway and Richard Vedder, "Ideas Versus Ideology: The Origins of Modern Labor Economics," *Journal of Labor Research* XXIV 4 (Fall 2003): 643–68.

2. Jeffrey W. Coker, *Confronting American Labor: The New Left Dilemma* (Columbia: University of Missouri Press, 2002); Michael E. McGerr, *A Fierce Discontent: The Rise and Fall of the Progressive Movement in America, 1870–1920* (New York: Free Press, 2003); Brandeis quoted in Philippa Strum, *Louis D. Brandeis: Justice for the People* (Cambridge: Harvard University Press, 1984), 103. On social science, see David C. Hammack and Stanton Wheeler, *Social Science in the Making Essays on the Russell Sage Foundation, 1907–1972* (New York: Russell Sage Foundation, 1994); Dorothy Ross, *The Origins of American Social Science* (New York: Cambridge University Press, 1991); Dorothy Ross, *Modernist Impulses in the Human Sciences, 1870–1930* (Baltimore: Johns Hopkins University Press, 1994); Thomas Bender, *Intellect and Public Life: Essays on the Social History of Academic Intellectuals in the United States* (Baltimore: Johns Hopkins University Press, 1993); Clarence E. Wunderlin, *Visions of a New Industrial Order: Social Science and Labor Theory in America's Progressive Era* (New York: Columbia University Press, 1992). Daniel Rodgers has suggested that Progressivism shared a set of common languages surrounding reform efforts. See Daniel T. Rodgers, "In Search of Progressivism," *Reviews in American History* 10, no. 4 (December 1982): 113–32; Alan Dawley, *Struggles for Justice: Social Responsibility and the Liberal State* (Cambridge: Harvard University Press, 1991).

3. Bruce E. Kaufman, "John R. Commons and the Wisconsin School on Industrial Relations Strategy and Policy," *Industrial and Labor Relations Review* 57, no. 1 October (2003): 79.

4. A good starting point on this debate is Leon Fink, *In Search of the Working Class: Essays in American Labor History and Political Culture* (Urbana: University of Illinois Press, 1994).

5. Joshua Benjamin Freeman, *In Transit: The Transport Workers Union in New York City, 1933–1966* (New York: Oxford University Press, 1989); Nelson Lichtenstein, *Labor's War at Home: The CIO in World War II* (Cambridge, UK: Cambridge University Press, 1982); and Michael Kazin, *Barons of Labor: The San Francisco Building Trades and Union Power in the Progressive Era* (Urbana: University of Illinois Press, 1987) have been referred to as a return of institutionalism.

6. Robert H. Wiebe, *The Search for Order, 1877–1920* (New York: Hill and Wang, 1967).

7. Lichtenstein and Harris, *Industrial Democracy*, 1.

8. Daniel E. Bender, *Sweated Work, Weak Bodies: Anti-Sweatshop Campaigns and Languages of Labor* (New Brunswick: Rutgers University Press, 2003). On the "new" immigrants in general, see Thomas Kessner, *The Golden Door: Italian and Jewish Immigrant Mobility in New York City, 1880–1915* (New York: Oxford University Press, 1977); John E. Bodnar, *The Transplanted a History of Immigrants in Urban America (Interdisciplinary Studies in History)* (Bloomington: Indiana University Press, 1985).

9. David Montgomery, *Workers' Control in America: Studies in the History of Work, Technology, and Labor Struggles* (New York: Cambridge University Press, 1979). On republicanism see Sean Wilentz, "Against American Exceptionalism: Class Consciousness and the American Labor Movement, 1790–1920," *International Labor and Working-Class History* 26 (Fall 1984): 1–24; Linda K. Kerker, "Working-Class Democrary in America: Sean Wilentz and the Jacksonian Worker," *International Labor and Working-Class History* 31 (Spring 1987): 69–76.

10. On workers' control, see David Montgomery, *Workers' Control in America: Studies in the History of Work, Technology, and Labor Struggles*.

11. Alan Dawley, *Struggles for Justice: Social Responsibility and the Liberal State* (Cambridge: Harvard University Press, 1991); and Graham Adams, *Age of Industrial Violence, 1910–15: The Activities and Findings of the United States Commission on Industrial Relations* (New York: Columbia University Press, 1966).

12. Shelton Stromquist, "Class Wars: Frank Walsh, the Reformers, and the Crisis of Progressivism," in Julie Greene, Eric Arnesen, and Bruce Laurie, eds., *Labor Histories: Class, Politics, and the Working-Class Experience* (Urbana: University of Illinois Press, 1998), 99. On the history of political economy, see Richard R. John, "Farewell to the 'Party Period': Political Economy in Nineteenth-Century America," *Journal of Policy History* 16:2 (2004): 117–25.

13. William J. Novak, *The People's Welfare Law and Regulation in Nineteenth-Century America* (Chapel Hill: University of North Carolina Press, 1996); Stephen Skowronek, *Building a New American State: The Expansion of National Administrative Capacities, 1877–1920* (New York: Cambridge University Press, 1982).

14. On Pullman, see Susan E. Hirsch, *After the Strike: A Century of Labor Struggle at Pullman* (Urbana: University of Illinois Press, 2003); Richard Schneirov, Shelton Stromquist, and Nick Salvatore, *The Pullman Strike and the Crisis of*

the 1890s: Essays on Labor and Politics (The Working Class in American History) (Urbana: University of Illinois Press, 1999). On Haymarket, see Paul Avrich, *The Haymarket Tragedy* (Princeton: Princeton University Press, 1984); Henry David, *The History of the Haymarket Affair: A Study in the American Social-Revolutionary and Labor Movements,* 2nd Ed. (New York: Russell & Russell, 1958); Carl Smith, *Urban Disorder and the Shape of Belief: The Great Chicago Fire, The Haymarket Bomb, and the Model Town of Pullman* (Chicago: University of Chicago Press, 1995). And on Ludlow, see Howard Gitleman, *The Legacy of the Ludlow Massacre: A Chapter in American Industrial Relations* (Philadelphia: University of Pennsylvania Press, 1988).

15. On labor and the law, see Karen Orren, *Belated Feudalism: Labor, the Law, and Liberal Development in the United States* (Cambridge, UK: Cambridge University Press, 1991); Victoria C. Hattam, *Labor Visions and State Power: The Origins of Business Unionism in the United States* (Princeton: Princeton University Press, 1993); Hattam, "Economic Visions and Political Strategies: American Labor and the State, 1865–1896," *Studies in American Political Development* 4 (1990): 83–129; Christopher L. Tomlins, *The State and the Unions: Labor Relations, Law, and the Organized Labor Movement in America, 1880–1960* (Cambridge, UK: Cambridge University Press, 1985); William E. Forbath, *Law and the Shaping of the American Labor Movement* (Cambridge: Harvard University Press, 1989); Randolph E. Bergdtrom, *Courting Danger: Injury and Law in New York City, 1870– 1910* (Ithaca, NY: Cornell University Press, 1992); William G. Ross, *A Muted Fury: Populists, Progressives, and Labor Unions Confront the Courts, 1890–1937* (Princeton: Princeton University Press, 1994). On the history of strikebreaking, see Stephen H. Norwood, *Strikebreaking and Intimidation Mercenaries and Masculinity in Twentieth-Century America* (Chapel Hill: University of North Carolina Press, 2002). In addition, see the recent Thomas R. Clark, *Defending Rights Law, Labor Politics, and the State in California, 1890–1925* (Detroit: Wayne State University Press, 2002).

16. Paul Boyer, *Urban Masses and Moral Order in America, 1820–1920* (Cambridge: Harvard University Press, 1978); Gabriel Kolko, *The Triumph of Conservatism: A Re-Interpretation of American History, 1900–1916* (New York: Free Press of Glencoe, 1963); Kolko, *Railroads and Regulation, 1877–1916* (Princeton: Princeton University Press, 1965).

17. On this, see the sophisticated work of Colin Gordon, *New Deals: Business, Labor, and Politics in America, 1920–1935* (New York: Cambridge University Press, 1994).

18. Ellis Hawley, *The New Deal and the Problem of Monopoly: A Study in Economic Ambivalence* (Princeton: Princeton University Press, 1966); Richard L. McCormick, *From Realignment to Reform: Political Change in New York State 1893– 1910* (Ithaca, NY: Cornell University Press, 1981). See also, Robert D. Johnston, *The Radical Middle Class: Populist Democracy and the Question of Capitalism in Progressive Era Portland* (Princeton: Princeton University Press, 2003); William G. Ross, *A Muted Fury: Populists, Progressives, and Labor Unions Confront the Courts, 1890–1937* (Princeton: Princeton University Press, 1994); and Elizabeth. Sanders,

Roots of Reform Farmers, Workers, and the American State, 1877–1917 (Chicago: University of Chicago Press, 1999).

19. On economists, see Clarence E. Wunderlin, *Visions of a New Industrial Order: Social Science and Labor Theory in America's Progressive Era* (New York: Columbia University Press, 1992).

20. On the economic issues, see Martin J. Sklar, *The Corporate Reconstruction of American Capitalism, 1890–1916: The Market, the Law and Politics* (New York: Cambridge University Press, 1988). On the social aspects, see Paul Boyer, *Urban Masses and Moral Order in America, 1820–1920* (Cambridge: Harvard University Press, 1978).

21. Lawrence Goodwyn, *Democratic Promise: The Populist Moment in America* (New York: Oxford University Press, 1976).

22. Mary O. Furner, "The Republican Tradition and the New Liberalism: Social Investigation, State Building, and Social Learning in the Gilded Age," in Michael James Lacey and Mary O. Furner, eds., *The State and Social Investigation in Britain and the United States* (Washington DC: Woodrow Wilson Center Series of Cambridge University Press, 1993). Also see Michael B. Katz, *In the Shadow of the Poorhouse: A Social History of Welfare in America* (New York: Basic Books, 1986). On worker self-activity, see Staughton Lynd, ed., *"We Are All Leaders": The Alternative Unionism of the Early 1930s* (Urbana: University of Illinois Press, 1996).

23. Lichtenstein and Harris, *Industrial Democracy in America*.

24. Steve Fraser, "The 'Labor Question,'" in Steve Fraser and Gary Gerstle, eds., *The Rise and Fall of the New Deal Order* (Princeton: Princeton University Press, 1989), 62.

25. Rosanne Currarino, "Labor Intellectuals and the Labor Question: Wage Work, and the Making of Consumer Society in America 1873–1905" (Ph.D. Dissertation, Rutgers University, 1999).

26. Herbert Gutman, "Labor History and the 'Sartre Question,'" reprinted in Ira Berlin, ed., *Power and Culture: Essays on the American Working Class* (New York, Patheon Books, 1987), 326–28.

27. David Fairris, *Shopfloor Matters: Labor-Management Relations in Twentieth Century American Manufacturing* (New York: Routledge, 1997), 1–16.

28. For an introduction to industrial democracy in America, see the work by Milton Derber, "The Idea of Industrial Democracy in America," *Labor History* 7, no. 3 (Fall 1966): 259–86; Derber, *The American Idea of Industrial Democracy, 1865–1965* (Urbana: University of Illinois Press, 1970). On the language of progressives, see Daniel Rodgers, "In Search of Progressivism," *Reviews in American History* (December 1982): 113–31.

29. Howard Dickman, *Industrial Democracy in America: Ideological Origins of National Labor Relations Policy* (La Salle, IL: Open Court, 1987), 215.

30. United States Commission on Industrial Relations, *Final Report of the Commission on Industrial Relations* (Washington, DC: Government Printing Office, 1916): 17–18.

31. Joseph A. McCartin, *Labor's Great War: The Struggle for Industrial Democracy and the Origins of Modern Labor Relations, 1912–1921* (Chapel Hill: University of University of North Carolina, 1998).

32. Lichtenstein and Harris, *Industrial Democracy in America*, 2.

33. Historians Daniel Rodgers and James Kloppenberg have clearly demonstrated what Kloppenberg calls the "via media," the relationship between American and European reform. Daniel T. Rodgers, *Atlantic Crossings Social Politics in a Progressive Age* (Cambridge: Belknap Press of Harvard University Press, 1998); James T. Kloppenberg, *Uncertain Victory: Social Democracy and Progressivism in European and American Thought, 1870–1920* (New York: Oxford University Press, 1986).

34. Sidney and Beatrice Webb, *Industrial Democracy* (New York: Augustus M. Kelley, 1965, 1897 [reprint 1920]). On the Webbs, see Royden Harrison, *The Life and Times of Sidney and Beatrice Webb 1858–1905, the Formative Years* (New York: St. Martin's Press, 2000); Jeanne MacKenzie, *A Victorian Courtship the Story of Beatrice Potter and Sidney Webb* (London: Weidenfeld and Nicolson, 1979); Margaret Cole, *The Webbs and Their Work* (Westport: Greenwood Press, 1985); R. H. Tawney, *The Webbs in Perspective*, Webb Memorial Lectures, 1952 (London: Athlone Press [distributed by Constable]; 1953).

35. David Montgomery, "Industrial Democracy or Democracy in Industry?: The Theory and Practice of the Labor Movement, 1870–1925," in Nelson Lichtenstein and Howell John Harris, eds., *Industrial Democracy in America: The Ambiguous Promise* (New York: Cambridge University Press, 1993), 30–32.

36. Harrison, *The Life and Times of Sidney and Beatrice Webb*, 240–45.

37. Harrison, *The Life and Times of Sidney and Beatrice Webb*, 260.

38. On the cross-Atlantic flow of ideas during the early twentieth century, see the work of Daniel T. Rodgers, *Atlantic Crossings: Social Politics in a Progressive Age* (Cambridge: Belknap Press of Harvard University Press, 1998); James T. Kloppenberg, *Uncertain Victory: Social Democracy and Progressivism in European and American Thought, 1870–1920* (New York: Oxford University Press, 1986); Kloppenberg, *The Virtues of Liberalism* (New York: Oxford University Press, 1998).

39. Selig Perlman, *A Theory of the Labor Movement* (Philadelphia: Porcupine Press, 1979): 291–92.

40. Ibid., 293.

41. Ibid., 296–97; and Sidney and Beatrice Webb, *Industrial Democracy*, Parts 1 and 2.

42. Bruce E. Kaufman, *The Origins and Evolution of the Field of Industrial Relations in the United States* (Ithaca, NY: IR Press, 1993), 33–34. On this matter Kaufman's claims find validation in the work of Michael B. Katz, *In the Shadow of the Poorhouse: A Social History of Welfare in America* (New York: Basic Books, 1986); Harry Braverman, *Labor and Monopoly Capital: The Degradation of Work in the Twentieth Century*, 25th Anniversary Ed. (New York: Monthly Review Press, 1998).

43. Christopher L. Tomlins, *The State and the Unions: Labor Relations, Law, and the Organized Labor Movement in America, 1880–1960* (Cambridge, UK: Cambridge University Press, 1985), 81.

44. For a recent discussion of this, see Philip Yale Nicholson, *Labor's Story in the United States (Labor in Crisis)* (Philadelphia: Temple University Press, 2004).

45. On the IWW, see Melvyn Dubofsky and Joseph Anthony McCartin, *We Shall Be All: A History of the Industrial Workers of the World*, Abridged Ed. (Urbana: University of Illinois Press, 2000). On the AFL see, for starters, Michael Kazin, *Barons of Labor: The San Francisco Building Trades and Union Power in the Progressive Era* (Urbana: University of Illinois Press, 1987); Melvyn Dubofsky, *Industrialization and the American Worker, 1865–1920* (Arlington Heights: Harlan Davidson, 1985, 1975); Dubofsky, *John L. Lewis: A Biography* (Urbana: University of Illinois Press, 1986). For recent work that looks at the IWW and the AFL in a comparative framework, see Peter Cole, "Shaping Up and Shipping Out: The Philadelphia Waterfront During and After the IWW Years, 1913–1940" (Ph.D. Dissertation, History, Georgetown University, 1997); and Howard Kimeldorf, *Battling for American Labor: Wobblies, Craft Workers, and the Making of the Union Movement* (Berkeley: University of California Press, 1999).

46. Steve Fraser, "From the 'New Unionism' to the New Deal," *Labor History* 25:3 (Summer 1984): 407; Fraser, "The 'New Unionism' and the New Economic Policy," in James E. Cronin and Carmen Sirianni, eds., *Work, Community, and Power: The Experience of Labor in Europe and American, 1900–1925* (Philadelphia: Temple University Press, 1983), 173–96. In addition, see Melvyn Dubofsky and Foster Rhea Dulles, *Labor in America: A History* (Wheeling, IL: Harlan Davidson, 2004), 191–94.

47. On the UMW, see Perry K. Blatz, *Democratic Miners: Work and Labor Relations in the Anthracite Coal Industry, 1875–1925* (Albany: State University of New York Press, 1994). On Hillman and the ACWU, see Steve Fraser, *Labor Will Rule: Sidney Hillman and the Rise of American Labor* (New York: Free Press, 1991).

48. For a sampling of the literature on the ethnicity of garment workers, see Daniel E. Bender, *Sweated Work, Weak Bodies: Anti-Sweatshop Campaigns and Languages of Labor* (New Brunswick: Rutgers University Press, 2003); Nan Enstad, *Ladies of Labor, Girls of Adventure: Working Women, Popular Culture, and Labor Politics at the Turn of the Twentieth Century* (New York: Columbia University Press, 1999); Hasia R. Diner, *Jewish Americans: The Immigrant Experience* (Westport, CT: Hugh Lauter Levin Associates, 2002); Diner, *A Time for Gathering the Second Migration, 1820–1880* (Baltimore: Johns Hopkins University Press, 1992); Jo Ann E. Argersinger, *Making the Amalgamated: Gender, Ethnicity, and Class in the Baltimore Clothing Industry, 1899–1939* (Baltimore: Johns Hopkins University Press, 1999); Daniel Soyer, "Class Conscious Workers as Immigrant Entrepreneurs: The Ambiguity of Class Among Eastern European Jewish Immigrants to the United States at the Turn of the Twentieth Century," *Labor History* 42, no. 1 (2001): 45–59; Charles Anthony Zappia, "Unionism and the Italian American Worker: A History of the New York City 'Italian Locals' in the International

Ladies' Garment Workers' Union, 1900–1914" (Ph.D. Dissertation, University of California at Berkeley, 1994); Louis Levine, *The Women's Garment Workers* (New York: B. W. Huebsch, 1924); Columba Marie Furio, "Immigrant Women and Industry: A Case Study, the Italian Women and the Garment Industry, 1880–1950" (Ph.D. Dissertation, New York University, 1979); Jennifer Guglielmo and Salvatore Salerno, *Are Italians White? How Race is Made in America* (New York: Routledge, 2003); Elizabeth Ewen, *Immigrant Women in the Land of Dollars: Life and Culture on the Lower East Side, 1890–1925* (New York: Monthly Review Press, 1985); Susan A. Glenn, *Daughters of the Shtetl: Life and Labor in the Immigrant Generation* (Ithaca, NY: Cornell University Press, 1990).

49. Sven Beckert, *The Monied Metropolis New York City and the Consolidation of the American Bourgeoisie, 1850–1896* (New York and Cambridge, UK: Cambridge University Press, 2001); and Thomas Kessner, *Capital City New York City and the Men Behind America's Rise to Economic Dominance, 1860–1900* (New York: Simon & Schuster, 2003).

50. Louis Brandeis, "Efficiency by Consent: To Secure Its Active Cooperation Labor Must Be Consulted," *Industrial Management* 55 (February 1918): 108–9.

51. Taylor quoted in Robert F. Hoxie, "Scientific Management and Labor Welfare," *Journal of Political Economy* 24:9 (November 1916): 837.

52. Howell John Harris, "Industrial Democracy and Liberal Capitalism, 1890–1925," in Nelson Lichtenstein and Howell John Harris, eds., *Industrial Democracy in America: The Ambiguous Promise* (New York: Cambridge University Press, 1993), 58.

53. David Brody, *Steel Workers in America: The Nonunion Era* (Cambridge: Harvard University Press, 1960); Editorial, *New Republic* 28 (August 1915): 91–92. On the larger issues of common interest and harmony, see Christopher J. Cyphers, *The National Civic Federation and the Making of a New Liberalism, 1900–1915* (Westport, CT: Praeger, 2002), 1–67.

54. Brandeis turned Wilson down. See Joseph A. McCartin, *Labor's Great War: The Struggle for Industrial Democracy and the Origins of Modern Labor Relations, 1912–1921* (Chapel Hill: University of University of North Carolina, 1998), 14.

55. See Chapters 5 through 7 in this volume and Leon Stein, *The Triangle Fire* (Ithaca, NY: Cornell University Press, 2001); Dave Von Drehle, *Triangle: The Fire That Changed America* (New York: Atlantic Monthly Press, 2003).

56. David von Drehle's recent book sees the strikes of 1909 and 1910, as well as the Protocol, as mere back story for the fire. He does not see these as two important and interconnected episodes. See *Triangle: The Fire that Changed America* New York: Atlantic Monthly Books, 2003.

57. Edwin G. Burrows and Mike Wallace, *Gotham* (New York: Oxford University Press, 1998); and Joshua Benjamin Freeman, *Working-Class New York Life and Labor Since World War II* (New York: New Press [distributed by W.W. Norton], 2000) for examples of what I would call "large" case studies on New York City.

58. On Homestead, see Paul Krause, *The Battle for Homestead, 1880–1992: Politics, Culture and Steel* (Pittsburgh: University of Pittsburgh Press, 1992).

59. Brandeis quoted in David W. Levy, "Brandeis and the Progressive Movement," in Nelson L. Dawson, ed., *Brandeis and America* (Lexington: University Press of Kentucky, 1989), 106–7; see also, Phillipa Strum, *Louis D. Brandeis: Justice for the People* (Cambridge: Harvard University Press, 1984), 95–96.

60. On these contradictions, see Daniel Bell, *The Cultural Contradictions of Capitalism* (New York: Basic Books, [1976], 1996). On Homestead and its importance, see Paul Krause, *The Battle for Homestead, 1880–1992: Politics, Culture and Steel* (Pittsburgh: University of Pittsburgh Press, 1992), passim. On nineteenth-century labor, see Bruce Laurie, *Artisans into Workers* (New York: Hill and Wang, 1995); Daniel Walkowitz, *Worker City, Company Town: Iron and Cotton-Worker Protest in Troy and Cohoes, New York, 1855–1884* (Urbana: University of Illinois Press, 1978); Alan Dawley, *Class and Community* (Cambridge: Harvard University Press, 1976); and Nick Salvatore, *Eugene V. Debs Citizen Socialist* (Urbana: University of Illinois Press, 1982) among others. On the subject of workplace dangers, see David and Gerald E. Moskowitz Rosner, *Dying for Work: Workers' Safety and Health in Twentieth-Century America* (Bloomington: Indiana University Press, 1987); and Mark Aldrich, *Safety First: Technology, Labor, and Business in the Building of American Work Safety, 1870–1939* (Baltimore: Johns Hopkins University Press, 1997).

61. Peter Filine's fine essay "An Obituary for the Progressive Movement," *American Quarterly* 22 (1970): 20–34. For a very recent overview of the period and the historical literature, see Steven J. Diner, *A Very Different Age: Americans of the Progressive Era* (New York: Hill and Wang, 1997).

62. Steve Fraser, "The 'Labor Question,'" in Steve Fraser and Gary Gerstle, eds., *The Rise and Fall of the New Deal Order* (Princeton: Princeton University Press, 1989), 76.

CHAPTER 1

1. Kathryn Kish Sklar, "Hull House in the 1890s: A Community of Women Reformers," *Signs* 10, no. 4 (Summer 1985): 658–77; Sklar, *Florence Kelley and the Nation's Work: The Rise of Women's Political Culture, 1830–1900* (New Haven: Yale University Press, 1995); Nancy Schrom Dye, "Creating a Feminist Alliance: Sisterhood and Class Conflict in the New York Women's Trade Union League, 1903–1914," in Milton Cantor and Bruce Laurie, eds., *Class, Sex, and the Women Worker* (Westport, CT: Greenwood Press, 1977), 225–46; Dye, "Feminism or Unionism? The New York Women's Trade Union League and the Labor Movement," *Feminist Studies* 3, no. 12 (1975): 111–25; Dye, "The Women's Trade Union League of New York, 1903–1920" (Ph.D. Dissertation, University of Wisconsin, 1974).

2. Alice Kessler-Harris, *Out to Work: A History of Wage-Earning Women in the United States* (New York: Oxford University Press, 1982); Nancy Schrom Dye, *As Equals and as Sisters: Feminism, the Labor Movement, and the Women's Trade Union League of New York* (Columbia: University of Missouri Press, 1980); Gladys Boone, *The Women's Trade Union League in Great Britain and the United States* (New York:

Columbia University Press, 1942); Allen Davis, "The Women's Trade Union League: Origins and Organization," *Labor History* 5:1 (Winter 2964): 3–17; Susan Glenn, *Daughters of the Shtetl: Life and Labor in the Immigrant Generation* (Ithaca, NY: Cornell University Press, 1990); Susan Lehrer, *The Origins of Protective Labor Legislation for Women, 1905–1925* (Albany: SUNY Press, 1987); Annelise Orleck, *Common Sense and a Little Fire: Women and Working-Class Politics in the United States, 1900–1965* (Chapel Hill: University of North Carolina Press, 1995); Maxine Schwartz Seller, "The Uprising of the Twenty Thousand: Sex, Class, and Ethnicity in the Shirtwaist Makers' Strike of 1909," in Dirk Hoerder, ed., *"Struggle a Hard Battle": Essays on Working Class Immigrants* (DeKalb: Northern Illinois University Press, 1986), 254–79; and Meredith Tax, *The Rising of the Women: Feminist Solidarity and Class Conflict, 1880–1917* (New York: Monthly Review Press, 1980).

3. Tax, *The Rising of the Women*.

4. The *Call* 15 December 1909, 2.

5. Glenn, *Daughters of the Shtetl*, 132–46; Daniel Horowitz, *The Morality of Spending: Attitudes Toward the Consumer Society in America, 1875–1940* (Baltimore: Johns Hopkins University Press, 1985), 13–66; Peter R. Shergold, *Working-Class Life: The "American Standard" in Comparative Perspective, 1899–1913* (Pittsburgh: University of Pittsburgh Press, 1982); and Dorothee Schneider, *Trade Unions and Community: The German Working Class in New York City, 1870–1900* (Urbana: University of Illinois Press, 1994).

6. The Sunday *Call* 29 December 1909.

7. Woods Hutchinson, "The Hygienic Aspects of the Shirtwaist Strike," the *Survey* XXII 2 January 1910, 544–50.

8. *Souvenir History*, 5

9. The *Outlook* XCIII 11 December 1909, 799.

10. Lemlich quoted in the *New York Evening Journal* 26 November 1909.

11. Orleck, *Common Sense*, 55

12. A sweatshop refers to any garment shop that is in violation of any labor, heath, or building codes.

13. Jesse Thomas Carpenter, *Competition and Collective Bargaining in the Needle Trades, 1910–1967* (Ithaca, NY: ILR Press, 1972); Richard A. Greenwald, "Bargaining for Industrial Democracy? Labor, the State, and the New Industrial Relations in Progressive Era New York" (Ph.D. Dissertation, New York University, 1998); Daniel E. Bender and Richard A. Greenwald, eds., *Sweatshop USA: The American Sweatshop in Historical and Global Perspective* (New York and London: Routledge, 2003); and the Governor's Advisory Commission, *Cloak, Suit, and Skirt Industry, New York City: Report of an Investigation* (New York: New York State, 1925).

14. Louis Levine, *The Women's Garment Workers: A History of the International Ladies' Garment Workers' Union* (New York: B. W. Huebsch, 1924), 148–50; Hyman Berman, "The Era of the Protocol: A Chapter in the History of the International Ladies' Garment Workers Union, 1910–1916" (Ph.D. Dissertation, Columbia University, 1956), 74; Constance D. Leupp, "The Shirtwaist Makers Strike," the *Survey* XXIII 18 December 1909, 383–86; the *Call* 27 August 1909.

15. McCreesch, "On the Picket Line," 146.

16. Quoted in ILGWU, *Proceedings of the Ninth Annual Convention* (Philadelphia, 1908), 1.

17. Cahan quoted in Dubofsky, *When Workers*, 46.

18. The *Call* for 21 August 1909. Meyer London, legal and labor relations adviser to union, recalled similarly: "We had unions some time ago—they existed on paper. We had agitators who were irrigators only. We had a movement that moved backwards. We talked about a social revolution and had a 70 hour week! We talked about reorganizing the whole world in a day, and down under our very noses, people slaved in sweat shops."

19. Levine, "Ladies' Garment Workers," *Women's Garment Workers*, 150.

20. The *Call* 6 and 8 September 1909.

21. Levine, *Women's Garment Workers*, 150–51.

22. Ibid., 150–51; the *Outlook* XCIII 11 December 1909, 800; the *Survey* XXIII 13 November 1909, 228; *Jewish Daily Forward* 28 September 1909, 8.

23. Levine, "Ladies' Garment Workers," *Women's Garment Workers*, 150–55.

24. Allen F. Davis, "The Women's Trade Union League: Origins and Organization," *Labor History* 5, no. 1 (Winter 1964): 3–17; Susan Estabrook Kennedy, *If All We Did Was Weep at Home: A History of White Working-Class Women in America* (Bloomington: Indiana University Press, 1979); Diane Kirby, "'The Wage-earning Woman and the State': The National Women's Trade Union League and Protective Labor Legislation, 1903–1923," *Labor History* 28, no. 1 (Winter 1987): 54–74; Robin Miller Jacoby, "The Women's Trade Union League and American Feminism," *Feminist Studies* 3, no. 12 (1975): 126–40; Nancy Schrom Dye, "Feminism or Unionism? The New York Women's Trade Union League and the Labor Movement," *Feminist Studies* 3, no. 12 (1975): 111–25; Dye, "Creating a Feminist Alliance: Sisterhood and Class Conflict in the New York Women's Trade Union League, 1903–1914," in Milton Cantor and Bruce Laurie, eds., *Class, Sex, and the Women Worker* (Westport, CT: Greenwood Press, 1977), 225–46; Dye, *As Equals and as Sisters: Feminism, the Labor Movement, and the Women's Trade Union League of New York* (Columbia: University of Missouri Press, 1980); Elizabeth Anne Payne, *Reform, Labor, and Feminism: Margaret Dreier Robins and the Women's Trade Union League* (Urbana: University of Illinois Press, 1988); Elizabeth Israels Perry, "Women's Political Choices After Suffrage: The Women's City Club of New York, 1915–1990," *New York History* 62, no. 4 (October 1990): 417–34; and Alice Kessler-Harris, *Out to Work: A History of Wage-Earning Women in the United States* (New York: Oxford University Press, 1982).

25. Editorial, *Jewish Daily Forward* 17 November 1909, 4.

26. Levine, *Women's Garment Workers*, 150–60; *New York World* 23 November 1909.

27. *New York Times* 23 November 1909, 16; *Jewish Daily Forward* 23 November 1909, 1, 8; the *Call* 22 and 23 November 1909.

28. *New York World* 23 November 1909, 7; William Mailly, "The Working Girl's Strike," *Independent* LXVII 23 December 1909, 1417.

29. *Jewish Daily Forward* 23 November 1909. The ILGWU and Local 25, in *Souvenir History*, 12, remembered the pledge without the overtly religious overtones: "If I turn traitor to the cause I now pledge, may this hand wither from the arm I now raise." See also, Hadassa Kosak, *Cultures of Opposition* (Albany: SUNY Press, 2000); as well as Irving Howe, *World of Our Fathers* (New York: Simon & Schuster, 1976); and Steven Cassedy, *To the Other Shore* (Princeton: Princeton University Press, 1997).

30. Sarah Comstock, "The Uprising of the Girls," *Collier's* XLIV 25 December 1909, 14–16; B. Weinstein, "Scenes from Strike Headquarters," *Jewish Daily Forward* 1 December 1909, 5.

31. Berman, "Era of the Protocol," 8; *New York World* 23 November 1909, 7; ibid., 24 November 1909, 2; *Jewish Daily Forward* 23 November 1909, 1.

32. *Souvenir History*, 12–13.

33. Quoted in Sue Annelise Clark and Edith Wyatt, *Making Both Ends* (New York: Macmillian, 1911), 65–67.

34. See Charles S. Bernheimer, *The Shirtwaist Strike: An Investigation Made for the Council and Head Worker of the University Settlement* (New York: University Settlement Studies, 1910), 3–5, for model settlement. Also see William Mailly, "The Working Girl Strike," *Independent* LXVII 23 December 1909, 1419.

35. See the *Jewish Daily Forward* 4 November 1909, 8. See also the *New York Herald* 6 November 1909, 4.

36. *New York World* 24 November 1909, 3; *Jewish Daily Forward* 24 November 1909, 1; and ibid., 25 November 1909, 1; *New York Herald* 25 November 1909, 5; "Battle Between Manufacturers and Women Workers," *Hampton's Magazine* XXIV (March 1910), 423–25; the *Outlook* XCIII, 799.

37. *New York Herald* 28 November 1909, II: 7; *New York World* 26 November 1909, 14; *New York Times* 27 November 1909, 3.

38. *New York Times* 28 November 1909, 71.

39. *New York Herald* 28 November 1909, II: 7.

40. Levine, Ladies' Garment Workers, *Women's Garment Workers*, 150–70.

41. *New York Times* 10 December 1909, 13; *Jewish Daily Forward* 27 November 1909, 8; the *Call* 12 December 1909; "The Philadelphia Shirtwaist Strike," the *Survey* 13 5 February 1910, 595–96.

42. 1909 striker interviewed and quoted in Levine, *Women's Garment Workers*, 144.

43. See note 3 as well as Nan Estad, *Ladies of Labor* (New York: Columbia University Press, 2000).

44. *Jewish Daily Forward* 3 October 1909, 1.

45. *Jewish Daily Forward* 12 August 1909, 1.

46. *Jewish Daily Forward* 11 September 1909, 1; and ibid., 17 September 1909, 1.

47. The *Call* 16 September 1909; McAlister Coleman, "All of Which I Saw," *Progressive* XIV May 1950, 24–25.

48. The *Call* 31 October 1909; Dubofsky, *When Workers Organize*, 53.

49. Malkiel, *Diary*, 95.

50. *New York World* 26 November 1909, 4; *New York Times* 6 January 1910, 5; and ibid., 7 January 1910, 6.

51. Dubofsky, *When Workers Organize*, 53–54.

52. For House quote, see *New York Times* 4 January 1910, 20. For similar statements by judges, see Annelise Clark and Edith Wyatt, "Shirtwaist Makers and their Strike," *McClure's Magazine* XXXVI November 1910, 70–86.

53. Malkiel, *Diary*, 113.

54. During the month of October, nonstriking waistmakers, those who had settled early, held a concert to raise money for the local's defense fund. See the *Call* 31 October 1909.

55. William Mailly, "The Working Girls Strike," *Independent* LXVII 23 December 1909, 1416; *New York Times* 16 December 1909, 3.

56. The *Call* 31 October 1909.

57. *New York Times* 5 November 1909, 1; the *Survey* XXIII 13 November 1909, 228; *New York World* 5 November 1909, 1; the *Call* 5 November 1909; and *Souvenir History*, 9–10.

58. For Weyl's and Hyman's statements, see the *New York Times* 4 December 1909, 20.

59. The *Call* 25 November 1909.

60. The *Call* 26 December 1909.

61. *New York Times* 21 December 1909.

62. *New York Times* 6 December 1909, 11; *Jewish Daily Forward* 6 December 1909, 1; Malkiel, *Diary*, 20–22.

63. "Girl Strikers Protest Against Magistrates," the *Survey* XXIII 8 January 1910, 485–90; *Souvenir History*, 20; Malkiel, *Diary*, 58–60, 72–74. These girls, once released from the workhouse, returned as heroes. See also the *New York Times* 23 December 1909, 7.

64. See those papers for 3 January 1909, especially the *New York Times* 3 January 1909, 3.

65. Nan Estad, *Ladies of Labor*.

66. Sarah Comstock, "The Uprising of the Girls," *Collier's* XLV 5 December 1909, 16; the *Call* 25 November 1909; *New York Times* 4 December 1909, 2; *New York World* 4 December 1909, 18; Malkiel, *Diary*, 15, 20–21; *Souvenir History*, 14–15; and Orlick, *Common Sense*, 61.

67. Letter of E.R.A. Seligman et al., *New York Times* 20 December 1909, 8; the *Times'* response, *New York Times* 21 December 1909, 8; Seligman and company's response, *New York Times* 24 December 1909, 3.

68. See *Century Illustrated Monthly Magazine* LXXIX March 1910, 791–92 for a critical account of the allies' efforts to aid the strikers; and Women's Trade Union League of New York, *Annual Report* (1909–10), 14; McCreesh, "On the Picket Line," 180–81; and Berman, "Era of the Protocol," 78.

69. Letter of Elizabeth Dutcher, chair of Picketing Committee of WTUL, in the *New York Times* 21 December 1909, 8; Martin Littleton, "The Legal Aspects: A Message to the Strikers," the *Survey* XXIII 22 January 1910, 555–8; *Jewish Daily*

Forward 15 February 1910, 1; *New York Times* (Magazine Section) 19 December 1909, 5; the *Call* 20 December 1909; and *Souvenir History*, 16.

70. Sarah Comstock, "The Uprising of the Girls," *Collier's* XLIV 25 December 1909, 20.

71. Malkiel, *Diary*, 41, 57; the *Call* 6 December 1909; ibid., 12 December 1909; and ibid., 20 December 1909; *Souvenir History*, 18.

72. Malkiel, *Diary*, 55.

73. Berman, "Era of the Protocol," 92.

74. See special editions of both papers: the *Call* 29 December 1909 and *Evening Journal* 6 January 1910.

75. See statements by I. B. Hyman of Association in the *New York Times* 4 December 1909, 20.

76. See the letter from John Mitchell and Marcus M. Marks to Solomon Shindler (Union) and I. B. Hyman (Association) in the *New York Times* 6 December 1909, 2.

77. *Jewish Daily Forward* 8 December 1909, 1; and ibid., 9 December 1909, 1.

78. *New York Times* 12 December 1909, 5.

79. Hillquit speech 27 December 1909 quoted in Philip Foner, *Women and the American Labor Movement, Vol.1* (New York: Free Press, 1979), 336.

80. *New York Times* 18 December 1909; and ibid., 19 December 1909, 2.

81. See Editorial, "The Open Shop," *New York Times* 16 December 1909, 8; "The Open Shop Again," ibid., 20 December 1909, 8; and Edward T. Devine, "The Shirtwaist Makers Strike," the *Survey* XXIII 15 January 1910, 505–6.

82. *New York Times* 15 December 1909, 8; ibid., 16 December 1909, 3; ibid., 23 December 1909, 1; and Boone, *The WTUL*, 84–85.

83. *New York Times* 24 December 1909, 3. For impact of Philadelphia strike on New York manufacturers, see the *New York Times* 20 December 1909, 2; and ibid., 21 December 1909, 1.

84. *New York Times* 28 December 1909, 5; Philip P. Davis, "The Shirtmakers Strike," *Chautauquan* LIX June 1910, 99–105.

85. *New York Times* 30 December 1909, 3; Bernheimer, *The Shirtwaist Strike*, passim.

86. *New York Times* 21 December 1909, 1; Mary Brown Sumner, "The Spirit of the Strikers," the *Survey* XXII 22 January 1910, 550–55; Miriam Finn Scott, "The Spirit of the Girl Strikers," the *Outlook* XCIV 19 February 1910, 392–97.

87. *New York Times* 4 January 1910, 20; ibid., 5 January 1910, 20; and ibid., 6 January 1910, 5; State of New York, Department of Labor, *Bulletin* XII 1910, 38–48.

88. *New York Times* 18 January 1910, 11.

89. *New York Times* 7 January 1910, 6; and ibid., 25 January 1910, 1.

90. *Jewish Daily Forward* 1 February 1910, 1; ibid., 2 February 1910, 1; and ibid., 7 February 1910, 1.

91. "Shirtwaist Strike in Philadelphia Settled," the *Survey* XXIII 19 February 1910, 757–58.

92. Colin Gordon's insightful work, *New Deals: Business, Labor, and Politics in America. 1920–1935* (Cambridge: Cambridge University Press, 1994).

93. Melvyn Dubofsky, *When Workers Organize* (Amherst: University of Massachusetts Press, 1968); Dubofsky, *The State and Labor in Modern America* (Chapel Hill: University of North Carolina Press, 1994).

94. Abraham Rosenberg, *Memoirs of the Clockmakers and Their Unions* (New York: Local 1, ILGWU, 1920), 183–85; B. Hoffman, *Fifty Years Cloak Operators' Union* (New York: Local 117, 1936), 170–71; Berman, "Era of the Protocol," 105–6.

95. To call this faction "conservative," as some scholars have, seems ill founded. Both factions claimed socialism as their political ideology. Both saw the union as a democratic institution to achieve socialism. Their differences were more over means than ends.

96. "Report of the Joint Board of Cloak, Skirt, Pressers Unions of New York," in *Proceedings of the Tenth Convention of the International Ladies Garment Workers Union* (Boston: ILGWU, 1910), 47–49.

97. "Report of the President," in *Proceedings of the Tenth Convention of the International Ladies Garment Workers Union* (Boston, ILGWU, 1910), 17; and Hoffman, *Fifty Years*, 169.

98. See "Report of Local 1," in *Proceedings of the Tenth Convention of the International Ladies Garment Workers Union* (Boston, ILGWU, 1910), 51–52; and "Report of Local 9," ibid., 56–57, for examples of this thinking.

99. See Rosenberg, *Memoirs*, 179–82; and "Men Who Made Women's clothing," the *Survey* XXIV (August 13, 1910): 701–3, for a fuller discussion of this trend.

100. "Minutes," *Special Meeting of a Committee to Investigate All Grievances of the Firm and the Workers of Joseph Rosenberg and Co.* February 8, 1915, 43 in Paul Abelson Papers, Catherwood Library, New York State School of Labor Relations, Cornell University. (Hereafter cited as Abelson Papers); Julius Hochman, "The Story of Labor: ILGWU—1900–1950," *Women's Wear Daily* 23 May 1950; Joel Seidman, *The Needle Trades*, 133; "The Cloakmakers' Strike," the *Outlook* XCV (July 23, 1910): 596–97; Edith Wyatt, "The New York Cloakmakers' Strike," *McClure's Magazine* XXXVI (April 1911): 708; "Reasons for a General Cloak Strike," *Jewish Daily Forward* 16 June 1910, 4.

101. Fosenberg, *Memoirs*, 190–91; Berman, "Era of the Protocol," 108–9. Neither Berman, while conducting research for his 1956 dissertation, nor I have been able to find many copies of the *New Post*. Most of what is known about this obviously valuable source comes from participants' observations and the earliest chroniclers of the events.

102. Jesse Thomas Carpenter has a complete discussion of jobbing, and inside- and outside-contracting. See his *Competition and Collective Bargaining*, 11–18.

103. This paragraph and the previous one are based on Rosenberg, *Memoirs*, 186–89; *Jewish Daily Forward* 24 June 1910, 1.

104. The ILGWU began in 1910 to establish a system based on hierarchy. In an effort to create a structure to effectively bargain with employers, it removed from the rank and file most of the control over labor relations.

105. "Report of the General Secretary-Treasurer," in *Proceedings of the Tenth Convention*, 26–29; Rosenberg, *Memoirs*, 192; Hoffman, *Fifty Years*, 177; *Jewish Daily Forward* 2 May 1910, 1.

106. This was to add to the two-dollar strike tax that was assessed in 1909.

107. "Report of Proceedings," in *Proceedings of the Tenth Convention*, 9, 70–73, 88, 95.

108. *Jewish Daily Forward* 21 June 1910, 1.

109. Hoffman, *Fifty Years*, 179–80; and Berman, "Era of the Protocol," 112.

110. Rosenberg, *Memoirs*, 195–96; *Jewish Daily Forward* 28 June 1910, 5; *New York Times* 30 June 1910; and *McClure's Magazine* XXVI, 709.

111. *New York Times* 30 June 1910, 11; *Jewish Daily Forward* 30 June 1910, 1; *New York World* 29 June 1910, 16.

112. On the voting and turnout, see the *Jewish Daily Forward* 5 July 1910, 1; and Rosenberg, *Memoirs*, 200–201.

113. Rosenberg, *Memoirs*, 202–6; Hoffman, *Fifty Years*, 182–85; *Jewish Daily Forward* 7 July 1910, 1, 9.

114. Rosenberg, *Memoirs*, 207–9; *New York Times* 8 July 1910, 1. On the number of strikers, the *New York Times* reported 60,000 workers. Yet as John Bryce McPherson showed, there were at least 15,000 allied workers in support trades, reefer, and raincoats that also joined the cloakmakers. See John Bryce McPherson, "The New York Cloakmakers' Strike," *Journal of Political Economy* XIX (March 1911): 154–55.

115. Rosenberg, *Memoirs*, 210–15; Morris Winchevsky, "Report of the Strike Fund Committee," *Jewish Daily Forward* 8 September 1910, 5.

116. *New York Times* 8 July 1910, 1, ibid., 12 July 1910, 5; and Berman, "Era of the Protocol," 117–19.

117. *New York Times* 2 July 1910, 5; *McClure's Magazine* XXXVI, 708–9.

118. Ibid.

119. Louis Levine, *Women's Garment Workers*, 196.

120. Benjamin Stolberg, *Tailor's Progress: The Story of a Famous Union and the Men Who Made It* (Garden City: Doubleday, 1944), 68.

121. Ibid.

CHAPTER 2

1. Nelson Lichtenstein and Howell John Harris, eds., *Industrial Democracy in America: The Ambiguous Promise* (Cambridge: Woodrow Wilson Center Series of Cambridge University Press, 1993), 5.

2. Melvyn Dubofsky, *When Workers Organize: New York City in the Progressive Era* (Amherst: University of Massachusetts Press, 1968), 58–68; Jesse Thomas

Carpenter, *Competition and Collective Bargaining in the Needle Trades, 1910–1967* (Ithaca, NY: Cornell University ILR Press, 1972), 1–54; Leon Stein, ed., *Out of the Sweatshop: The Struggle for Industrial Democracy* (New York: Quadrangle Books, 1977), 87–175; Louis Levine, *The Women's Garment Workers* (New York: Huebsch, 1924), 168–319; Gus Tyler, *Look For the Union Label*(New York: M.E. Sharpe, 1995), 63–85; Julius Henry Cohen, *Law and Order in Industry* (New York: MacMillan Company, 1916); Benjamin Stolberg, *Tailor's Progress*, (New York: Doubleday, 1944), 59–91; Arthur A. Goren, *New York Jews and the Quest for Community: The Kehillah Experiment, 1908–1922* (New York: Columbia University Press, 1970), 186–213; Philippa Strum, *Louis D. Brandeis: Justice for the People* (Cambridge: Harvard University Press, 1984), 159–95; and J. M. Budish and George Soule, *The New Unionism in the Clothing Industry* (New York: Harcourt, Brace and Howe, 1920), 101–55.

3. Correspondence between Michael J. Reagan and Alexander Bloch, July 8, 1910, and Michael J. Reagan and A. F. Lefcourt, July 15, 1910; Louis Brandeis Papers (Brandeis Papers); Hyman Berman, "The Era of the Protocol: A Chapter in the History of the International Ladies Garment Workers Union, 1910–1916," (Ph.D. Dissertation, Columbia University, 1956), 122–23; *New York Times* 13 July 1910, 3.

4. Berman, "Era of the Protocol," 123–25, particularly his quotes involving discussions between Simpson and Filene on July 14, 1910; Donald Wilhelm, "Meyer Bloomfield," *American Magazine* LXXIII, (March 1912): 553–54.

5. Kim McQuaid's fine essay on the shared vision of the two Filene brothers: "An American Owenite: Edward A. Filene and the Parameter of Industrial Reform, 1890–1937," *American Journal of Economics and Sociology* 35 (1976).

6. Carpenter, *Competition and Collective Bargaining*; Phillippa Strum, *Brandeis: Beyond Progressivism* (Lawrence: University of Kansas Press, 1993); Carpenter, *Louis D. Brandeis: Justice of the People* (Cambridge: Harvard University Press. 1984); Carpenter, "The Legacy of Louis Dembitz Brandeis, People's Attorney," 81 *American Jewish History* (Spring/Summer 1994): 406–27.

7. Arthur A Goren, "Jewish Labor Movement and Kehillah," in *New York Jews and the Quest for Community: The Kehillah Experiment, 1908–1922* (New York: Columbia University Press, 1970), 186–213. The quote is from page 197.

8. "Memorandum of Conference Between Meyer London and Principles," July 21, 1910 (Brandeis Papers). The Bloomfield letter quote is from Alpheus Thomas Mason, *Brandeis: A Free Man's Life* (New York: Viking Press, 1946), 292.

9. Louis D. Brandeis, quoted in the *Echo* (March 19, 1913).

10. Stolberg, *Tailor's Progress*, 55.

11. Letter from Louis D. Brandeis to Alfred Brandeis, July 24, 1910, quoted in Melvin I. Urofsky and David W. Levy, eds., *Letters of Louis D. Brandeis Volume II, 1907–1912: People's Attorney* (Albany: SUNY Press, 1972), 365.

12. "Notes of Telephone Conversations Between A. Lincoln Filene and L. D. Brandeis," July 22, 1910, and "Draft of Proposed Labor Agreement," July 23, Papers of Louis D. Brandeis, Garment Workers Files, (Microfilm Edition), hereafter cited as Brandeis Papers.

13. Berman, "Era of the Protocol," pp. 126–27. For the Brandeis quote, see L. D. Brandeis to J. H. Cohen, July 24, 1910, Berman, 127; also see Mason, *Brandeis*, 292.

14. The *New York Call* 26 July 1910, for this and the next paragraph.

15. Ibid. In addition, see Solberg, *Tailor's Progress* for an interesting discussion of the personalities of these union leaders.

16. *New York Times* 26 July 1910, 4; *New York Call* 26 July 1910, 1; *Jewish Daily Forward* 26 July 1910, 1; Rosenberg, *Memoirs*, 223–24; and Hoffman, *Fifty Years Cloak Operators' Union* (New York: Local 117, 1936), 193–94.

17. Julius Henry Cohen to Louis D. Brandeis, July 27, 1910 (Brandeis Papers).

18. Meyer London and J. H. Cohen to L. D. Brandeis, July 27, 1910, and L. D. Brandeis to M. Cohen and J. H. Cohen, July 27, 1910 (Brandeis Papers); Mason, *Brandeis*, 294.

19. Edith Wyatt in *McClure's Magazine* XXXVI, 710–11.

20. *New York Times* 29 July 1910. See also the *New York Globe* and *New York World* 29 July 1910 for the belief that the strike would soon be over—a few days more at most.

21. Brandeis's opening remarks for the conference on July 28, quoted in Mason, *Brandeis*, 294.

22. Mason, *Brandeis*, 295–96.

23. Mason, *Brandeis*, 295–96.

24. Quoted in Mason, *Brandeis*, 296–97.

25. Ibid.; Berman, "Era of the Protocol," 129–30. Brandeis quote is from page 130; David W. Levy, "Brandeis and the Progressive Movement," in Nelson L. Dawson, ed., *Brandeis and America* (Lexington: University Press of Kentucky), 108–9; and Strum, *Louis D. Brandeis*, 94–113.

26. Mason, *Brandeis*, 298.

27. Ibid, 131; L. D. Brandeis to Alfred Brandeis, July 31, 1910, in *Brandeis Letters*, 368.

28. Cohen to Brandeis, August 1, 1910, with tentative agreement, Brandeis to Cohen, August 1, 1910, with revised agreement, Cohen to London, August 1, 1910, with corrected agreement in ibid., 132.

29. The *Call* 3 August 1910; *Jewish Daily Forward* 30 July 1910, 4; and ibid., 3 August 1910, 1.

30. Reprinted letter of Meyer London to Julius Henry Cohen, August 3, 1910, in the *Jewish Daily Forward* 5 August 1910.

31. Mason, *Brandeis*, 298–99; See Berman, "Era of the Protocol," 133. On Moskowitz, see J. Salwyn Schapiro, "Henry Moskowitz: Social Reformer in Politics," the *Outlook* CII (October 26, 1912): 446–49; Hamilton Holt, "Henry Moskowitz: A Useful Citizen," the *Independent* LXXVII (January 12, 1914): 66–67.

32. Rosenberg, *Memoirs*, 219–21; *Jewish Daily Forward* 12 August 1910, 4.

33. *Jewish Daily Forward* 3 August 1910, 8; *New York Times* 25 August 1910, 2; Morris Winchevsky, "Report of the Strike Fund Committee," *Jewish Daily Forward* 8 September 1910, 5; and Berman, " Era of the Protocol," 135.

34. *New York Times* 2 August 1910, 6; ibid., 3 August 1910, 12; ibid., 5 August 1910, 8; the *Outlook* XCV (August 20, 1910): 856.

35. *New York Times* 6 August 1910, 14; ibid., 8 August 1910, 14.

36. *New York Times* 9 August 1910, 3; ibid., 10 August 1910, 2; ibid., 11 August 1910, 6; and *New York World* 9 August 1910, 5.

37. Letter from John Purroy Mitchel to William F. Baker, August 12, 1910, as printed in the *New York Times* 13 August 1910, 2.

38. Letter from John Purroy Mitchel to Chief Magistrates McAdoo and Kempner, August 13, 1910 printed in the *New York Times* 14 August 1910, 2.

39. *New York Times* 14 August 1910, 2; Paul J. Bonwit to John P. Mitchel August 13, 1910, printed in the *New York Times* 17 August 1910, 5.

40. *New York Times* 25 August 1910, 2.

41. Cohen, *Law and Order in Industry*, 12–13; Daniel R. Ernst, *Lawyers Against Labor: From Individual Rights to Corporate Liberalism* (Urbana: University of Illinois Press, 1995). See also Christopher Tomlins, *The State and the Unions* (New York: Cambridge University Press, 1985) and William Forbath, *Law and the Shaping of American Labor* (Cambridge: Harvard University Press, 1989).

42. *New York Times* 7 August 1910, 6; ibid., 14 August 1910, 2; *Jewish Daily Forward* 13 August 1910, 1. For the case summary, see Max M. Schwarcz as treasurer of the Cloak, Suit, and Skirt Manufacturers' Protective Association, Plaintiff, v. the International Ladies' Garment Workers' Union et al., Defendants. Supreme Court, County of New York, August 1910, 68 Misc. 528 (534).

43. Berman, "Era of the Protocol," 140

44. Ibid., 141.

45. Ibid.

46. Henry Moskowitz to Meyer Bloomfield, August 12, 1910, as quoted in Berman, "Era of the Protocol," 142; Henry Moskowitz to Meyer Bloomfield, August 12, 1910, and A. Lincoln Filene to Louis Marshall, August 18, 1910 as quoted in Berman, "Era of the Protocol," 142.

47. *New York Times* 20 August 1910, 1; *New York World* 23 August 1910, 7; ibid., 26 August 1910, 4.

48. *New York World* 21 August 1910, 4; *New York Times* 26 August 1910, 16; *McClure's Magazine* XXXVI, 712; and letter from Meyer Bloomfield to A. Lincoln Filene, August 21, 1910 as quoted in Berman, "Era of the Protocol," 143–44.

49. For this paragraph as well the following see, for the language of the preferential shop and the evolution of the draft language, Berman, "Era of the Protocol," 428.

50. Berman, "Era of the Protocol," 428.

51. *New York Times* 28 August 1910, 1, 3; John Bruce McPherson, "The New York Cloakmakers' Strike" *Journal of Political Economy* 19(3) (March 1911) 153–187. *New York Times* 28 August 1910, 3; *Jewish Daily Forward* 28 August 1910; Rosenberg, *Memoirs*, 238–42; *Jewish Daily Forward* 26 August 1910, 1; *Wahrheit* 27 August 1910, 1; *New York Evening Post* 26 August 1910, 3; Hoffman, *Fifty Years*, 201–3; *New York World* 27 August 1910, 5; ibid., 28 August 1910, 2.

52. Supreme Court, Special Term, New York County, Max M. Schwarcz, as Treasurer of the Cloak, Suit, and Skirt Manufacturer's Protective Association, Plaintiff, v. International Ladies' Garment Workers' Union, et al. Decedents, 68 (Misc) 528–34. Quote from page 534; see also, *New York Times* 28 August 1910, 1; *New York World* 28 August 1910, 2.

53. Editor on the *New York Evening Post*, quoted in Edith Wyatt, *McClure's Magazine* XXXVI, 713; see also Editorial "A Startling Labor Decision," *New York Times* 28 August 1910, 8; and Editorial, "Enjoining a Strike," the *Outlook* XCVI (September 19, 1910): 52.

54. *New York Times* 30 August 1910, 6; 2 September 1910, 5; letter from Mayor John P. Mitchel to William F. Baker, 30 August 1910 in the *New York Times* 31 August 1910, 5; *New York World* 31 August 1910, 3.

55. Moskowitz and Filene, for example, were horrified at the injunction. They believed that Goff would side with the union. But Filene and the others were relative newcomers to labor relations and assumed that the courts would be "neutral." This injunction, and other court actions that soon followed, forced them to advocate a new more privatized system of IR. *New York Times* 28 August 1910, 3; ibid., 29 August 1910, 6; *New York World* 29 August 1910, 5.

56. A. Lincoln Filene to Louis D. Brandeis, August 31, 1910, as quoted in Berman, "Era of the Protocol," 150.

57. Letter from Meyer London to John P. Mitchel, 1 September 1910, in the *New York Times* 2 September 1910, 5.

58. Berman, "Era of the Protocol," 151.

59. "Outcome of the Cloakmakers' Strike," the *Outlook* XCVI (September 17, 1910): 99–101; Hoffman, *Fifty Years*, 207–8; Rosenberg, *Memoirs*, 245.

60. *New York Times* 3 September 1910, 1; *Jewish Daily Forward* 3 September 1910, 1.

61. *New York Times* 6 September 1910, 9; *Jewish Daily Forward* 4 September 1910, 1; ibid., 5 September 1910, 1; ibid., 6 September 1910, 1.

62. Stolberg, *Tailor's Progress*, 117.

63. Stolberg, *Tailor's Progress*, 117.

64. See Philippa Strum, "Worker Participation," in *Louis D. Brandeis*, 159–95.

65. Cohen, *Law and Order in Industry*, 91.

66. For a similar point, see Colin Gordon's brilliant *New Deals: Business, Labor, and Politics in America, 1920–1935* (New York: Cambridge University Press, 1994).

67. Stolberg, *Tailor's Progress*, 73–74.

68. C. Howard, "Solution of the Labor Problem," *North American Review* CXCII (September 1910): 341–48; H. H. Lusk, "Industrial War," *Forum* XLVIII (November 1912): 553–64; E. P. Wheeler, "Industrial Peace or War," *Atlantic Monthly* CXI (April 1913): 532–39; G. B. Hugo, "Conditions Fundamental to Industrial Peace, *Annals of the American Academy* XLIV (November 1912): 18–27; and Washington Gladden, "Industry and Democracy," the *Outlook* XCVII (March 1911): 589–95, for a sampling of the purely positive public reception of this settlement.

69. Louis D. Brandeis to Ray Standard Baker, February 26, 1912, in Melvin I. Urofsky, ed., *The Letters of Louis D. Brandeis Volume II* (Albany: SUNY Press), 562–63.

70. Louis D. Brandeis to Ray Standard Baker, February 26, 1912, in Urofsky, ed., *The Letters of Louis D. Brandeis Volume II*, 562–63.

71. The most obvious place to see this is Brandeis's own *The Curse of Bigness*. Useful sources to help place Brandeis within the larger Progressive movement are Melvin I. Urofsky's work *A Mind of One Piece: Brandeis and American Reform* (New York: Scribner's, 1971), *Louis D. Brandeis and the Progressive Tradition* (Boston: Little, Brown, 1981), and "To Guide by the Light of Reason: Mr. Justice Brandeis—An Appreciation," *American Jewish History* 81 (Spring\Summer, 1994): 365–93; Phillipa Strum's work, *Brandeis: Beyond Progressivism* (Lawrence: University of Kansas Press, 1994), *Louis D. Brandeis: Justice for the People* (Cambridge: Harvard University Press, 1984), and "The Legacy of Louis Dembitz Brandeis, People's Attorney" *American Jewish History* 81 (Spring\Summer, 1994): 406–27; Stephen W. Bakerville's intellectual biography, *Of Laws and Limitations* (Rutherford: Fairleigh Dickinson University, 1994); Gerald Berk's "Neither Markets nor Administration: Brandeis and the Antitrust Reforms of 1914," *Studies in American Political Development* 8 (Spring, 1994):24–59; and the older work of Alpheus Thomas Mason, *Brandeis and the Modern State* (Washington: National Home Library, 1936), and *Brandeis: A Free Man's Life* (New York: Viking Press, 1946).

72. Gail Bederman, *Manliness and Civilization: A Cultural History of Gender and Race in the United States, 1880–1917* (Chicago: University of Chicago Press, 1995).

73. Brandeis to Paul Kellogg, December 19, 1911, *Letters* Vol. II, 522; and Brandeis to Lawrence Fraser Abbott, September 6, 1910, ibid., 371–72.

74. Cohen would, during the 1920s, argue that the Protocol model could be successfully adapted to diplomacy, therefore ending world wars, as it had industrial ones.

75. Bruce E. Kaufman, *The Origins and Evolution of the Field of Industrial Relations* (Ithaca, NY: ILR Press, 1993); Jonathan Zeitlin, "Labour History to the History of Industrial Relations," *Economic History Review* 2nd Series XL, 2 (1987): 159–84; Perry Blatz, *Democratic Miners: Work and Labor Relations in the Anthracite Coal Industry, 1875–1925* (Albany: SUNY Press, 1994); Clarence E. Wunderlin, Jr., *Visions of a New Industrial Order: Social Science and Labor Theory in America's Progressive Era* (New York: Columbia University Press, 1992); Howard M. Gitelman, *Legacy of the Ludlow Massacre: A Chapter in American Industrial Relations* (Philadelphia: University of Pennsylvania Press, 1988); James Naylor, *The New Democracy: Challenging the Social Order in Industrial Ontario* (Toronto: University Press of Toronto, 1991); Colin Davis, *Power at Odds: The 1922 National Railroad Shopmen's Strike* (Urbana: University of Illinois Press, 1997); Joseph McCartin, *Labor's Great War: The Struggle for Industrial Democracy and the Making of Modern Labor Relations, 1912–1921* (Chapel Hill: University of North Carolina Press, 1998); McCartin, "Industrial Democracy and the Vision of a Progressive State: An

Etymological Reflection on Progressivism," Paper presented January 4, 1997, at the annual meeting of the AHA in New York (in my possession. I would like to thank Dr. McCartin for sharing his unpublished work with me).

76. Robert Weibe, *A Search for Order, 1877–1920* (New York: Hill and Wang, 1967); Gabriel Kolko, *The Triumph of Conservatism: A Reinterpretation of American History, 1900–1916* (London: Free Press, 1963); James Livingston, *Origins of the Federal Reserve System: Money, Class, and Corporate Capitalism, 1890–1913* (Ithaca, NY: Cornell University Press, 1986), Livingston, "The Social Analysis of Economic History and Theory: Conjectures on Late Nineteenth-Century American Development," *American Historical Review* 92 (February 1992): 69–95; and Livingston, *Pragmatism and the Political Economy of Cultural revolution, 1850–1940* (Chapel Hill: University of North Carolina, 1994); Martin J. Sklar, *The Corporate reconstruction on American Capitalism, 1890–1916: The Market, the Law, and Politics* (New York: Cambridge University Press, 1988); Sklar, *The United States as a Developing Country: Studies in U.S. History in the Progressive Era and the 1920s* (New York: Cambridge University Press, 1992); and Colin Gordon, *New Deals.*

77. Wunderlin, *Visions of a New Industrial Order*, passim, but especially 95–112.

78. Colin Gordon, *New Deals*, and Stanley Vitoz, *New Deal Labor Policy and the Industrial Economy* (Chapel Hill: University of North Carolina Press, 1987).

79. Julius Henry Cohen, "Protocols in the Cloak, Suit, and Skirt Industry and in the Dress and Waist Industry," *Transaction of the Efficiency Society, Inc.* (New York, 1913); Cohen, *An American Labor Policy* (New York: MacMillan, 1919); Cohen, *Law and Order in Industry* (New York: MacMillan, 1916); Cohen, *They Built It Better Than They Knew* (New York: Julian Messner, 1946).

80. Julius Henry Cohen, "Control of Sanitary Condition," the *Survey* XXIX (February 1913):632.

81. Charles H. Winslow, *Conciliation, Arbitration and Sanitation in the Cloak, Suit and Skirt Industry of New York City.* Bulletin of the United States Bureau of Labor Statistics no. 98 (Washington, DC: Government Printing Office, 1912).

82. Ibid., 253–70; George M. Price, *First Annual Report of the Joint Board of sanitary Control* (New York: Joint Board of Sanitary Control, 1911): 1–64; Henry Moskowitz, "Joint Board of Sanitary Control," *Annals of the American Academy* XLIV (November 1912): 39–58; Paul Kellogg, "Pioneering by Employers," the *Survey* XXVI (August 19, 1911): 712–17; Julius Henry Cohen, "Control of Sanitary Standards," the *Survey* XXIX (February 1, 1913): 631–32; George M. Price, "Factory Inspection," the *Survey* XXVI (May 6, 1911): 219–28; and "Garment Workers," the *Survey* XXXI (December 20, 1913): 313.

83. Steve Fraser's essay, "The Labor Question," in Steve Fraser and Gary Gerstle, eds., *The Rise and Fall of the New Deal Order* (Princeton: Princeton University Press, 1989).

84. Ibid., 55–84.

85. Levine, *Women's Garment Workers*, 219–20; George M. Price, *Special Report on Sanitary Conditions in the Shops of the Dress and Waist Industry in New York* (New York: Joint Board of Sanitary Control, 1913): 4–8; N. I. Stone, *Wages and*

Regularity of Employment and Standardization of Piece Rates in the Dress and Waist Industry, Bulletin of the U.S. Bureau of Labor Statistics no. 146 (Washington DC: Government Printing Office, 1914): 20–30.

86. Alice Kessler-Harris, "Organizing the Unorganizable: Three Jewish Women and their Union," in Milton Cantor and Bruce Laurie, eds., *Class, Sex, and the Woman Worker* (Westport, CT: Greenwood Press, 1977); and Kessler-Harris, *Out to Work: A History of Wage-Earning Women in America* (New York: Oxford University Press, 1982).

87. Annelise Orleck, *Common Sense and a Little Fire: Women and Working-Class Politics in the United States, 1900–1965* (Chapel Hill: University of North Carolina, 1995).

88. Berman, "Era of the Protocol," 159; *Ladies' Garment Worker* IV February 1913, 9–12; The Eleventh Convention, ILGWU, *Report of Proceedings* (Toronto: ILGWU, 1912), especially resolutions 27 and 61 authorizing the strikes. In addition, see "Reports of Abe Mitchel and Saul Elstein to the General Executive Board," *Ladies' Garment Worker* IV January 1913, 21–24.

89. *American Cloak and Suit Review* III June 1912, 275; and Berman, "Era of the Protocol," 162–63.

90. *American Cloak and Suit Review* III June 1912, 275–76.

91. Charles H. Winslow, *Conciliation, Arbitration and Sanitation in the Dress and Waist Industry of New York City,* Bulletin of the U.S. Bureau of Labor Statistics no. 145 (Washington, DC: Government Printing Office, 1914): 14.

92. "Conferees' Report and Recommendations" in *Minutes of Meetings Held Between Representatives of the Dress and Waist Manufacturers' Association and the ILGWU. 1912–1913,* 33–45. ILGWU Papers, Catherwood Library, New York State School of Industrial Relations, Cornell University (ILGWU Papers).

93. Theresa Wolfson, "Role of the ILGWU in Stabilizing the Women's Garment Industry," *Industrial and Labor Relations Review* 4 (1950): 33–43.

94. Winslow, *Conciliation,* 14–22.

95. *Jewish Daily Forward* 19 December 1912, 1; for the GEB Report, see *Ladies' Garment Worker* IV January 1913, 10, 21–22. Mitchel quote is from 21–22.

96. For the men's clothing strike of 1912–13 I have relied on the unpublished work of David Osborn, "The New York City Men's Garment Strike of 1912–13," May 1987 (in my possession. I wish to thank Dr. Osborn, formally of the LaGuardia\Wagner Archives at CUNY, for sharing with me his unpublished paper.) Also see Steve Fraser, *Labor Shall Rule: Sidney Hill and the Rise of American Labor* (New York: Free Press, 1990).

97. *Jewish Daily Forward* 23 December 1912, 8; ibid., 5 January 1913, 1; ibid., 8 January 1912, 1; ibid., 9 January 1912, 1; and *New York Times* 9 January 1913, 5; ibid., 6 January 1913, 1; ibid., 10 January 1913, 22; and finally, *New York World* 6 January 1913, A1.

98. *New York Times* 13 January 1913, 3; ibid., 14 January 1913, 7. See also, the *Jewish Daily Forward* 9 January 1913, 10. The strike vote was indeed lopsided: 11,839 for the strike, and only 542 opposed to it.

99. *Jewish Daily Forward* 12 January 1913, 1; ibid., 14 January 1913, 1; ibid., 15 January 1913, 1. See also, the *New York Times* 15 January 1913, 5.

100. *Jewish Daily Forward* 15 January 1913, 1; ibid., 16 January 1913, 1. See also, the *New York Times* 16 January 1913, 3.

101. *Jewish Daily Forward* 16 January 1913, 1; *New York Times* 16 January 1913, 1; and the Socialist Labor Party's the *Daily People* 19 January 1913, 3.

102. *New York Times* 19 January 1913, II, 3; and Winslow, *Conciliation*, 38.

103. *New York Times* 22 January 1913, 2; ibid., 23 January 1913, 7; ibid., 25 January 1913, 24; and ibid., 26 January 1913, 9.

104. Michael Miller Topp, *Those Without A Country: The Political Culture of Italian American Syndicalists* (Minneapolis: University of Minnesota Press, 2001); *New York Times* 19 January 1913, II, 3; ibid., 20 January 1913, 2; ibid., 21 January 1913, 24; *Daily People*, 20 January 1913, 2; and for the hard sell the union took, see Morris Winchefsky, "A QuietRevolution of the Waist Dress Industry," *Ladies' Garment Worker* IV April 1913, 19.

105. Harry Lang, *"62": Biography of a Union* (New York: Local 62, ILGWU, 1940): 97–114; the *Outlook* CIII (January 18, 1913): 102–3; and *New York Times* 11 January 1913, 7.

106. *New York Times* 10 January 1913, 22; and *Jewish Daily Forward* 10 January 1913, 1; ibid., 11 January 1913, 1.

107. *Jewish Daily Forward* 14 January 1913, 1; and *New York Times* 12 January 1913, V, 7; ibid., 15 January 1913, 5; ibid., 16 January 1913, 3; and ibid., 17 January 1913, 10.

108. *Ladies' Garment Worker* IV (April 1913): 1–3; *Jewish Daily Forward* 14 January 1913, 1; ibid., 15 January 1913, 1; ibid., 16 January 1913, 1; ibid., 19 January 1913, 1; ibid., 21 January 1913, 1. In addition, see the *New York Times* 14 January 1913, 7; and the *Outlook* CIV (May 17, 1913): 7.

109. Congressional Record for the 62nd Congress, 3rd Session, IV, p. 2136, HR796; *New York Times*, 31 January 1913, 4; ibid., 22 January 1913, 1; *Jewish Daily Forward* 22 January 1913, 1; and the *Outlook* CII (February 1, 1913): 253–58.

110. *New York Times* 25 January 1913, 24; and Theodore Roosevelt to Michael Chaap, January 25, 1913 in E. Morrison, ed., *Letters of Theodore Roosevelt* (Cambridge: Harvard University Press, 1954), VII, 696–701.

111. *New York Times* 22 January 1913, 2; ibid., 26 January 1913, 9; ibid., 30 January 1913, 15; ibid., 31 January 1913, 4; see as well the *Jewish Daily Forward* 26 January 1913, 4; ibid., 31 January 1913, 1; and ibid., 1 February 1913, 1.

112. *New York Times* 7 February 1913, 9; *Jewish Daily Forward* 4 February 1913, 1. For an example of public pressure, see the *New York Times* 30 January 1913, 5.

113. *New York Times* 9 February 1913, III, 3; ibid., 10 February 1913, 8; ibid., 12 February 1913, 8; *Jewish Daily Forward* 6 February 1913, 1; ibid., 12 February 1913, 1; as well as the *Ladies' Garment Worker* IV (April 1913): 1–3.

114. Harry Lang, *"62,"* 112–25; *New York Times* 31 January 1913, 4.

115. *Jewish Daily Forward* 1 February 1913, 1; ibid., 3 February 1913, 1; ibid., 7 February 1913, 1; ibid., 10 February 1913, 1; ibid., 12 February 1913, 1. Also

see the *New York Times* 31 January 1913, 4; ibid., 11 February 1913,10; ibid., 12 February 1913, 8. For the background on this, see Lang, *"62,"* 127–40.

116. *New York Times* 13 January 1913, 12 and 20; ibid., 15 February 1913, 8; and the *Jewish Daily Forward* 14 February 1913, 8; and ibid., 15 February 1913, 1.

117. *New York Times* 19 February 1913, 9.

118. *New York Times* 11 March 1913, 22; ibid., 12 March 1913, 10; ibid., 13 March 1913, 22; ibid., 14 March 1913, 7; and the *Jewish Daily Forward* 10 March 1913, 1; ibid., 12 March 1913, 1; ibid., 13 March 1913,1; ibid., 14 March 1913, 1.

119. Of the 1,101 disputes reported during the period, 308 involved the piece-rate. See Winslow, *Conciliation*, 230–31.

120. Ibid., 54–56; and "The Wage Scale," *American Cloak and Suit Review*, V (May 1913): 113–14.

121. See Protocol clauses 16–18 in the Appendix of Berman, "Era of the Protocol," for details.

122. Julius Henry Cohen especially worried about this as early as 1910. Brandeis was convinced that the Board of Grievances would solve all problem and "there may be no occasion for the Arbitration Board to meet." Cohen had hoped so, but worried all the well. See Brandeis's letter to Cohen November 9, 1910 in Melvin I. Urofsky, ed., *The Letters of Louis D. Brandeis Volume II 1907–1912* (Albany: SUNY Press, 1972), 281–82. See Cohen letter to Brandeis dated October 10, 1910 as cited in Berman, "Era of the Protocol," 211.

123. "Our New York Locals," *Ladies' Garment Worker* I (December 1910): 8; and "Is the Grievance Committee a Failure?," ibid., (February 1911): 4.

124. Moskowitz's letters to A. Lincoln Filene and Jane Addams on November 12, 1910, as cited in Berman, "Era of the Protocol," 214; see *Minutes of Conference Between Cloak, Suit and Skirt Manufacturers' Protective Association and the International Ladies' Garment Workers Union* December 14, 1910, 1–54 in the Paul Abelson Papers, Catherwood Library, Cornell University, New York State School of Industrial and Labor Relations Library (Hereafter cited as Abelson Papers).

125. *Brief to Board of Arbitration, in the Matter of the Complaint of the Manufacturers Against the Unions, Cloak, Suit and Skirt Industry January 17, 1911* (Abelson Papers); also see Cohen to A. Lincoln File, January 17, 1911, as quoted in Berman, "Era of the Protocol," 215, note 1; Moskowitz to Brandeis January 15, 1911, and Cohen to Brandeis, January 21 and 26, 1911, as cited in Berman, "Era of the Protocol," 215; See *Brief Answer and Countercharges, in the Matter of the Complaint of the Manufacturers Against the Unions, Before the Board of Arbitration, Cloak, Suit and Skirt Industry*, 1–5.

126. Winslow, *Conciliation*, 251–52.

127. *Board of Arbitration, Cloak, Suit and Skirt Industry, Opening Arguments and Discussion in the Matter of the Complaint of Manufacturers Against the Unions March 4, 1911* (Abelson Papers).

128. On Hillquit, see Richard W. Fox, "The Paradox of Progressive Socialism: The Case of Morris Hillquit, 1901–1914," *American Quarterly* 26:2 (1974): 127–40; Mark E. Kann, "Challenging Lockean Liberalism in America: The Case of Debs and Hillquit," *Political Theory* 8 (May 1980): 202–23; and Irwin Yellowitz,

"Morris Hillquit: American Socialism and Jewish Concerns," *American Jewish History* 68:2 (1978): 163–88.

129. *Board of Arbitration, Cloak, Suit and Skirt Industry, Decision in Matter of Complaint of Manufacturers Against the Unions, March 14, 1911* (Abelson Papers), 1–14 . The quote is from pages 13–14.

130. Berman, in his 1956 Dissertation on the Protocol, makes no reference at all to the Triangle Fire. See Berman's "Era of the Protocol."

131. Winslow, *Conciliation*, 225–27; and *Rules and Plan of Procedure Adopted By the Board of Grievances, Approved by the Board of Arbitration, Clauses 4 and 11*. (No date, but most likely from March 1911 in Abelson Papers.)

132. Ibid.; see also "Solution for Industrial Peace," in Holt's own the *Independent* LXXIV (February 6, 1912): 273–75; Iris Weed, "Instead of Strikes," *Everybodies'* XXIX (July 1913): 131–22; Helen Sumner, "Court for Garment Trades," *New Republic* IV (September 19, 1915): 176–78.

133. Charles H. Winslow, *Industrial Court of the Cloak, Suit and Skirt Industry of New York City,* Bulletin of the U.S. Bureau of Labor Statistics no. 144 (Washington, DC: Government Printing Office, 1914): 8–22. In the majority of the cases, those handled by the clerks, little information exists except the final decision. These were often clear-cut, such as workers' refusal to abide by an accepted wage scale or manufacturers ignoring sanitary conditions. The cases that did go to the full Board, especially those that went further to the Arbitration Board, tended to involve larger issues.

134. Ibid., 24–27; see also, John A. Dyche, "Report of the Secretary-Treasurer, ILGWU," *Report of the Proceedings, 12th Convention* (Cleveland, ILGWU, June 1–14, 1914): 57–59; as well as Brandeis to Moskowitz, March 25, 1912, Brandeis to Hillquit, March 28,1912, and Brandeis to Holt, March 28, 1912, in *Brandeis Letters,* 569–72.

135. Because of this practice, we have no real indication of just how many wildcat strikes there were. See Dyche, "Report," *12th Convention,* 58–59; and see *Ladies' Garment Worker* II (February 1911): 4, for a sample of the growing hostility toward the Protocol. See also Brandeis to Moskowitz, March 25, 1912, in *Brandeis Letters,* 570.

136. Brandeis to Ray Stanndard Baker, February 26, 1912, *Brandeis Letters,* 563.

CHAPTER 3

1. *Regularity of Employment in Women's Ready-to-Wear Garment Industries* Bulletin of the United States Bureau of Labor Statistics no. 183 (Washington, DC: Government Printing Office, 1916): 21–23.

2. "Report of Proceedings," *Eleventh Convention Report June 3–12, 1912* (Toronto: ILGWU, 1912), 53–54; *American Cloak and Suit Review* II (June 1911): 147–48; *Ladies' Garment Worker* II (April 1911): 11; *Ladies' Garment Worker* (May 1911): 4, 7; Sol Rosman, "Will There a General Strike of Ladies' Tailors," *Ladies'*

Garment Worker II (July 1911): 14–15; *Ladies' Garment Worker* II (August 1911): 22–23; "Minutes of the General Executive Board Meeting Held at Cleveland, Ohio, September 10111, 1911," *Ladies' Garment Worker* (October 1911):17–18; A. Rosebury, "Glorious Victory of Ladies' Tailors," *Ladies' Garment Worker* II (October 1911): 1–2; Sol Rosman, "Victory of the Ladies' Tailors," *Ladies' Garment Worker* II (November 1911): 8.

3. *Treaty of Peace Between the Merchant's Society of Ladies' Tailors and Dressmakers of New York and the Ladies' Tailors and Dressmakers Union, Local 38, ILGWU,* September 18, 1911, passim. Paul Abelson Papers, Collection 5192, Kheel Center for Labor-Mangament Documentation and Archives, Catherwood Library, New York State School of Industrial and Labor Relations, Cornell University. (Hereafter cited as Abelson Papers.)

4. "Direct Action of Local 38 Executives," *Ladies' Garment Worker* II (December 1911): 26–27. The Cohen quote is from Cohen to Brandeis December 7, 1911, as quoted in Hyman Berman, "Era of the Protocol: A Chapter in the History of the International Ladies' Garment workers' Union, 1910–1916" (Ph.D. Dissertation, Columbia University, 1956), 249.

5. Moskowitz to Brandeis December 7, 1911, and Brandeis to Markowitz December 10, 1911. Papers of Louis D. Brandeis, Garment Workers Files (Microfilm). (Hereafter cited as Brandeis Papers.); *Statement Showing Net Result of Operations of 16 Members, Examined for the Year Ending September 19, 1911, Merchants' Society of Ladies' Tailors and Dressmakers, New York, Prepared by Investigators' Agency, Inc.; and Auditors Supplementary Report to Board of Arbitration in Ladies' Tailoring Industry, January 24, 1912,* passim (Abelson Papers). On Dyche, see *Ladies' Garment Worker* (December 1911): 26–27 and his "Report of the Secretary-Treasurer," *Eleventh Convention Report,* 30–31.

6. Moskowitz to Brandeis, January 18, 1912, Bandeis Papers. For Rosenberg's and Dyche's activity, see *Ladies' Garment Worker* (December 1912): 14–15. See Julius Henry Cohen, *Memorandum and Brief for the Employers in the Matter of the Arbitration Between the Merchants' Society of Ladies' Tailors and Dressmakers and Local 38 of the ILGWU, February 5, 1912,* 7–21; Meyer London, *Memorandum and Brief of the Union in the Matter of the Arbitration Between the Merchants' Society of Ladies' Tailors and Dressmakers and Local 38 of ILGWU* (No date, but most likely late January 1912), 8–9; and *Proceedings Before the Board of Arbitration,* January 27, 1912, 370–438 (Abelson Papers).

7. *Decision of the Board of Arbitration,* February 27, 1912, 1–14 (Abelson Papers).

8. "Statement of facts on Local 38 Situation," *Eleventh Convention Report,* 56–57.

9. Moskowitz to Brandeis, March 11, 1912, Brandeis Papers.

10. "New York Ladies' Tailors," *Ladies' Garment Worker* III (May 1912): 29–32; "President's Report," *Eleventh Convention Report,* 16; and "The Report of the Committee of Three on Local 38," ibid., 55–56.

11. On this battle of words, see *Ladies' Garment Worker* (May 1912): 31–32 for Rossman; and for Dyche, see his "Report of the Secretary-Treasurer," *Eleventh Convention Report,* 30–31.

12. See "Minutes of General executive Board Held March 30–31, 1912," *Ladies' Garment Worker* (April 1912) and (May 1912). Both issues covered the "Local 38 Situation," as it became known, in great detail.

13. *Decision of the Board of Arbitration*, April 4, 1912, 306 (Abelson Papers). Ironically, the clauses granting the shop owners power to fire were Hillquit's. See Hillquit to Brandeis, March 23, 1912, Brandeis Papers; and Brandeis to Hillquit, March 28, 1912, *Letters of Louis D. Brandeis*, 571–72.

14. "Report of the President" and "Report of the Secretary-Treasurer," in *Reports and Proceedings of the Twelfth Convention, ILGWU, June 1–13, 1914* (Cleveland, OH: ILGWU, 1914): 17–59; as well as the *Ladies' Garment Worker* III (January 1912): 15–16.

15. "Monthly Bulletin of Stirring Events," *Ladies' Garment Worker* III (March 1912): 13.

16. Berman, "Era of the Protocol," 271; John Dickinson and Morris Kolchin, *Report of Investigation of the Governor's Advisory Commission in the Cloak, Suit and Skirt Industries of New York City* (New York: Evening Post Printing, 1925): passim; and Nancy L. Green, *Ready-to-Wear and Ready-to-Work: A Century of Industry and Immigrants in Paris and New York* (Durham: Duke University Press, 1997): 146–55.

17. Levine, *Ladies' Garment Worker*, 246; and "A Protocol Label for Cloak and Suits," *Ladies' Garment Worker* III (May 1912): 17–18.

18. *Ladies' Garment Worker* III (May 1912): 16–17; and ibid. (June 1912): 16.

19. *Complaint of the Joint Board in the case of Carl Bonwit to the Chief Clerk, Protective Association, May 3rd 1912* (Abelson Papers); "Report of the Secretary-Treasurer," *Twelfth Convention Report*, 63; and Julius Henry Cohen to Brandeis, May 9, 1912, as quoted in Berman, "Era of the Protocol," 276.

20. Brandeis to Moskowitz, May 10, 1912, in *Letters of Louis Brandeis*, 616–17. On Dyche, see his "Report of the Secretary-Treasurer," *Twelfth Convention Report*, 62.

21. "Report of the President," *Twelfth Convention Report*, 15–18; and "Report of the Secretary-Treasurer," ibid., 51–53.

22. No complete collection of the *New Post* has survived in the archival collections. A few issues are scattered in the papers of various Protocolists and a few survived as part of the Board of Arbitration's official records (saved by and deposited in Paul Abelson's papers at the ILR School of Cornell University). The best source for the ensuing war of words are the *Ladies' Garment Worker* and Dr. Hoffman's autobiography, *Fifty Years Cloak Operators' Union*, which reprints many of his editorials. For examples of these early fights, see Hoffman, *Fifty Years* (New York: Local 117, 1936): 234–36; and *Ladies' Garment Worker* III (May 1912): 17.

23. "Report of the Secretary-Treasurer," *Twelfth Convention Report*, 62–66; Hoffman, *Fifty Years*, 236–37; *Ladies' Garment Worker* III (September 1912): 17–18; Levine, *Ladies' Garment Worker*, 251 and "Report of the Label and Boycott Committee," *Twelfth Convention Report*, 94–95.

24. Moskowitz to Brandeis, July 9, 1912, as cited in Berman, "Era of the Protocol," 281.

25. Berman, "Era of the Protocol," 281–83.

26. Cohen to Brandeis, September 7, 1912, as quoted in Berman, "Era of the Protocol," 283; "Report of the Secretary-Treasurer," *Twelfth Convention Report*, 66; Hoffman, *Fifty Years*, 237; and *Ladies' Garment Worker* III (November 1912): 17.

27. Dyche's unpublished interview as quoted in Berman, "Era of the Protocol," 283.

28. Robert Zeigler, *The CIO, 1935–1955* (Chapel Hill: University of North Carolina Press, 1995), argues quite effectively that rank-and-file workers of the 1930s became liberals, rather than radicals. I would argue that the antecedents to this are found among many of the garment workers that I have studied.

29. "Report on J. R. Stratton Stoppage Prepared by John Dyche, October 26, 1912," *Final Report and Testimony of the United States Commission on Industrial Relations*. 64th Congress, 1st Session, Senate Document 415. (Washington, DC: Government Printing Office, 1916) II, 1122–23, 1047–48, 1095, and 1109; and "Report of the Secretary-Treasurer," *Twelfth Convention Report*, 67.

30. Hoffman, *Fifty Years*, 239; and "Report of the Secretary-Treasurer," *Twelfth Convention Report*, 68–69.

31. *Conference Minutes Between the Representatives of Protective Association and Joint Board and ILGWU, December 11, 1912*, 1–135 (Abelson Papers); "Report of the Secretary-Treasurer," *Twelfth Convention Report*, 70; Hoffman, *Fifty Years*, 239; and Letter Between Moskowitz and Brandeis, December 23, 1912, as cited in Berman, "Era of the Protocol," 290.

32. *Ladies' Garment Worker* III (November 1912): 3; "Testimony of Isaac A. Hourwich, "*Report of the US Commission on Industrial Relations*, II, 1094; and "Report of the President," *Twelfth Convention Report*, 18–19.

33. George Kennan, "How Russia Losses Good Citizens, Isaac A. Hourwich," the *Outlook* CIV (July 26, 1913): 714–17; I. M. Rubinow, "Isaac A. Hourwich," in *Encyclopedia of the Social Sciences* (New York: MacMillan, 1932) VII, 494; *Jewish Daily Forward* (January 12, 1913): 8; and Hoffman, *Fifty Years*, 240; See *American Cloak and Suit Review* V (January 1913): 236–37; "Report of the President," *Twelfth Convention Report*, 15–17; "Report of the Secretary-Treasurer," ibid., 52–56; Meyer London, "The Last Strikes and Settlements," *Zukunft* XVIII (April 1913): 335; and Henry Moskowitz's Letter to Brandeis, January 17, 1913, both in Brandeis Papers. Also see the *Ladies' Garment Worker* October through December for coverage of the growing rift.

34. *Jewish Daily Forward* (January 24, 1913): 1; Hoffman, *Fifty Years*, 241. The quote is from "Testimony of Isaac A. Hourwich," *Report of the U.S. Commission on Industrial Relations*, II, 1096.

35. "Testimony of Isaac A. Hourwich," *Report of U.S. Commission on Industrial Relations*, II, 1097; and *Minutes of Joint Board of Cloakmakers Union, February 1, 1913*, Joint Board Collection, ILGWU Papers, New York State School of Industrial and Labor Relations, Cornell University. (Hereafter referred to as Joint Board Papers.)

36. *Jewish Daily Forward* (January 24, 1913): 1; Hoffman, *Fifty Years*, 241. The quote is from "Testimony of Isaac A. Hourwich," *Report of the U.S. Commission on Industrial Relations*, II, 1096.

37. "Minutes of the Board of Grievances, January 27, 1913," passim. The quote is from "Testimony of Isaac A. Hourwich," *Report of the U.S. Commission on Industrial Relations*, II, 1102–3.

38. The letter, dated January 29, 1913, stated that the ILG "acted merely as attorney in fact for its New York Locals." It further argued that because of the federated nature of the ILG, it could not be a legal party to any such agreement. Only a local had such authority. Letter is reprinted in "Report of the Secretary-Treasurer," *Twelfth Convention Report*, 70–71. Also see Hoffman, *Fifty Years*, 243.

39. Moskowitz to Brandeis, January 29, 1913, Brandeis Papers.

40. Conference between Members of the Board of Arbitration, New York, February 3 and 4, 1913, 192–215 (Abelson Papers).

41. "Testimony of Paul Abelson," *Report of the U.S. Commission on Industrial Relations*, II, 1074. It is because of this near obsession with record keeping that the bulk of the Protocol materials survives today. In this effort, he had an unlikely alley: Abelson. See also "Testimony of Isaac A. Hourwich," *Report of the U.S. Commission on Industrial Relations*, II, 1097–1108; and "Testimony of Julius Henry Cohen, ibid., II, 1115.

42. "Testimony Regarding Cloak, Suit, and Skirt Industry," *Report of the U.S. Commission on Industrial Relations*, II, 1025–1161.

43. "Report of the Secretary-Treasurer," *Twelfth Convention Report*, 65–78. The quote is from page 65; Hoffman, *Fifty Years*, 248–49.

44. Hourwich to Abelson, April 15, 1913, in *Minutes of Special Meeting of the Board of Grievances, April 18, 1913*, 4 (Abelson Papers); Hourwich to L. E. Rosenfield, April 15, 1913, and Rosenfield to Hourwich, April 17, 1913, reprinted in *Minutes of Special Meeting of the Board of Grievances, April 18, 1913*, 4F-H (Abelson Papers).

45. Ibid., 6–6B; Moskowitz to Brandeis, May 1, 1913, as quoted in Berman, "Era of the Protocol," 307.

46. *Ladies' Garment Worker* IV (June 1913): 18; I. Hourwich, "The Good and Bad Aspects of the Protocol," *New Post* (May 23, 1913) as quoted in Berman, "Era of the Protocol," 308.

47. Brandeis to Moskowitz, May 10, 1913, Brandeis Papers.

48. Hourwich to Brandeis, May 11, 1913; Hourwich to Brandeis, May 12, 1913; and Hourwich to Brandeis, May 21, 1913, Brandeis Papers.

49. *Proposed Amendments to Protocol, May 17, 1913*. Enclosed with a letter from Hourwich to Brandeis, May 21, 1913, Brandeis Papers.

50. Hourwich to Brandeis, May 27, 1913, Brandeis Papers.

51. Moskowitz to Brandeis, May 29, 1913, Brandeis Papers; Moskowitz to Brandeis, May 28, 1913, Brandeis Papers; Hoffman, *Fifty Years*, 247–48; "Testimony of Julius Henry Cohen, "*Report of the U.S. Commission on Industrial*

Relations, II, 1116; "Testimony of Abe Bisno," ibid., II, 1136–41; and "Testimony of Isaac A. Hourwich," ibid., II, 1151–52.

52. Hoffman, *Fifty Years*, 247.

53. *Members, Board of Arbitration. August 3–6, 1913* (Abelson Papers); and "Testimony of Louis Brandeis Before the U.S. Commission on Industrial Relations, February 2, 1914," unpublished. In *U.S. Commission on Industrial Relations Papers*, Record Group 174, National Archives.

54. "Testimony of Isaac A. Hourwich," *Report of the U.S. Commission on Industrial Relations*, II, 1150–51; and Hoffman, *Fifty Years*, 250.

55. On this strike, see the *New York Times* for 3 August 1913, II, 2; ibid., 13 August 1913, 13; ibid., 14 August 1913, 5; ibid., Editorial, "A Sweatshop Workers' Strike," 16 August 1913, 8; ibid., 16 August 1913, 16; ibid., 20 August 1913, 4; ibid., 22 August 1913, 11; ibid., 23 August 1913, 7; ibid., 28 August 1913, 5. See also the *Jewish Daily Forward* 14 August 1913, 1; ibid., 15 August 1913, 1; and ibid., 24 August 1913, 8.

56. Hoffman, *Fifty Years*, 251–52; Dyche to Brandeis, September 2, 1913, and Moskowitz to Brandeis, September 21, 1913, as quoted in Berman, "Era of the Protocol," 325. One of the reasons Hourwich did not take the new position was because he was well aware of how and why it was offered to him.

57. Julius Henry Cohen, *Memorandum of Remarks Before the Board of Arbitration, October 4, 1913* (Abelson Papers).

58. *Board of Arbitration, Decision October 5, 1913* (Abelson Papers). The strike was at the firm of Levey and Friedberg.

59. *Jewish Daily Forward* 5 November 1913, 1; and Moskowitz to Brandeis, October 9, 1913, as quoted in Berman, "Era of the Protocol," 331.

60. Hoffman, *Fifty Years*, 254.

61. Moskowitz to Brandeis, November 24, 1913, and November 29, 1913, Brandeis Papers; and Hoffman, *Fifty Years*, 254–56; *Jewish Daily Forward* 17 December 1913, 1.

62. Moskowitz to Brandeis, December 11, 1913, Brandeis Papers. See also B. Hoffman, *Fifty Years*, 257.

63. Moskowitz to Brandeis, December 18, 1913, Brandeis Papers.

64. "Testimony of Isaac A. Hourwich," *Report of the U.S. Commission on Industrial Relations*, II, 1151–56.

65. Ibid., 1151–56.

66. General Executive Board of the ILGWU, *A Statement RE the Hourwich Affair, January 5, 1914*, 1–6 (ILGWU Papers.) And the *New York Times* 5 January 1914, 7.

67. See the *New York Times* 8 January 1914, 20; ibid., 10 January 1914, 4; See also, the *Jewish Daily Forward* 7 January 1914, 1; and ibid., 10 January 1914, 1.

68. See Moskowitz to Brandeis, January 10, 1914, and Walter Weyl to Brandeis, January 12, 1914, Brandeis Papers. See also the *New York Times* 1 February 1914, V, 6.

69. Mrs. J. Borden Harriman, "Hither and Yan," *Century Magazine* CVII (December 1923): 299–300; "Hearing in the Cloak, Suit and Skirt Industry,"

Report of the U.S. Commission on Industrial Relations, II, 1025–26; and "Report of Hearings in New York Relative to Industrial Relations in the Cloak and Suit Trade," General Records, Department of Labor. RG 174, National Archives.

70. Brandeis quoted in T. Mason, *Brandeis: A Freeman's Life* (New York: Viking Press, 1946), 310.

71. See Berman, "Era of the Protocol," 344; *Jewish Daily Forward* 20 January 1914, 1, 8; *New York Times* 22 January 1914, 7, 10.

72. *New York Times* 21 January 1914, 1; ibid., 24 January 1914, 5; see also the *Jewish Daily Forward* 21 January 1914, 1.

73. *New York Times* 25 January 1914, II, 8; ibid., 26 January 1914, 6, 9; see also the *Jewish Daily Forward* 25 January 1914, 1.

74. On Hillman, see the Steve Fraser biography, *Labor Shall Rule.*

75. *New York Times* 4 February 1914, 10; ibid., 10 February 1914, 11; and the *Jewish Daily Forward* 10 February 1914, 1; ibid., 16 February 1914, 1.

76. "Report of the Proceedings," *Twelfth Convention Report,* 176–205, 229–33; and Hoffman, *Fifty Years,* 262–64.

77. *Board of Arbitration, Dress and Waist Industry, Proceedings and Decision on Conference Agreements, January 31, 1916,* 2–17 (Abelson Papers).

78. Ibid., 18–27.

79. See the *New York Times* 7 February 1916, 8; ibid., 8 February 1916, 6; ibid., 9 February 1916, 5; ibid., 10 February 1916, 7; ibid., 12 February 1916, 7; ibid., 13 February 1916, I, 13; ibid., 25 February 1916, 13; *Jewish Daily Forward* 10 February 1916, 1; ibid., 13 February 1916, 1; ibid., 25 February 1916, 1. The strike also received national attention. See "When a Strike is Just a Holiday," the *Survey* XXXV (February 19, 1916): 597; and "Remarkable Strike," the *Outlook* CXII (February 23, 1916): 409–10.

80. Julius Henry Cohen, "Revised Protocol in the Dress and Waist Industry," *Annals of the American Academy* LXIX (January 1917): 183–96; "What Others Think of Our New Protocol," *Gleichheit* 14 March 1916, 5; and Robert Valentine, "Accomplishments of the New Protocol," ibid., 9 June 1916, 3.

81. What he wanted was nothing less than standardized production in the ladies' garment industry under the direction of his Board. He firmly believed that through greater efficiency and scientific management, both sides would gain and the Protocol would be an absolute success. Robert Valentine, *Tentative Final Draft of Report of Protocol Standards, September 1916,* 1–34 (Abelson Papers).

82. Berman, "Era of the Protocol," 374 ff.

83. For information on Schlesinger and Sigman, see Joel Steidman, *The Needle Trades* (New York: Farrar and Rinehart, 1942), 95–152; Jesse Carpenter, *Competition and Collective Bargaining in the Needle Trades, 1910–1967* (Ithaca, NY: ILR Press, 1972); and "Benjamin Schlesinger," in *Encyclopedia of the Social Sciences* (New York: MacMillan, 1913), XIII, 573; and "Morris Sigman," ibid., 51–52.

84. Berman, "Era of the Protocol," 377.

85. Steven Fraser, *Labor Will Rule: Sidney Hillman and the Rise of American Labor* (New York: Free Press, 1991), 82–113.

86. *Board of Arbitration, Cloak and Suit Industry, Complaint of Union in RE Nathan Schuss and Company, November 29, 1914,* passim; *Answer of Union's Complaint in RE Nathan Schuss and Company, December 18, 1914,* passim (Abelson Papers).

87. *Board of Grievances, Proceedings in the Matter of RE Nathan Schuss and Company, November 25, 1914,* 37–113 (Abelson Papers).

88. *Plan for Regularization of Employment and For Increasing the Earnings of Those Regularly Employed, Submitted by Association to Union at Joint Conference, February 17, 1915* (Abelson Papers).

89. *Plan for Regulation of Employment and for Increasing the Earning of Those Regularly Employed, Submitted by Union to Association at Joint Conference, March 16, 1915* (Abelson Papers).

90. American Cloak and Suit Review IX (March 1915): 156–59.

91. See Berman, "Era of the Protocol," 398.

92. Henry Gordon, "The Industrial Relations in the Cloak Industry," *Women's Wear Daily* (May 14, 1915).

93. *New York Times* 20 May 1915, 13; ibid., 21 May 1915, 8; and the *Jewish Daily Forward* 20 May 1915, 1; ibid., 21 May 1915, 1.

94. *New York Times* 23 May 23 1915, II, 5; ibid., 6 June 1915, VII, 9; ibid., 13 June 1915, II, 6; and Berman, "Era of the Protocol," 402–3.

95. Walter Weyle, "Substitute for the Protocol," *New Republic* III (June 12, 1915): 142–43; "End of Protocol," ibid., (May 29, 1915): 84–85; "Stand By the Protocol," the *Independent* LXXXII (May 31, 1915): 82; and Berman, "Era of the Protocol," 403.

96. *New York Times* 29 June 1915, 6; ibid., 2 July 1915, 22; ibid., 3 July 1915, 5; ibid., 7 July 1915, 9.

97. *Council of Conciliation, Cloak, Suit and Skirt Industry, Report and Recommendations, July 23, 1915,* 1–2 (Abelson Papers).

98. The biggest difference was the time frame: this agreement ended in two years. *Jewish Daily Forward* 25 July 1915, 1–8.

99. *New York Times* 2 August 1915, 5; ibid., 3 August 1915, 9; ibid, 4 August 1915, 4 and 20; *Jewish Daily Forward* 4 August 1915, 1; "Settlement in the Cloak Industry," *New York Times* 7 August 1915, 6; "Strike Averted in Garment Trade," the *Survey* XXXIV (July 31, 1915): 390; "Triumph for Arbitration," the *Outlook* CXIII (August 14, 1915): 491–92.

100. Julius Henry Cohen to Brandeis, August 21, 1915, and Moskowitz to Brandeis to Brandeis, August 23, 1915, as cited in Berman, "Era of the Protocol," 409–10.

101. *New York Times* 31 August 1915, 4.

102. From August to May, 91 shop strikes and lockouts rocked New York City. At the same time, the association demanded that the number of paid holidays workers were allowed be reduced from ten to five. The Council later agreed. When Columbus Day (one of the newly reclassified workdays) came, most workers stayed home. *New York Times* 9 October 1915, 14; ibid., 12 October 1915, 4; ibid., 13 October 1915, 5.

103. *Council of Conciliation, Cloak, Suit and Skirt Industry, Hearings and Decisions Relating to the Preferential Union Shop, February 16–18, 1916*, passim (Abelson Papers).

104. E. J. Wile to Felix Adler, March 2, 1916, as quoted in Berman, "Era of the Protocol," 412–13.

105. *New York Times* 8 March 1916, 14; ibid., 11 March 1916, 5; *Jewish Daily Forward* 8 March 1916, 1; ibid., 10 March 1916, 1; ibid., 4 April 1916, 1; and "End of the Cloak and Suit Protocol," the *Survey* XXXV (March 18, 1916): 712.

106. *New York Times* 26 April 1916, 9; ibid., 27 April 1916, 22; *Jewish Daily Forward* 27 April 1916, 1; ibid., 28 April 1916, 1; and "Cloak and Suit Makers Lockout," the *Independent* LXXXVI (May 15, 1916): 233–34.

107. On the numerous efforts to prevent the strike, see the *New York Times* 3 May 1916, 7; ibid., 13 May 1916, 5; "Statement of Faculty of Political Science, Columbia University," ibid., 3 July 1916, 18; *Jewish Daily Forward* 3 May 1916, 1; and "Out of the Mouths of the Faculty," the *Independent* LXXXVI (June 19, 1916): 464–65.

108. *New York Times* 20 July 1916, 7; ibid., 21 July 1916, 7; ibid., 22 July 1916, 5; ibid., 2 August 1916, 5; also see the following journals and magazines for August and September: the *Survey*, the *New Republic*, the *Outlook*, and the *Independent*. In addition, see the coverage in the *Jewish Daily Forward*.

109. *New York Times* 3 August 1916, 12; ibid., 4 August 1916, 2; *Jewish Daily Forward* 3 August 1916, 1; ibid., 4 August 1916, 1–8; ibid., 7 August 1916, 1; ibid., 8 August 1916, 1; "Garment Makers Back to Work," the *Survey* XXVI (August 12, 1916): 493–94; "Settlement That Does Not Settle," the *Independent* LXXXVII (August 14, 1916): 214; and "Stability in the Garment Trades," the *Nation* CIII (August 10, 1916): 123.

PART II

1. Mike Davis, "The Barren Marriage of American Labour and the Democratic Party," *New Left Review* I 124 (November/December 1980): 43–84.

CHAPTER 4

1. *New York Times* 26 March 1911, 1. This quote is from the front-page photo caption on the fire.

2. See Alice Kessler-Harris, *Out to Work: A History of Wage-Earning Women in the United States* (New York: Oxford University Press, 1982), 108–217; Meredith Tax, *Rivington Street* (New York: Morrow, 1982) and *Union Square* (New York: Avon, 1988); Anne Marion MacLean, *Wage-Earning Women* (New York: MacMillan Company, 1910), 31–54; Theresa S. Malkiel, *The Diary of a Shirtwaist Striker* (Ithaca, NY: ILR Press, 1990 [1910]); and Meredith Tax's *The Rising of*

the Women: Feminist Solidarity and Class Conflict, 1880–1917 (New York: Monthly Review Press, 1980), among others.

3. Leon Stein, *The Triangle Fire* (New York: Carroll and Graf, 1962), passim. Stein was the editor of the ILGWU paper *Justice* and interviewed many survivors for his book. For a more recent account (one that still follows Stein's claims), see David Von Drehle's recent *Triangle: The Fire That Changed America* (New York: Atlantic Monthly Press, 2003).

4. Stein, *Triangle Fire*, 33. Stein discovered that the scrap dealer Triangle used, Louis Levy, usually picked up six times a year.

5. Stein, *Triangle Fire*, 3–4.

6. See Tamara K. Hareven, *Family Time Industrial Time: The Relationship Between Family and Work in a New England Industrial Community* (Cambridge: Cambridge University Press, 1982); and the work of Virginia Yans-McLaughlin, "Patterns of Work and Family Organization: Buffalo's Italians," *Journal of Interdisciplinary History* 2 (Autumn 1971–72): 299–314; Yans-McLaughlin, "A Flexible Tradition: South Italian Immigrants Confront a New Experience," *Journal of Social History* 7 (Summer 1974): 429–45; and Yans-McLaughlin, *Family and Community: Italian Immigrants in Buffalo, 1880–1930* (Ithaca, NY: Cornell University Press).

7. Stein, *Triangle Fire*, 31–42.

8. Ibid., 38.

9. Rose Grantz quoted in Stein, *Triangle Fire*, 54–58.

10. Stein, *Triangle Fire*, 14–18.

11. The thought of that choice, to jump to death or stay and be burned to death, was one that stayed with many who witnessed the fire. Similarly, the events of September 11, 2001, brought about similar discussions as images of people jumping from the upper floors of the World Trade Center buildings were seen on TV and printed in newspapers.

12. *New York Times* 26 March 1911, 1.

13. *New York Times* 26 March 911, 2.

14. Stein, *Triangle Fire*, 16.

15. Stein, *Triangle Fire*, 18.

16. Ibid., 18.

17. Martha Bensely Bruere, "The Triangle Fire," *Life and Labor* (May 1911): 137.

18. Stein, *Triangle Fire*, 168.

19. The *American* 28 March 1911, 5.

20. Bruere, "The Triangle Fire," 137.

21. Stein, *Triangle Fire*, 21.

22. *New York Times* 26 March 1911, 2.

23. Stein, *Triangle Fire*, 18.

24. Ibid, 18, full description is on 16–18.

25. *New York Times* 26 March 1911, 2.

26. *New York Daily Tribune* 26 March 1911, 2.

27. *New York Times* 29 March 1991.

28. *Tribune* 26 March 1911, 2.

29. "Visitors Reports on Triangle Fire Victims and Their Families." Leonora O'Reilly Papers, Records of the WTUL and Their Principle Leaders, Reel 13 (O'Reilly Papers).

30. *New York Times* 26 March 1911, 2.

31. Stein, *Triangle Fire*, 65.

32. *Tribune* 26 March 1911, 1–2; Stein, *Triangle Fire*, 54. *New York Times* 26 March 1911, 1–2.

33. See the *New York Times* and the *Tribune* for March 26, 1911.

34. Gullo quoted in Stein, *Triangle Fire*, 55.

35. Ibid., 47.

36. *New York Times* 29 March 1911.

37. *New York Times* 26 March 1911, 3; ibid., 27 March 1911, 1.

38. *New York Times* 26 March 1911, 3.

39. *New York American* 26 March 1911, 5.

40. *New York Times* 27 March 1911; Stein, *Triangle Fire*, 95–101.

41. Ibid., 104; *New York Times* and *Tribune* for 26 and 27 March 1911.

42. Quoted in Stein, *Triangle Fire*, 74.

43. The *World* 26 March 1911.

44. Stein, *Triangle Fire*, 73–94; *New York Times* 27 March 1911, 1.

45. Stein, *Triangle Fire*, 71.

46. The *Call* ran many such calls for aid. See the *Call* 28 March 1911, "Appeal for Aid."

47. See the *Call* for a full list of monies raised to aid the families of the dead and injured, March 28, April 1, 4, and 14, 1911.

48. *Annual Report of the Charity Organization Society of New York, 1911* (New York: COS, 1911), 47–48.

49. Hadassa Kosak, "The Rise of the Jewish Working Class, New York, 1881–1905" (Ph.D. Dissertation, CUNY Graduate Center, 1987), especially chapters 2–3.

50. *Report of the Joint Committee, Ladies-Waist and Dressmakers' Local 25 on the Triangle Fire Disaster* (January 15, 1913), 5. ILGWU Papers, Catherwood Library, New York State School of Industrial Relations, Cornell University.

51. Ibid., 48. The union distributed the rest of the funds to nonmembers. Exact numbers were $17,187.19 and $15,286.49.

52. Michael Katz, *In the Shadow of the Poor House: A Social History of Welfare in America* (New York: Basic Books, 1986), 58–85.

53. Red Cross Emergency Relief Committee of the Charities Organization Society of New York, *Emergency Relief After the Washington Place Fire, New York, March 25, 1911* (New York: COS, 1912), 7, 12, 89. Again, the exact numbers are $103,899.38 and $80,556.16.

54. *New York Times* 29 March 1911.

55. On the role of these two organizations, see Rose Schneiderman with Lucy Goldwaite, *All for One* (New York: Eriksson, 1967), 98.

56. The *Call* 28 March 1911.

57. See Stein, *Triangle Fire*, 255, and most of the New York daily papers following the fire.

58. The *Call* 29 March 1911; and ibid., 31 March 1911. Some identifications were made, however.

59. The *Call* 3 April 1911.

60. The *Call* 3 April 1911; and Stein, *Triangle Fire*, 141.

61. Wise quoted in Stein, *Triangle Fire*, 142–43.

62. Speech quoted in Schneiderman and Goldwaite, *All for One*, 100–101.

63. For a useful discussion of the emergence of the public sphere, see Craig Calhoun, ed., *Habermas and the Public Sphere* (Cambridge: MIT Press, 1992); Thomas Bender, "Wholes and Parts: The Need for Synthesis in American History," *Journal of American History* 73 (June 1986): 120–36; and Judith R. Walkowitz, *City of Dreadful Delight: Narratives of Sexual Danger in Late-Victorian London* (Chicago: University of Chicago Press, 1992).

64. *New York Times* 29 March 1911.

65. The term "general strike" was used by the *Call* 1 April 1911.

66. The *Call* 3 and 4 April 1911.

67. The *Call* 28 March 1911.

68. Quoted in the *Call* 27 March 1911.

69. *New York Times* 29 March 1911.

70. Henry Biscoff, "The Reformers, the Workers, and the Growth of the Positive State: A History of the Labor Legislation Movement in New York State, 1865–1911" (Ph.D. Dissertation, University of Chicago, 1964), 247–48.

71. See the *Call* 29 March 1911 for this analysis.

72. Gary Gerstle, *Working-Class Americanism: The Politics of Labor in a Textile City, 1914–1960* (Cambridge: Cambridge University Press, 1989); Joseph McCartin, "Labor's Great War: Workers, Unions, and the State, 1916–1920" (Ph.D. Dissertation, SUNY Binghamton, 1990); and David Montgomery's *Worker Citizen: The Experience of Workers in the United States with Democracy and the Free Market During the Nineteenth Century* (Cambridge: Cambridge University Press, 1993).

73. Stein, *Triangle Fire*, 95.

74. Montgomery, *Citizen Worker*; Gerstle, *Working-Class Americanism*; McCartin, "Labor's Great War"; Karen Orren, *Belated Feudalism: Labor, the Law, and Liberal Development on the United States* (Cambridge: Cambridge University Press, 1991); see also James Naylor, *The New Democracy: Challenging the Social Order in Industrial Ontario, 1914–25* (Toronto: University of Toronto Press, 1991).

75. *New York Times* 28 March 1911.

76. The *American* 6 April 1911, 6.

77. The *Call* 5 April 1911; and Stein, *Triangle Fire*, 149.

78. The *Call* 29 March 1911, 1.

79. Ibid.

80. The *Call* 1 April 1911.

81. The *Call* 6 April 1911.

82. Nancy Schrom-Dye, *As Equals and As Sisters: Feminism, the Labor Movement, and the Women's Trade Union League of New York.* (Columbia: University of Missouri Press, 1980); Gary Edward Endelman, "Solidarity Forever: Rose Schneiderman and the Women's Trade Union League" (Ph.D. Dissertation, University of Delaware, 1978); and Elizabeth Anne Payne, *Reform, Labor, and Feminism: Margaret Dreier Robins and the Women's Trade Union League* (Urbana: University of Illinois Press, 1988).

83. *New York Times* 5 April 1911; and New York *Tribune* 6 April 1911.

84. *New York Times* 27 March 1911, 1.

85. *New York Times* 26 March 1911, 2.

86. See the *Evening Post*, *New York Times*, and *Tribune* from March 26–19, 1911.

87. *Tribune* 26 March 1911, 2.

88. *Tribune* 27 March 1911, 2.

89. *Tribune* 27 March 1911.

90. Ibid.

91. On the intra-agency struggles see the *Times* and the *Tribune* for March 26–28, 1911.

92. See the *American* 28 March 1911, 1.

93. Editorial, *New York Times* 29 March 1911.

94. The *American* 27 March 1911, 3.

95. Ibid.

96. *New York Tribune* 26 March 1911, 1.

97. The best account on the connection between New York's workers and unions and the middle-class reformers is Melvyn Dubofsky, *When Workers Organize: New York City in the Progressive Era* (Amherst: University of Massachusetts Press, 1968).

98. *New York Times* 27 March 1911.

99. *New York Tribune* 27 March 1911, 4.

100. Mary Dreier to Leonora O'Reilly, April 18, 1911, O'Reilly Papers, Collection 5, Reel 5.

101. See Audre Lorde, "Learning From the 60s," in her collection *Sister Outsider: Essays and Speeches* (Freedom, CA: Crossing Press, 1984), especially 137.

102. See Nancy Schrom Dye, *As Equals and As Sisters* and Annelise Orleck, *Common Sense and a Little Fire: Women and Working-Class Politics in the United States, 1900–1965* (Chapel Hill: University of North Carolina Press, 1995); and Orleck, "Common Sense and a Little Fire: Working Women's Political Activism in the Twentieth Century United States" (Ph.D. Dissertation, New York University, 1989).

103. O'Reilly to Wagner dated May 15, 1911, O'Reilly Papers, Collection 5, Reel 5. Wagner and other Tammany Hall politicians were not at all interested in these events.

104. *New York Times* 29 March 1911.

105. O'Reilly Papers, Collection 5, Reel 13.

106. O'Reilly to Waldo April 19, 1911, O'Reilly Papers, Collection 5, Reel 5.

107. Street to O'Reilly, April 15, 1911, O'Reilly Papers, Collection 5 Reel 5.

108. Miller to O'Reilly, May 9 and May 25, O'Reilly Papers, Collection 5 Reel 5.

109. The *Call* 27 March 1911, 3.

110. *New York Times* 30 March 1911, 1.

111. See the *Tribune* for the week following the fire. These boxes ran daily.

112. Mirian F. Scott, "The Factory Girl's Danger," the *Outlook* 5 April 1911, 817–21.

113. All quoted in Stein, *Triangle Fire*, 113–14. Also see the local press during the week following the fire.

114. Stein, *Triangle Fire*, 179.

115. Kathy Peiss, *Cheap Amusements: Working Women and Leisure in Turn-of-the Century New York* (Philadelphia: Temple University Press, 1986); and Elizabeth Ewen, *Immigrant Women in the Land of Dollars: Life and Labor on the Lower East Side, 1890–1925* (New York: Monthly Review Press, 1981). Both detail the process by which these women define their own identity.

116. Stein, *Triangle Fire*, 180. The court records for the trial are no longer in existence. The Municipal Archives has lost the transcripts. Stein was one of the last to use them for his book. I had hoped that his papers might have copies, or at least notes, but they have not yet been donated to an archive.

117. Stein, *Triangle Fire*, 181.

118. Ibid., 177.

119. Ibid., 200.

120. On the "Seabury Committee" investigations into Mayor Jimmy Walker, see David M. Ellis et al., *A History of New York State* (Ithaca, NY: Cornell University Press, 1957), 414–16.

121. Ibid., 205.

122. Ibid., 207.

123. The *Call* 31 March 1911. On the state compensation law, see the *Call* March 29, 1911. On the National Civic Federation, one of the best treatments remains David Montgomery, "Machinists, the Civic Federation and the Socialist Party," in his *Workers Control in America* (Cambridge: Cambridge University Press, 1979).

124. On the New Deal Order, see Steve Frazer and Gary Gerstle, eds., *The Rise and Fall of the New Deal Order* (Cambridge: Cambridge University Press, 1989).

125. See Theda Skocpol, *Protecting Soldiers and Mothers: The Political Origins of Social Policy in the United States* (Cambridge, MA: Harvard University Press, 1992), especially p. 58.

CHAPTER 5

1. Alan Dawley, *Struggles for Social Justice: Social Responsibility and the Liberal State* (Cambridge: Harvard University Press, 1991), 3–4.

2. On the "labor problem" see Steven Fraser's "The Labor Problem," in Steven Fraser and Gary Gerstle, eds., *The Rise and Fall of the New Deal order, 1930–1980* (Princeton: Princeton University Press, 1989), 55–84.

3. Michael B. Katz, *In The Shadow of the Poorhouse: A Social History of Welfare in America* (New York: Basic Books, 1986); and Edward D. Berkowitz, *American's Welfare State: From Roosevelt to Reagan* (Baltimore: Johns Hopkins University Press, 1991); Mimi Abromovitz, *Regulating the Lives of Women: Social Welfare Policy From Colonial Times to the Present* (Boston: South End Press, 1988); Theda Skocpol, *Protecting Soldiers and Mothers: The Political Origins of Social Policy in the United States* (Cambridge: Harvard University Press, 1992); Molly Ladd-Taylor, *Mother-Work: Women, Child-Welfare, and the State, 1890–1930* (Urbana: University of Illinois Press, 1995); Linda Gordon, *Pitied But Not Entitled: Single Mothers and the History of Welfare* (New York: Free Press, 1994); Kriste Lindenmeyer, *"A Right to Childhood": The U.S. Children's Bureau and Child Welfare, 1912–1946* (Urbana: University of Illinois Press, 1997); and Joanne L. Goodwin, *Gender and the Politics of Welfare Reform: Mothers' Pensions in Chicago, 1911–1929* (Chicago: University of Chicago Press, 1997).

4. On this, see Alan Brinkley, *The End of Reform: New Deal Liberalism in Recession and War* (New York: Knopf, 1995) as the most recent significant statement on this historical debate surrounding liberalism.

5. Philip R. VanderMeer, "Bosses, Machines, and Democratic Leadership: Party Organization and Managers in Indiana, 1880–1910," *Social Science History* 12:4 (Winter 1988): 395–427; Terrence J. McDonald, "The Problem of the Political in Recent Urban History: Liberal Pluralism and the Rise of Functionalism," *Social History* 10:3 (October 1985): 323–45; and Philip J. Ethington, "Urban Constituencies, Regimes, and Policy Innovation in the Progressive Era: An Analysis of Boston, Chicago, New York and San Francisco," *Studies in American Political Development* 7 (Fall 1993): 275–315.

6. Samuel P. Hays's now classic essay "The Politics of Reform in Municipal Government in the Progressive Era," *Pacific Northwest Quarterly* 55 (October 1964): 157–69.

7. Paul Boyer, *Urban Masses and Moral Order in America, 1820–1920* (Cambridge: Harvard University Press, 1978); Carl Smith, *Urban Disorder and the Shape of Belief: The Great Chicago Fire, The Haymarket Bomb, and the Model Town of Pullman* (Chicago: University of Chicago Press, 1995); and the *New York Times* 27 March 1911.

8. See Nancy Strom Dye, *As Equals and as Sisters: Feminism, the Labor Movement, and the Women's Trade Union League of New York* (Columbia: University of Missouri Press, 1980); and Elizabeth Ann Payne, *Reform, Labor, and Feminism: Margaret Dreier Robins and the Women's Trade Union League* (Urbana: University of Illinois Press, 1988) for a description of the WTUL and its relationship to labor.

9. *New York Times* 27 March 1911; ibid., 29 March 1911; the *Call* 27 March 1911; see also, the WTUL of New York, *Annual Report, 1911–1912*, 17–19.

10. Ibid.

11. Boyer, *Urban Masses*; Michel B. Katz, *In the Shadow of the Poorhouse*; Katz, *Poverty and Policy in American History* (New York: Academic Press, 1983); *New York Times* 19 April 1911; the *Call* 19 April 1911; Henry Morgenthau's *All in a Lifetime* (New York: Doubleday, 1922), 94–129.

12. FIC, *Preliminary Report of the Factory Investigating Commission, 1912* (3 Volumes, Albany: Argus, 1912): II, 622.

13. See Claire Brandler Walker, "A History of Factory Legislation and Inspection in New York State, 1886–1911" (Ph.D. Dissertation, Columbia University, 1969).

14. See Alfred E. Smith, *Up to Now: An Autobiography* (New York: Viking Press, 1929), 91; and J. Joseph Hutchmarcher, *Senator Robert F. Wagner and the Rise of Urban Liberalism* (New York: Atheneum, 1968), 4–6. In addition, see the *New York Times* 9 May 1911 and the *Call* 9 May 1911, as well as *Laws of the State of New York* (1911), ch. 561.

15. *Laws of the State of New York* (1911), ch 561; Hutchmarcher, *Senator Robert F. Wagner*; Robert A. Slayton, Empire *Statesman: The Rise and Redemption of Al Smith* (New York: Free Press, 2001).

16. Morgenthau, *All in a Lifetime*, 108.

17. *New York Times* 19 August 1911; and FIC *Preliminary Report*, I, 14–15.

18. Elizabeth Israels Perry, *Belle Moskowitz: Feminine Politics and the Exercise of Power in the Age of Alfred E. Smith* (New York: Oxford University Press, 1987). In addition, see Thomas Kerr, "New York Factory Investigating Commission and the Progressives," (Ph.D. Dissertation, Syracuse University, 1965), 28–31; FIC, *Preliminary Report*, I, 125–26; and *First Annual Report of the Joint Board of Sanitary Control, October 1911*, 18.

19. Robert F. Wesser's *A Response to Progressivism: The Democratic Party and New York Politics, 1902–1918* (New York: New York University Press, 1986); Richard L. McCormick, *From Realignment to Reform: Political Change in New York, 1893–1910* (Ithaca, NY: Cornell University Press, 1981); and Robert F. Wesser, "Charles Evans Hughs and New York Politics: 1905–1910" (Ph.D. Dissertation, University of Rochester, 1961).

20. Henry L. Stimson and McGeorge Bundy, *On Active Service in Peace and War* (New York: Harper Brothers, 1948); Henry Moskowitz, "Henry L. Stimson," the *Independent* LXIX (October 7, 1910): 904–7.

21. The *Outlook* CII (September 21, 1912): 107–11; J. Salwyn Schapiro, "Social Reformer in Politics," ibid., (October 26, 1912): 446–49; and Albany *Knickerbocker Press* 4 September 1912; ibid., 5 September 1912; ibid., 7 September 1912.

22. Nancy Joan Weiss's *Charles Francis Murphy, 1858–1924: Respectability and Responsibility in Tammany Politics* (North Hampton, MA: Smith College Press, 1968); and J. Joseph Hutchmacher, "Charles Evans Hughs and Charles Francis Murphy: The Metamorphosis of Progressive Reform," *New York History* 46:1 (January 1965): 25–40.

23. Weiss, *Charles Francis Murphy*, 43–54; Wesser, *A Response*, 21–43; and see also "Tammany's Opportunity," the *Outlook* XCVI (October 1910): 334–36; Kerr,

"New York Factory," 66; J. Joseph Hutchmarcher, *Senator Robert F. Wagner and the Rise of Urban Liberalism* (New York: Atheneum, 1968), 3–37; Oscar Handlin, *Al Smith and His America* (Boston: Little Brown, 1958), 39–65; Robert Moses, *A Tribute to Governor Smith* (New York: Simon and Schuster, 1962), passim; Richard O'Connor, *The First Hurrah: A Biography of Alfred E. Smith* (New York: G.P. Putnam's Sons, 1970), 33–77; Smith, *Up To Now*, 69–112; Norman Hapsgood and Henry Moskowitz, *Up From the City Streets: Alfred E. Smith: A Biographical Study in Contemporary Politics* (New York: Harcourt, Brace, 1927), 40–99; Emily Smith Warner with Daniel Hawthorne, *The Happy Warrior: A Biography of My Father Alfred E. Smith* (Garden City: Doubleday, 1956), 43–81; Henry F. Pringle, *Alfred E. Smith: A Critical Study* (New York: Marcy-Masius, 1927), 75–124; Henry Moskowitz, *Alfred E. Smith: An American Career* (New York: Thomas Seltzer, 1924), 25–42; Perry, *Belle Moskowitz*, passim; Albany *Knickerbocker Press*, 29 October 1911. The quote is from ibid., 7 November 1911. See also, the *New York Times* 31 October 1911; ibid., 2 November 1911; ibid., 3 November 1911.

24. Melvyn Dubofsky, "Success and Failure of Socialism in New York City, 1900–18: A Case Study," *Labor History* XI (Fall 1968): 361–75; Charles Leinenweber, "Socialists in the Streets: The New York City Socialist Party in Working Class Neighborhoods, 1908–1918," *Science and Society* 41:2, 152–71. Also see the *New York Times* 9 November 1911.

25. Kerr, "New York Factory," 73–77.

26. McCormick, *From Realignment to Reform*; Michael McGerr, *The Decline of Popular Politics: The American North, 1865–1928* (New York: Oxford University Press, 1986); and Paula Baker, "The Domestication of Politics: Women and American Political Society, 1780–1920," *American Historical Review* 89 (June 1984): 620–47.

27. FIC, *Preliminary Report*, III, 1038–39; and FIC, *Fourth Report*, 1915, I, 73. See also Elkus, *Annals of the American Academy of Political and Social Science* XVIII (July 1913): 54–65.

28. FIC, *Preliminary Report*, I, 16–27, III, 815. Also see the *New York Times* editorial on 30 March 1912.

29. FIC, *Second Report, 1913*, I, 14–22, 264; ibid., II, 399–408; ibid., III, 1.

30. Lillian D. Wald and Henry Moskowitz, "Taking Stock in New York's Factories," the *Survey* XXVII (March 16, 1912): 1928–29; "A report of the Factory Commission," the *Nation* XCIV (March 7, 1912): 228–29; *New York Times* 29 March 1912. See also the Consumers' League of the City of New York, *Report for the Year 1914* (New York: Consumers' League, 1915): 12–15 and "Resolution of Consumers' League," in FIC, *Second Report*, II, 1338–39.

31. Julia Greene, "The Strike at the Ballot Box: The American Federation of Labor's Entrance into Election Politics, 1906–1909," *Labor History* 32:2 (Spring 1991): 165–92; and her 1990 Yale Dissertation: "The Strike at the Ballot Box: Politics and Partisanship in the American Federation of Labor, 1881–1916." Greene's work builds on the earlier revisionist work of Gary Fink. See Fink, "The Rejection of Volunteerism," *Industrial and Labor Relations Review* 26 (1982): 805–19.

32. Kerr, "New York Factory," 82.

33. *New York Times* 6 September 1912. Also see "New York's Progressive Convention: Unbossed and Unafraid," the *Outlook* CII (September 14, 1912): 50–51.

34. *New York Times* 13 August 1912; ibid., 22 September 1912; ibid., 23 September 1912; ibid., 24 September 1912; ibid., 28 September 1912; Albany *Knickerbocker Press* 2 September 1912; ibid., 13 September 1912; ibid., 18 September 1912; ibid., 19 September 1912; ibid., 21 September 1912; ibid., 24 September 1912; ibid., 26 September 1912; ibid., 27 September 1912; ibid., 28 September 1912. See also State of New York, *Public Papers of William Sulzer, Governor, 1913* (Albany: J. B. Lyon, 1914), iii–xxix.

35. *New York Times* and Albany *Knickerbocker Press* 1 October 1912; ibid., 2 1912; ibid., 3 October 1912.

36. *New York Times* 3 October 1913.

37. Kerr, New York Factory," 91–93.

38. FIC, *Fourth Report*, I, 5–8; and FIC, *Third Report*, 11–43.

39. FIC, *Fourth Report*, I, 5–8 for a complete rundown of what the commission did.

40. Ibid.; see also State of New York, *Public Papers of William Sulzer*, 32; *New York Times* 4 May 1913.

41. New York State Federation of Labor, *Official Proceedings: Fifteenth Annual Convention, 1913* (New York State Federation, 1913), 135 and *American Federationist* II (February 1913): 141–42.

42. *New York Times* 9 February 1913; ibid., 12 February 1913; Consumer's League of the City of New York, *Report for the Year 1913* (New York: Consumers' League, 1914), 9; and Kerr, "New York Factory," 97–98.

43. *New York Times* 17 February 1913; ibid., 10 March 1913; and the *Call* 12 February 1913; and ibid., 1 March 1913.

44. Kerr, "New York Factory," 97–100; and Wesser, *A Response*. See also Albany *Knickerbocker Press* 12 March 1913; and Jacob A. Friedman, *The Impeachment of Governor William Sulzer* (New York: Columbia University Press, 1939), 39–147.

45. Albany *Knickerbocker Press* 7 August 1913; ibid., 9 August 1913; ibid., 11 August 1913; ibid., 12 August 1913; ibid., 14 August 1913; *New York Times* 4 May 1913; ibid., 31 July 1913; ibid., 7 August 1913; ibid., 9 August 1913.

46. Morgenthau, *All in a Lifetime*, 172; Albany *Knickerbocker Press* 13 August 1913; ibid., 25 September 1913; ibid., 26 September 1913; ibid., 8 October 1913; and *New York Times* 25 September 1913; ibid., 27 September 1913.

47. *New York Times* 17 October 1913; ibid., 18 October 1913; ibid., 19 October 1913; Albany *Knickerbocker Press* 16 October 1913; ibid., 17 October 1913 and Morgenthau, *All in a Lifetime*, 171.

48. Albany *Knickerbocker Press* 4 September 1913; ibid., 5 September 1913; ibid., 19 September 1913; "Where it Leaves Murphy," the *Nation* XCVII (August 21, 1913): 158; "The Struggle in New York to End the Reign of Tammany," *Current Opinion* IV (October 1913): 223–26.

49. Gregory Mason "New York City Fusion Tickets," the *Outlook* CV (September 6, 1913): 23–28; "Trained Social Workers Take Charge of New York City Government," the *Survey* XXXI (January 10, 1914): 430–32; *New York Times* 20 October 1913; ibid., 21 October 1913; ibid., 2 November 1913; and Albany *Knickerbocker Press* 4 November 1913; ibid., 5 November 1913.

50. Edgar J. Marlin, *New York Red Book, 1914* (Albany: J. B. Lyon, 1914), 692–702.

51. *New York Times* 5 November 1913; ibid., 6 November 1913; Albany *Knickerbocker Press* 6 November 1913; "Tammany's Waterloo," *Literary Digest* XIXII (November 15, 1913): 927–29; and "War on Murphy," ibid. (February 21, 1914): 361–63.

52. "Judge Who Would Serve the People," the *Independent* LXXVI (October 30, 1913): 217; and *New York Times* 5 October 1913.

53. Buffalo *Courier* and *Express* 7, 9, 10 December 1913.

54. *American Labor Legislation Review* I (March 1912): 81–104 and Kerr, New York Factory," 107–8.

55. Samuel Gompers, "Women's Work, Rights, and Progress," *American Federationalist* XX (August 1913): 624–27; *Garment Worker* (October 23, 30; November 6, 13, 20, 27; December 4, 11, 18, 25, 1914).

56. Albany *Knickerbocker Press* 30 March 1914; ibid., 31 March 1914 and *New York Times* 11 November 1913; ibid., 13 December 1913; ibid., 29 March 1914.

57. Kerr, "New York Factory," 112; Albany *Knickerbocker Press* 20 August 1914; ibid., 13 October 1914; ibid., 17 October 1914; ibid., 20 October 1914; ibid., 24 October 1914; ibid., 27 October 1914; and the *New York Times* 20 October 1914; ibid., 25 October 1914; ibid., 28 October 1914; ibid., 3 November 1914; ibid., 4 November 1914; ibid., 5 November 1914.

58. Kerr, "New York Factory," 113–16. Kerr did an excellent breakdown of the 1914 vote in New York, although he does not digest the vote nor does he explain its meaning.

59. Ibid.

60. Ibid., II, 6–27.

61. FIC, *Fourth Report*, I, 10–16.

CHAPTER 6

1. Richard L. McCormick, "The Discovery That Business Corrupts Politics: A Reappraisal of the Origins of Progressivism," *American Historical Review* 86:2 (April 1981). Also see the work of Morton Keller, *Regulating a New Economy: Public Policy and Economic Change in America, 1900–1933* (Cambridge: Harvard University Press, 1990); Kellor, *Regulating a New Society: Public Policy and Social Change in America, 1900–1933* (Cambridge: Harvard University Press, 1994).

2. New York Factory Investigating Commission (FIC), *Second Report of the Factory Investigating Commission* (Albany: J. B. Lyon Company, Printers, 1913),

I, 12; FIC, *Preliminary Report of the Factory Investigating Commission, 1912* (3 Volumes, Albany: Argus, 1912), I, 728, II, 329, III, 1529; Randolph E. Bergstrom, *Courting Danger: Injury and Law in New York City, 1870–1910* (Ithaca, NY: Cornell University Press, 1992), 31–86, and 144–66; FIC, *Preliminary Report*, I, 43, 681, 728–31, II 239, III, 1065–72, 1527–29.

3. FIC, *Second Report*, II, 1320–29; "Make Workers Safe From Fire," *Searchlight* II (June 4, 1912): 1–2.

4. Frances Perkins' "The Committee on Safety," in Joint Board of Sanitary Control, *Manufacturers' Bulletin for Fire Prevention*, No. 2 (March 1915): 8–9; Consumers' League of New York, *Report, June 1910-February 26, 1913* (New York: Consumers' League, 1913): 6–7; WTUL, *Annual Report, 1912–1913* (New York: WTUL, 1913): 21; ibid, *Annual Report, 1913–1914*, 7; and FIC, *Second Report*, II, 1338–39; FIC, *Preliminary Report*, I, 733, II, 648–50, 910, 920, III, 1809–20, FIC, *Second Report*, III 445–62, 478–86, 621–26, 775–80, 1074–84, 1087–91, 1113–22, IV, 1332–34, 1380–93, 1415–28, 1442–52, 1857–69, 2001–04, 2020–26, 2029–32, 2035–42, 2044–61, 2075–82, 2156; FIC, *Preliminary Report*, I, 740–43, II, 548–50, 564–69, 817–22; Albany *Knickerbocker Press*, 2 March 1912; Buffalo *Courier*, 28 November 1911; and Buffalo, *Express*, 28 November 1911.

5. George Price, "Fifteen Years of Progress," in *Fifteenth Anniversary of the Joint Board of Sanitary Control, 1910–1925* (New York: Joint Board, 1926): 28; Joint Board of Sanitary Control, *First Annual Report of the Joint Board of Sanitary Control, October 1911* (New York: Joint Board, 1911): 22–23; and Joint Board, *Second Annual Report of the Joint Board of Sanitary Control, December 1912* (New York: Joint Board, 1912): 22–23. See also "Fire Protection," *Life and Labor* (June 1911): 180–82; and the *Call* 27 March 1911; and ibid., 28 March 1911.

6. New York State Department of Labor, *Tenth Annual Report of the Commissioner of Labor for the Twelve Months Ended September 30, 1910* (Albany: State Department of Labor, 1911): 54; New York State Department of Labor, *Eleventh Annual Report of the Commissioner of Labor for the Twelve Months Ended September 30, 1911* (Albany: State Department of Labor, 1912); and the *Call* 29 March 1911.

7. New York State Federation of Labor, *Official Proceedings, Fifteenth Annual Convention, 1911*, 78; "Fire Prevention," the *Survey* (May 16, 1911): 2; and the *Call* 31 May 1911.

8. *New York Times* 3 April 1914; and chapter 3 of this book.

9. FIC, *Preliminary Report*, I, 15–29, 175–ff, II, 108–26, 594–602, 623–29; and FIC, *Second Report*, I, 15.

10. FIC, *Preliminary Report*, I, 28–35, 169, II, 863–67, III, 1039–45; and FIC, *Second Report*, I, 58–64, II, 423–25.

11. FIC, *Preliminary Report*, I, 161–63, 174–97, 660–89, 728–43, II, 104–8, 135–53, 196–215, 234–36, 506–16, 629–36, III, 567–78, 1502–12, 1905–37; and FIC, *Second Report*, II, 615–56.

12. FIC, *Preliminary Report*, I, 170–84, 707–17, II 14–43, 104–130, 213–15, 506–16, 623–36, 830, III, 1114–21, 1335–50, 1533–35, 1792–1802, 1905–14, 1925–37; and FIC, *Second Report*, II, 615–56, III, 462–67, IV, 1462–78; FIC, *Preliminary Report*, I,

174–75, 185–97, 660–89, II, 135–37, 196–215, 234–36, 385–99, 580–82, III, 1351–52, 1481–91, 1502–35, 1792–1802; FIC, *Second Report*, I, 68–72, II, 615–56, 1329, 1334–37, III, 1122–26, IV, 1428–42, and 1462–92. See also the *New York Times* March 12, 1913.

13. Frances Perkins, *The Roosevelt I Knew* (New York: Viking Press, 1946), 22–23.

14. FIC, *Preliminary Report*, I, 38; FIC, *Preliminary Report*, I, 663; *Second Report*, IV, 1405; *New York Times* 19 March 1913; ibid., 23 March 1913; Buffalo *Courier*, 7 December 1912; ibid., 10 December 1912; Buffalo *Express*, 7 December 1912; ibid., 10 December 1912; and "Proposed Bills Being Drafted," *Monthly Bulletin* III (January 1913): 284–85; and "Jeremiah and Job," ibid., (March 1913): 345–47. The *Monthly Bulletin* was a publication of the Real Estate Board, which was a vocal and active member of the anti-FIC coalition.

15. Ibid., 817–18; and *Laws of the State of New York* (1912): ch. 329.

16. FIC, *Preliminary Report*, I, 818; and *Laws of the State of New York* (1912): ch. 330.

17. FIC, *Preliminary Report*, I, 818–19, and *Laws of the State of New York* (1912): ch. 332; FIC, *Preliminary Report*, I, 82 ff; and *Laws of the State of New York*, (1912): ch. 325.

18. FIC, *Preliminary Report*, I, 823–25; and State of New York, *Public Papers of Governor Dix*, 1912, 158–59.

19. FIC, *Second Report*, I, 327–45; and *Laws of the State of New York* (1913): chs. 461 and 695.

20. "New York Factory Bills: Symposium," the *Survey* XXIX (February 22, 1913): 725–36; George M. Price, *Modern Factory* (New York: John Wiley, 1914), 501; FIC, *Second Report*, I, 12 (quote); and FIC, *Preliminary Report*, I, 13.

21. John B. Andrew's annual "Report of Work," published each January in the AALL's *American Labor Legislation Review*. Also see John M. Glenn, Lillian Brant, and F. Emerson Andrews, *Russell Sage Foundation, 1907–1946* (New York: Russell Sage Foundation, 1947): I, 152–60. While the AALL's papers are well preserved and microfilmed, no recent full-scale study has emerged. One of the best treatments of this group is found in Clarence E. Wunderlin, Jr., *Visions of a New Industrial Order: Social Science and Labor Theory in America's Progressive Era* (New York: Columbia University Press, 1992), especially chapter 2: "The Emerging Synthesis."

22. George Price, *Handbook on Sanitation* (New York: John Wiley, 1901, 1911); ILGWU, *Annual Report of the Union Health Center, 1943* (New York: Union Health Center, 1943): 5; George M. Price, "A General Survey of the Sanitary Conditions of the Shops in the Cloak Industry," *First Annual Report of the Joint Board of Sanitary Control, October, 1911* (New York: Joint Board, 1912): 70; Kerr, "New York Factory," 140. On the growing field of workers' health, see David Rosner and Gerald Moskowitz's pioneering collection, *Dying for Work: Workers' Safety and Health in Twentieth-Century America* (Bloomington: Indiana University Press, 1987).

23. FIC, *Preliminary Report*, I, 23–25, 116–24, 591–93, and 1946–49.

24. FIC, *Second Report*, I, 14–18, 227, II, 401–4, 412–15, 487–532.

25. FIC, *Preliminary Report*, I, 45–54, 112–26, 277–334, 631–43, II, 127–49, 269–305, 422–56, 535–44, 782–803, 822–33, 957–74, III, 1031–33, 1046–48, 1287–1290, 1390–1402, 1535–59. Price's quote is from *Second Report*, II, 416.

26. FIC, *Second Report*, I, 227–28.

27. Alan Dawley claimed that one way to see the Progressive Era was as a "reign of the Middle Class"; that through cultural institutions, reform organizations, and political influences, the middle class regained, or held onto, power. See his *Struggles for Justice: Social Responsibility and the Liberal State* (Cambridge: Harvard University Press, 1991), 19–23.

28. FIC, *Preliminary Report*, I, 277–78, 328–31, III, 1949–50, 1632–42; *Second Report*, I, 231–33. The quote is from *Preliminary Report*, I, 71; FIC, *Preliminary Report*, I, 147, 627–31, 758–64, II, 98–99, 263–69, 422–29, 802–3, 824–29, 957–74, III, 1031–39, 1089–98, 1360–64, 1373–80, 1450–59, 1498–1501, 1609–17, 1760–70.

29. FIC, *Preliminary Report*, I, 73–74, 147, II, 127–35, 269–305, 429–41, III, 1952; *Second Report*, I 229–30, II, 426–30; and New York State Department of Labor, *Eleventh Annual Report, 1911*, 22; ibid., *Twelfth Annual Report of the Commissioner of Labor for the Twelve Months Ended September 30, 1912* (Albany: State Department of Labor, 1913): 71–72.

30. Mark Aldrich, *Safety First: Technology, Labor, and Business in the Building of American Work Safety, 1870–1939* (Baltimore: Johns Hopkins University Press, 1997); Richard A Greenwald, "Workers, Health and Community: Danbury Connecticut's Struggle with Industrial Disease," *Labor's Heritage* 2:3 (July 1990); David Rosner and Gerald Moskowitz. In particular, see their *Deadly Dust: Silicosis and the Politics of Occupational Disease in Twentieth Century America* (Princeton: Princeton University Press, 1994) and their edited collection, *Dying for Work*.

31. John B. Andrews, "Introduction to Symposium on Industrial Diseases," *American Labor Legislation Review* II (June 1912): 181–82.

32. FIC, *Preliminary Report*, I, 17– 18, 142–43, 244–48, 334, II, 549–601, 846–60, 1045–80, 1623–32, III, 627–50; FIC, *Second Report*, II, 459–513, 533–40.

33. FIC, *Preliminary Report*, I 368–72, 532–48, 565–69; FIC, *Second Report*, I, 16–18.

34. FIC, *Preliminary Report*, I 147–49, 643–46, II 456–67, 523–35, 636–45, 833–53, III, 1089–98, 1360–64, 1373–80, 1450–59, 1498–1501, 1609–17, 1623–32, 1677–87; FIC, *Second Report*, I, 248–49, II, 514–40, 1083, 1137–40, III, 650–59.

35. *Lochner v. New York* 198 US 45 (1905).

36. FIC, *Preliminary Report*, I, 78–80, 211–20, 350–54, II, 676–97; FIC, *Second Report*, I, 216–24.

37. Robert B. Down's Afterward to Upton Sinclair, *The Jungle* (New York: Signet Classic, 1988 edition), 345; FIC, *Preliminary Report*, I, 24, 204, 350–53; FIC, *Second Report*, I, 216–24; New York State Consumers' League, *Bulletin* (May 1911); *New York Times* 19 April and 15 November 1911; and New York State Department of Labor, *Eleventh Annual Report*, 24.

38. FIC, Preliminary Report, II, 553–55, 737–40; FIC, Second Report, IV, 1246–70, 1289–96, 1341–48, 1774, 1789–90, 2123–25, 2283–85, 2303–11.

39. FIC, Preliminary Report, I, 81–82, 140–42, 234–68; FIC, Second Report, II, 216–26.

40. FIC, Preliminary Report, II, 278.

41. FIC, Preliminary Report, I, 128.

42. That science would be used to make the argument was clear, as was the educational aspect. "Education," as one FIC commissioner stated, "will bring about the desired results in this field." FIC, Second Report, I, 242 (quote), IV, 2088, and 2116 (Wagner quote).

43. FIC, Preliminary Report, I, 764, II, 153–67, 842–46, III, 1002–03, 1617–23, 1672–76, 1700–1710; FIC, Second Report, III, 660–89, 845 (first quote), 1091–1111, 1213 (last quote), IV, 1965–83, 1988–95, 2065–67.

44. FIC, Preliminary Report, I, 827–29; and Laws of the State of New York (1912) ch. 334, 335, 336; FIC, Preliminary Report, I, 830–32, 835–37.

45. George Price to John B. Andrews, July 17, 1911, American Association of Labor Legislation (Micro Film Collection) Reel 7. Rabbi Stephan Wise as quoted in Leon Stein, The Triangle Fire (New York: Carroll and Graff, 1962), 142–43.

46. When I refer to "labor laws," I include in that category, as did the reformers themselves, legislation concerning safety and health as well as hours and wages. Progressive reformers surrounding the FIC had a broader understanding of labor than was once thought.

47. John Coleman as quoted in the Buffalo Express November 29, 1911. See FIC, Preliminary Report, II, 776–80, 798–99, 822–24, 879–82, III, 1005, 1092–1108, 1500, 1326–28, 1498–1501, 1666–71.

48. FIC, Preliminary Report, II, 776–80, 798–99, 822–24, 879–882, III, 1005, 1092, 1095–1108, 1326–28, 1498–1501, 1666–71.

49. FIC, Preliminary Report, II, 54–73, 273, 413–22, 614–15, 698–99, 834–36, 885–903, III, 739–46, 1129–60, 1184–1200, 1256–62, 1292–99, 1316–22, 1331–ff, 364–70, 1393–1425, 1433–50, 1463–71, 1850–66, 1954. See also FIC, Second Report, III, 207–13, 671–73, 787–90, IV, 1149–51.

50. FIC, Preliminary Report, I, 588–91, 603–10, 611–25, 691–92, II, 76–77, 87–88, 133, 138, 245, 341–43, 419–21, 425–27, 437–38, 469–72, 539, 629–63, III, 1564, 1609–12, 1643–44, 1711–13, 1721–30, 1754–70, 1922–30, 1967–78.

51. American Labor Legislation Review, VII (June 1917): 247–48; Laws of the State of New York (1908), ch. 520; ibid., (1910), ch. 514; ibid., (1911), chs. 565 and 729; New York State Department of Labor, Tenth Annual of Report of the Commissioner of Labor for the Twelve Months Ended September 30, 1910 (Albany: State Department of Labor, 1911): 12–13, 18, 23–24, 30–33; ibid., Eleventh Annual Report (Albany: State Labor Department, 1912): 20–35; ibid., Twelfth Annual Report (Albany: State Labor Department, 1913): 10–52; ibid., Thirteenth Annual Report (Albany: State Labor Department, 1914): 35–38; and FIC, Preliminary Report, II, 54–73. On rapid growth of the economy, see Martin J. Sklar, The Corporate Reconstruction of American Capitalism, 1890–1916: The Market, the Law, and Politics

(New York: Cambridge University Press, 1988); Elizabeth Brandeis, "Labor Legislation" in John R. Commons, ed., *History of Labor in the United States, 1896–1932* (New York: Augustus M. Kelley, 1966, reprint of 1935), 644–55; Wunderlin, *Visions of a New Industrial Order*; McCartin, op. cit.; State Department of Labor, *Eleventh Annual Report* (Albany: State Department of Labor, 1912): 38; ibid., *Fourteenth Annual Report* (Albany: State Labor Department, 1915): 12. The other state that had followed the Wisconsin approach was Massachusetts; FIC, *Preliminary Report*, I, 23, 754–57; John B. Andrews to Abram I. Elkins, October 13, 1911; Andrews to Dr. George M. Price, January 2, 1911; Andrews to Mary Dreier, January 2, 1912 (AALL Papers University Microfilms).

52. FIC, *Second Report*, III, 1, 34–37, 60–68, 97–115, 611–21, IV, 1781–82, 2339–58. See also *American Labor Legislation Review* VII (June 1917): 250; FIC, *Preliminary Report*, I, 36–38, 64–73, 66 (quote).

53. FIC, *Second Report*, II, 1302–8, III, 1–68, 97–115, 611–21, IV, 1127–32, 1144–47, 1166–67, 1173–84, 1215–22, 1365–80, 1633–39, 2042–43, 2067–74. See also *Weekly Bulletin of the Clothing Trades* 18 October 1912. And because the opposition to the FIC was strongest in Buffalo, see the Buffalo *Courier* 10 December 1912.

54. Albany *Knickerbocker Press*, 27 September 1912; ibid., 3 October 1912 for party platforms. See also the *New York Times* 2 January 1913; and State of New York, *Public Papers if William Sulzer, Governor, 1913* (Albany: J. B. Lyon, 1914), 32.

55. This and the following discussion of the bill are based on FIC, *Second Report*, I, 26–50. For the bill and the FIC's rationalization for it, see pp. 298–320 in FIC, *Second Report*, I, 26–27, 52, 292–93.

56. IC, *Second Report*, I, 28–30, 292.

57. FIC, *Second Report*, I, 304–5.

58. FIC, *Second Report*, I, 298–320. The informal recommendations are on p. 31.

59. New York State Department of Labor, *Thirteenth Annual Report*, 7–10; Department of Labor, *Fourteenth Annual Report*, 33, 44–47, 100, 128–71; Department of Labor, *New York Labor Bulletin: The Industrial Board Number 56* (September 1913): 383–92; *American Labor Legislation Review* VII (June 1917): 377; and Consumers' League of the City of New York, *Report, 1913*, 9–10.

60. "Tammany and the Factory Fire Laws," the *Survey* XXX (August 2, 1913): 557–58; *New York Times* 24 July 1913; Albany *Knickerbocker Press* 3 August 1913; and Consumers' League of the City of New York, *Report, 1913*, 9–10.

61. FIC, *Second Report*, I, 292; FIC, *Third Report*, 12–13, 43–44. The members of the Advisory Panel included two former labor commissioners and six respected reformers, including Pauline Goldmark.

62. FIC, *Third Report*, 45–51, quote is from page 51. For the Bill itself, see 417–601.

63. FIC, *Fourth Report*, I, 10; New York State Federation of Labor, *Official Proceedings, Fifty-First Annual Convention, 1914* (New York: New York Federation of Labor, 1914): 49; and *New York Times* 22 June 1914.

64. FIC, *Fourth Report*, I, 13–22, 51–52.

65. FIC, *Fourth Report*, I, 52–62, 709. The 1915 bill can be found on pages 93–290.

66. FIC, *Fourth Report*, I, 79–89; New York Industrial Commission, *New York Labor Laws of 1915* Number 72 (July 1915): 9. See also Albany *Knickerbocker Press* 25 April 1915.

67. FIC, *Second Report*, III, 2–15, IV, 1210–15; Paul Kennedy, "Inspectors to Supervise Factories," the *Survey* XXVII (February 3, 1912): 1669; "New York Factory Bureau," the *Survey* XXVIII (May 11, 1912): 266–68; "Tammany Tiger's Paw on Labor Laws in New York State," the *Survey* XXXIII (August 15, 1914): 499–502; See also Florence Kelley, *Modern Industry in Relation to the Family, Health, Education, Morality* (New York: Longmans, 1914), 68.

CHAPTER 7

1. Factory Investigating Commission, *Second Report*, II, 1006. This was the testimony of a twelve-year-old worker.

2. Mary Chamberlain, "Children in Bondage," *Good Housekeeping* LVI (May 1913): 618–25; and FIC, *Second Report*, I, 132–39, 154–58, II, 770–89, 820–23, III, 313–38, 997–1018; FIC, *Second Report*, IV, 1573–76, 1792 (quote).

3. FIC, *Second Report*, IV, 2095–96.

4. Gail Bederman, *Manliness and Civilization: A Cultural History of Gender and Race in the United States, 1880–1917* (Chicago: University of Chicago Press, 1995), 77–120.

5. Frances Perkins' *Reminiscences, 1951–55*, Book I, p. 58. Columbia University Oral History Project, Butler Library, Columbia University.

6. Theda Skocpol, *Protecting Soldiers and Mothers: The Political Origins of Social Policy in the United States* (Cambridge: Harvard University Press, 1992), especially 1–62.

7. FIC, *Preliminary Report*, I, 93–95 271–78, 293–95, 832–33, III, 1474–76, 1636–38; FIC, *Second Report*, I, 366–67 III, 339–70, 538–46, IV, 1689–90; and *Laws of the State of New York* (1913), ch. 197; Melvin I. Urofsky, "State Courts and Protective Legislation During the Progressive Era: A Reevaluation," *Journal of American History* 72:1 (June 1985): 63–91.

8. Consumers' League of the City of New York, *Report for the Year 1911* (New York: Consumers' League, 1912): 13, 29–32; and FIC, *Preliminary Report*, I, 646–48, III, 1613.

9. FIC, *Second Report*, III, 813. For Gompers' actions on this issue, see New York State Federation of Labor, *Official Proceedings Forty-Ninth Annual Convention, 1912*, 132.

10. FIC, *Second Report*, III, 793– 806–7, 824–31, 854–57, IV, 1801–2, 1835–50, 2063.

11. FIC, *Second Report*, I, 263 (quote). For background on this, see ibid., I, 260–63, IV, 1787; FIC *Preliminary Report*, I, 107, II, 789–90, III, 1203–5, 1212; and Buffalo *Express* 30 May 1912.

12. *Laws of the State of New York* (1913), ch. 464.

13. FIC, *Preliminary Report*, I, 272–73, 362–593, 807, II, 331, 428, 540, 800, 962–64, III, 1287–90, 1599–1600, 1804; FIC, *Second Report*, II, 1274–88; Clara M. Boyer, *History of Labor Legislation in Three States*, Bulletin of the U.S. Department of Labor Women's Bureau, no. 66 (Washington, DC: Government Printing Office, 1929): 111–13; and *The Weekly Bulletin of the Clothing Trades* (October 4, 1912). For the FIC recommendations and the law itself, see FIC, *Preliminary Report*, I, 93, 99–100, 833; and see *Laws of the State of New York* (1912), ch. 331; FIC, *Preliminary Report*, I, 271–78, III, 1636–38.

14. *Laws of the State of New York*, (1886), ch. 409; ibid., (1889), ch. 560; ibid., (1890), ch. 398; ibid., (1892), ch. 673; ibid., (1899), ch. 192; ibid., (1906), ch. 507; and Melvin Urofsky, "State Courts and Protective Legislation," op.cit.

15. Mary Van Kleeck, "Working Hours for Women in Factories," *Charities and the Commons* (October 1906): 13–21; New York State Federation of Labor, *Official Proceedings, 1912*, 62. See also Boyer, *History of Labor Legislation*, 66–81; and, finally, the law exempted the canning industry: FIC, *Preliminary Report*, I, 295–99, 551, 569, 649–55, II, 54, 84–85, 296–97, 372, 381, 440, 486, 504, 533–42, 561, 641, 669, 842, 846, 852–53, 800–809, 962–71, III, 993–96, 1021, 1098, 1128–29, 1224–27, 1251–55, 1604–8, 1292, 1402, 1457, 1588, 1604–8, 1804, 1903–4. *Laws of the State of New York* (1912), ch. 539; FIC, *Second Report*, I, 213–15.

16. *Laws of the State of New York* (1896), ch. 384; ibid., (1908), ch. 520; and ibid., (1910), ch. 387. See also Boyer, *History of Labor Legislation*, 70–71.

17. FIC, *Preliminary Report*, III, 1614–15; and FIC, *Second Report*, I, 264.

18. FIC, *Second Report*, I, 18, 277–79, II, 1197–1200, 1213–54.

19. FIC, *Second Report*, I, 289–90; and *Laws of the State of New York* (1913), ch. 145.

20. FIC, *Third Report*, 53–54; Consumer's League of the City of New York, *Report of the Year 1914* (New York: Consumer's League, 1915): 30–31; New York State Department of Labor, *Thirteenth Annual Report of the Commissioner of Labor for the Twelve Months Ended September 30, 1913* (Albany: State Department of Labor, 1914): 81, 118; Boyer, *History of Labor Legislation*, 83; and *Laws of the State of New York* (1914), ch. 331.

21. *Laws of the State of New York* (1899), ch. 560; ibid., (1896) ch. 384; ibid., (1899) ch. 192.

22. *People v. Williams*, 189 New York 131 (1907); and *Muller v. Oregon*, 208 US 412 (1908); see also FIC, *Second Report*, I, 203–6; and *Laws of the State of New York* (1907) ch. 506. After the court struck down the 1899 law, the state legislature reenacted the law for minors.

23. Josephine Goldmark, "Report of the Committee on Legislation," in Consumer's League, *Fourteenth Report for the Two Years Ending December 31, 1913* (New York: Consumer's League, 1914): 32–33; see also Susan Lehrer, *Origins of Protective Labor Legislation for Women, 1905–1925* (Albany: SUNY Press, 1987), 38–39; Vivien Hart, *Bound by Our Constitution: Women, Workers, and the Minimum Wage* (Princeton: Princeton University Press, 1994), 10–12; Kathryn Kish

Sklar, "Two Political Cultures in the Progressive Era," in Linda K. Kerber, Alice Kessler-Harris, and Kathryn Kish Sklar, eds., *U.S. History as Women's History: New Feminist Essays* (Chapel Hill: University of North Carolina Press, 1995), 36–62; Kathryn Kish Sklar, "The Historical Foundations of Women's Power in the Creation of the American Welfare State, 1830–1930," in Seth Koven and Sonya Michel, eds., *Mothers of a New World: Maternalist Politics and the Origins of Welfare States* (New York: Routledge, 1999), 43–93; and Alice Kelsser-Harris, "The Paradox of Motherhood: Night Work Restrictions in the United States," in *Protecting Women: Labor Legislation in Europe, the United States, and Australia, 1880–1920* (Urbana: University of Illinois Press, 1995), 337–58.

24. FIC, *Preliminary Report*, I, 97–99, 649–55, III, 1596–97; FIC, *Second Report*, I, 16, 193–98, 277–79, II, 439–43, 451–58, III, 543, IV, 1649–71, 1726.

25. FIC, *Second Report*, I, 193, 198, 212.

26. Annie Marion MacLean, *Wage-Earning Women* (New York: Arno Press, [1910] 1974), 177–78.

27. Don Lescohier, *The Labor Market* (New York: Macmillan, 1919), 88; Michael B. Katz, *In the Shadow of the Poorhouse: A Social History of Welfare in America* (New York: Basic Books, 1986), 181. Also see Harry Braverman, *Labor and Monopoly Capitalism* (New York: Monthly Review Press, 1997), 280.

28. FIC, *Second Report*, I, 203–6, 366, II, 444, III, 370–89, IV, 1656, 2162–65. See also *Laws of the State of New York* (1913), ch. 83.

29. *Laws of the State of New York* (1913), ch. 493; ibid., (1914), ch. 331; and see FIC, *Fourth Report*, I, 10.

30. FIC, *Preliminary Report*, I, 776, II, 600–606; FIC, *Second Report*, IV, 1357–58.

31. "One Day Rest in Seven," *American Labor Legislation Review*, II (December 1912): 518–33; Consumer's League of the City of New York, *The Work of the Consumer's League of the City of New York, 1915* (New York: Consumer's League, 1916): 5; FIC, *Preliminary Report*, II, 838; and FIC, *Second Report*, I, 29, IV, 1167, 1354–64, 2012–15. John B. Andrews, "Outline for Work, 1913," *American Labor Legislation Review* IV (February 1914): 146–57; and also *Laws of the State of New York* (1913), ch. 740.

32. See Katz, *In the Shadow of the Poorhouse*, 113–45 for a full discussion of these efforts.

33. New York State Department of Labor, *Eleventh Annual Report of the Commissioner of Labor for the Twelve Months Ended September 30, 1911* (Albany: State Department of Labor, 1912), 54; ibid., *Twelfth Annual Report of the Commissioner of Labor for the Twelve Months Ended September 30, 1912* (Albany: State Department of Labor, 1913), 21, 67, 116–17; ibid., *Thirteenth Annual report*, 40–42; see also *New York State Department of Labor, Industrial Commission, Annual Report of the Industrial Commission, 1915* (Albany: State Department of Labor, 1916), 223.

34. George A. Kall, "New Child Labor Legislation in New York," the *Survey* XXXI (October 25, 1913): 89–90; Fred S. Hall, *Forty Years, 1902–1942: The Work of the New York Guild Labor Committee* (Brattleboro: E. L. Hildreth, 1943).

35. FIC, *Preliminary Report*, II, 331, 850–51, 971, III, 1037, 1354; FIC, *Second Report*, I, 180–92, 391–93, III, 115–22; and *Laws of the State of New York* (1913), ch. 464. For the history and evolution of child labor laws in New York, see *Laws of the State of New York* (1886), ch. 409; ibid., (1887), ch. 462; ibid., (1889), ch. 560; ibid., (1899), ch. 375; ibid., (1903), ch. 561; ibid., (1906), ch. 375; ibid., (1909), ch. 299. See also Kriste Lindenmeyer, *"A Right to Childhood": The U.S. Children's Bureau and Child Welfare, 1912–46* (Urbana: University of Illinois Press, 1997) for a larger discussion of this issue.

36. FIC, *Preliminary Report*, I, 101–3, 833–35, II, 362–63, 428, 539, 712–13, 858–62, III, 1049–54, 1138, 1237–51, 1597, 1784–87, 1889–98; and *Laws of the State of New York* (1912), ch. 333.

37. FIC, *Preliminary Report*, II, 539, 858–59, III, 1889–98; FIC, *Second Report*, I, 179–92, 359–60, II, 550–51, III, 115–22, IV, 1719–26, 1786; and *Laws of the State of New York* (1913), ch. 200.

38. FIC, *Second Report*, I, 176–79, 191, 360–65; and *Laws of the State of New York* (1913), ch. 101, 144.

39. New York State Consumer's League, *Our Working Child* (New York: Consumer's League, 1906): 10ff; George A. Hall, "New York Child Labor Legislation," *Charities and the Commons*, XVIII (July 20, 1907): 434–36.

40. FIC, *Preliminary Report*, II, 803, III, 1600, 1614, 1902–4; FIC, *Second Report*, II, 1201–3, IV, 1151–53; FIC, *Third Report*, 52–53; FIC, *Fourth Report*, I, 10. See also *Laws of the State of New York* (1914), ch. 331.

41. Christine Stansell, "The Origins of the Sweatshop: Women and Early Industrialization in New York City," in Michael H. Frisch and Daniel J. Walkowitz, eds., *Working-Class America: Essays on Labor, Community, and American Society* (Urbana: University of Illinois Press, 1983), 78–103.

42. FIC, *Preliminary Report*, I, 83–86. The Court of Appeals overturned the 1883 law in *In Re Jacobs*, 98 *New York* 98 (1885); FIC, *Second Report*, I, 119; New York State Department of Labor, *Twelfth Annual Report*, 17–19, 51–56. See also Eileen Boris, *Home to Work: Motherhood and the Politics of Industrial Homework in the United States* (New York: Cambridge University Press, 1994), 21–80.

43. New York State Consumer's League, *Bulletin* (October 1911); Mary Van Kleeck, "Child Labor in New York City Tenements," *Charities and the Commons*, XIX (January 19, 1908): 1405–20; Mary Van Kleeck, "Child Labor in House Industries," *National Child Labor Committee Proceedings, 1910*, 145–49; Josephine C. Goldmark, *Impatient Crusader: Florence Kelley's Life Story* (Urbana: University of Illinois Press, 1953), 121–26; and FIC, *Preliminary Report*, I, 573–80, III, 1760–70; and FIC, *Second Report*, I, 114–15; and FIC, *Third Report*, 4.

44. FIC, *Preliminary Report*, I, 25–26, 124, 145, 270–77, 585–98, 689–90.

45. FIC, *Preliminary Report*, I, 85–91.

46. FIC, *Second Report*, I, 15, 90–111, II, 413, 669–711, 729–32, 737–38, IV, 1535–48. Also see Eileen Boris, *Home to Work*, 1–20.

47. FIC, *Preliminary Report*, I, 582, III, 1591–97, 1734, 1744–46, 1803; FIC, *Second Report*, II, 695, 739–55, IV, 1548–58, 1562–72, 1594–1604, 1627–29, 1692–98.

48. FIC, *Preliminary Report*, III, 1978–86; FIC, *Second Report*, IV, 1504–6, 1594–99, 1614–23.

49. FIC, *Preliminary Report*, II, 665–70, III, 1089–98, 1450–59, 1591–97, 1730, 1760–70, 1803–4, 1878–86, 1937–46, 1978–86; FIC, *Second Report*, IV, 1548–72, 1610–14, 1624–27, 1692–98, 1761–68, 2268–82. See also the *New York Tribune* 8 December 1912; for other newspaper coverage, see Buffalo *Courier* 7 December 1912; the *Call* 8 December 1912; the *World* 6 December 1912; ibid., 7 December 1912; the *Sun* 5 December 1912; ibid., 6 December 1912; *New York Journal* 6 December 1912; the *American* 6 December 1912, the *Globe* 6 December 1912, and the Albany *Knickerbocker Press* 7 December 1912.

50. FIC, *Second Report*, I, 116–23, 345–56, IV, 1504, 1632; and *Laws of the State of New York* (1913), chs. 260, 529.

51. FIC, *Second Report*, I, 124–26.

52. FIC, *Second Report*, I, 124–26, 169–73, II, 762–69.

53. National Consumer's League, *Women and Children in Canneries* (New York: National Consumer's League, 1907); Josephine Goldmark, "Report of the Committee on Legislation," in Consumer's League, *Thirteenth Report*, 28; Consumer's League of the City of New York, *Report for the Year, 1910*, 25–26; Pauline Goldmark, *Do Children Work in Canneries?* (New York: Consumer's League, 1907), 3–15; FIC, *Preliminary Report*, II, 662–65, III, 1614–15, 1898–1901. On Potter and the FIC's work, see Zenos Potter, "Child Labor in the Canneries of New York State," *Child Labor Bulletin*, I (June 1912): 135–39; FIC, *Second Report*, I, 15–16, 126–131, II, 758, III, 945–60.

54. FIC, *Second Report*, I, 124–36, II, 762–94 (quote on 794), III, 214–34, 945–60, 991–97.

55. FIC, *Second Report*, I, 143–58, II, 809–31, III, 961–73.

56. FIC, *Second Report*, I, 215, II, 833–35, 876, III, 1004–16.

57. FIC, *Second Report*, IV, 1945.

58. Al Smith, *Up to Now* (New York: Viking Press, 1929), 95.

59. Samuel Gompers, "Child Labor in the New York Canneries," *American Federationist* (February 1913): 133–36; FIC, *Second Report*, I, 170.

60. Albany *Knickerbocker Press*, 27 November 1912; ibid., 30 November 1912; Buffalo *Courier*, 10 December 1912; the *American*, 12 December 1912; *New York Times*, 27 November 1912; ibid., 7 December 1912; ibid., 16 December 1912; ibid., 1 January 1913; and the *Call*, 5 December 1912.

61. FIC, *Second Report*, I, 142–43, 213–15, 246, 345–47, 356–58; and *Laws of the State of New York* (1913), chs. 195, 465, 529.

62. New York State Department of Labor, *Fourteenth Annual Report*, 132–64; and *New York Times*, 18 March 1915; *New York Times*, 1 April 1915; ibid., 9 April 1915; and Albany *Knickerbocker Press*, 1 April 1 1915; ibid., 9 April 1915. Albany *Knickerbocker Press*, 12 April 1915; ibid., 16 April 1915; ibid., 23 April 1915; *New York Times* 12 April 1915; ibid., 14 April 1915; ibid., 17 April 1915; ibid., 18 April 1915; ibid., 20 April 1915; ibid., 21 April 1915; ibid., 23 April 1915. See State of New York, *Public Papers of Charles Seymour Whitman, Governor*,

1915 (Albany: J. B. Lyon, 1916), 100; *Laws of the State of New York* (1915), ch. 386; and Consumer's League, *Work of the Consumer's League of the City of New York, 1915* (New York: Consumer's League, 1916), 15. *People v. Jacob Balofsky*, 167 N.Y. App. Div. 913 (1915); *People v. Charles Schweinler Press*, 214 N.Y. 395 (1915); and Josephine Goldmark, "New York Night Work Law for Women Upheld," the *Survey* XXXIV (August 1, 1914): 450.

63. Harry Millis, "Some Aspects of the Minimum Wage," *Journal of Political Economy* XXII (February 1914): 132–55.

64. Henry Seager, "The Minimum Wage as Part of a Program for Social Reform," *Annals of the American Academy of Political and Social Science* XLVIII (July 1913): 3–12; and Harry Millis, "Some Aspects of the Minimum Wage," *Journal of Political Economy* XXII (February 1914): 132–55.

65. Florence Kelley, *Modern Industry in Relation to the Family, Health, Education, Morality* (New York: Longmans, 1914); and Thomas R. Byrne, "The Social Thought of Robert F. Wagner" (Ph.D. Dissertation, Georgetown University, 1951).

66. Michael B. Katz, "Reorganizing the Labor Market," in *In the Shadow of the Poorhouse: a Social History of Welfare in America* (New York: Basic Books, 1986): 179–205; Harry, Braverman, *Labor and Monopoly Capitalism* (New York: Monthly Review Press, 1977). Katz and Braverman were picking up on one strand of the reformers rhetoric. See John Bates Clark, "The Minimum wage," *Atlantic Monthly* CXII (September 1913): 289–97; Samuel Lindsay, "Minimum Wage as a Legislative Proposal in the United States," *Annals of the American Academy of Political and Social Science* XLVIII (July 1913): 45–53; Henry R. Seager, "The Theory of the Minimum Wage," *American Labor Legislation Review* III (February 1913): 81–91; Sidney Webb, "The Economic Theory of a Legal Minimum Wage," *Journal of Political Economy* XX (December 1912): 973–98. Of great importance is John R. Commons and John B. Andrews, *Principles of Labor Legislation* (New York: Harper, 1916): 170–71.

67. A. Pigou, "Principles of the Minimum Wage," *Living Age* CCLXXVII (April 26, 1913): 195–205; Commons and Andrews, "Principles," 167–96; Florence Kelley, "Minimum Wage Laws," *Journal of Political Economy* II (December 1912): 999–1010; and John Ryan, "Minimum Wages and Minimum Wage Boards," the *Survey* XXIV (September 3, 1910): 810–20.

68. Irene Osgood Andrews, "Minimum Wage Legislation"; FIC, *Third Report*, 249–87. On the general issue, see Elizabeth Brandeis, "Labor Legislation," Vol. 3 in *History of Labor in the United States, 1896–1932* (1935; New York: Augustus Kelley, 1966): 501–39; Florence Kelley, *Minimum Wage Boards* (New York: Consumers' League, 1911); Kelley, "Report for the Special Committee on Minimum Wage Boards," in Consumers' League, *Fourteenth Report for the Two Years Ending December 31, 1913* (New York: Consumers' League, 1914): 52–61; Josephine C. Goldmark, *Impatient Crusader: Florence Kelley's Life Story* (Urbana: University of Illinois Press, 1953), 132–45; and for background of Kelley, see Kathryn Kish Sklar, *Florence Kelley and the Nation's Work: The Rise of Women's Political Culture,*

1830–1900 (New Haven: Yale University Press, 1995); John Ryan, "Guaranteeing a Living Wage by Law," *Life and Labor* II (March 1912): 84–85; Margaret Dreier Robbins, "The Minimum Wage," *Life and Labor* III (June 1913): 168–72. Also see Elizabeth Anne Payne, *Reform, Labor, and Feminism: Margaret Dreier Robins and the Women's Trade Union League* (Urbana: University of Illinois Press, 1988).

69. Florence Kelley, *The Present Status of Minimum Wage Legislation* (New York: Consumers' League, 1913); Kelley, *The Case for the Minimum Wage* (New York: Consumers' League, 1915); Brandeis, *History of Labor*, 523–39; Andrews, "Minimum Wage Legislation," in FIC, *Third Report*, 169–216. On the political position of reformers during this period, see Richard L. McCormick, *From Realignment to Reform: Political Change in New York State 1893–1910* (Ithaca: Cornell University Press, 1981); and David C. Hammack, *Power and Society: Greater New York at the Turn of the Century* (New York: Columbia University Press, 1982); Sue Ainslie Clark and Edith Wyatt, "Working-Girls' Budgets," *McClure's* XXXV (October 1910): 595–614; "The Working-Girl and the Minimum Wage," *Life and Labor* III (January 1913): 27; Florence Kelley, "Minimum Wage Laws," *Journal of Political Economy* XX (December 1912): 999–1010; Consumers' League of the City of New York, *Report for the Year 1910* (New York: Consumers' League, 1911); Consumer's League, *Report for the Year 1911* (New York: Consumers' League, 1912): 17–18; New York State Consumer's League, *Bulletin* (October 1911). See also *New York Times* 2 January 1913 and "Governor Sulzer on Minimum Wage Boards," the *Outlook* CIII (January 1913): 52.

70. FIC, *Preliminary Report*, II, 125–26, 151–52, 542, 639, 803–10, 860, 966–71, 1290–92; III, 1097, 1123–24, 1255–56, 1280–82, 1452–53; FIC, *Second Report*, III, 534–37; IV, 1133–36. See also, Consumers' League of the City of New York, *Report for the Year 1912* (New York: Consumers' League, 1913): 9–22, 36–37; Consumers' League, *Report for the Year 1913* (New York: Consumers' League, 1914): 10–18; WTULNY, *Annual Report, 1911–1912* (New York WTUL, 1912): 23.

71. FIC, *Second Report*, I, 164–67, 279–86; II, 866–72, 1254–63 (Dreier quote is from 1263); see also FIC, *Preliminary Report*, III, 1063, 1073, 1075, 1107–8, 1123, 1292, 1430.

72. *Laws of the State of New York* (1913), ch. 137; FIC, *Third Report*, 1; FIC, *Fourth Report*, I, 7–8, 33; Brandeis, *History of Labor*; Christopher L. Tomlins, *The State and the Unions: Labor Relations, Law, and the Organized Labor Movement in America, 1880–1960* (New York: Cambridge University Press, 1985); William E. Forbath, *Law and the Shaping of the American Labor Movement* (Cambridge: Harvard University Press, 1991); Victoria C. Hattam, *Labor Visions and State Power: The Origins of Business Unionism in the United States* (Princeton: Princeton University Press, 1993); Karen Orren, *Belated Feudalism: Labor, the Law, and Liberal Development in the United States* (New York: Cambridge University Press, 1991); David Montgomery, *Citizen Worker: The Experience of Workers in the United States with Democracy and the Free Market During the Nineteenth Century* (New York: Cambridge University Press, 1993); Daniel R. Ernst, *Lawyers Against Labor: From Individual Rights to Corporate Liberalism* (Urbana: University of Illinois Press,

1995); and the essays in *Labor Law in America: Historical and Critical Essays*, edited by Christopher L. Tomlins and Andrew J, King (Baltimore: Johns Hopkins University Press, 1992).

73. Thomas Jefferson Kerr, "New York Factory Investigating Commission and the Progressives" (D.S.S. Dissertation, Syracuse University, 1964), 242.

74. FIC, *Fourth Report*, II, 26–27; *Laws of the State of New York* (1914), ch. 110.

75. FIC, *Third Report* 16–26; and Kerr, "New York Factory," 243.

76. FIC, *Third Report*, 18–29; FIC, *Fourth Report*, I, 18; IV, 2540; FIC, *Third Report*, 12–13; FIC, *Fourth Report*, I, 17–36, 41–42; II, 6–18, 27–29. See also Howard Woolson, "Wages in New York," in Florence Kelley, ed., *The Case for the Minimum Wage* 23–28; and "New York Factory Investigating Commission," the *Survey* XXXI (March 21, 1914): 783–84.

77. FIC, *Fourth Report*, II, 51–117.

78. FIC, *Fourth Report*, II, 147–74.

79. FIC, *Third Report*, 42–43 (FIC quote is from 42), 101 (Woolson quote is from 101); FIC, *Fourth Report*, II, 28–29, 34–35175–225, 301–57, 361–429.

80. See Irene Osgood Andrews, "The Relation of Irregular Employment to the Living Wage for Women," in FIC, *Fourth Report*, II, 497–635; and Frank Streightoff, "Report on the Cost of Living," in FIC, *Fourth Report*, IV, 1461–1671.

81. See Ester Packard, "Living on Six Dollars a Week," in FIC, *Fourth Report*, IV, 1675–92; and Marie Orenstein, "How the Working Girl of New York Lives," ibid., IV, 1693–1711. On morality and prostitution, see ibid., I, 25–26, 389–417.

82. FIC, *Fourth Report*, I, 21–40, 418–89, (quote from 40), IV, 1241–60, V, 2572–2605; and FIC, *Fourth Report*, I, 539–846.

83. FIC, *Fourth Report*, I, 681–783.

84. AFL, *Report of the Proceeding of the Thirty-Second Annual Convention of the AFL, 1912* (Washington, DC: AFL, 1912): 94, 251; AFL, *Thirty-Third Annual Convention*, 59–64, 299–300; AFL, *Thirty-Fourth Annual Convention*, 63–64.

85. FIC, *Fourth Report*, I, 456, V, 2622–28, 2671–76, 2717–53, 2848–65, 2907–22; See also "Many Minds on the Minimum Wage," the *Survey* XXXIII (January 23, 1915): 435; William R. Wilcox, "Working Conditions in New York Stores," *National Civic Federation Review* IV (July 15, 1913): 1–32; Mary Van Kleeck, "Working Conditions in New York Stores," the *Survey* XXXI (October 11, 1913): 50–51; Elizabeth Dutcher, "Department Store Clerks," the *Survey* XXXI (December 20, 1913): 336–39; and the *Monitor* I (August 1915): 1–5.

86. FIC, *Fourth Report*, I, 47.

87. FIC, *Fourth Report*, I, 291–98; FIC, *Fourth Report*, I, 48.

88. Kerr, "New York Factory," 258; Walter Lippman, "Campaign Against Sweating," *New Republic* II (March 27, 1915): 1–8; "Fears of the Minimum Wage" the *Survey* XXXIV (May 22, 1915): 184; and WTUL, *Annual Report, 1914–1915* (New York: WTUL, 1915): 11.

89. Frances Perkins' *Reminiscences*, Book I, 58; also see Howell Harris, "The Snarls of Liberalism? Politicians, Bureaucrats, and the Shaping of Federal Labour Relations Policy in the United States, ca. 1915–1947," in Steven Tolliday and

Jonathan Zeitlin, eds., *Shopfloor Bargaining and the State: Historical and Comparative Perspectives* (New York: Cambridge University Press, 1985), 148–92.

CONCLUSION

1. Samuel Gompers as quoted in the *New York Times* June 30, 1910, 10.

2. Louis Levine, *The Women's Garment Workers: A History of the International Ladies' Garment Workers' Union* (New York: B. W. Huebsch, 1924), 196.

3. Benjamin Stolberg, *Tailor's Progress: The Story of a Famous Union and the Men who made it*, (Garden City, NY: Doubleday, 1944), 68.

4. Gus Tyler, *Look for the Union Label: A History of the International Ladies' Garment Workers' Union* (Armonk, NY: M. E. Sharpe, 1995), 73.

5. On this, see Bruce E. Kaufman, *The Origins and Evolution of the Field of Industrial Relations in the United States* (Ithaca, NY: ILR Press, 1993).

6. Louis D. Brandeis to Lawrence Fraser Abbott, September 6, 1919, in Melvin I. Urofsky and David W. Levy, eds., *The Letters of Louis D. Brandeis: Volume II, 1907–1912: People's Attorney* (Albany: SUNY Press, 1972), 371–72.

7. Stolberg, *Tailor's Progress*, 68.

8. Colin Gordon, *New Deals: Business, Labor, and Politics in America, 1920–1935* (Cambridge: Cambridge University Press, 1994). Especially chapter 3, "Workers Organizing Capitalists: Regulatory Unionism in American Industry, 1920–1932," 87–127.

9. See David Brody, *Steel Workers in America: The Nonunion Era* (Cambridge: Harvard University, 1960) for an earlier assessment of "regulatory unionism."

10. Jesse Thomas Carpenter, *Competition and Collective Bargaining in the Needle Trades, 1910–1967* (Ithaca, NY: ILR Press, 1972), xix.

11. Sidney and Beatrice Webb, *Industrial democracy* (New York: Augustus M. Kelley Booksellers, 1965 [reprint 1897]).

12. The fire is usually lumped into the literature on American labor massacres: Nelson Lichtenstein writes, "The milestones that mark the course of American labor history are those of heroic failure or great tragedy." The fire, for Lichtenstein, is one of those tragedies. But if this is the only significance of the fire, then it truly is a tragedy. They fire did kill 146 young, mostly immigrant women, and that is tragic. But the fire was also a catalyst for change and must be viewed in the larger context of the newly emerging IR system. See Nelson Lichtenstein, *Labor's War at Home: The CIO in World War II* (Cambridge: Cambridge University Press, 1982), 8.

13. The model seems to be George Tuttle's magnificent work on the Chicago Race Riots of 1919. See Paul Krause, *The Battle for Homestead, 1880–1892: Politics, Culture and Steel* (Pittsburgh: University of Pittsburgh Press, 1992); Howard Gitelman, *The Legacy of the Ludlow Massacre: A Chapter in American Industrial Relations* (Philadelphia: University of Pennsylvania Press, 1988).

14. J. Joseph Hutchmacher, "Charles Evans Hughs, and Charles Francis Murphy, The Metamorphosis of Progressivism," *New York History* 46:1 (January

1965): 25–40; and Hutchmacher, *Senator Robert F. Wagner and the Rise of Urban Liberalism* (New York: Atheneum, 1968); see also John Buenker's *Urban Liberalism and Progressive Reform.* (New York: Charles Scribner's Sons, 1973); Buenker, "Urban Liberalism in Rhode Island, 1900–1919," *Rhode Island History* 30:2 (1971): 34–51.

15. Alan Dawley, *Struggles for Justice: Social Responsibility and the Liberal State* (Cambridge: Harvard University Press, 1991); and Theda Skocpol, *Protecting Soldiers and Mothers: The Political Origins of Social Policy in the United States* (Cambridge: Harvard University Press, 1992).

16. On the origins of the welfare state in America see the works of Michael B. Katz, *In The Shadow of the Poorhouse: A Social History of Welfare in America* (New York: Basic Books, 1986); Katz, *The Undeserving Poor: From the War on Poverty to the War on Welfare* (New York: Pantheon Books, 1989); Katz, ed., *The "Underclass" Debate: Views from History* (Princeton: Princeton University Press, 1993); Edward D. Berkowitz and Kim McQuaid, *Creating the Welfare State: The Political Economy of 20th-Century Reform* (Lawrence: University Press of Kansas, 1992); Linda Gordon and Theda Skocpol, "Gender, State and Society: A Debate with Theda Skocpol," 2:3 *Contention* (Spring 1993): 139–89; Skocpol's *Protecting Soldiers and Mothers: The Political Origins of Social Policy in the United States* (Cambridge: Harvard University Press, 1992); Gordon's *Pitied But Not Entitled: Single Mothers and the History of Welfare* (New York: Free Press, 1994); Gordon, ed., *Women, the State and Welfare* (Madison: University of Wisconsin Press, 1990); Mimi Abromovitz, *Regulating the Lives of Women: Social Welfare from Colonial Times to the Present* (Boston: South End Press, 1988); Rosalind Rosenberg, "Domesticating the State," in her *Divided Lives: American Women in the Twentieth-Century* (New York: Hill and Wang, 1992); Seth Koven and Sonya Michel, eds., *Mothers of the New World: Materialist Politics and the Origins of the Welfare State* (London and New York: Routledge Press, 1993); and Robert G. Moeller, *Protecting Motherhood: Women and the Family in the Politics of Postwar West Germany* (Berkeley: University of California Press, 1993).

17. Daniel Czitrom, "Underworlds and Underdogs: Big Tim Sullivan and Metropolitans In New York, 1889–1913," *Journal of American History* 78:2 (September, 1991): 536–58; Robert F. Wesser, *A Response to Progressivism: The Democratic Party and New York Politics, 1902–1918* (New York, 1986); J. Joseph Hutchmacher, "Urban Liberalism and the Age of Reform," *Mississippi Valley Historical Review* 49 (September 1962): 231–41; Buenker, *Urban Liberalism*; Martin Shefter, "The Emergence of the Political Machine: An Alternative View," in Willis D. Hawley et al., eds., *Theoretical Perspectives on Urban Politics* (Englewood Cliffs, NJ: Prentice Hall, 1976); Stephen P. Erie, *Rainbow's End: Irish-Americans and the Dilemmas of Urban Machine Politics* (Berkeley, University of California Press, 1988); Thomas Henderson, *Tammany Hall and the New Immigrants: The Progressive Years* (New York: Arno Press, 1976); Melvyn Dubofsky, "Success and Failure of Socialism in New York City, 1900–1918: A Case Study," *Labor History* 9:3 (Fall 1968): 361–75; and Augustus Cerillo, Jr., "The Reform of Municipal Government

in New York City: From Seth Low to John Purroy Mitchel," *New York Historical Society Quarterly* (57 1973): 51–71; Philip J. Ethnigton, "Urban Constituencies, Regimes, and Policy Innovation in the Progressive Era: An Analysis of Boston, Chicago, New York City and San Francisco," *Studies in American Political Development* 7 (Fall 1993): 275–315; Richard Scheirov, "Rethinking the Relation of Labor to the Politics of Urban Social Reform in Late-Nineteenth-Century America: The Case of Chicago," *International Labor and Working-Class History* 46 (Fall 1994): 93–108.

18. Susan Ware's *Beyond Suffrage: Women in the New Deal* (Cambridge: Harvard University Press, 1981); Ware, *Partner and I: Molly Dewson, Feminism, and the New Deal* (New Haven: Yale University Press, 1987); and Volume I of Blanche Wiesen Cook's *Eleanor Roosevelt* (New York: Viking Press, 1992).

19. Frances Perkins, Oral History, Columbia University.

20. Herbert G. Gutman, "Labor and the 'Sartre Question'" in Herbert G. Gutman (edited by Ira Berlin) *Power and Culture: Essays on the American Working Class* (New York: Pantheon, 1987), 326.

21. Quoted in Steven Fraser, "The Labor Question," in Steven Fraser and Gary Gerstle, eds., *The Rise and Fall of the New Deal Order, 1930–1980* (Princeton: Princeton University Press, 1989), 58.

22. Nelson Lichtenstein and Howell John Harris, eds., *Industrial Democracy in America: The Ambiguous Promise* (Cambridge: Woodrow Wilson Center Series of Cambridge University Press, 1993), 5.

23. Melvyn Dubofsky, *When Workers Organize: New York City in the Progressive Era* (Amherst: University of Massachusetts Press, 1968), 58–68; Jesse Thomas Carpenter, *Competition and Collective Bargaining in the Needle Trades, 1910–1967* (Ithaca, NY: Cornell University ILR Press, 1972), 1–54; Leon Stein, ed., *Out of the Sweatshop: The Struggle for Industrial Democracy* (New York: Quadrangle Books, 1977), 87–175; Louis Levine, *The Women's Garment Workers*, 168–319; Gus Tyler, *Look for the Union Label*, 63–85; Julius Henry Cohen, *Law and Order in Industry*, (New York: The MacMillan Company, 1916); Benjamin Stolberg, *Tailor's Progress*, 59–91; Arthur A. Goren, *New York Jews and the Quest for Community: The Kehillah Experiment, 1908–1922* (New York: Columbia University Press, 1970), 186–213; Philippa Strum, *Louis D. Brandeis: Justice for the People* (Cambridge: Harvard University Press, 1984), 159–95; and J. M. Budish and George Soule, *The New Unionism in the Clothing Industry* (New York: Harcourt, Brace and Howe, 1920), 101–55. Also see Chapter 1 of this book.

Bibliography

Adams, Graham. *Age of Industrial Violence, 1910–15 the Activities and Findings of the United States Commission on Industrial Relations*. New York: Columbia University Press, 1966.

Albrecht, Sandra L. "Forms of Industrial and Economic Democracy: A Comparison of Prevailing Approaches." *Mid-American Review of Sociology* 8, no. 2 (1983): 43–66.

Alchon, Guy. *The Invisible Hand of Planning: Capitalism, Social Science, and the State in the 1920s*. Princeton: Princeton University Press, 1985.

———. "Policy History and the Sublime Immodesty of the Middle-Aged Professor." *Journal of Policy History* 9, no. 3 (356–74, 1997): theory.

Aldrich, Mark. *Safety First: Technology, Labor, and Business in the Building of American Work Safety, 1870–1939*. Baltimore: Johns Hopkins University Press, 1997.

Allen, Oliver E. *The Tiger: The Rise and Fall of Tammany Hall*. Reading, MA: Addison-Wesley, 1993.

Allen, William Harvey. *Al Smith's Tammany Hall: Champion Political Vampire*. New York: Institute for Public Service, 1928.

Amberg, Stephen. *The Union Inspiration in American Politics: The Autoworkers and the Making of a Liberal Industrial Order*. Philadelphia: Temple University Press, 1994.

Ansell, Christopher K., and Arthur L. Burns. "Bosses of the City Unite!: Labor Politics and Political Machine Consolidation, 1870–1910." *Studies in American Political Development* 11 (Spring 1997): 1–43.

Argersinger, Jo Ann E. *Making the Amalgamated: Gender, Ethnicity and Class in the Baltimore Clothing Industry, 1899–1939*. Baltimore: Johns Hopkins University Press, 1999.

Argersinger, Peter H. *Structure, Process, and Party: Essays in American Political History*. Armonk, NY: M.E. Sharpe, 1992.

Argersinger, Peter H. "From Political Management to Administrative Politics: Progressive Reform in New York." *Reviews in American History* 10, no. 3 (1982): 391–95.

Arnesen, Eric, Julie Greene, and Bruce Laurie. *Labor Histories: Class, Politics, and the Working-Class Experience*. Urbana: University of Illinois Press, 1998.

Aronowitz, Stanley. *From the Ashes of the Old: American Labor and America's Future*. New York: Houghlin Mifflin, 1998.

———. *How Class Works: Power and Social Movement*. New Haven: Yale University Press, 2003.

Aronson, David I. "The City Club of New York, 1882–1912." Ph.D. Dissertation, New York University, 1975.

Asard, Erik. "American Unions and Industrial Democracy: The 'Business Unionism' Thesis Reexamined." *Statsvetenskaplig Tidskrift* 85, no. 3 (1982): 155–64.

Ashford, Douglas E. "The Historical and Political Foundations of the Welfare State: A Lost Opportunity for the Left." *Journal of Policy History* 5, no. 3 (1993): 311–34.

Atleson, James B. "The Law of Collective Bargaining and Wartime Labor Regulations." In *American Labor in the Era of World War II*, edited by Sally M. Miller and Daniel A. Cornford. Contribution in Labor Studies, Number 45. Westport, CT: Greenwood Press, 43–68.

Avrich, Paul. *The Haymarket Tragedy.* Princeton: Princeton University Press, 1984.

Bae, Young-Soo. "Men's Clothing Workers in Chicago, 1871–1929: Ethnicity, Class and a Labor Union." Ph.D. Dissertation, Harvard University, 1989.

Baker, Paula. "The Domestication of Politics: Women and American Political Society, 1780–1920." *American Historical Review* 89 (June 1984): 620–47.

Baker, Ray Stannard. *The New Industrial Unrest: Reasons and Remedies.* New York: Doubleday, 1920.

Banta, Martha. *Taylored Lives: Narrative Productions in the Age of Taylor, Veblen, and Ford.* Chicago: University of Chicago Press, 1993.

Baron, Ava, Editor. *Work Engendered: Toward a New History of American Labor.* Ithaca, NY: Cornell University Press, 1991.

Barrett, James R. "Unity and Fragmentation: Class, Race, and Ethnicity on Chicago's South Side, 1900–1922." In *"Struggle a Hard Battle": Essays on Working-Class Immigrants*, edited by Dirk Hoerder, 229–53. DeKalb: Northern Illinois University Press, 1986.

Barrish, Phillip. " 'The Genuine Article': Ethnicity, Capital, and the Rise of David Levinsky." *American Literary History* (Winter 1993): 643–62.

Barrow, Clyde W. "Beyond Progressivism: Charles A. Beard's Social Democratic Theory of American Political Development." *Studies in American Political Development* 8, no. 2 (Fall 1994): 231–80.

———. "Building a Workers' Republic: Charles A. Beard's Critique of Liberalism in the 1930s." *Polity* 30, no. 1 (Fall 1997): 29–57.

———. "The Diversionary Thesis and the Dialectic of Imperialism: Charles A. Beard's Theory of American Foreign Policy Revisited." *Studies in American Political Development* 11 (Fall 1997): 248–91.

———. "State Theory and the Dependency Principle: An Institutionalist Critique of the Business Climate Concept." *Journal of Economic Issues* 32, no. 1 (March 1998): 107–45.

Baskerville, Stephen W. *Of Laws and Limitations: An Intellectual Portrait of Louis Dembitz Brandeis.* Rutherford, NJ: Fairleigh Dickinson University Press, 1994.

Baum, Charlotte, Paula Hyman, and Sonya Michel. *The Jewish Woman in America.* New York: New American Library, 1975.

Bayor, Ronald H. *Fiorello H. LaGuardia: Ethnicity and Reform*. Arlington Heights, IL: Harlan Davidson, 1993.

Beck, John P., and Janet Schneider. "None of Us Alone Knows as Much as All of Us Together: Participatory Learning for Worker Participation." *Labor Studies Journal* 8, no. 3 (Winter 1984): 287–300.

Becker, Linda Gail. " 'Invisible Threads': Skill and the Sicursive Marginalization of the Garment Industry's." Ph.D. Dissertation, University of Washington, 1997.

Beckert, Sven. *The Monied Metropolis New York City and the Consolidation of the American Bourgeoisie, 1850–1896*. Cambridge, UK New York, NY: Cambridge University Press, 2001.

Bederman, Gail. *Manliness and Civilization: A Cultural History of Gender and Race in the United States, 1880–1917*. Chicago: University of Chicago Press, 1995.

Beito, David T. *From Mutual Aid to the Welfare State: Fraternal Societies and Social Services, 1890–1967*. Chapel Hill: University of North Carolina Press, 2000.

Bender, Daniel E. *Sweated Work, Weak Bodies Anti-Sweatshop Campaigns and Languages of Labor*. New Brunswick, NJ: Rutgers University Press, 2004.

Bender, Daniel E., and Richard A. Greenwald, Editors. *Sweatshop USA: The American Sweatshop in Historical and Global Perspective*. New York London: Routledge, 2003.

Bender, Thomas. *Intellect and Public Life: Essays on the Social History of Academic Intellectuals in the United States*. Baltimore: Johns Hopkins University Press, 1993.

Bensel, Richard Franklin. *Sectionalism and American Political Development*. Madison: University of Wisconsin Press, 1984.

———. *Yankee Leviathan: The Origins of Central State Authority in America, 1859–1877*. Cambridge: Cambridge University Press, 1990.

Benson, Herman. "Strengthening Democracy in Unions." *Working USA* 5, no. 4 (Spring 2002): 71–83.

Benson, Lee, Joel H. Silbey. "Toward a Theory of Stability and Change in American Voting Patterns: New York State, 1792–1970." In *The History of American Electoral Behavior*, edited by Joel H. Silbey, Allan G. Bogue, and William H. Flanigan, 78–105. Princeton: Princeton University Press, 1978.

Bergdtrom, Randolph E. *Courting Danger: Injury and Law in New York City, 1870–1910*. Ithaca, NY: Cornell University Press, 1992.

Berk, Gerald. "Adversaries by Design: Railroads and the American State." *Journal of Policy History* 5, no. 3 (1993): 333–54.

———. *Alternative Tracks: The Constitution of American Industrial Order, 1865–1917*. Baltimore: Johns Hopkins University Press, 1994.

Berkowitz, Edward, and Kim McQuaid. "Businessman and Bureaucracy: The Evolution of the American Social Welfare System, 1900–1940." *Journal of Economic History* XXXVIII, no. 1 (1978): 120–41.

Berkowitz, Edward D. "How to Think About the Welfare State." *Labor History* 32, no. 4 (Fall 1991): 489–502.

———. "Social Welfare and the American State." In *Federal Social Policy: The Historical Dimension*, edited by Donald T. Critchlow and Ellis W. Hawley, 171–200. University Park: Pennsylvania State University Press, 1988.

Berkowitz, Edward D., and Kim McQuaid. *Creating the Welfare State: The Political Economy of Twentieth-Century Reform*. Lawrence: University Press of Kansas, 1992 (1988).

Berman, Hyman. "A Cursory View of the Jewish Labor Movement: An Historiographical Survey." *American Jewish Historical Quarterly* 2 (Dec. 1962): 79–97.

———. "Era of the Protocol: A Chapter in the History of the International Ladies' Garment Workers' Union, 1910–1916." Ph.D. Dissertation, Columbia University, 1956.

Berrol, Selma. *East Side/East End: Eastern European Jews in London and New York, 1870–1920*. Westport, CT: Praeger, 1994.

———. "When Uptown Met Downtown: Julia Richman's Work in the Jewish Community of New York, 1880–1912." *American Jewish History* 70, no. 1 (1980): 35–51.

Best, Harry. *The Men's Garment Industry of New York and the Strike of 1913*. New York: University Settlement Society, 1914.

Bischoff, Henry. "The Reformers, the Workers, and the Growth of the Positive State: A History of the Labor Legislation Movement in New York State, 1865–1915." Ph.D. Dissertation, University of Chicago, 1964.

Blatz, Perry K. *Democratic Miners: Work and Labor Relations in the Anthracite Coal Industry, 1875–1925*. Albany: State University of New York Press, 1994.

Block, Fred. "The Ruling Class Does Not Rule: Notes on the Marxist Theory of the State." In *The Political Economy: Readings in the Politics and Economics of American Public Policy*, edited by Thomas Ferguson and Joel Rogers, 32–46. Armonk, NY: M.E. Sharpe, 1984, 1977.

Block, Richard N. "Labor Law, Economics, and Industrial Democracy: A Reconciliation." *Industrial Relations* 34, no. 3 (July 1995): 402–16.

Blumberg, Dorothy Rose. *Florence Kelley: The Making of a Social Pioneer*. New York: Augustus M. Kelley, 1966.

Blumberg, Paul. *Industrial Democracy the Sociology of Participation*. New York: Schocken Books, 1973.

Bodnar, John E. *The Transplanted a History of Immigrants in Urban America*. Interdisciplinary Studies in History. Bloomington: Indiana University Press, 1985.

Boomhower, Ray E. "'A Business Without a Boss': William Powers Hapgood and the Columbia Conserve Company." *Traces* (Winter 2001): 4–13.

Boone, Gladys. *The Women's Trade Union Leagues in Great Britain and the United States of America*. New York: Columbia University Press, 1942.

Boone, Gloria M. "The Reform Rhetoric of Samuel Seabury of New York: The Battle Against Tammany Hall and Municipal Corruption," Ohio State University, 1982.

Boris, Eileen. "The Home as a Workplace: Deconstructing Dichotomies." *International Review of Social History* 39 (1994): 415–28.

———. *Home to Work: Motherhood and the Politics of Industrial Homework in the United States*. Cambridge: Cambridge University Press, 1994.

———. "Tenement Homework on Army Uniforms: The Gendering of Industrial Democracy During World War I." *Labor History* 32, no. 2 (Spring 1991): 231–52.

Botsman, Peter. "Rethinking the Class Struggle: Industrial Democracy and the Politics of Production." *Economic and Industrial Democracy* 10 (1989): 123–42.

Boyer, Paul. *Urban Masses and Moral Order in America, 1820–1920*. Cambridge, MA: Harvard University Press, 1978.

Boyle, Kevin, Editor. *Organized Labor and American Politics, 1894–1994: The Labor-Liberal Alliance*. Albany: SUNY Press, 1998.

Brandeis, Elizabeth. "Labor Legislation." In *History of Labor in the United States, 1896–1932*, edited by John R. Commons. Volume III. New York: Augustus M. Kelley, 1966, 1935.

Brandeis, Louis Dembitz. *"Half Brother, Half Son": The Letters of Louis D. Brandeis to Felix Frankfurter*. Norman: University of Oklahoma Press, 1991.

———. *Letters of Louis D. Brandeis*. Albany: State University of New York Press, 1971–78.

Brandes, Joseph. "From Sweatshop to Stability: Jewish Labor Between Two World Wars." *YIVO Annual of Jewish Social Sciences* 16 (1976): 1–149.

Brandes, Stuart D. *American Welfare Capitalism, 1880–1940*. Chicago: University of Chicago Press, 1976 (1970).

Brandler, Walker Claire. "A History of Factory Legislation in New York State, 1886–1911," Ph.D. Dissertation, Columbia University, 1969.

Braun, Kurt. *Union-Management Co-Operation: Experiences in the Clothing Industry*. Washington, DC: Brookings Institution, 1947.

Braverman, Harry. *Labor and Monopoly Capital the Degradation of Work in the Twentieth Century*. 25th anniversary ed. New York: Monthly Review Press, 1998.

Breisach, Ernst. *American Progressive History: An Experiment in Modernization*. Chicago: University of Chicago Press, 1993.

Bridges, Amy. "Creating Cultures of Reform." *Studies in American Political Development* 8, no. 1 (Spring 1994): 1–23.

Brinkley, Alan. *The End of Reform: New Deal Liberalism in Recession and War*. New York: Alfred A. Knopf, 1995.

———. "The New Deal." *Wilson Quarterly* 6 (Spring 1982): 51–61.

Brody, David. *Industrial America in the Twentieth Century; Documents, Edited and Selected by David Brody*. New York: Crowell, 1967.

———. *In Labor's Cause: Main Themes on the History of the American Worker*. New York: Oxford University Press, 1993.

———. "Labor History, Industrial Relations, and the Crisis of American Labor." *Industrial and Labor Relations Review* 43, no. 1 (October 1989): 7–18.

———. "The Second Industrial Divide: A Review." *Reviews in American History* 13, no. 4 (1985): 612–1615.

———. *Steel Workers in America: The Nonunion Era.* Cambridge, MA: Harvard University Press, 1960.

———. "Why No Shop Committees in America: A Narrative History." *Industrial History* 40, no. 3 (July 2001): 356–76.

———. *Workers in Industrial America: Essays on the Twentieth Century Struggle.* New York: Oxford University Press, 1993.

Brown, M. Craig, and Charles N. Halaby. "Machine Politics in America, 1870–1945." *Journal of Interdisciplinary History* XVII, no. 3 (Winter 1987): 587–612.

Buell, Janet W. "Alva Belmont: From Socialite to Feminist." *The Historian* 52, no. 2 (1990): 219–41.

Buenker, John. "The Progressive Era: A Search for a Synthesis." *Mid-America* 51 (1969): 175–93.

Buenker, John D. "Questing for Democracy and Community in Progressive Era Cities." *Journal of Urban History* 26, no. 6 (September 2000): 843–50.

———. *Urban Liberalism and Progressive Reform.* New York: Charles Scribner's Sons, 1973.

———. "Urban Liberalism in Rhode Island, 1909–1919." *Rhode Island History* 30, no. 2 (1971): 34–51.

———. "The Urban Political Machine and Woman Suffrage: A Study in Political Authority." *The Historian* 33, no. 2 (1971): 264–79.

Buhle, Mari Jo. *Women and American Socialism, 1870–1920.* Urbana: University of Illinois Press, 1981.

Buhle, Mari Jo, et al., Editors. *The American Radical.* New York: Routledge, 1994.

Buhle, Mari Jo, et al., Editors. *Encyclopedic of the American Left.* New York: Garland, 1990.

Buhle, Paul. *Taking Care of Business: Samuel Gompers, George Meany, Lane Kirkland and the Tragedy of American Labor.* New York: Monthly Review Press, 1999.

Bularzik, Mary J. "The Bonds of Belonging: Leonora O'Reilly and Social Reform." *Labor History* 24, no. 1 (1983): 60–83.

Burawoy, Michael. *Marxist Inquiries: Studies of Labor, Class, and States.* Chicago: University of Chicago Press, 1982.

Burne, Thomas R. "The Social Thought of Robert F. Wagner." Ph.D. Dissertation, Georgetown University, 1951.

Burrows, Edwin G., and Mike Wallace. *Gotham.* New York: Oxford University Press, 1998.

Butler, Elizabeth Beardsley. *Women and the Trades.* New York: Arno, 1969, 1909.

Cahan, Abraham. *The Rise of David Levinsky.* New York: Harper and Brothers, 1917.

Callcott, Mary Stevenson. *Child Labor Legislation in New York <Microform>: The Historical Development and the Administrative Practices of Child Labor Laws in the State of New York, 1905–1930.* New York: Macmillan, 1931.

Campbell, Ballard. "The State Legislature in American History: A Review Essay." *Historical Methods Newsletter* 9, no. 4 (September 1976): 185–94.

Cantor, Milton, and Bruce Laurie, Editors. *Class, Sex, and the Woman Worker.* Contributions in Labor History, Number 1. Westport, CT: Greenwood Press, 1977.

Carnoy, Martin. "Education, Industrial Democracy and the State." *Economic and Industrial Democracy* 2 (1981): 243–60.

Carpenter, Jesse Thomas. *Competition and Collective Bargaining in the Needle Trades, 1910–1967.* Ithaca, NY: ILR Press, 1972.

Carson, Mima. *Settlement Folk: Social Thought and the American Settlement Movement, 1885–1930.* Chicago: University of Chicago Press, 1990.

Cassidy, Kevin J. "Economic Conversion: Industrial Policy and Democratic Values." *Policy Studies Review* 9, no. 4 (Summer 1990): 775–86.

Castrovinci, Joseph L. "Prelude to Welfare Capitalism: The Role of Business in the Enactment of Workmen's Compensation Legislation in Illinois, 1905–12." *Social Service Review* 50 (March 1976): 80–102.

Cerillo, Augustus. "The Reform of Municipal Government in New York City: From Seth Low to John Purroy Mitchel." *New York Historical Society Quarterly* 57 (1973): 51–71.

Cerillo, Jr., Augustus. "The Impact of Reform Ideology: Early Twentieth Century Municipal Government in New York City." In *The Age of Urban Reform: New Perspectives on the Progressive Era*, edited by Michael H. Ebner and Eugene M. Tobin. Port Washington, NY: Kennikat Press, 1977.

———. "Reform in New York City: A Study of Urban Progressivism." Ph.D. Dissertation, Northwestern University, 1969.

Chambers II, John Whiteclay. *The Tyranny of Change: America in the Progressive Era, 1900–1917.* New York: St. Martins Press, 1980.

Clark, Claudia. *Radium Girls: Women and Industrial Health Reform, 1910–1935.* Chapel Hill: University of North Carolina Press, 1997.

Clark, Thomas R. *Defending Rights Law, Labor Politics, and the State in California, 1890–1925.* Detroit: Wayne State University Press, 2002.

Clawson, Dan. *Bureaucracy and the Labor Process: The Transformation of U.S. Industry, 1860–1920.* New York: Monthly Review Press, 1980.

Clegg, Hugh Armstrong. *Industrial Democracy and Nationalization a Study Prepared for the Fabian Society.* Oxford: Blackwell, 1951.

———. *A New Approach to Industrial Democracy.* Oxford: Blackwell, 1960.

———. *The System of Industrial Relations in Great Britain.* 3d ed. Oxford: Blackwell, 1976.

———. *Trade Unionism Under Collective Bargaining a Theory Based on Comparisons of Six Countries.* Warwick Studies in Industrial Relations. Oxford: B. Blackwell, 1976.

Cobble, Dorothy Sue. "A Self Possessed Woman: A View of FDR's Secretary of Labor, Madame Perkins." *Labor History* 29, no. 2 (Spring 1988): 225–29.

Cohen, Andrew. "Secondary Associations and Democratic Governance." *Politics and Society* 20, no. 4 (December 1992): 393–472.

———. "State, Civil Society, and Labor Union Development in Chicago, 1900–1940." Presented at the Law and Society. University of Wisconsin–Madison: Institute for Legal Studies, 1998.

———. "The Struggle for Order: Law, Labor and Resistance to the Corporate Ideal, Chicago, 1900–1940." Ph.D. Dissertation, History, University of Chicago, 1999.

Cohen, Joshua, and Joel Rogers. *On Democracy: Toward a Transformation of American Society*. New York: Penguin Books, 1983.

Cohen, Julius Henry. *An American Labor Policy*. New York: MacMillan Company, 1919.

———. *Law and Order in Industry: Five Years Experience*. New York: The Mac-Millan Company, 1916.

———. *A League to Enforce Industrial Peace*. New York: Academy of Political Science, 1916.

———. "The Revised Protocol in the Dress and Waist Industry." *Annals of the American Academy of Political and Social Science* LXIX (1917): 183–96.

Cohen, Lizabeth. *Making a New Deal: Industrial Workers in Chicago, 1919–1939*. New York: Cambridge University Press, 1990.

Cohen, Miriam. "Italian-American Women in New York City, 1900–1950: Work and School." In *Class, Sex, and the Women Worker*, edited by Milton Cantor and Bruce Laurie, 120–43. Westport, CT: Greenwood Press, 1977.

———. *Workshop to Office: Two Generations of Italian Women in New York City, 1900–1950*. Ithaca, NY: Cornell University Press, 1992.

Cohen, Miriam, and Michael Hanagan. "Politics, Industrialization and Citizenship: Unemployment Policy in England, France and the United States, 1890–1950." *International Review of Social History* 40, no. Supplement 3 (1995): 91–129.

Cohen, Naomi W. *Encounter with Emancipation: The German Jews in the United States, 1830–1914*. Philadelphia: Jewish Publication Society, 1984.

Colburn, David R., and George E. Pozzetta, Editors. *Reform and Reformers in the Progressive Era*. Westport, CT: Greenwood Press, 1984.

Cole, Margaret. *The Webbs and Their Work*. Westport, CT: Greenwood Press, 1985.

Coleman, John J. "State Formation and the Decline of Political Parties: American Parties in the Fiscal State." *Studies in American Political Development* 8, no. 2 (Fall 2994): 195–230.

Collom, Ed. "Clarifying the Cross-Class Support for Workplace Democracy." *Berkeley Journal of Sociology* 45 (September 2001): 71–103.

———. "Two Classes and One Vision?: Managers' and Workers' Attitudes Toward Workplace Democracy." Presented at the American Sociological Association. Washington, DC, August, 2000.

Collom, Vincent Edward. "Social Inequality and the Politics of Production: Americans' Attitudes Toward Workplace Democracy." Ph.D. Dissertation, Sociology, University of California, Riverside, 2001.

Commons, John R. *Labor and Administration*. New York: Augustus M. Kelley, 1964, 1913.

Commons, John R., and John B. Andrews. *Principle of Labor Legislation*. New York: Harper and Brothers, 1936, 1918.

Congdon, Tim. "The Economics of Industrial Democracy." *New Society* October 30 1975: 255–57.

Connable, Alfred, and Edward Silberfarb. *Tigers of Tammany: Nine Men Who Ran New York*. New York: Holt, Rinehart and Winston, 1967.

Connolly, James J. *The Triumph of Ethnic Progressivism: Urban Political Culture in Boston, 1900–1925*. Cambridge, MA: Harvard University Press, 1998.

Coppin, Clayton. "Strategic Uses of Public Policy: Business and Government in the Progressive Era." *Business History Review* 62, no. 3 (Autumn 1988): 541–43.

Cressey, Peter, and John MacInnes. "Voting for Ford: Industrial Democracy and the Control of Labour." *Capital and Class* 11 (Summer 1980): 5–33.

Critchlow, Donald T. "Social-Policy History: Past and Present." In *Federal Social Policy: The Historical Dimension*, edited by Donald T. Critchlow and Ellis W. Hawley, 9–34. University Park: Pennsylvania State University Press, 1988.

Crocker, Ruth Huthinson. "The Settlements: Social Work, Culture, and Ideology in the Progressive Era: Review Essay." *History of Education Quarterly* 31, no. 2 (Summer 1991): 253–60.

Crunden, Robert M. *Ministers of Reform: The Progressives' Achievement in American Civilization, 1889–1920*. Urbana: University of Illinois Press, 1984.

Cullis, Philip. "The Limits of Progressivism: Louis Brandeis, Democracy and the Corporation." *Journal of American Studies* 30 (December 1996): 381–404.

Czitron, Daniel. "Underworlds and Underdogs: Big Tim Sullivan and Metropolitan Politics in New York, 1889–1913." *The Journal of American History* 78, no. 2 (September 1991): 536–58.

Dahrendorf, Ralf. *Class and Class Conflict in Industrial Society*. Stanford, CA: Stanford University Press, 1959.

Daniel, Cletus E. *The ACLU and the Wagner Act: An Inquiry into the Depression-Era Crisis of American Liberalism*. Ithaca: New York State School of Industrial and Labor.

Davies, Stephen. "Two Conceptions of Welfare: Voluntarism and Incorporationism." *Social Philosophy and Policy* 14, no. 2 (1997): 39–68.

Davis, Allen F. *Spearheads of Reform: The Social Settlements and the Progressive Movement, 1890–1914*. New York: Oxford University Press, 1967.

———. "The Women's Trade Union League: Origins and Organization." *Labor History* 5, no. 1 (Winter 1964): 3–17.

Davis, Colin J. *Power at Odds: The 1922 National Railroad Shopmen's Strike*. Urbana: University of Illinois Press, 1997.

Davis, Mike. *Prisoners of the American Dream Politics and Economy in the History of the U.S. Working Class*. London: Verso, 1986.

Dawley, Alan. *Changing the World American Progressives in War and Revolution*. Politics and Society in Twentieth-Century America. Princeton: Princeton University Press, 2003.

———. *Struggles for Justice: Social Responsibility and the Liberal State*. Cambridge, MA: Harvard University Press, 1991.

Dawson, Nelson L. *Brandeis and America*. Lexington: University Press of Kentucky, 1989.

de Marquez, Viviane B. "Politics, Bureaucracy, and Industrial Democracy: A Comparartive Framework for the Analysis of Worker Control in Latin America." *Sociology of Work and Occupations* 8, no. 2 (May 1981): 165–79.

Denis, Alexander. *"Tammany Hall": And Other Miscellaneous Poems.* New York: A. Denis, 1847.

Derber, Milton. *The American Idea of Industrial Democracy, 1865–1965.* Urbana: University of Illinois Press, 1970.

———. "The Idea of Industrial Democracy in America." *Labor History* 7, no. 3 (Fall 1966): 259–86.

Derber, Milton, and Edwin Young, Editors. *Labor and the New Deal.* Madison: University of Wisconsin Press, 1961.

Derickson, Alan. "Making Human Junk: Child Labor as a Health Issues in the Progressive Era." *The American Journal of Public Health* 82, no. 9 (Sept. 1992): 1280–90.

———. *Workers' Health, Workers' Democracy: The Western Miners' Struggle, 1891–1925.* Ithaca, NY: Cornell University Press, 1988.

Dickman, Howard. *Industrial Democracy in America: Ideological Origins of National Labor Relations Policy.* La Salle, IL: Open Court, 1987.

DiGanetano, Alan. "Urban Political Reform: Did It Kill the Machine?" *Journal of Urban History* 18, no. 1 (November 1991): 37–67.

Diggins, John P. *The Rise and Fall of the American Left.* New York: W.W. Norton, 1992.

Diggins, John Patrick. "Republicanism and Progressivism." *American Quarterly,* September 1985, 572–98.

Diner, Hasia R. *Hungering for America Italian, Irish, and Jewish Foodways in the Age of Migration.* Cambridge, MA: Harvard University Press, 2001.

———. *Jewish Americans the Immigrant Experience.* Westport, CT: Hugh Lauter Levin Associates, 2002.

———. *Jews in America. Religion in American Life.* New York: Oxford University Press, 1999.

———. *Lower East Side Memories: A Jewish Place in America.* Princeton: Princeton University Press, 2000.

———. *A Time for Gathering: The Second Migration, 1820–1880.* Baltimore: Johns Hopkins University Press, 1992.

———. *Women and Urban Society: A Guide to Information Sources.* Urban Studies Information Guide Series. Detroit: Gale Research, 1979.

Diner, Hasia R., Jeffrey Shandler, and Beth S. Wenger. *Remembering the Lower East Side: American Jewish Reflections.* Bloomington: Indiana University Press, 2000.

Diner, Steven J. *A Very Different Age: Americans of the Progressive Era.* New York: Hill and Wang, 1997.

Domhoff, G. William. "The Wagner Act and Theories of the State: A New Analysis Based on Class-Segment Theory." *Political Power and Social Theory* 6 (1987): 159–85.

Downs, Anthony. "An Economic Theory of Political Action in a Democracy." *Journal of Political Economy* 65 (1957): 135–50.

Dubinsky, David, and A. H. Raskin. *David Dubinsky: A Life with Labor*. New York: Simon & Schuster, 1977.

Dubofsky, Melvyn. *Industrialization and the American Worker, 1865–1920*. Arlington Heights, IL: Harlan Davidson, 1985, 1975.

———. *John L. Lewis: A Biography*. Urbana: University of Illinois Press, 1986.

———. "The Lattimer Massacre and the Meaning of Citizenship." *Pennsylvania History* 68 (Winter 2002): 52–57.

———. "Organized Labor and the Immigrant in New York City, 1900–1918." *Labor History* 2, no. 2 (Spring 1961): 182–201.

———. *The State and Labor in Modern America*. Chapel Hill: University of North Carolina Press, 1994.

———. "Success and Failure of Socialism in New York City, 1900–18: A Case Study." *Labor History* IX (Fall 1968): 361–75.

———. *When Workers Organize: New York City in the Progressive Era*. Amherst: University of Massachusetts Press, 1968.

Dubofsky, Melvyn, and Joseph Anthony McCartin. *We Shall Be All a History of the Industrial Workers of the World*. Abridged ed. The Working Class in American History. Urbana: University of Illinois Press, 2000.

Dye, Nancy Schrom. "Creating a Feminist Alliance: Sisterhood and Class Conflict in the New York Women's Trade Union League, 1903–1914." In *Class, Sex, and the Women Worker*, edited by Milton Cantor and Bruce Laurie, 225–46. Westport, CT: Greenwood Press, 1977.

———. *As Equals and as Sisters: Feminism, the Labor Movement, and the Women's Trade Union League of New York*. Columbia: University of Missouri Press, 1980.

———. "Feminism or Unionism? The New York Women's Trade Union League and the Labor Movement." *Feminist Studies* 3, no. 12 (1975): 111–25.

———. "The Women's Trade Union League of New York, 1903–1920." Ph.D. Dissertation, University of Wisconsin, 1974.

Einhorn, Robin L. "Industrial Relations in the Progressive Era: The United States and Great Britain." *Social Service Review* 58, no. 1 (March 1984): 98–116.

Eisenach, Eldon J. *The Lost Promise of Progressivism*. Lawrence: University Press of Kansas, 1994.

Eisenstein, Louis, and Elliot Rosenberg. *A Stripe of Tammany's Tiger*. New York: R. Speller, 1966.

Eisner, J. Michael. *William Morris Leiserson: A Biography*. Madison: University of Wisconsin Press, 1967.

Endelman, Gary Edward. "Solidarity Forever: Rose Schneiderman and the Women's Trade Union League." Ph.D. Dissertation, University of Delaware, 1978.

Enstad, Nan. "Fashioning Political Identities: Cultural Studies and the Historical Construction of Political Subjects." *American Quarterly* 50, no. 4 (December 1998): 745–82.

———. *Ladies of Labor, Girls of Adventure: Working Women, Popular Culture, and Labor Politics at the Turn of the Twentieth Century*. New York: Columbia University Press, 1999.

Epstein, Melech. *Jewish Labor in the U.S.A. (1882–1952).* New York: Trade Union Sponsoring Committee, 1950–53.

———. *Profiles of Eleven.* Detroit: Wayne State University Press, 1965.

Erickson, Nancy S. "Muller V. Oregon Reconsidered: The Origins of a Sex-Based Doctrine of Liberty of Contract." *Labor History* 30, no. 2 (Spring 1989): 228–50.

Ernst, Daniel R. *Lawyers Against Labor: From Individual Rights to Corporate Liberalism.* Urbana: University of Illinois Press, 1995.

Ethington, Philip J. *The Public City: The Political Construction of Urban Life in San Francisco, 1850–1900.* New York: Cambridge University Press, 1994.

———. "Urban Constituencies, Regimes, and Policy Innovation in the Progressive Era: An Analysis of Boston, Chicago, New York City, and San Francisco." *Studies in American Political Development* 7 (Fall 1993): 275–315.

Ewen, Elizabeth. *Immigrant Women in the Land of Dollars: Life and Culture on the Lower East Side, 1890–1925.* New York: Monthly Review Press, 1985.

Faue, Elizabeth. *Community of Suffering and Struggle: Women, Men, and the Labor Movement in Minneapolis, 1915–1945.* Chapel Hill: University of North Carolina, 1991.

———. *Writing the Wrongs: Eva Valesh and the Rise of Labor Journalism.* Ithaca, NY: Cornell University Press, 2002.

Feingold, Henry. *A Time for Searching: Entering the Mainstream. The Jewish People in America.* Baltimore: Johns Hopkins University Press, 1992.

Feinman, Ronald L. *Twilight of Progressivism: The Western Republican Senators and the New Deal.* Baltimore: Johns Hopkins University Press, 1981.

Fenton, Edwin. *Immigrants and Unions, a Case Study: Italians and American Labor, 1870–1920.* New York: Arno Press, 1975.

Ferguson, Thomas. "From Normalcy to New Deal: Industrial Structure, Party Competition, and American Public Policy in the Great Depression." *International Organization* 38, no. 1 (Winter 1984): 41–94.

Ferguson, Thomas, Editor. *The Political Economy: Readings in the Politics and Economics of American Public Policy.* Armonk, NY: M.E. Sharpe, 1984.

Ferguson, Thomas, and Joel Rogers. *The Political Economy: Readings in the Politics and Economics of American Public Policy.* Armonk, NY: M.E. Sharpe, 1984.

Feruson, Thomas. "From Normalcy to New Deal: Industrial Structure, Party Competition, and American Public Policy in the Great Depression." *International Organization* 38, no. 1 (1984): 41–94.

Filene, Peter G. "An Obituary for the Progressive Movement." *American Quarterly* 22 (1970): 20–34.

Finegold, Henry, and Theda Skocpol. *State and Party in America's New Deal.* Madison: University of Wisconsin Press, 1995.

Finegold, Kenneth. *Experts and Politicians: Reform Challenges to Machines Politics in New York, Cleveland, and Chicago.* Princeton Studies in American Politics. Princeton: Princeton University Press, 1995.

Fink, Gary M. "The Rejection of Volunteerism." *Industrial and Labor Relations Review* 26 (1972): 805–19.

Fink, Leon. *In Search of the Working Class: Essays in American Labor History and Political Culture*. Urbana: University of Illinois Press, 1994.

———. "'Intellectuals' Versus 'Workers': Academic Requirements and the Creation of Labor History." *American Historical Review* 96, no. 2 (April 1991): 395–421.

———. *Progressive Intellectuals and the Dilemmas of Democratic Commitment*. Cambridge, MA: Harvard University Press, 1998.

Fishback, Price V., and Shawn Everett Kantor. *A Prelude to the Welfare State: The Origins of Workers' Compensation*. Chicago: University of Chicago Press, 2000.

Fitzpartick, Ellen. "Rethinking the Intellectual Origins of American Labor History." *American Historical Review* 96, no. 2 (April 1991): 422–28.

Fitzpatrick, Ellen F. *Endless Crusade: Women Social Scientists and Progressive Reform*. New York: Oxford University Press, 1990.

Flanagan, Maureen A. "Gender and Urban Political Reform: The City Club and the Woman's City Club of Chicago in the Progressive Era." *American Historical Review* 95 (1990): 1032–50.

Flick, Alexander C., Editor. *Wealth and Commonwealth*. Vol. 8 of *History of the State of New York*. New York: Columbia University Press, 1935.

Foner, Philip S. *The AFL in the Progressive Era, 1910–1915*. New York, International Publishers.

———. *Women and the American Labor Movement: From Colonial Times to the Eve of World War I*. New York: Free Press, 1979.

Fones-Wolf, Elizabeth, and Ken Fones-Wolf. "Rank-and-File Rebellions and AFL Interference in the Affairs of National Unions: The Gompers Era." *Labor History* 35, no. 2 (Spring 1994): 237–59.

Forbath, William E. "Courts, Constitutions, and Labor Politics in England and America: A Study of the Constitutive Power of Law." *Law and Social Inquiry* 16, no. 1 (1991): 1–34.

———. *Law and the Shaping of the American Labor Movement*. Cambridge, MA: Harvard University Press, 1989.

Forcey, Charles. *The Crossroads of Liberalism: Croly, Weyl, Lippmann, and the Progressive Era, 1900–1925*. New York: Oxford University Press, 1961.

Forester, Tom. "Whatever Happened to Industrial Democracy." *New Society* 53, no. 922 (July 17 1980): 120–22.

Fox, Daniel M. *The Discovery of Abundance: Simon N. Patten and the Transformation of Social Theory*. Ithaca, NY: Cornell University Press, 1967.

Fox, Richard W. "The Paradox of 'Progressive' Socialism: The Case of Morris Hillquit, 1901–1914." *American Quarterly* 26, no. 2 (1974): 127–40.

Frank, Dana. "Housewives, Socialists, and the Politics of Food: The 1917 New York Cost-of-Living Protests." *Feminist Studies* 11, no. 2 (Summer 1985): 255–85.

Frankel, Jonathan. "Class War and Community: The Socialists in American-Jewish Politics, 1897–1918." In *Prophecy and Politics: Socialism, Nationalism and the Russian Jews, 1862–1917*, 453–547. Cambridge: Cambridge University Press, 1981.

Fraser, Steve. "The 'Labor Question'." In *The Rise and Fall of the New Deal Order*, edited by Steve Fraser and Gary Gerstle, 55–84. Princeton: Princeton University Press, 1989.

———. *Labor Will Rule: Sidney Hillman and the Rise of American Labor*. New York: Free Press; Toronto: Maxwell Macmillan Canada, 1991.

———. "Landslayt and Paesani: Ethnic Conflict and Cooperation in the Amalgamated Clothing Workers of America." In *'Struggle a Hard Battle': Essays on Working-Class Immigrants*, edited by Dirk Hoerder, 280–302. DeKalb: Northern Illinois University Press, 1986.

Fraser, Steve, and Gary Gerstle, Editors. *The Rise and Fall of the New Deal Order, 1930–1980*. Princeton: Princeton University Press, 1989.

Fraser, Steve, and Joshua Benjamin Freeman. *Audacious Democracy Labor, Intellectuals, and the Social Reconstruction of America*. Boston: Houghton Mifflin, 1997.

Fraser, Steven Clark. "Sidney Hillman and the Origins of the 'New Unionism.'" Ph.D. Dissertation, Rutgers University, 1983.

Freeman, Joshua Benjamin. *Working-Class New York Life and Labor Since World War II*. New York: New Press, 2000.

Frieburger, William Joseph. "The Lone Socialist Vote: A Political Study of Meyer London," University of Cincinnati, 1980.

Fried, Albert. *The Rise and Fall of the Jewish Gangster in America*. Revised ed. New York: Columbia University Press, 1993 (1980).

Fried, Barbara H. *The Progressive Assault on Laissez Faire: Robert Hale and the First Law and Economics Movement*. Cambridge, MA: Harvard University Press, 1998.

Friedman, Jacob Alexis. *The Impeachment of Governor William Sulzer*. New York: Columbia University Press, 1939.

Friedman-Kasaba, Kathie. *Memories of Migration: Gender, Ethnicity, and Work in the Lives of Jewish and Italian Women in New York, 1870–1924*. Albany: SUNY Press, 1996.

Frisch, Michael H. "Urban Theorists, Urban Reform, and American Political Culture in the Progressive Period." *Political Science Quarterly* 97, no. 2 (Summer 1982): 295–315.

Frisch, Michael H., and Daniel J. Walkowitz, Editors. *Working-Class America: Essays on Labor, Community, and American Society*. Urbana: University of Illinois Press, 1983.

Furio, Columba Marie. "Immigrant Women and Industry: A Case Study, the Italian Women and the Garment Industry, 1880–1950." Ph.D. Dissertation, New York University, 1979.

Furner, Mary O. *Advocacy and Objectivity: A Crisis in the Professionalization of American Social Science, 1865–1905*. Lexington: University Press of Kentucky, 1975.

———. "Knowing Capitalism: Public Investigation and the Labor Question in the Long Progressive Era." In *The State and Economic Knowledge: The American and British Experience*, edited by Mary O. Furner and Barry Supple.

Woodrow Wilson International Center for Scholars. Cambridge: Cambridge University Press, 1990.

———. *The State and Economic Knowledge: The American and British Experiences.* Washington, DC: Woodrow Wilson International Center for Scholars.

Furner, Mary O., and Barry Supple. "Ideas, Institutions, and the State in the United States and Britain: An Introduction." In *The State and Economic Knowledge: The American and British Experience*, edited by Mary O. Furner and Barry Supple. Woodrow Wilson International Center for Scholars. Cambridge: Cambridge University Press, 1990.

Gabaccia, Donna. *From the Other Side: Women, Gender, and Immigrant Life in the U.S., 1820–1990.* Bloomington: Indiana University Press, 1994.

———. *From Sicily to Elizabeth Street: Housing and Social Change Among Italian Immigrants, 1880–1930.* Albany: State University of New York Press, 1984.

———. *Immigrant Women in the United States: A Selectively Annotated Multidisciplinary Bibliography.* Westport, CT: Greenwood Press, 1989.

———. *Militants and Migrants: Rural Sicilians Become American Workers.* New Brunswick, NJ: Rutgers University Press, 1988.

———. "Neither Padrone Slaves nor Primitive Rebels: Sicilians on Two Continents." In *'Struggle a Hard Battle': Essays on Working-Class Immigrants*, edited by Dirk Hoerder, 95–120. DeKalb: Northern Illinois University Press, 1986.

Gabaccia, Donna, Editor. *Seeking Common Ground: Multicultral Studies of Immigrant Women in the United States.* Westport, CT: Greenwood Press, 1992.

Gabaccia, Donna R., and Fraser Ottanelli. "Diaspora or International Proletariat? Italian Labor, Labor Migrations, and the Making of Multiethnic States, 1815–1939." *Diaspora* 6, no. 1 (Spring 1997): 61–84.

Galambos, Louis. "The Emerging Organizational Synthesis in Modern American History." *Business History Review* XLIV, no. 3 (1970): 279–90.

Gambino, Richard. *Blood of My Blood: The Dilemma of the Italian-Americans.* Garden City, NY: Doubleday, 1974.

Gerstle, Gary. "The Protean Character of American Liberalism." *American Historical Review* 99, no. 4 (October 1994): 1043–73.

Gilbert, James. "Defining Industrial Democracy: Work Relations in Twentieth-Century America." *International Labor and Working-Class History* 35 (Spring 1989): 81–91.

Gitleman, Howard. *The Legacy of the Ludlow Massacre: A Chapter in American Industrial Relations.* Philadelphia: University of Pennsylvania Press, 1988.

Glenn, Susan A. *Daughters of the Shtetl: Life and Labor in the Immigrant Generation.* Ithaca, NY: Cornell University Press, 1990.

Glickman, Lawrence B. *A Living Wage: American Workers and the Making of Consumer Society.* Ithaca, NY: Cornell University Press, 1998.

Godley, Andrew. "The Global Diffusion of the Sewing Machine, 1850–1914." *Research in Economic History* 20 (2001): 1–45.

Goldberg, Gorden J. "Meyer London and the National Social Insurance Movement, 1914–1922." *American Jewish Historical Quarterly* 65, no. 1 (1975): 59–73.

Golfield, Michael. "Explaining New Deal Labor Policy." *American Political Science Review* 84, no. 4 (December 1990): 1297–1315.

Goodwin, Joanne L. *Gender and the Politics of Welfare Reform: Mothers' Pensions in Chicago, 1911–1929.* Chicago: University of Chicago Press, 1997.

Goodwyn, Lawrence. *Democratic Promise the Populist Moment in America.* New York: Oxford University Press, 1976.

Gordon, Colin. "The Lost City of Solidarity: Metropolitan Unionism in Historical Perspective." *Politics and Society* 27, no. 4 (December 1999): 561–85.

———. *New Deals: Business, Labor, and Politics in America, 1920–1935.* New York: Cambridge University Press, 1994.

———. "Why No Corporatism in the United States? Business Disorganized and Its Consequences." *Business and Economic History* 27, no. 1 (Fall 1998): 29–46.

Gordon, Lynn. "Women and the Anti-Child Labor Movement in Illinois, 1890–1920." *Social Service Review* 51 (June 1977): 228–48.

Gordon, Lynn D. "The Gibson Girl Goes to College: Popular Culture and Women's Higher Education in the Progressive Era, 1890–1920." *American Quarterly* 39 (Summer 1987): 211–30.

Goren, Arthur A. *New York Jews and the Quest for Community: The Kehillah Experiment, 1908–1922.* New York: Columbia University Press, 1970.

Governor's Advisory Commission. *Cloak, Suit, and Skirt Industry, New York City: Report of an Investigation.* New York: New York State, 1925.

Green, Nancy L., Editor. *Jewish Workers in the Modern Diaspora.* Berkeley: University of California Press, 1998.

———. *Ready-to-Wear and Ready-to-Work: A Century of Industry and Immigrants in Paris and New York.* Durham, NC: Duke University Press, 1997.

———. "Women and Immigrants in the Sweatshop: Categories of Labor Segmentation Revisited." *Comparative Studies in Society and History* 38 (July 1996): 411–33.

Greenbaum, Fred. "Ambivalent Friends: Progressive Era Politicians and Organized Labor, 1902–1940." *Labor's Heritage* 6 (Summer 1994): 62–76.

Greenberg, Edward S. "Industrial Democracy and the Democratic Citizen." *Journal of Politics* 43, no. 3 (1981): 964–81.

Greene, Julie. "The Strike at the Ballot Box: Politics and Partisanship in the American Federation of Labor, 1881–1916," Yale University, 1990.

———. "The Strike at the Ballot Box: The American Federation of Labor's Entrance into Election Politics, 1906–1909." *Labor History* 32, no. 2 (Spring 1991): 165–92.

———. *Pure and Simple Politics: The American Federation of Labor and Political Activism.* New York: Cambridge University Press, 1998.

———. "Dinner-Pail Politics: Employers, Workers, and Partisan Culture in the Progressive Era." In *Labor Histories: Class, Politics, and the Working-Class Experience,* edited by Julie Greene and Bruce Laurie Eric Arnesen. Urbana: University of Illinois Press, 1998.

———. "Negotiating the State: Frank Walsh and the Transformation of Labor's Political Culture in Progressive America." In *Organized Labor and American*

Politics, 1894–1994: The Labor-Liberal Alliance, edited by Kevin Boyle, 71–102. Albany: SUNY Press, 1998.

Greenfeld, Judith. "The Role of the Jews in the Development of the Clothing Industry in the United States." *Yivo Annual of Jewish Social Science* 2–3 (1948-9): 180–205.

Greenwald, Richard A. "Bargaining for Industrial Democracy? Labor, the State, and the New Industrial Relations in Progressive Era New York." Ph.D. Dissertation, New York University, 1998.

Gregory, Charles Oscar. *Labor and the Law.* New York: W.W. Norton, 1979.

Gutman, Herbert G. *Power and Culture: Essays on the American Working Class.* Berlin, Ira. New York: Pantheon Press, 1987.

———. *Work, Culture, and Society in Industrializing America: Essays in American Working-Class and Social History.* New York: Vintage Books, 1977, c1976.

Guzda, Henry P. "Industrial Democracy: Made in the U.S.A." *Monthly Labor Review* 107, no. 5 (May 1984): 26–33.

Hamilton, Alice. *Exploring the Dangerous Trades: The Autobiography of Alice Hamilton, MD.* Boston: Northeastern University Press, 1985, 1943.

Hammack, David C., and Stanton Wheeler. *Social Science in the Making: Essays on the Russell Sage Foundation, 1907–1972.* New York: The Foundation, 1994.

Handlin, Oscar. *Al Smith and His America.* Boston: Northeastern University Press, 1987 (Reprint 1958).

Hapgood, Hutchins. *The Spirit of the Ghetto.* Cambridge, MA: Harvard University Press, 1967 (1902).

Hapgood, Norman, and Henry Moskowitz. *Up From the City Streets: Alfred E. Smith.* New York: Hardcourt, Brace and Company, 1927.

Hapke, Laura. "The American Working Girl and the New York Tenement Tale of the 1890s." *Journal of American Culture* 15, no. 2 (1992): 43–50.

———. "A Shop is Not a Home: Nineteenth-Century American Sweatshop Discourse." *American Nineteenth Century History* 2, no. 3 (Autumn 2001): 47–66.

Harris, Howell John. *Bloodless Victories: The Rise and Fall of the Open Shop in the Philadelphia Metal Trades, 1890–1940.* New York: Cambridge University Press, 2000.

———. "Give Us Some Less of That Old-Time Corporate History." *Labor History* 28, no. 1 (Winter 1987): 75–83.

———. "Industrial Democracy and Liberal Capitalism, 1890–1925." In *Industrial Democracy in America: The Ambiguous Promise,* edited by Nelson Lichtenstein and Howell John Harris, 43–66. New York: Cambridge University Press, 1993.

———. *The Right to Manage: Industrial Relations Policies of American Business in the 1940s.* Madison: University of Wisconsin Press, 1982.

Harrison, Royden. *The Life and Times of Sidney and Beatrice Webb 1858–1905, the Formative Years.* New York: St. Martin's Press, 2000.

Hart, Vivien. "Minimum-Wage Policy and Constitutional Inequality: The Paradox of the Fair Labor Standards Act of 1938." *Journal of Policy History* 1, no. 3 (1989): 319–43.

Hasenfeld, Yeheskel. "The Welfare State, Citizenship, and Bureaucratic Encounters." *American Review of Sociology* 13 (1987): 387–415.

Hattam, Victoria. "Economic Visions and Political Strategies: American Labor and the State, 1865–1896." *Studies in American Political Development* 4 (1990): 83–129.

———. *Labor Visions and State Power: The Origins of Business Unionism in the United States.* Princeton: Princeton University Press, 1993.

———. "Reply to Lovell: Politics of Commitment or Calculation?" *Studies in American Political Development* 8, no. 1 (Spring 1994): 103–10.

Hawley, Ellis. "The Discovery and Study of a 'Corporate Liberalism'." *Business History Review* LII, no. 3 (Autumn 1978): 309–20.

———. "Economic Inquiry and the State in New Era America: Antistatist Corporatism and Positive Statism in Uneasy Coexistence." In *The State and Economic Knowledge: The American and British Experiences*, edited by Mary O. Furner and Barry Supple, 287–324. Woodrow Wilson International Center for Scholars. Cambridge: Cambridge University Press, 1990.

———. *The New Deal and the Problem of Monopoly: A Study in Economic Ambivalence.* Princeton: Princeton University Press, 1966.

———. "Social Policy and the Liberal State in Twentieth-Century America." In *Federal Social Policy: The Historical Dimension*, edited by Donald T. Critchlow and Ellis W. Hawley, 117–40. University Park: Pennsylvania State University Press, 1988.

Haydu, Jeffrey. "Employers, Unions, and American Exceptionalism: Pre-World War I Open Shops in the Machine Trades in Comparative Perspective." *International Review of Social History* XXIII (1988): 25–41.

———. *Making American Industry Safe for Democracy: Comparative Perspectives on the State and Employee Representation in the Era of World War I.* Urbana: University of Illinois, 1997.

Hays, Samuel P. "The Politics of Reform in Municipal Government in the Progressive Era." *Pacific Northwest Quarterly* 55 (October 1964): 157–69.

———. *The Response to Industrialism: 1885–1914.* Chicago: University of Chicago Press, 1957.

Hazen, Margarett Hindle, and Robert K. Hazen. *Keepers of the Flame: The Role of Fire in American Culture, 1775–1925.* Princeton: Princeton University Press, 1992.

Heinze, Andrew R. *Adapting to Abundance: Jewish Immigrants, Mass Consumption, and the Search for American Identity.* New York: Columbia University Press, 1990.

Helfgott, Roy B. "Trade Unionism Among the Jewish Garment Workers of Britain and the United States." *Labor History* 2 (Spring 1961): 202–14.

Henderson, Thomas M. *Tammany Hall and the New Immigrants: The Progressive Years.* New York: Arno Press, 1976.

———. "Immigrant Politician: Salvatore Costillo, Progressive Ethnic." *The International Migration Review* 13, no. 1 (1979): 81–102.

Henderson, Thomas McLean. "Tammany Hall and the New Immigrants, 1910–1921." Ph.D. Dissertation, University of Virginia, 1973.

Herberg, Will. "The Jewish Labor Movement in the United States." *American Jewish Yearbook* (1952): 3–74.

Hillquit, Morris. *Socialism Summed Up.* New York: The H. K. Fly Company, 1913.

Hillquit, Morris, et al. *The Double Edge of Labor's Sword Discussion and Testimony on Socialism and Trade-Unionism Before the Commission on Industrial Relations.* Chicago: Socialist Party, National Office, 1914.

Himmelberg, Robert E. *The Origins of the National Recovery Administration: Business, Government, and the Trade Association Issue, 1921–1933.* New York: Fordham University Press, 1993 (1976).

Hobson, Wayne K. "Professionals, Progressives and Bureaucratization: A Reassessment." *The Historian* 39 (August 1977): 639–58.

Hofstadter, Richard. *The American Political Tradition and the Men Who Made It.* New York: Vintage Books, 1974.

———. *The Progressive Movement, 1900–1915.* New York: Simon & Schuster, 1986, c1963.

———. *Social Darwinism in American Thought.* Boston: Beacon Press, 1955.

Hogler, Raymond L. "Labor History and Critical Labor Law: An Interdisciplinary Approach to Workers' Control." *Labor History* 30, no. 2 (Spring 1989): 185–92.

Holt, Wythe. "The New American Labor Law History." *Labor History* 30, no. 2 (Spring 1989): 275–93.

Horne, Roger D. "Practical Idealism at the Zenith of Progressivism: John R. Commons as an Industrial Reformer." *Mid-America* 76, no. 1 (Winter 1994): 53–70.

Horowitz, David A. *Beyond Left and Right: Insurgency and the Establishment.* Urbana: University of Illinois Press, 1997.

Hourwich, Isaac A. *Immigration and Labor: The Economic Aspects of European Immigration to the United States.* New York: G.P. Putnam's Sons, 1912.

Howe, Irving. *World of Our Fathers.* New York: Harcourt Brace Jovanovich, 1976.

Howell, Chris. *Regulating Labor: The State and Industrial Relations Reform in Postwar France.* Princeton: Princeton University Press, 1996.

Hoxie, Robert Franklin. *Scientific Management and Labor.* New York and London: D. Appleton and Company, 1915.

Huddleston, John. "Industrial Democracy." *Parliamentary Affairs* 25, no. 3 (1972): 224–33.

Huthmacher, J. Joseph. "Charles Evans Hughs and Charles Francis Murphy: The Metamorphosis of Progressive Reform." *New York History* 46, no. 1 (January 1965): 25–40.

———. *Senator Robert F. Wagner and the Rise of Urban Liberalism.* New York: Athenaeum, 1968.

———. "Senator Robert F. Wagner and the Rise of Urban Liberalism." *American Jewish Historical Quarterly* 58, no. 3 (1969): 330–46.

————. "Urban Liberalism and the Age of Reform." *Mississippi Valley Historical Review* 49, no. 2 (1962–1963): 231–41.

Hyman, Paula E. *Gender and Assimilation in Modern Jewish History: The Roles and Representation of Women.* Seattle: University of Washington Press, 1995.

————. "Immigrant Women and Consumer Protest: The New York City Kosher Meat Boycott of 1902." *American Jewish History* 70, no. 1 (1980): 91–105.

Ingalls, Robert P. "New York and the Minimum-Wage Movement, 1933–1937." *Labor History* 15, no. 2 (1974): 179–98.

Jacoby, Robin Miller. "The Women's Trade Union League and American Feminism." *Feminist Studies* 3, no. 12 (1975): 126–40.

Jacoby, Sanford. "Unnatural Extinction: The Rise and Fall of the Independent Local Union." *Industrial Relations* 40, no. 3 (July 2001): 377–404.

Jacoby, Sanford, Editor. *Masters to Managers: Historical and Comparative Perspectives on American Employers.* New York: Columbia University Press, 1991.

Jeffreys-Jones, Rhodri. *Violence and Reform in American History.* New York: New Viewpoints, 1978.

————. "Violence in American History: Plug Uglies in the Progressive Era." In *Perspectives in American History*, edited by Donald Fleming and Bernard Bailyn, 465–583. Charles Warren Center for Studies in American History, Vol. VIII. Cambridge, MA: Harvard University Press, 1974.

Jeffries, John W. "The 'New' New Deal and American Liberalism, 1937–1945." *Political Science Quarterly* 105, no. 3 (1990): 397–418.

Jensen, Frances. "The Triangle Fire and the Limits of Progressivism." Ph.D. Dissertation, University of Massachusetts, Amherst, 1996.

Jensen, Joan M., and Sue Davidson, Editors. *A Needle, a Bobbin, a Strike: Women Needleworkers in America.* Philadelphia: Temple University Press, 1984.

Johnston, Robert D. *The Radical Middle Class Populist Democracy and the Question of Capitalism in Progressive Era Portland, Oregon.* Princeton: Princeton University Press, 2003.

————. "Re-Democratizing the Progressive Era: The Politics of Progressive Era Political Historiography". *Journal of the Gilded Age and Progressive Era* 1, no. 1 (January 2002): 68–92.

Jordon, John M. *Machine-Age Ideology: Social Engineering and American Liberalism, 1911–1939.* Chapel Hill: University of North Carolina Press, 1994.

Joselit, Jenna Weissman. "The Landlord as Czar: Pre-World War I Tenant Activity." In *The Tenant Movement in New York City, 1904–1984*, edited by Ronald Lawson and Mark Naison, 39–50. New Brunswick, NJ: Rutgers University Press, 1986.

————. *Our Gang: Jewish Crime and the New York Jewish Community, 1900–1940.* Bloomington: Indiana University Press, 1983.

————. *The Wonders of America: Reinventing Jewish Culture, 1880–1950.* New York: Hill and Wang, 1994.

Kahn, Jonathan. *Budgeting Democracy: State Building and Citizenship in America, 1890–1928.* Ithaca, NY: Cornell University Press, 1997.

Katz, Michael B. *Improving Poor People: The Welfare State, the "Underclass," and Urban Schools as History.* Princeton: Princeton University Press, 1995.

———. *In The Shadow of the Poorhouse: A Social History of Welfare in America.* New York: Basic Books, 1986.

———. *Poverty and Policy in American History.* New York: Academic Press, 1983.

———, Editor. *The "Underclass" Debate: Views from History.* Social Science Research Council (U.S.). Committee for Research on the Urban Underclass. Princeton: Princeton University Press, 1993.

Kaufman, Bruce E. "John R. Commons and the Wisconsin School on Industrial Relations Strategy and Policy." *Industrial and Labor Relations Review* 57, no. 1 (October 2003): 3–29.

———. *The Origins and Evolution of the Field of Industrial Relations in the United States.* Ithaca, NY: ILR Press, 1993.

Kaufman, Stuart Bruce. *Samuel Gompers and the Origins of the American Federation of Labor, 1848–1896.* Westport, CT: Greenwood Press, 1973.

Kazin, Michael. *Barons of Labor: The San Francisco Building Trades and Union Power in the Progressive Era.* Urbana: University of Illinois Press, 1987.

———. "Struggling with the Class Struggle: Marxism and the Search for a Synthesis of U.S. Labor History." *Labor History* 28, no. 4 (Fall 1987): 497–514.

Keller, Morton. *Affairs of State: Public Life in Late Nineteenth Century America.* Cambridge: Belknap Press of Harvard University Press, 1977.

———. "Brandeis—Reformer." *American Jewish History* 81 (Spring/Summer 1994): 394–405.

———. *Regulating a New Economy: Public Policy and Economic Change in America, 1900–1933.* Cambridge, MA: Harvard University Press, 1990.

———. *Regulating a New Society: Public Policy and Social Change in America, 1900–1933.* Cambridge, MA: Harvard University Press, 1994.

———. "Social Policy in Nineteenth-Century America." In *Federal Social Policy: The Historical Dimension,* edited by Donald T. Critchlow and Ellis Hawley, 99–116. University Park: Pennsylvania State University Press, 1988.

Kenneally, James J. "Women and Trade Unions 1870–1920: The Quandary of the Reformer." *Labor History* 14, no. 1 (1973): 42–55.

Kennedy, Susan Estabrook. *If All We Did Was Weep at Home: A History of White Working-Class Women in America.* Bloomington: Indiana University Press, 1979.

———. " 'The Want It Satisfies Demonstrates the Need of It': A Study of Life and Labor of the Women's Trade Union League." *International Journal of Women's Studies* 3, no. 4 (1980): 391–406.

Kerr, Thomas Jefferson. "New York Factory Investigating Commission and the Progressives." Ph.D. Dissertation, Syracuse University, 1965.

Kessler-Harris, Alice. "Organizing the Unorganizable: Three Jewish Women and Their Union." In *Class, Sex, and the Women Worker,* edited by Milton Cantor and Bruce Laurie, 144–65. Westport, CT: Greenwood Press, 1977.

——. *Out to Work: A History of Wage-Earning Women in the United States.* New York: Oxford University Press, 1982.

Kessner, Thomas. *Capital City New York City and the Men Behind America's Rise to Economic Dominance, 1860–1900.* New York: Simon & Schuster, 2003.

——. *The Golden Door: Italian and Jewish Immigrant Mobility in New York City, 1880–1915.* New York: Oxford University Press, 1977.

Kim, Jin Hee. "Labor Law and Labor Policy in New York State, 1920s–1930s." Ph.D. Dissertation, Binghamton University, SUNY, 1999.

Kimeldorf, Howard. *Battling for American Labor: Wobblies, Craft Workers, and the Making of the Union Movement.* Berkeley: University of California Press, 1999.

——. "Bring the Union Back In (Or Why We Need Old Labor History)." *Labor History* 32, no. 1 (1991): 91–128. With Comments by: Alice Kessler-Harris, David Montgomery, Bruce Nelson, Michael Kazin, and Daniel Nelson.

——. *Reds or Rackets?: The Making of Radical and Conservative Unions on the Waterfront.* Berkeley: University of California Press, 1988.

Kirby, Diane. "'The Wage-Earning Woman and the State': The National Women's Trade Union League and Protective Labor Legislation, 1903–1923." *Labor History* 28, no. 1 (Winter 1987): 54–74.

Kirby, Diane Elizabeth. "Alice Henry: The National Women's Trade," University of California, Santa Barbara, 1982.

Kloppenberg, James T. *Uncertain Victory Social Democracy and Progressivism in European and American Thought, 1870–1920.* New York: Oxford University Press, 1986.

——. *The Virtues of Liberalism.* New York: Oxford University Press, 1998.

Kocks, Dorothee E. *Dream a Little Land and Social Justice in Modern America.* Berkeley: University of California Press, 2000.

Kolko, Gabriel. *Railroads and Regulation, 1877–1916.* New York: W.W. Norton, 1970.

——. *Railroads and Regulation, 1877–1916.* Princeton: Princeton University Press, 1965.

——. *The Triumph of Conservatism: A Reinterpretation of American History, 1900–1916.* London: The Free Press of Glencoe, 1963.

——. *Wealth and Power in America: An Analysis of Social Class and Income Distribution.* Westport, CT: Greenwood Press, 1962, (1981).

Korman, Gerd. "New Jewish Politics for an American Labor Leader: Sidney Hillman, 1942–1946." *American Jewish History* 82, nos. 1–4 (1994): 195–213.

Kosak, Hadassa. *Cultures of Opposition: Jewish Immigrant Workers, New York City, 1881–1905.* Albany: State University of New York Press, 2000.

Kovacik, Karen. "Words of Fire for Our Generation: Contemporary Working-Class Poets on the Triangle Fire." *Women's Studies Quarterly* XXVI, no. 1 & 2 (Spring/Summer 1998): 137–58.

Koven, Seth, and Sonya Michel, Editors. *Mothers of a New World: Maternalist Politics and the Origins of Welfare States.* New York: Routledge Press, 1993.

Krause, Paul. *The Battle for Homestead, 1880–1892: Politics, Culture and Steel.* Pittsburgh: University of Pittsburgh Press, 1992.

Kraut, Alan M. "Silent Travelers: Germs, Genes, and American Efficiency." *Social Science History* 12, no. 4 (Winter 1988): 377–94.

———. *Silent Travelers: Germs, Genes, and the 'Immigrant Menace.'* New York: Basic Books, 1994.

Lacey, Michael James, and Mary O. Furner. *The State and Social Investigation in Britain and the United States.* Washington. DC: Woodrow Wilson Center Press; Cambridge.

Ladd-Taylor, Molly. *Mother-Work: Women, Child-Welfare, and the State, 1890–1930.* Urbana: University of Illinois Press, 1995.

———. *Raising A Baby the Government Way: Mothers' Letters to the Children's Bureau, 1915–1932.* New Brunswick, NJ: Rutgers University Press, 1986.

Lagemann, Ellen Condliffe. *A Generation of Women: Education in the Lives of Progressive Reformers.* Cambridge, MA: Harvard University Press, 1979.

Lane, A.T. *Solidarity or Survival?: American Labor and European Immigrants, 1830–1924.* Westport, CT: Greenwood Press, 1987.

Lane, Robert E. "From Political to Industrial Democracy?" *Polity* 42, no. 4 (1985): 623–48.

Laslett, John H.M. "Three Anglo-American Radicals and the Dilemmas of Syndicalism and Social Democracy." *Lanour/Le Travail* 25 (1990): 237–44.

Lawson, Ronald. "The Rent Strike in New York City, 1904–1980: The Evolution of a Social Movement." *Journal of Urban History* 10, no. 3 (1984): 235–58.

Leeder, Elaine J. *The Gentle General: Rose Pesotta, Anarchist and Labor Organizer.* Albany: State University of New York Press, 1993.

———. "The Gentle Warrior: Rose Pesotta, Anarchist and Labor Organizer." Ph.D. Dissertation, Cornell University, 1985.

Leff, Mark H. "Revisioning U.S. Political History." *American Historical Review* 100, no. 3 (June 1995): 829–53.

Lehrer, Susan. *Origins of Protective Labor Legislation for Women, 1905–1925.* Albany: SUNY Press, 1987.

Leinenweber, Charles. "The Class and Ethnic Bases of New York City Socialism, 1904–1915." *Labor History* 22 (Winter 1981): 31–56.

———. "Socialists in the Streets: The New York City Socialist Party in Working Class Neighborhoods, 1908–1918." *Science and Society* 41, no. 2 (1977): 152–71.

Leitch, John. *Man to Man: The Story of Industrial Democracy.* New York: B.C. Forbes Company, 1919.

Lembcke, Jerry. *Capitalist Development and Class Capacities: Marxist Theory and Union Organization.* New York: Greenwood Press, 1988.

Lerner, Elinor. "Jewish Involvement in the New York City Woman Suffrage Movement." *American Jewish History* 70, no. 4 (1981): 442–61.

———. "Jewish Women in the New York City Woman Suffrage Movement." *American Jewish History* 70, no. 4 (1981): 442–61.

Lescohier, Don D. "Working Conditions." In *History of Labor in the United States, 1896–1932,* edited by John R. Commons. Volume III. New York: Augustus M. Kelley, 1966, 1935.

Leviatin, David. *Followers of the Trail: Jewish Working-Class Radicals in America.* New Haven: Yale University Press, 1989.

Levine, Louis. *The Women's Garment Workers.* New York: B.W. Huebsch, 1924.

Lichtenstein, Nelson. *Labor's War at Home: The CIO in World War II.* Cambridge: Cambridge University Press, 1982.

Lichtenstein, Nelson, and Howell John Harris, Editors. *Industrial Democracy in America: The Ambiguous Promise.* Cambridge: Cambridge University Press, 1993.

Liebman, Arthur. *Jews and the Left.* New York: John Wiley and Sons, 1976.

Link, Arthur Stanley. *Progressivism.* Arlington Heights, IL: Harlan Davidson, 1983.

Lippmann, Walter. *Drift and Mastery an Attempt to Diagnose the Current Unrest.* New York: M. Kennerley, 1914.

Lipset, Seymour Martin, and Earl Raab. *Jews and the New American Scene.* Cambridge, MA: Harvard University Press, 1995.

Lipsky, Abram. "The Political Mind of Foreign-Born Americans." *Popular Science Monthly* 85 (Oct. 1914): 397–403.

Lissak, Rivka S. *Pluralism and Progressives: Hull House and the New Immigrants, 1890–1919.* Chicago: University of Chicago Press, 1989.

Livesay, Harold C. *Samuel Gompers and Organized Labor in America.* Boston: Little Brown, c1978.

Livingston, James. *Pragmatism and the Political Economy of Cultural Revolution, 1850–1940.* Chapel Hill: University of North Carolina Press, 1994.

———. *Pragmatism, Feminism, and Democracy Rethinking the Politics of American History.* New York: Routledge, 2001.

———. "The Social Analysis of Economic History and Theory: Conjectures on Late Nineteenth-Century American Development." *American Historical Review* 92 (February 1992): 69–95.

Lovell, George. "The Ambiguities of Labor's Legislative Reforms in New York State in the Late 19th Century." *Studies in American Political Development* 8, no. 1 (Spring 1994): 81–102.

Lowi, Theodore J. "Machine Politics—Old and New." *The Public Interest* 9 (1967): 83–92.

———. "The State in Political Science: How We Become What We Study." *American Political Science Review* 86, no. 1 (March 1992): 1–7.

Lubove, Roy. *The Struggle for Social Security, 1900–1935.* Pittsburgh. University of Pittsburgh Press: 1986.

Lyddon, Dave. "Industrial-Relations Theory and Labor History." *International Labor and Working-Class History* 46 (Fall 1994): 122–41.

Lynd, Staughton, Editor. *"We Are All Leaders": The Alternative Unionism of the Early 1930s.* Urbana: University of Illinois Press, 1996.

MacKenzie, Jeanne. *A Victorian Courtship the Story of Beatrice Potter and Sidney Webb.* London: Weidenfeld and Nicolson, 1979.

MacLean, Nancy. "The Culture of Resistance: Female Institution Building in the International Ladies' Garment Workers Union, 1905–1925." *Michigan Occasional Papers* (Women's Studies Program) XX1 (Winter 1982): 1–152.

Madison, Charles A. "Joseph Barondess to David Dubinsky: From Sweatshop to Industrial Leadership." In *American Labor Leaders: Personalities and Forces in the Labor Movement*, edited by Charles A. Madison, 199–234. New York: Frederick Ungar Publishing, 1950.

Malkiel, Theresa. *The Diary of a Shirtwaist Striker*. Ithaca, NY: ILR Press, 1990, 1910.

Mandel, Bernard. *Samuel Gompers: A Biography*. Yellow Springs, OH: Antioch Press, 1963.

Marilley, Suzanne M. *Woman Suffrage and the Origins of Liberal Feminism in the United States, 182–1920*. Cambridge, MA: Harvard University Press, 1996.

Markowitz, Gerald E., and David Rosner, Editors. *Slaves of the Depression: Workers' Letters About Life on the Job*. Ithaca, NY: Cornell University Press, 1987.

Martin Christopher. "Making Colleagues of Antagonists: Edward Filene and the Promise of Industrial Democracy." Presented at the Social Science History Association. Pittsburgh, October 2000.

———. "New Unionism at the Grassroots: The Amalgamated Clothing Workers of America in Rochester, New York, 1914–1929." Presented at the Researching New York: Empire State History. Albany: SUNY-Albany, October 1999.

Mason, Alpheus Thomas. *Brandeis and the Modern State*. Washington, DC: National Home Library Foundation, 1936.

———. *Brandeis: A Free Man's Life*. New York: Viking Press, 1946.

Mattina, Anne F. "Rights as Well as Duties: The Rhetoric of Leonora O'Reilly." *Communication Quarterly* 42, no. 2 (Spring 1994): 196–205.

Mattson, Kevin. *Creating a Democratic Public the Struggle for Urban Participatory Democracy During the Progressive Era*. University Park: Pennsylvania State University Press, 1998.

Mayer, Robert. "Michael Walzer, Industrial Democracy, and Complex Equality." *Political Theory* 29, no. 2 (April 2001): 237–61.

McCartin, Joseph A. "Abortive Reconstruction: Federal War Labor Policies, Union Organization, and the Politics of Race, 1917–1920." Paper Presented at the Labor History Workshop, Penn State University, March 1996, 1995.

———. "Abortive Reconstruction: Federal War Labor Policies, Union Organization, and the Politics of Race, 1917–1920." *Journal of Policy History* 9, no. 2 (1997): 155–83.

———. "Industrial Democracy and the Vision of a Progressive State: An Etymological Reflection on Progressivism." Paper Presented at the American Historical Association. New York City, 4 January 1997.

———. *Labor's Great War: The Struggle for Industrial Democracy and the Origins of Modern Labor Relations, 1912–1921*. Chapel Hill: University of University of North Carolina, 1998.

McCormick, Richard L. *From Realignment to Reform: Political Change in New York, 1893–1910*. Ithaca, NY: Cornell University Press, 1981.

———. *The Party Period and Public Policy: American Politics from the Age of Jackson to the Progressive Era*. New York: Oxford University Press, 1986.

———. *Political Parties and the Modern State*. New Brunswick, NJ: Rutgers University Press, 1984.

———. "The Realignment Synthesis in American History." *Journal of Interdisciplinary History* 13 (Summer 1982): 85–105.

McCreesh, Carolyn D. *Women in the Campaign to Organize Garment Workers, 1880–1917*. Modern American History. New York: Garland, 1985.

———. "On the Picket Line: Militant Women Campaign to Organize Garment Workers, 1880–1917," University of Maryland, 1975.

McGerr, Michael E. *The Decline of Popular Politics: The American North, 1865–1928*. New York: Oxford University Press, 1986.

———. *A Fierce Discontent: The Rise and Fall of the Progressive Movement in America, 1870–1920*. New York: Free Press, 2003.

McKnight, Gerald. "The Perils of Reform Politics: The Abortive New York State Constitutional Reform Movement of 1915." *New-York Historical Society Quarterly* 63, no. 3 (1979): 202–27.

McQuaid, Kim. "An American Owenite: Edward A. Filene and the Parameter of Industrial Reform, 1890–1937." *American Journal of Economics and Sociology* 35 (1976).

Mendel, Ronald. "Workers in Gilded Age New York and Brooklyn, 1886–1898," Ph.D. Dissertation, Graduate Center, City University of New York, 1989.

Menes, Abraham. "The East Side and the Jewish Labor Movement." In *Voices from the Yiddish: Essays. Memoirs, Diaries*, edited by Irving Howe and Eliezer Greenberg, 202–18. Ann Arbor: University of Michigan Press, 1972.

Mettler, Suzanne. " 'Federalism, Gender, and the Fair Labor Standards Act of 1938'." *Polity* XXVI, no. 4 (1994): 635–54.

———. "The Stratification of Social Citizenship: Gender and Federalism in the Formation of Old Age Insurance and Aid to Dependent Children." *Journal of Policy History* 11, no. 1 (1999): 31–58.

Milkis, Sidney M., and Daniel J. Tichenor. " 'Direct Democracy' and Social Justice: The Progressive Party Campaign of 1912." *Studies in American Political Development* 8, no. 2 (Fall 1994): 282–340.

Milkman, Ruth. *Women, Work and Protest: A Century of U.S. Women's Labor History*. New York: Routledge, 1985.

Miller, Sally M. "From Sweatshop Worker to Labor Leader: Theresa Malkiel, a Case Study." *American Jewish History* 68, no. 2 (1978): 189–205.

Miller, Zane L. "The Ethnic Revival and Urban Liberalism." *Reviews in American History* 2, no. 3 (1974): 418–24.

Mink, Gwendolyn. *Old Labor and New Immigrants in American Political Development: Union, Party, and State, 1875–1920*. Ithaca, NY: Cornell University Press, 1986.

——. *The Wages of Motherhood: Inequality in the Welfare State, 1917–1942*. Ithaca, NY: Cornell University Press, 1995.

Mohr, John W., and Vincent Duquenne. "The Duality of Culture and Practice: Poverty Relief in New York City, 1888–1917." *Theory and Society* 26, no. 2–3 (305–56, 1997): welfare, labor, urban, progress, 19th, 20th.

Montgomery, David. *The Fall of the House of Labor: The Workplace, the State, and American Labor Activism, 1865–1925*. Cambridge, UK; New York: Cambridge University Press, 1987.

——. "Industrial Democracy or Democracy in Industry?: The Theory and Practice of the Labor Movement, 1870–1925." In *Industrial Democracy in America: The Ambiguous Promise*, edited by Nelson Lichtenstein and Howell John Harris, 20–42. New York: Cambridge University Press, 1993.

——. "Labor and the Political Leadership of New Deal America." *International Review of Social History* 39 (1994): 335–60.

——. "Nationalism, American Patriotism, and Class Consciousness Among Immigrant Workers in the United States in the Epoch of World War I." In *Struggle a Hard Battle': Essays on Working-Class Immigrants*, edited by Dirk Hoerder, 327–52. DeKalb: Northern Illinois University Press, 1986.

——. "The 'New Unionism' and the Transformation of Workers' Consciousness in America, 1909–1922." *Journal of Social History* 7 (1974): 509–29.

——. *Workers' Control in America: Studies in the History of Work, Technology, and Labor Struggles*. Cambridge, UK; New York: Cambridge University Press, 1979.

Moody, J. Carroll, and Alice Kessler-Harris. *Perspectives on American Labor History: The Problem of Synthesis*. DeKalb: Northern Illinois University Press, 1989.

Moore, Deborah Dash. *At Home in America: Second Generation*. New York: Columbia University Press, 1981.

Moore, Elizabeth A. Payne. " 'Life and Labor': Margaret Dreier Robins and the Women's Trade Union League," University of Illinois at Chicago Circle, 1981.

Morris, Joe. "Industrial Democracy in West Germany." *Canadian Labour* (February 1972): 9–11.

Moskowitz, Henry. *Alfred E. Smith: An American Career*. New York: Thomas Seltzer, 1924.

Muncy, Robin. *Creating a Female Dominion in American Reform, 1890–1935*. New York: Oxford University Press, 1991.

——. "Gender and Professionalization in the Origins of the U.S. Welfare State: The Careers of Sophonisba Brekinridge and Edith Abbott, 1890–1935." *Journal of Policy History* 2, no. 3 (1990): 290–315.

Murphy, Marjorie. "Work, Protest, and Culture: New Work on Working Women's History." *Feminist Studies* 13, no. 3 (Fall 1987): 657–67.

Myers, Gustavus. *The History of Tammany Hall*. New York: Burt Franklin, 1968, 1917.

Nadel, Stanley. "Reds Versus Pinks: A Civil War in the International; Ladies Garment Workers Union." *New York History* 66, no. 1 (January 1985): 38–47.

Nasaw, David. *The Chief the Life of William Randolph Hearst.* Boston: Houghton Mifflin, 2000.

Naylor, James. *The New Democracy: Challenging the Social Order in Industrial Ontario.* Toronto: University of Toronto Press, 1991.

Neli, Humbert S. "The Italian Padrone System in the United States." *Labor History* 5, no. 2 (Spring 1964): 153–67.

Nelson, Bruce. *Shifting Fortunes: The Rise and Fall of American Labor, from the 1820s to the Present.* Chicago: Ivan R. Dee, 1997.

———. "Working-Class Agency and Racial Inequality." *International Review of Social History* 41 (1996): 407–20.

Nelson, Daniel. "Scientific Management, Systematic Management, and Labor, 1880–1915." *Business History Review* XLVIII, no. 4 (Winter 1974): 479–99.

Nicholson, Philip Yale. *Labor's Story in the United States. Labor in Crisis.* Philadelphia: Temple University Press, 2004.

Noble, David F. *Forces of Production: A Social History of Industrial Automation.* New York: Oxford University Press, 1986.

Novak, William J., and American Council of Learned Societies. *The People's Welfare Law and Regulation in Nineteenth-Century America. Studies in Legal History.* Chapel Hill: University of North Carolina Press, 1996.

Oestreicher, Richard. "Urban Working-Class Political Behavior and Theories of American Electoral Politics, 1870–1940." *The Journal of American History* 74, no. 4 (March 1988): 1257–86.

Orleck, Annelise. *Common Sense and a Little Fire: Women and Working-Class Politics in the United States, 1900–1965.* Chapel Hill: University of North Carolina Press, 1995.

Orloff, Ann Shola. "Gender and the Social Rights of Citizenship: The Comparative Analysis of Gender Relations and Welfare States." *American Sociological Review* 58 (June 1993): 303–28.

Orren, Karen. *Belated Feudalism: Labor, the Law, and Liberal Development in the United States.* Cambridge: Cambridge University Press, 1991.

———. "Union Politics and Postwar Liberalism in the United States, 1946–1979." *Studies in American Political Development* 1 (1986): 215–52.

Orren, Karen, and Stephen Skowronek. "Beyond the Iconography of Order: Notes for a 'New Institutionalism'." In *The Dynamics of American Politics: Approaches and Interpretations,* 311–30. Boulder, CO: Westview Press, 1994.

———. "Editor's Preface." *Studies in American Political Development* 1 (1986): VII–VIII.

O'Brien, Ruth. "Industrial Democracy in the U.S." *Journal of Policy History* 12, no. 3 (2000): 400–404.

———. "Taking the Conservative State Seriously: State Building and Restrictive Labor Practices in Postwar America." *Labor Studies Journal* 21, no. 4 (1997): 33–63.

———. " 'A Sweat Shop of the Whole Nation': The Fair Labor Standard Act and the Failure of Regulatory Unionism." *Studies in American Political Development* 15 (Spring 2001): 33–52.

O'Connor, Richard. *The First Hurrah: A Biography of Alfred E. Smith*. New York: G.P. Putnam's Sons, 1970.

O'Leary, Kevin G. "Herbert Croly and Progressive Democracy." *Polity* 26, no. 4 (Summer 1994): 533–52.

Pabon, Carlos. "Regulating Capitalism: The Taylor Society and Political Economy in the Interwar Years." Ph.D. Dissertation, University of Massachusetts, 1992.

Parker, Albert C.E. "Empire Stalemate: Voting Behavior in New York State, 1860–1892," Washington University, 1975.

Parmet, Wendy E. "From Slaughter-House to Lochner: The Rise and Fall of the Constitutionalization of Public Health." *The American Journal of Legal History* 40 (Oct. 1995): 476–505.

Parrini, Carl P., and Martin J. Sklar. "New Thinking About the Market, 1896–1904: Some American Economists on Investment and the Theory of Surplus Capital." *Journal of Economic History* XLIII, no. 3 (September 1983): 559–78.

Patterson, James T. *America's Struggle Against Poverty, 1900–1985*. Cambridge, MA: Harvard University Press, 1981.

———. "America's 'Underclasses,' Past and Present: A Historical Perspective." *Proceedings of the American Philosophical Society* 141, no. 1 (March 1996): 13–29.

Paulsen, George E. "Ghost of the NRA: Drafting National Wage and Hour Legislation in 1937." *Social Science Quarterly* 67, no. 2 (June 1996): 241–54.

Paulsson, Martin. *The Social Anxieties of Progressive Reform: Atlantic City, 1854–1920*. New York: New York University Press, 1994.

Payne, Elizabeth Anne. *Reform, Labor, and Feminism: Margaret Dreier Robins and the Women's Trade Union League*. Urbana: University of Illinois Press, 1988.

Pearlman, Michael. *To Make Democracy Safe for America: Patricians and Preparedness in the Progressive Era*. Urbana: University of Illinois Press, 1984.

Pedersen, Susan. *Family, Dependence, and the Origins of the Welfare State: Britain and France, 1914–1945*. Cambridge: Cambridge University Press, 1994.

Peiss, Kathy. *Cheap Amusements: Working Women and Leisure in Turn-of-the Century New York*. Philadelphia: Temple University Press, 1986.

Perlman, Selig. *A Theory of the Labor Movement*. Philadelphia: Porcupine Press, 1979.

Perlman, Selig, and Phillip Taft. "Labor Movements." In *History of the Labor in the United States, 1896–1932*, edited by John R. Commons. Volume IV. New York: Augustus M. Kelley, 1966, 1935.

Perry, Elizabeth Israels. *Belle Moskowitz: Feminine Politics and the Exercise of Power in the Age of Alfred E. Smith*. New York: Oxford University Press, 1987.

———. "Men Are From the Gilded Age, Women Are From the Progressive Era." *Journal of the Gilded Age and Progressive Era* 1, no. 1 (January 2002): 25–47.

———. "Women's Political Choices After Suffrage: The Women's City Club of New York, 1915–1990." *New York History* 62, no. 4 (October 1990): 417–34.

Pesotta, Rose. *Bread upon the Waters*. Ithaca, NY: ILR Press, 1987, 1944.

Peterson, Joyce Shaw. "Matilda Robbins: A Women's Life in the Labor Movement, 1900–1920." *Labor History* 34, no. 1 (Winter 1993): 33–56.

Petras, Elizabeth McLean. "The Shirt on Your Back: Immigrant Workers and the Reorganization of the Garment Industry." *Social Justice* 19, no. 1 (1992): 76–114.

Phelan, Craig. *Divided Loyalties: The Public and Private Life of Labor Leader John Mitchell*. Albany: State University of New York Press, 1994.

———. "The Making of a Labor Leader: John Mitchell and the Anthracite Strike of 1900." *Pennsylvania History* 63 (Winter 1996): 53–77.

Pilzer, Jay M. "The Jews and the Great 'Sweated Labor' Debate: 1888–1892." *Jewish Social Studies* 41, nos. 3–4 (1979): 257–74.

Plotke, David. *Building a Democratic Political Order: Reshaping American Liberalism in the 1930s and 1940s*. New York: Cambridge University Press, 1996.

———. "The Wagner Act, Again: Politics and Labor, 1937–37." *Studies in American Political Development* 3 (1989): 103–56.

Plumb, Glenn Edward, and William G. Roylance. *Industrial Democracy a Plan for Its Achievement*. New York: B.W. Huebsch, Inc., 1923.

Pollack, Ervin H., Editor. *The Brandeis Reader*. New York: Oceana Publications, 1956.

Poole, Michael. "Industrial Democracy: A Comparative Analysis." *Industrial Relations* 18, no. 3 (Fall 1979): 262–72.

———. "Theories of Industrial Democracy: The Emerging Synthesis." *The Sociological Review* 30, no. 2 (May 1980): 181–207.

Pozzetta, George E. *Immigrant Radicals: The View From the Left*. New York: Garland, 1991.

———. "The Italian Immigrant Press of New York City: The Early Years, 1880–1915." *Journal of Ethnic Studies* 1, no. 3 (1973): 32–46.

———. "The Italians of New York City, 1890–1914." Ph.D. Dissertation, University of North Carolina, 1971.

Pratt, Norma Fain. *Morris Hillquit: A Political History of an American Jewish Socialist*. Westport, CT: Greenwood Press, 1979.

Quadagno, Jill. "Theories of the Welfare State." *American Review of Sociology* 13 (1987): 109–28.

Radice, Lisanne. *Beatrice and Sidney Webb Fabian Socialists*. New York: St. Martin's Press, 1984.

Ramirez, Bruno. *When Workers Fight: The Politics of Industrial Relations in the Progressive Era, 1898–1916*. Westport, CT: Greenwood Press, 1978.

Reed, Louis S. *The Labor Philosophy of Samuel Gompers*. Port Washington, NY: Kennikat Press, 1966, 1930.

Reznick, Allan Edward. "Lillian D. Wald: The Years at Henry Street," University at Wisconsin, 1973.

Rischin, Moses. "The Jewish Labor Movement in America: A Social Interpretation." *Labor History* 4 (Fall 1963): 227–47.

———. *The Promised City: New York's Jews, 1870–1914*. Cambridge, MA: Harvard University Press, 1962.

Roberts, Benjamin C. *Towards Industrial Democracy: Europe, Japan and the United States*. Montclair, NJ: Allanheld, Osmun Publishers, 1979.

Robertson, David Brian. "The Bias of American Federalism: The Limits of Welfare-State Development in the Progressive Era." *Journal of Policy History* 1, no. 3 (1989): 261–91.

———. "The Return to History and the New Institutionalism in American Political Science." *Social Science History* 17, no. 1 (Spring 1993): 1–35.

Rodgers, Daniel. "In Search of Progressivism." *Reviews in American History* (December 1982): 113–31.

Rodgers, Daniel T. *Atlantic Crossings Social Politics in a Progressive Age.* Cambridge, MA: Belknap Press of Harvard University Press, 1998.

———. "In Search of Progressivism." *Reviews in American History* 10, no. 4 (December 1982): 113–32.

———. *The Work Ethic in Industrial America, 1850–1920.* Chicago: University of Chicago Press, 1974.

Rogers, Joel. "Divide and Conquer: Further 'Reflections on the Distinctive Character of American Labor Laws.'" *Wisconsin Law Review* 1 (1990): 1–147.

Rogin, Michael. "Voluntarism: The Political Functions of an Antipolitical Doctrine." *Industrial and Labor Relations Review* 15 (1962): 521–35.

Ronald Lawson, Editor. *The Tenant Movement in New York City, 1904–1984.* New Brunswick, NJ: Rutgers University Press, 1986.

Rosner, David, and Gerald E. Moskowitz. *Dying for Work: Workers' Safety and Health in Twentieth-Century America.* Bloomington: Indiana University Press, 1987.

Ross, Dorothy. *Modernist Impulses in the Human Sciences, 1870–1930.* Baltimore: Johns Hopkins University Press, 1994.

———. *The Origins of American Social Science.* New York: Cambridge University Press, 1991.

Ross, Steven J. "The Politicization of the Working Class: Production, Ideology, Culture and Politics in Late Nineteenth-Century Cincinnati." *Social History* 11, no. 2 (May 1986): 171–95.

Ross, William G. *A Muted Fury: Populists, Progressives, and Labor Unions Confront the Courts, 1890–1937.* Princeton: Princeton University Press, 1994.

Rothschild, Teal. "Alliances Across Skill, Gender, and Ethnicity: A Structural and Identity Based Analysis of Two Strikes in the New York City Garment Industry, 1885–1921." Ph.D. Dissertation, Graduate Faculty for Political and Social Science, New School, 2000.

Rothstein, Lawrence. "Industrial Justice Meets Industrial Democracy: Liberty of Expression at the Workplace in the U.S. and France." *Labor Studies Journal* 13, no. 3 (1988): 18–39.

Rotundo, Ronald D. "The 'Liberal' Label: Roosevelt's Capture of a Symbol." *Public Policy* 17 (1968): 377–408.

Ryan, Susan M. "'Rough Ways and Rough Work': Jacob Riis, Social Reform, and the Rhetoric of Benevolent Violence." *ATQ* 11, no. 3 (September 1997): 191–212.

Salerno, Salvatore. "The Early Labor Radicalism of the Industrial Workers of the World a Socio-Cultural Critique," Ph.D. Dissertation, Blandeis University, 1986.

———. *Red November, Black November Culture and Community in the Industrial Workers of the World*. SUNY Series in American Labor History. Albany: State University of New York Press, 1989.

Salvatore, Nick. *Eugene V. Debs: Citizen and Socialist*. Urbana: University of Illinois Press, 1982.

Sanders, Elizabeth. *Roots of Reform Farmers, Workers, and the American State, 1877–1917*. American Politics and Political Economy. Chicago: University of Chicago Press, 1999.

Sanders, Ronald. *The Downtown Jews*. New York: Harper and Row, 1969.

Sarvasy, Wendy. "Beyond the Difference Versus Equality Policy Debate: Postsuffrage Feminism, Citizenship, and the Quest for a Feminist Welfare State." *Signs* 17, no. 2 (Winter 1992): 329–62.

Schneirov, Richard. "Free Thought and Socialism in the Czech Community in Chicago, 1875–1887." In *'Struggle a Hard Battle': Essays on Working-Class Immigrants*, edited by Dirk Hoerder, 121–42. DeKalb: Northern Illinois University Press, 1986.

———. "The Odyssey of William English Walling: Revisionism, Social Democracy, and Evolutionary Pragmatism." *Journal of the Gilded Age and Progressive Era* 2, no. 4 (October 2003): 403–30.

———. "Political Cultures and the Role of the State in Labor's Republic: The View From Chicago, 1848–1877." *Labor History* 32 (Summer 1991): 376–400.

———. "Rethinking the Relations of Labor to the Politics of Urban Social Reform in Late Nineteenth-Century America: The Case of Chicago." *International Labor and Working-Class History* 46 (Fall 1994): 93–108.

Schneirov, Richard, Shelton Stromquist, and Nick Salvatore, Editors. *The Pullman Strike and the Crisis of the 1890s Essays on Labor and Politics*. The Working Class in American History. Urbana: University of Illinois Press, 1999.

Schofield, Ann. *"To Do and to Be": Ladies, Immigrants, and Workers, 1893–1986*. Boston: Northeastern University Press, 1997.

———. " 'To Do and to Be': Mary Dreier, Pauline Newman, and the Psychology of Feminist Activism." *The Psychohistory Review* 18, no. 1 (1989): 33–55.

Schuller, Tom. "Common Discourse?: The Language of Industrial Democracy." *Economic and Industrial Democracy* 2 (1981): 261–91.

Schwartz, Anita. "The Secular Seder: Continuity and Change Among Left-Wing Jews." In *Between Two Worlds: Ethnographic Essays on American Jewry*, edited by Jack Kugelmass, 105–27. Ithaca, NY: Cornell University Press, 1998.

Schwarz, Jordan A. *The New Dealers: Power Politics in the Age of Roosevelt*. New York: Knopf, 1993.

———. *The Ordeal of Twentieth-Century America: Interpretive Readings*. Boston: Houghton Mifflin, 1974.

———. "The Woman and Liberal and the Liberal as Woman." *Reviews in American History* 17, no. 1 (1989): 109–12.

Scranton, Philip. "Manufacturing Diversity: Production System, Markets, and an American Consumer Society, 1870–1930." *Technology and Culture* 35 (475–505 1994).

Seidman, Joel Isaac. *Democracy in the Labor Movement.* 2d ed. Bulletin (New York State School of Industrial and Labor Relations). Ithaca: New York State School of Industrial and Labor Relation, Cornell University, 1969.

Seller, Maxine. *Immigrant Women.* Albany: State University of New York Press, 1994.

Seller, Maxine Schwartz. "The Uprising of Twenty Thousand: Sex, Class, and Ethnicity in the Shirtwaist Makers' Strike of 1909." In *'Struggle a Hard Battle': Essays on Working-Class Immigrants,* edited by Dirk Hoerder, 254–79. DeKalb: Northern Illinois University Press, 1986.

Seltzer, Andrew J. "The Effects of the Fair Labor Standards Act of 1938 on the Southern Seamless Hosiery and Lumber Industries." *The Journal of Economic History* 57, no. 2 (June 1997): 396–415.

Seltzer, Robert M., and Norman J. Cohen, Editors. *The Americanization of the Jews.* New York: New York University Press, 1995, 1995.

Shalev, Michael. "The Social Democratic Model and Beyond: Two 'Generations' of Comparative Research on the Welfare State." *Comparative Social Research* 6 (1983): 315–51.

Shapiro, Robert D. *A Reform Rabbi in the Progressive Era: The Early Career of Stephen S. Wise.* New York: Garland, 1988.

Shefter, Martin. "The Electoral Foundations of the Political Machine: New York City, 1884–1897." In *The History of American Electoral Behavior,* edited by Joel H. Silbey, Allan G. Bogue, and William H. Flanigan, 263–98. Princeton: Princeton University Press, 1978.

———. *Political Parties and the State: The American Historical Experience.* Princeton: Princeton University Press, 1995.

Sibley, Joel H. "The State and Practice of American Political History at the Millennium: The Nineteenth-Century as a Test Case." *Journal of Policy History* 11, no. 1 (1999): 1–30.

Sklar, Katherine Kish. *Florence Kelley and the Nation's Work: The Rise of Women's Political Culture, 1830–1900.* New Haven: Yale University Press, 1995.

———. "The Historical Foundations of Women's Power in the Creation of the American Welfare State, 1830–1930." In *Mothers of a New World: Maternalist Politics and the Origins of Welfare States,* edited by Seth Koven and Sonya Michel, 43–93. New York: Routledge, 1993.

———. "Hull House in the 1890s: A Community of Women Reformers." *Signs* 10, no. 4 (Summer 1985): 658–77.

Sklar, Martin J. *The Corporate Reconstruction of American Capitalism, 1890–1916: The Market, the Law and Politics.* New York: Cambridge University Press, 1988.

———. "Thoughts on Capitalism and Socialism: Utopian and Realistic." *Journal of the Gilded Age and Progressive Era* 2, no. 4 (October 2003): 361–76.

———. *The United States as a Developing Country: Studies in U.S. History in the Progressive Era and the 1920s.* New York; Cambridge: Cambridge University Press, 1992.

Skocpol, Theda. "Did Capitalists Shape Social Security." *American Sociological Review* 50, no. 4 (August 1985): 572–78.

———. "The Origins of Social Policy in the United States: A Polity-Centered Analysis." In *The Dynamics of American Politics: Approaches and Interpretations,* 182–206. Boulder, CO: Westview Press, 1994.

———. "Political Response to Capitalist Crisis: Neo-Marxist Theories of the State and the Case of the New Deal." *Politics & Society* 10 (1980): 155–201.

———. *Protecting Soldiers and Mothers: The Political Origins of Social Policy in the United States.* Cambridge, MA: Harvard University Press, 1992.

———. *Social Policy in the United States: Future Possibilities in Historical Perspective.* Princeton: Princeton University Press, 1995.

———. "Soldiers, Workers, and Mothers: Gendered Identities in Early U.S. Social Policy." *Contention* 2, no. 3 (Spring 1993): 157–83.

———. *Vision and Method in Historical Sociology.* New York: Cambridge University, 1979.

Skocpol, Theda, and Edwin Amenta. "States and Social Policies." *American Review of Sociology* 12 (1986): 131–57.

Skocpol, Theda, and John Ikenberry. "The Political Formation of the American Welfare State in Historical and Comparative Perspective." *Comparative Social Research* 6 (1983): 87–150.

Skowronek, Stephen. *Building a New American State: The Expansion of National Administrative Capacities, 1877–1920 Building a New American State: The Expansion of National.* Cambridge [Cambridgeshire]; New York: Cambridge University.

Slayton, Robert A. *Empire Statesman: The Rise and Redemption of Al Smith.* New York: Free Press, 2001.

Smith, Carl. *Urban Disorder and the Shape of Belief: The Great Chicago Fire, the Haymarket Bomb, and the Model Town of Pullman.* Chicago: University of Chicago Press, 1995.

Smith, Daniel Arthur. "Insular Democracy: Labor-Management Councils in the American States." Ph.D. Dissertation, Political Science, University of Wisconsin–Madison, 1994.

Smith, Judith E. *Family Connection: A History of Italian and Jewish Immigrant Lives in Providence Rhode Island, 1900–1940.* Albany: State University of New York Press, 1985.

Smith, Mortimer. *William Jay Gaynor: Mayor of New York.* Chicago: Henry Regnery Company, 1951.

Sorin, Gerald. *The Prophetic Minority: American Jewish Immigrant Radicals, 1880–1920.* Bloomington: Indiana University Press, 1985.

———. "A Time for Building: The Third Migration, 1880–1920." In *The Jewish People in America*, edited by Henry L. Finegold. Baltimore: Johns Hopkins University Press, 1992.

Soyer, Daniel. "Class Conscious Workers as Immigrant Entrepreneurs: The Ambiguity of Class Among Eastern European Jewish Immigrants to the United States at the Turn of the Twentieth Century." *Labor History* 42, no. 1 (2001): 45–59.

———. *Jewish Immigrant Associations and American Identity in New York, 1880–1939*. Cambridge, MA: Harvard University Press, 1997.

———. "Landsmanshaftn and the Jewish Labor Movement: Cooperation, Conflict, and the Building of Community." *Journal of American Ethnic History* 7, no. 2 (Spring 1988): 22–45.

Spargo, John. *Bolshevism the Enemy of Political and Industrial Democracy*. New York London: Harper and Brothers, 1919.

Spencer, Thomas T. " 'Old' Democrats and New Deal Politics: Claude G. Bowers. James A. Farley, and the Changing Democratic Party, 1933–1940." *Indiana Magazine of History* 92 (March 1996): 26–45.

Spratt, Margaret A. "The Pittsburgh YWCA and Industrial Democracy in the 1920s." *Pennsylvania History* 59, no. 1 (1992): 5–20.

Sprinker, Michael, and Mike Davis. *Reshaping the US Left: Popular Struggles in the 1980s*. Year Left. London New York: Verso, 1988.

Stave, Bruce M. *Urban Bosses, Machines, and Progressive Reformers*. Malabar, FL: R.E. Krieger Pub. Co., 1984.

Stave, Bruce M., and John M. Allswang. "A Reassessment of the Urban Political Boss: An Exchange of View." *History Teacher* 21, no. 3 (1988): 293–312.

Stearns, Peter N., and Daniel J. Walkowitz, Editors. *Workers in the Industrial Revolution: Recent Studies of Labor in the United States and Europe*. New Brunswick, NJ: Transaction Books, 1974.

Stein, Emanuel, and Jerome Davis. *Labor Problems in America*. New York: Farrar & Rinehart, 1940.

Stein, Leon. *Out of the Sweatshop the Struggle for Industrial Democracy*. New York: Quadrangle/New York Times Book Co., 1977.

———. *The Triangle Fire*. New York: Carroll and Graf, 1962.

Stein, Leon, and Philip Taft. *Workers Speak: Self Portraits*. American Labor (New York, NY). New York: Arno, 1971.

Stephan-Norris, Judith, and Maurice Zeitlin. "Insurgency, Radicalism, and Democracy in America's Industrial Unions." *Social Forces* 75, no. 1 (September 1996): 1–32.

———. "Union Democracy, Radical Leadership, and the Hegemony of Capital." *American Sociological Review* 60 (December 1995): 829–50.

Stettner, Edward A. *Shaping Modern Liberalism: Herbert Croly and Progressive Thought*. Lawrence: University Press of Kansas, 1993.

Stoddard, Lothrop. *Master of Manhattan: The Life of Richard Croker*. New York: Longmans, 1931.

Storrs, Landon R. *Civilizing Capitalism: The National Consumers' League, Women's Activism, and Labor Standards in the New Deal Era*. Chapel Hill: University of North Carolina Press, 2000.

———. "Gender and the Development of the Regulatory State: The Controversy over Restricting Women's Night Work in the Depression Era South." *Journal of Policy History* 10, no. 2 (1998): 179–206.

Stromquist, Shelton. "Class Wars: Frank Walsh, the Reformers, and the Crisis of Progressivism." In *Labor Histories: Class, Politics, and the Working-Class Experience*, edited by Julie Greene Eric Arnesen, and Bruce Laurie, 97–124. Urbana: University of Illinois Press, 1998.

———. "The Crucible of Class: Cleveland Politics and the Origins of Municipal Reform in the Progressive Era." *Journal of Urban History* 23, no. 2 (January 1997): 192–220.

Strum, Philippa. *Brandeis: Beyond Progressivism*. Lawrence: University of Kansas Press, 1993.

———. "The Legacy of Louis Dembitz Brandeis, People's Attorney." *American Jewish History* 81 (Spring/Summer 1994): 406–27.

———. *Louis D. Brandeis: Justice for the People*. Cambridge, MA: Harvard University Press, 1984.

Sturmthal, Adolf F. "Unions and Industrial Democracy." *Annals, AAPSS* 431 (May 1977): 12–31.

Sumner, Helen L. *History of Women in Industry in the United States*. New York: Arno Press, 1974, 1910.

Szjkowski, Zosa. "The Jews and New York City's Mayoralty Election of 1917." *Jewish Social Studies* 32 (Oct. 1970): 286–306.

Taft, Philip. *The A.F. of L. in the Time of Gompers*. New York: Harper and Brothers, 1957.

Tarrow, Sidney G. "Lochner Versus New York: A Political Analysis." *Labor History* 5, no. 2 (1964): 277–312.

Tawney, R.H. *The Webbs in Perspective*. Webb Memorial Lectures, 1952. [London]: Athlone Press [distributed by Constable], 1953.

Tax, Meredith. *The Rising of the Women: Feminist Solidarity and Class Conflict, 1880–1917*. New York: Monthly Review Press, 1980.

———. *Rivington Street*. New York: Morrow, 1982.

———. *Union Square*. New York: Avon Books, 1988.

Taylor, Albion Guilford. *Labor Problems and Labor Law*. New York: Prentice Hall, 1939.

Taylor, Shawn. "Horace Kallen's Workers' Education for Industrial Democracy." *Labor Studies Journal* 23, no. 3 (Fall 1998): 84–102.

Taylor, William R. *In Pursuit of Gotham: Culture and Commerce in New York*. New York: Oxford University Press, 1992.

Taylor-Gooby, Peter. "Welfare State Regimes, and Welfare Citizenship." *Journal of European Social Policy* 1, no. 2 (1991): 93–105.

Tentler, Leslie Woodcock. *Wage-Earning Women: Industrial Work and Family Life in the United States, 1900–1930*. New York: Oxford University Press, 1979.

Thelen, David. "Social Tensions and the Origins of Progressivism." *Journal of American History* 56 (1969): 323–41.

Thelen, David P. *The New Citizenship: Origins of Progressivism in Wisconsin, 1885–1900*. Columbia: University of Missouri Press, 1972.

———. "Urban Politics: Beyond Bosses and Reformers." *Reviews in American History* 7, no. 3 (1979): 406–12.

Thomas, Rebecca L. "John J. Eagan and Industrial Democracy at Acipco." *Alabama Review* XLIII, no. 4 (October 1990): 270–88.

Thomas, William B., and Kevin J. Moran. "The Politicization of Efficiency Concepts in the Progressive Period, 1918–1922." *Journal of Urban History* 17, no. 4 (August 1991): 390–409.

Thornton, Robert M. "William Jay Gaynor: Libertarian Mayor of New York." *The Freeman* 20, no. 3 (1970): 156–64.

Tolliday, Steven, and Jonathan Zeitlin. *Shop Floor Bargaining and the State Historical and Comparative Perspectives*. Cambridge [Cambridgeshire] New York: Cambridge University Press, 1985.

Tomlins, Christopher L. *Law, Labor, and Ideology in the Early American Republic*. Cambridge: Cambridge University Press, 1993.

———. *The State and the Unions: Labor Relations, Law, and the Organized Labor Movement in America, 1880–1960*. Cambridge: Cambridge University Press, 1985.

Tomlins, Christopher L., and Andrew King. *Labor Law in America: Historical and Critical Essays*. Baltimore: Johns Hopkins University Press, 1992.

Tone, Andrea. *The Business of Benevolence: Industrial Paternalism in Progressive America*. Ithaca, NY: Cornell University Press, 1997.

Toplin, Robert Brent. "The Guns of Industrial America." *Reviews in American History* 7, no. 4 (1979): 542–46.

Trattner, Walter I. *From Poor Law to Welfare State: A History of Social Welfare in America*. New York: Free Press, 1994, 1974.

———. *Louis D. Brandeis and the Progressive Tradition*. Boston: Little Brown, 1981.

Urofsky, Melvin I. *A Mind of One Piece: Brandeis and American Reform*. New York: Charles Scribner's Sons, 1971.

———. "'To Guide by the Light of Reason': Mr. Justice Brandeis—An Appreciation." *American Jewish History* 81 (1994): 365–93.

Valentine, Cynthia E. "Industrial Union Democracy—Does It Help or Hinder the Movement for Industrial Democracy." *The Insurgent Sociologist* 8, no. 2–3 (Fall 1978): 40–51.

Vandermeer, Philip R. "Bosses, Machines, and Democratic Leadership: Party Organization and Managers in Indiana, 1880–1910." *Social Science History* 12, no. 4 (Winter 1988): 395–428.

Vittoz, Stanley. *New Deal Labor Policy and the American Industrial Economy*. Chapel Hill: University of North Carolina Press, 1987.

Von Drehle, Dave. *Triangle the Fire That Changed America*. New York: Atlantic Monthly Press, 2003.

Walker, Claire Brandler. "A History of Factory Legislation and Inspection in New York State, 1866–1911." Ph.D. Dissertation, Columbia University, 1969.

Walkowitz, Daniel J. *Worker City, Company Town: Iron and Cotton-Worker Protest in Troy and Cohoes, New York, 1855–84*. Urbana: University of Illinois Press, 1978.

Walkowitz, Judith. *City of Dreadful Delight: Narratives of Sexual Danger in Late-Victorian London*. Chicago: University of Chicago Press, 1992.

Wallace, Mike. *A New Deal for New York*. New York: Bell & Weil and Publishers, 2002.

Wandersee, Winifred D. " 'I'd Rather Pass a Law Than Organize a Union': Frances Perkins and the Reformist Approach to Organized Labor." *Labor History* 34, no. 1 (Winter 1993): 5–32.

Ware, Susan. *Beyond Suffrage, Women in the New Deal*. Cambridge, MA: Harvard University Press, 1981.

———. *Partner and I: Molly Dewson, Feminism, and New Deal Politics*. New Haven, CT: Yale University Press, 1987.

Webb, Sidney and Beatrice. *Industrial Democracy*. New York: Augustus M. Kelley, 1965, 1897 (reprint 1920).

Webb, Sidney, et al. *The Letters of Sidney and Beatrice Webb*, edited by Norman MacKenzie. Cambridge New York: Cambridge University Press, 1978.

Weiler, N. Sue. "Walkout: The Chicago Men's Garment Workers' Strike, 1910–1911." *Chicago History*.

Weinberg, Sydney Stahl. *The World of Our Mothers: The Lives of Jewish Immigrant Women*. Chapel Hill: University of North Carolina Press, 1988.

Weinstein, James. *The Decline of Socialism in America, 1912–1925*. New Brunswick, NJ: Rutgers University Press, 1984.

———. *For a New America; Essays in History and Politics from Studies on the Left, 1959–1967*, edited by James Weinstein and David W. Eakins. New York: Random House, 1970.

Weiss, Nancy J. *Charles Francis Murphy, 1858–1924; Respectability and Responsibility in Tammany Politics*. Northhampton, MA: Smith College, 1968.

Weisser, Michael. *A Brotherhood of Memory: Jewish Landsmanshaftn in the New World*. New York: Basic Books, 1985.

Werner, M.R. *Tammany Hall*. Garden City, NY: Doubleday, Doran and Co., 1928.

Wertheimer, Barbara Mayer. *We Were There: The Story of Working Women in America*. New York: Pantheon Books, 1977.

Wesser, Robert F. *Charles Evans Hughes; Politics and Reform in New York, 1905–1910*. Ithaca, NY: Cornell University Press, 1967.

———. *A Response to Progressivism: The Democratic Party and New York Politics, 1902–1918*. New York: New York University Press, 1986.

Westbrook, Robert B. *John Dewey and American Democracy*. Ithaca, NY: Cornell University Press, 1991.

———. "Schools for Industrial Democrats: The Social Origins of John Dewey's Philosophy of Education." *American Journal of Education* 100 (August 1992): 408–19.

Wiebe, Robert H. *Businessmen and Reform: A Study of the Progressive Movement.* Chicago: Quadrangle Books, 1968.

———. *The Opening of American Society: From the Adoption of the Constitution to the Eve of Disunion.* New York: Knopf, 1984.

———. *The Search for Order, 1877–1920.* New York: Hill and Wang, 1967.

———. *The Segmented Society; an Introduction to the Meaning of America.* New York: Oxford University Press, 1975.

———. *Self-Rule: A Cultural History of American Democracy.* Chicago: University of Chicago Press, 1995.

Williams, Talcott. *Tammany Hall.* New York: G.P. Putnam's Sons, 1898.

Wineburg, Bob. *A Limited Partnership: The Politics of Religion, Welfare, and Social Science.* New York: Columbia University Press, 2001.

Wolfson, Theresa. "Role of the ILGWU in Stabilizing the Women's Garment Industry." *Industrial and Labor Relations Review* 4 (1950): 33–43.

Wunderlin, Clarence E. *Visions of a New Industrial Order: Social Science and Labor Theory in America's Progressive Era.* New York: Columbia University Press, 1992.

Yans-McLaughlin, Virginia. *Family and Community: Italian Immigrants in Buffalo, 1880–1930.* Ithaca, NY: Cornell University Press, 1977.

———. "A Flexible Tradition: South Italian Immigrants Confront a New Experience." *Journal of Social History* 7 (Summer 1974): 429–45.

———. "Italian Women and Work: Experience and Perception." In *Class, Sex, and the Women Worker,* edited by Milton Cantor and Bruce Laurie, 101–19. Westport, CT: Greenwood Press, 1977.

———. "Patterns of Work and Family Organization: Buffalo's Italian Immigrants." *Journal of Interdisciplinary History* 2 (Autumn 1971–72): 299–314.

Yellowitz, Irwin, Editor. *Essays in the History of New York City: A Memorial to Sidney Pomerantz.* Port Washington, NY: Kennikat Press, 1978.

———. *Industrialization and the American Labor Movement, 1850–1900.* Port Washington, NY: Kennikat Press, 1977.

———. *Labor and the Progressive Movement in New York State, 1897–1916.* Ithaca, NY: Cornell University Press, 1965.

———. "Morris Hillquit: American Socialism and Jewish Concerns." *American Jewish History* 68, no. 2 (1978): 163–88.

———. *The Position of the Worker in American Society, 1865–1896.* Englewood Cliffs, NJ: Prentice Hall, 1969.

Young, Angela Nugent. "Interpreting the Dangerous Trades; Workers Health in America and the Career of Alice Hamilton, 1910–1935." Ph.D. Dissertation, Brown University, 1982.

Zappia, Charles Anthony. "Unionism and the Italian American Worker: A History of the New York City 'Italian Locals' in the International Ladies' Garment Workers' Union, 1900–1914." Ph.D. Dissertation, University of California at Berkeley, 1994.

Zeitlin, Jonathan. "From Labour History to the History of Industrial Relations." *Economic History Review* XL, no. 2 (1987): 159–84.

Zieger, Robert H. "Historians and the U.S. Industrial Relations Regime." *Journal of Policy History* 9, no. 4 (1997): 475–89.

———. "CIO Leaders and the State, 1935–55." In *American Labor in the Era of World War II*, edited by Sally M. Miller and Daniel A. Cornford, 29–42. Contributions to Labor Studies, Number 45. Westport, CT: Greenwood Press, 1995.

Zink, Harold. *City Bosses in the United States: A Study of Twenty Municipal Bosses.* Durham, NC: Duke University Press, 1930.

Zunz, Olivier. *Making America Corporate, 1870–1920.* Chicago: University of Chicago Press, 1990.

———. "The Synthesis of Social Change: Reflections on American Social History." In *Reliving the Past: The Worlds of Social History*, edited by Olivier Zunz. Chapel Hill: The University of North Carolina Press, 1985.

Index